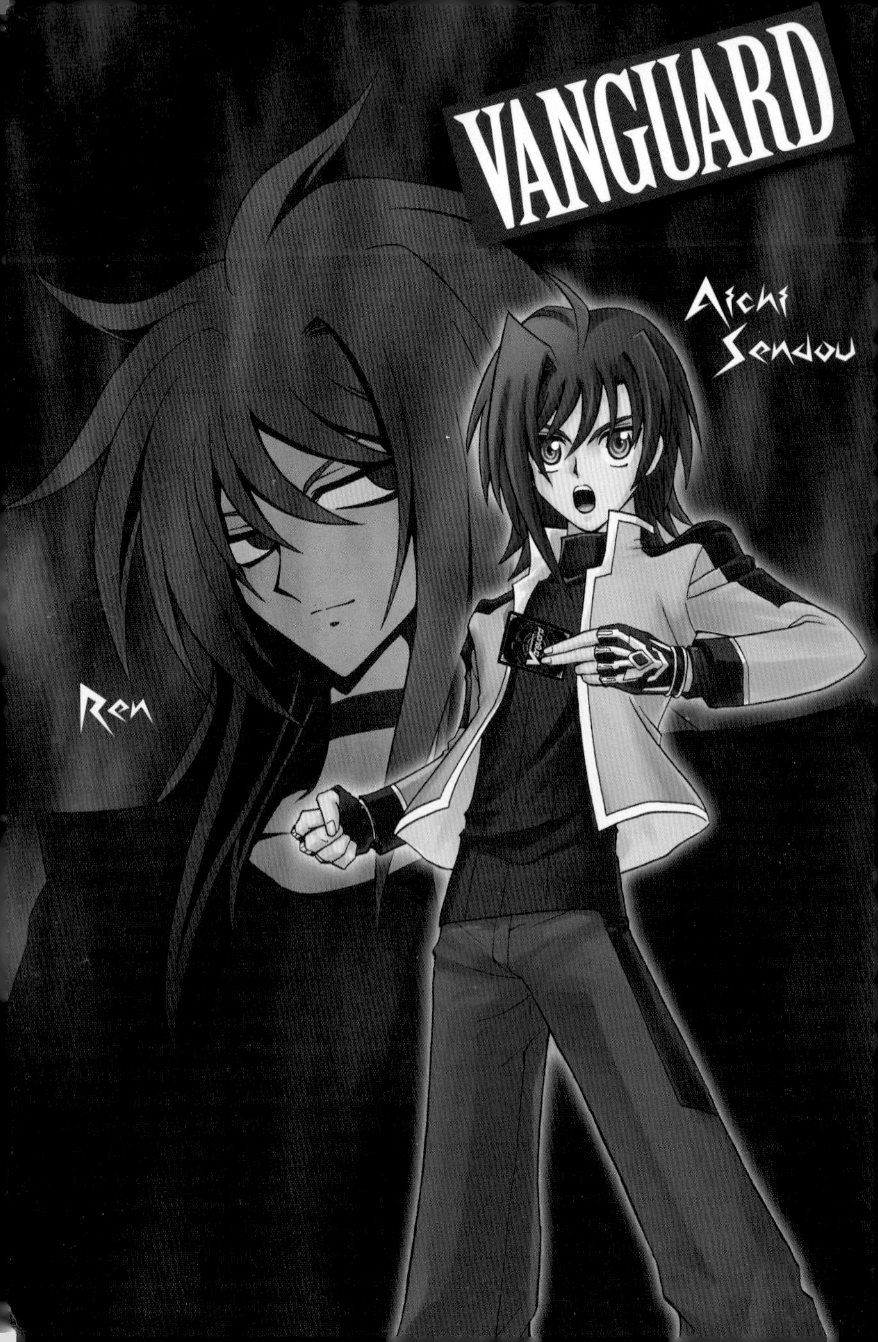
VANGUARD
Aichi Sendou
Ren

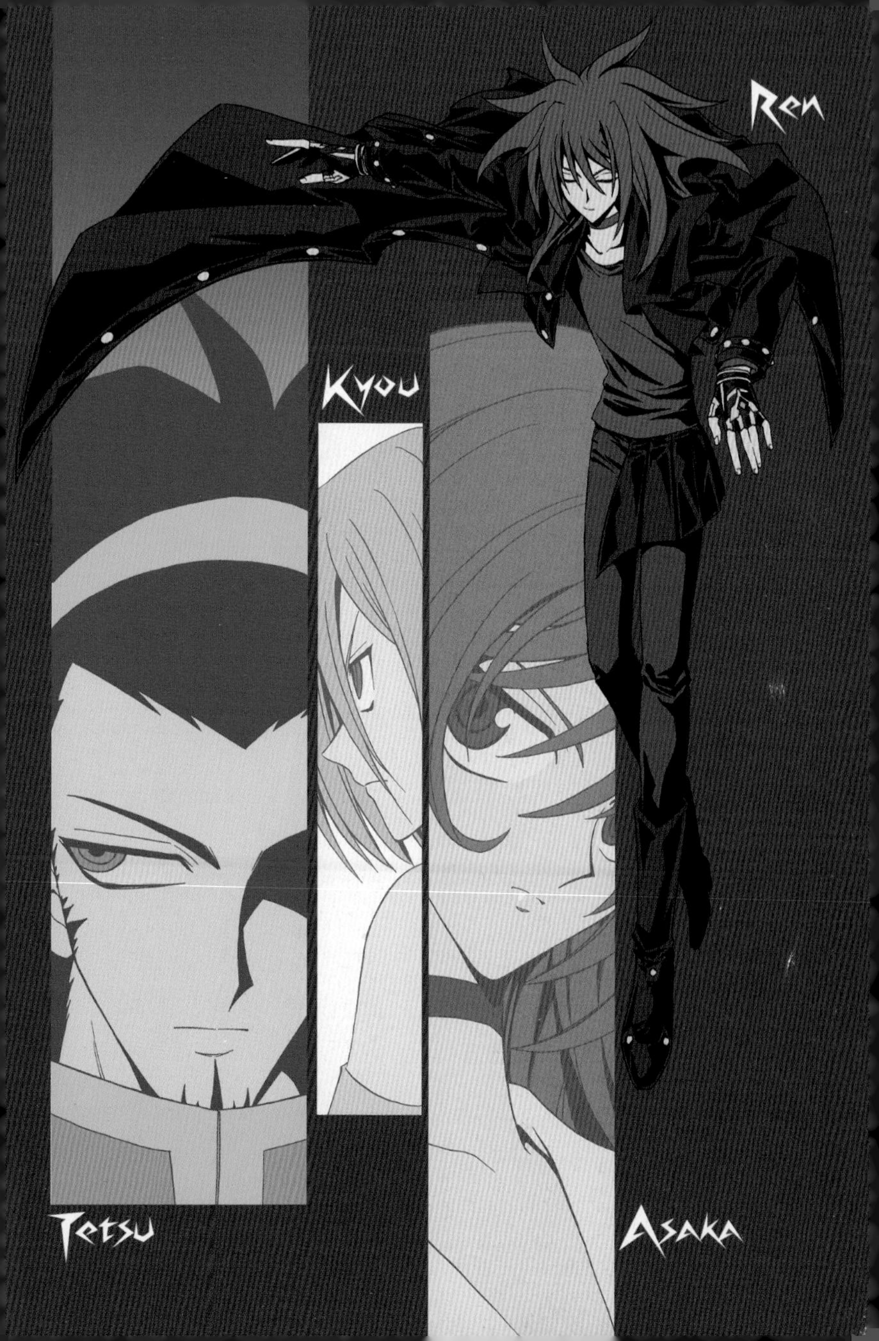
Ren
Kyou
Asaka
Tetsu

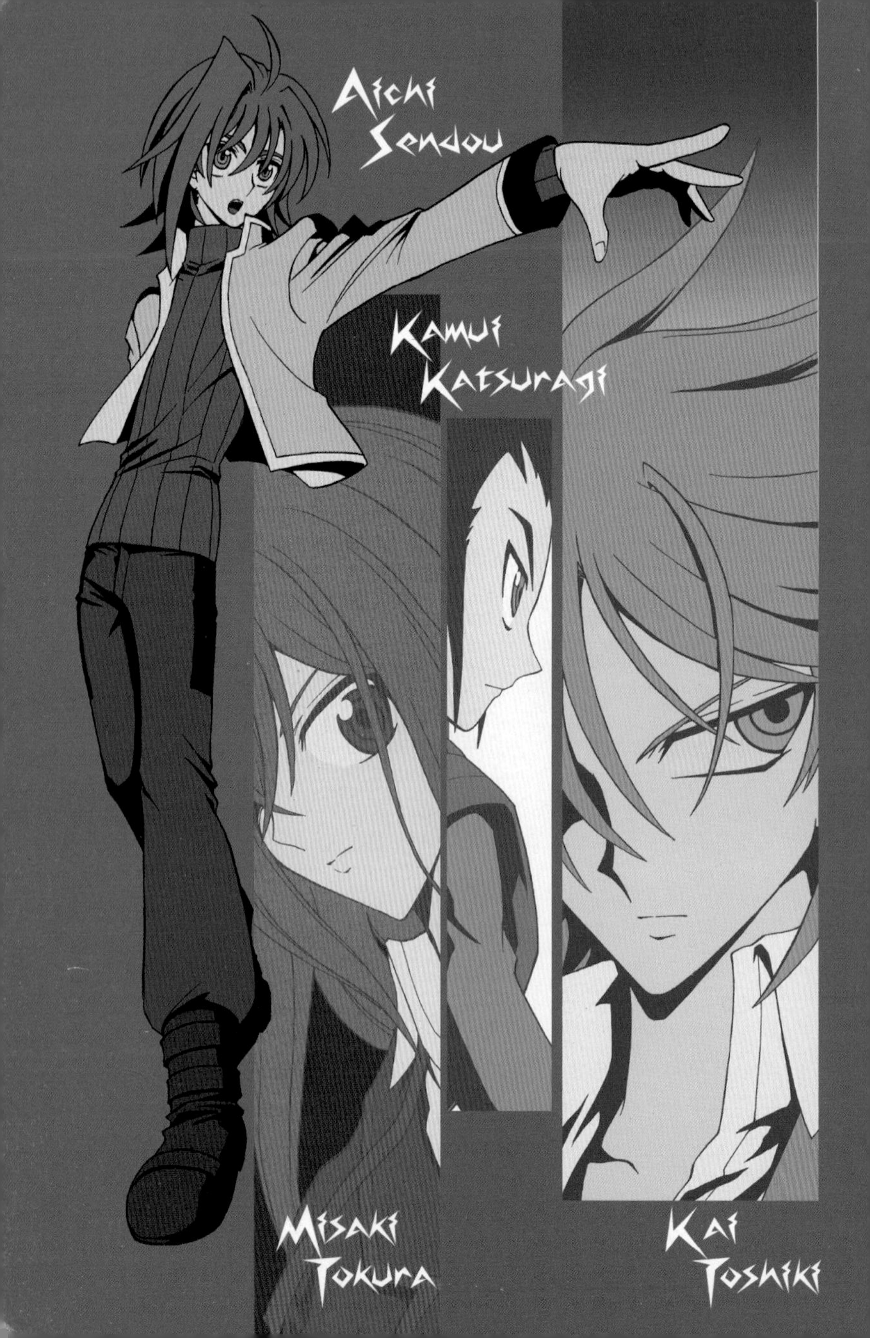
Aichi Sendou
Kamui Katsuragi
Kai Toshiki
Misaki Tokura

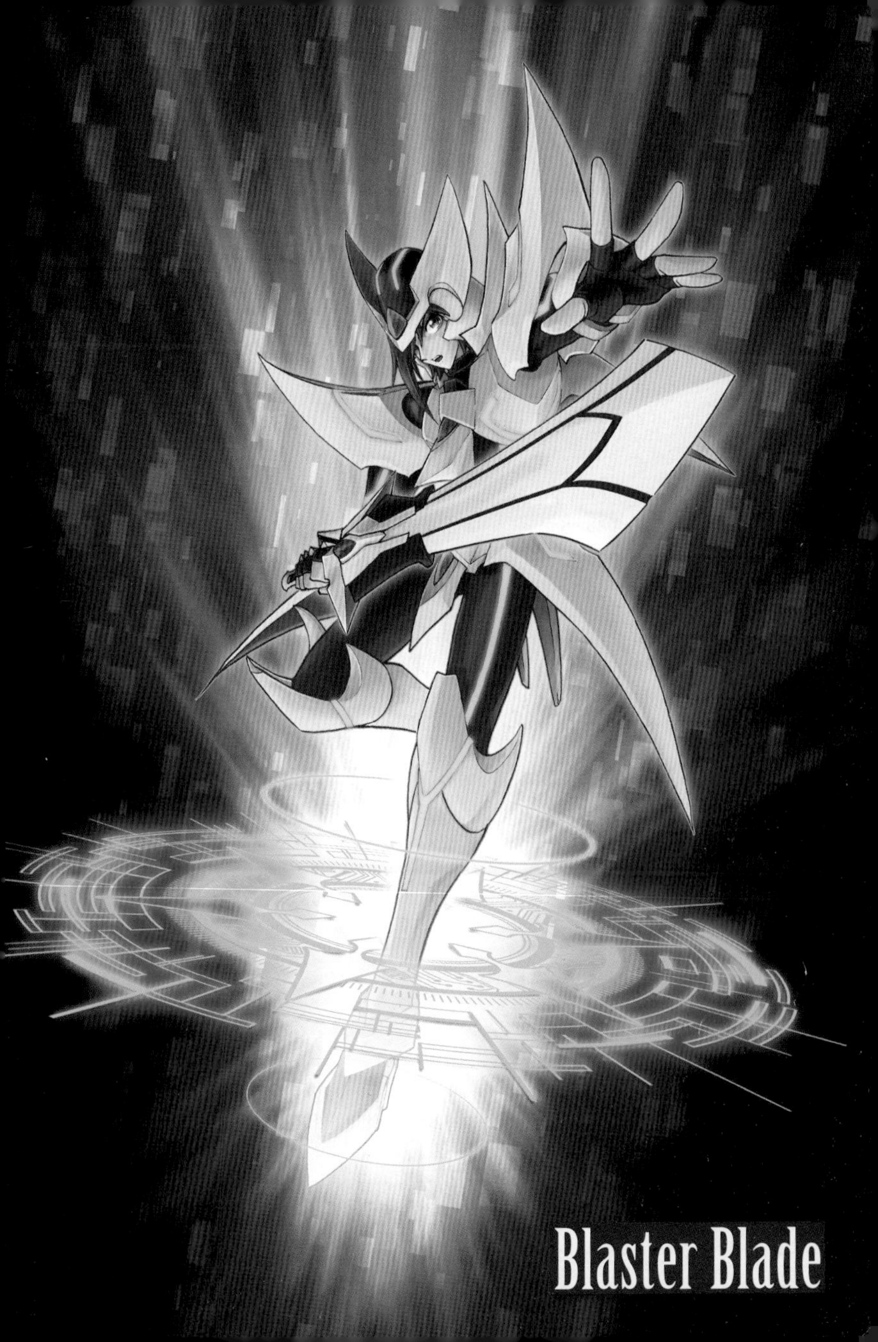
Blaster Blade

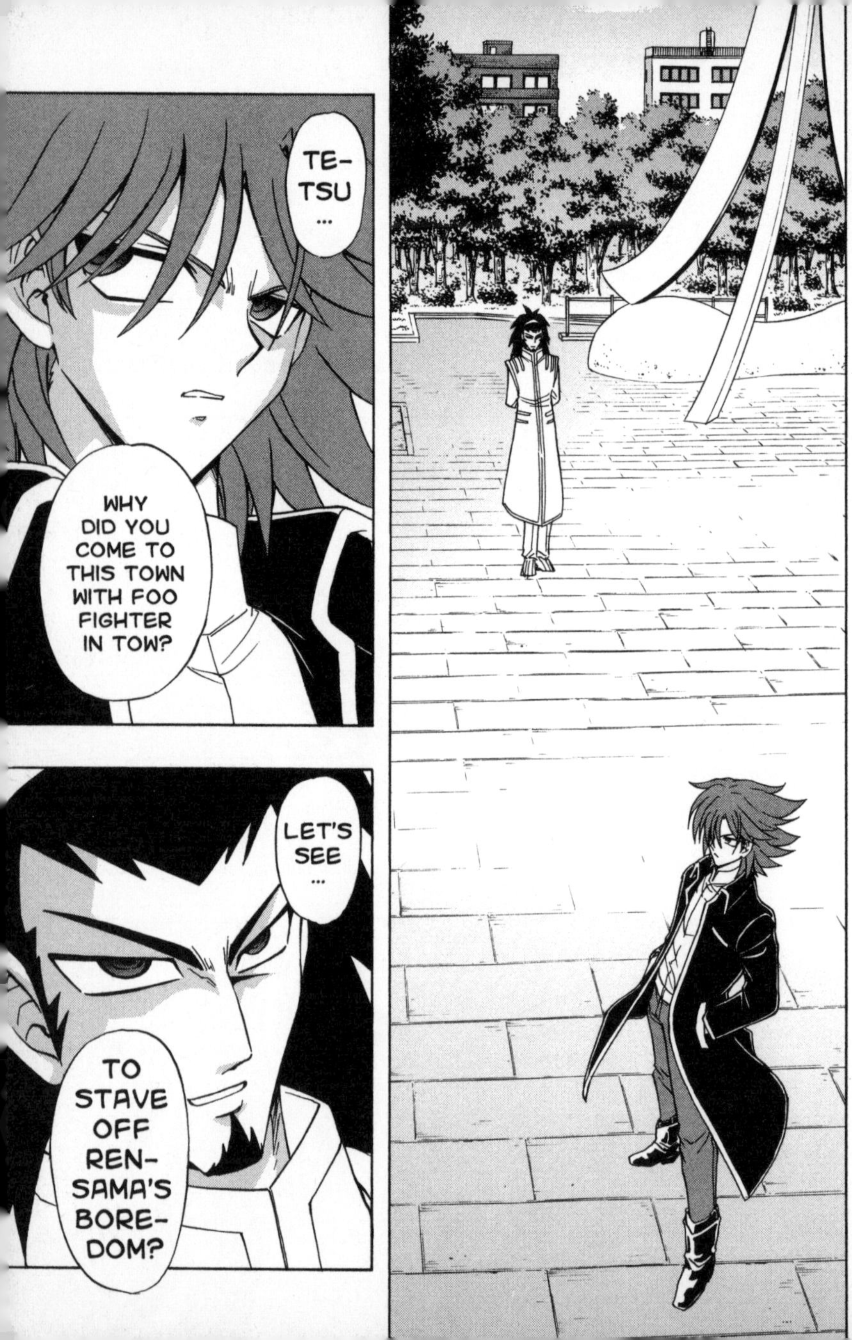
TE-TSU ...
WHY DID YOU COME TO THIS TOWN WITH FOO FIGHTER IN TOW?
LET'S SEE ...
TO STAVE OFF REN-SAMA'S BORE-DOM?

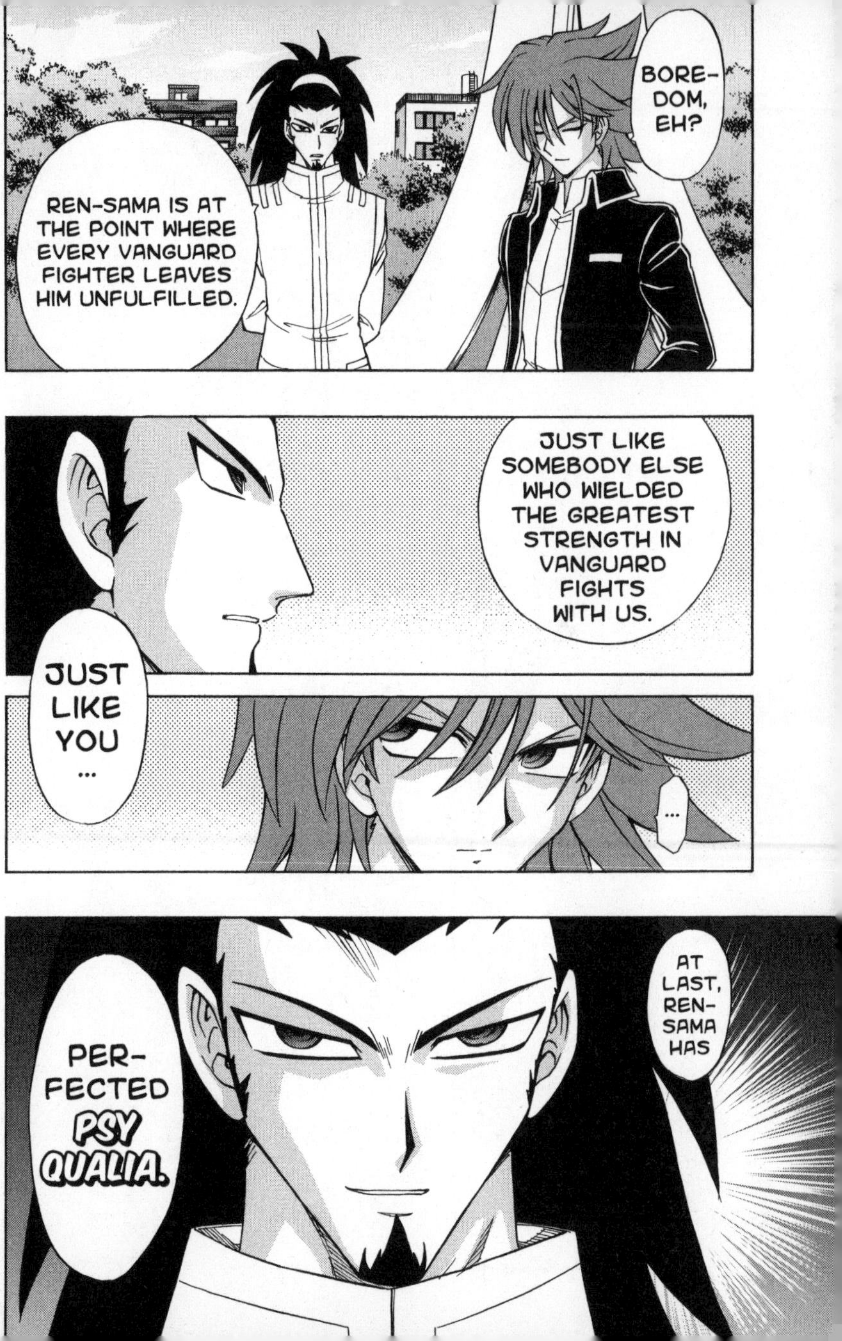
BORE-DOM, EH?
REN-SAMA IS AT THE POINT WHERE EVERY VANGUARD FIGHTER LEAVES HIM UNFULFILLED.
JUST LIKE SOMEBODY ELSE WHO WIELDED THE GREATEST STRENGTH IN VANGUARD FIGHTS WITH US.
JUST LIKE YOU ...
...
AT LAST, REN-SAMA HAS
PER-FECTED PSY QUALIA.

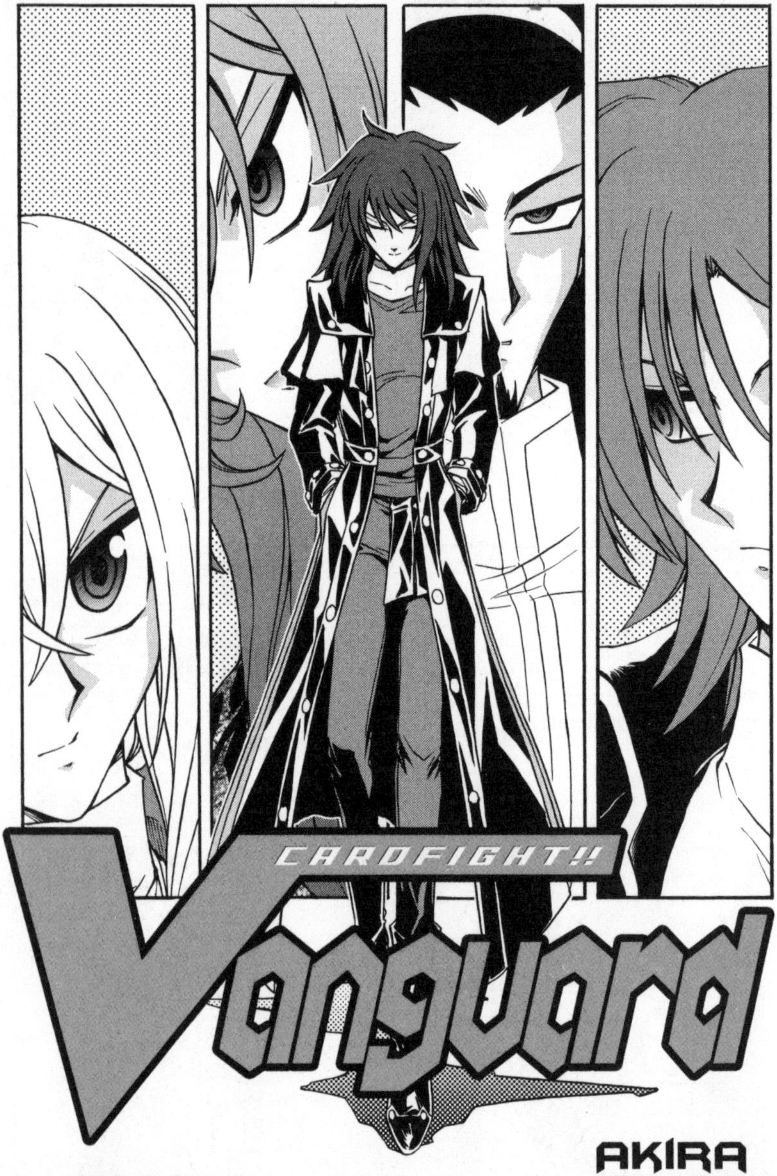
CARDFIGHT!!
Vanguard

AKIRA
ITOU

#010 GIRLS' FIGHT

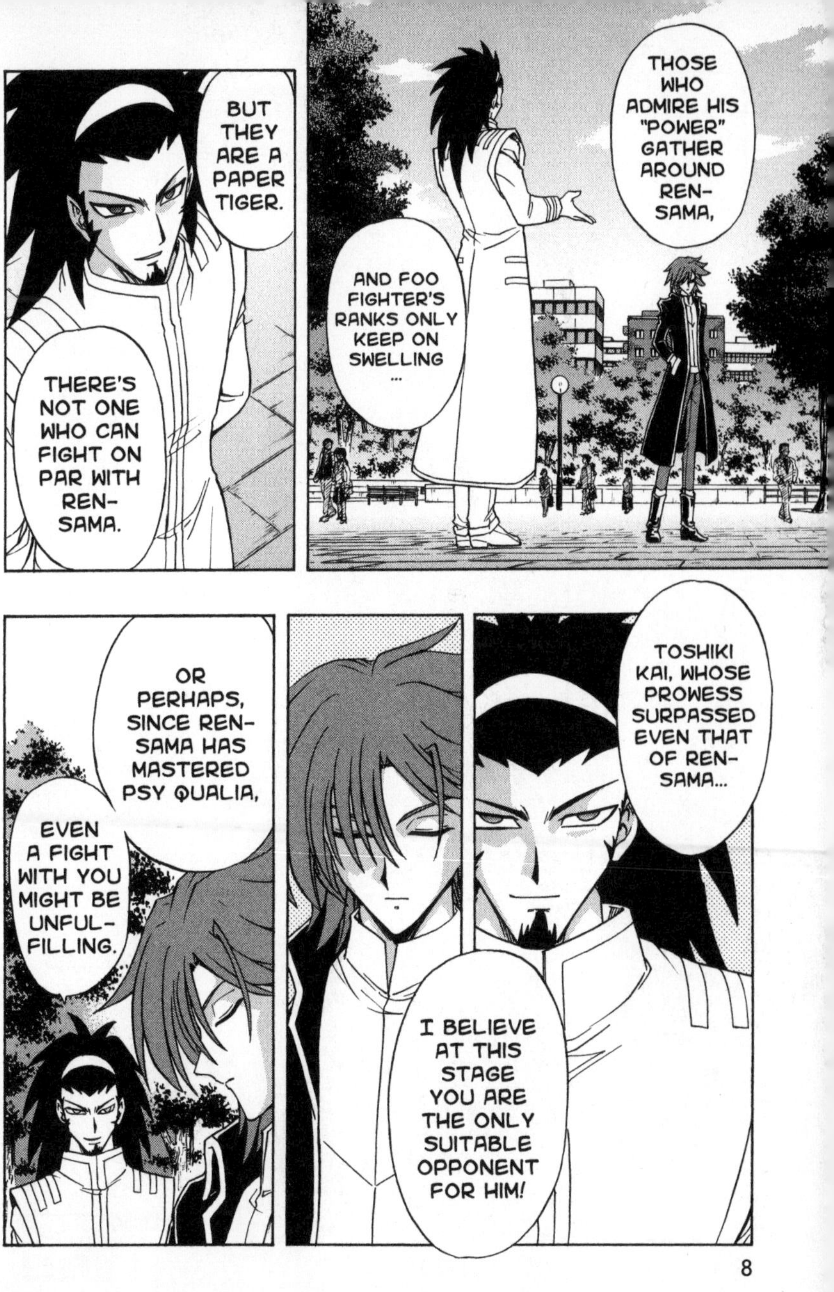
THOSE WHO ADMIRE HIS "POWER" GATHER AROUND REN-SAMA,
AND FOO FIGHTER'S RANKS ONLY KEEP ON SWELLING ...
BUT THEY ARE A PAPER TIGER.
THERE'S NOT ONE WHO CAN FIGHT ON PAR WITH REN-SAMA.
TOSHIKI KAI, WHOSE PROWESS SURPASSED EVEN THAT OF REN-SAMA...
I BELIEVE AT THIS STAGE YOU ARE THE ONLY SUITABLE OPPONENT FOR HIM!
OR PERHAPS, SINCE REN-SAMA HAS MASTERED PSY QUALIA,
EVEN A FIGHT WITH YOU MIGHT BE UNFUL-FILLING.

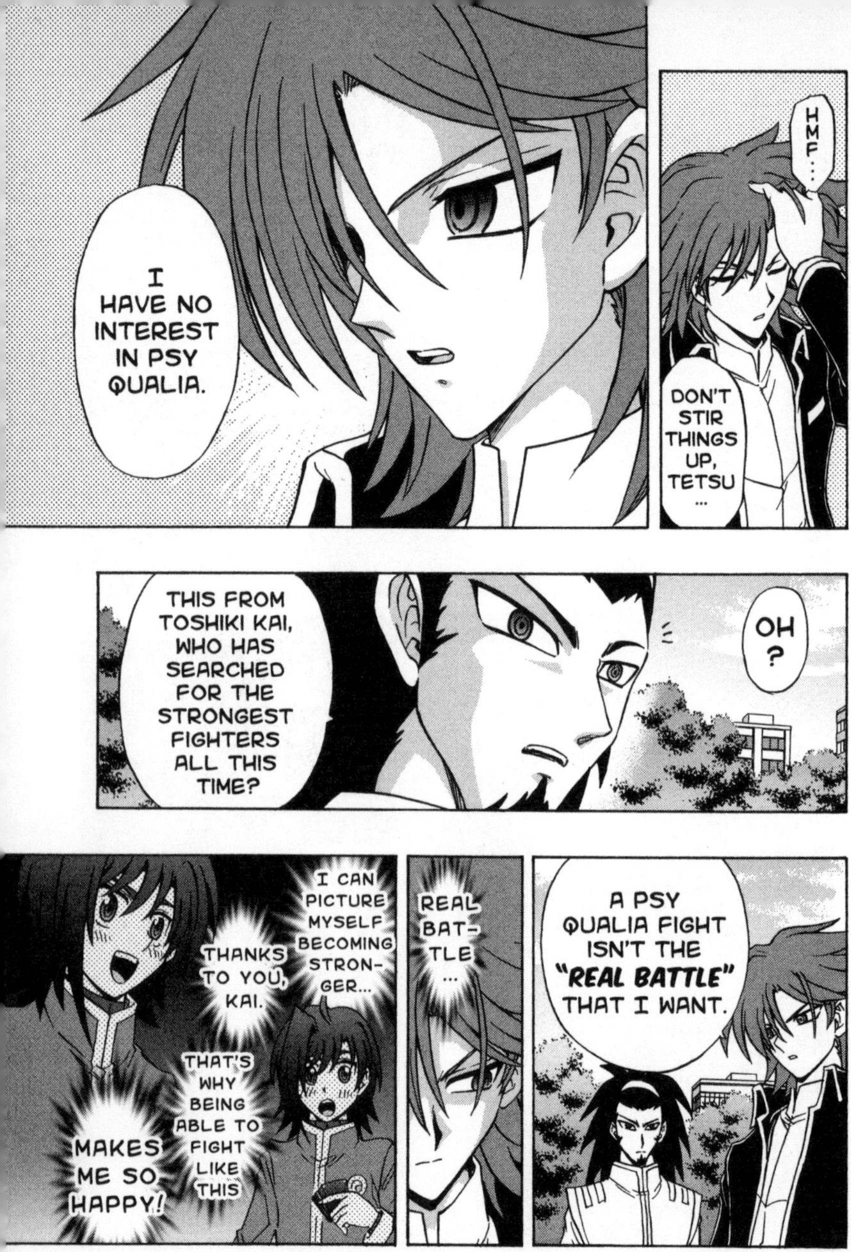
HMF...
DON'T STIR THINGS UP, TETSU...
I HAVE NO INTEREST IN PSY QUALIA.
OH?
THIS FROM TOSHIKI KAI, WHO HAS SEARCHED FOR THE STRONGEST FIGHTERS ALL THIS TIME?
A PSY QUALIA FIGHT ISN'T THE "***REAL BATTLE***" THAT I WANT.
REAL BAT-TLE...
I CAN PICTURE MYSELF BECOMING STRON-GER...
THANKS TO YOU, KAI.
THAT'S WHY BEING ABLE TO FIGHT LIKE THIS
MAKES ME SO HAPPY!

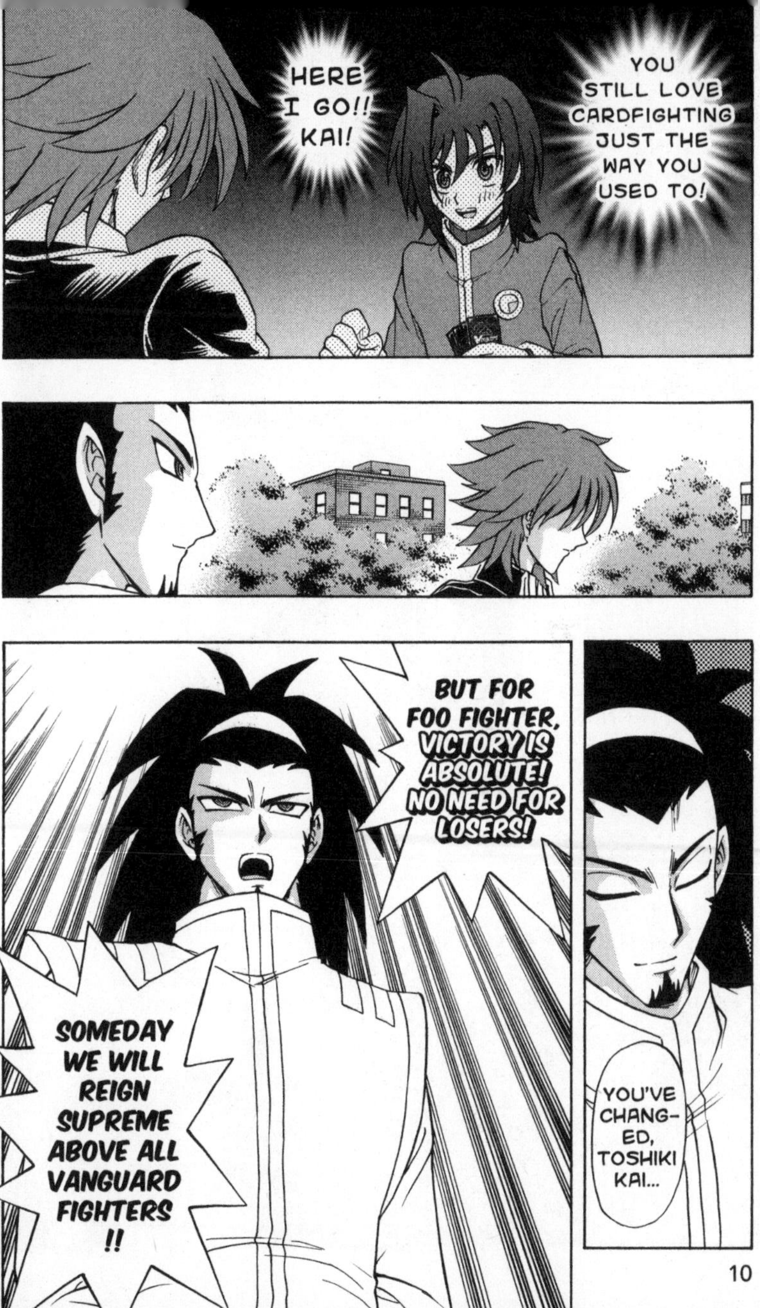
YOU STILL LOVE CARDFIGHTING JUST THE WAY YOU USED TO!
HERE I GO!! KAI!
YOU'VE CHANG-ED, TOSHIKI KAI...
BUT FOR FOO FIGHTER, VICTORY IS ABSOLUTE! NO NEED FOR LOSERS!
SOMEDAY WE WILL REIGN SUPREME ABOVE ALL VANGUARD FIGHTERS !!

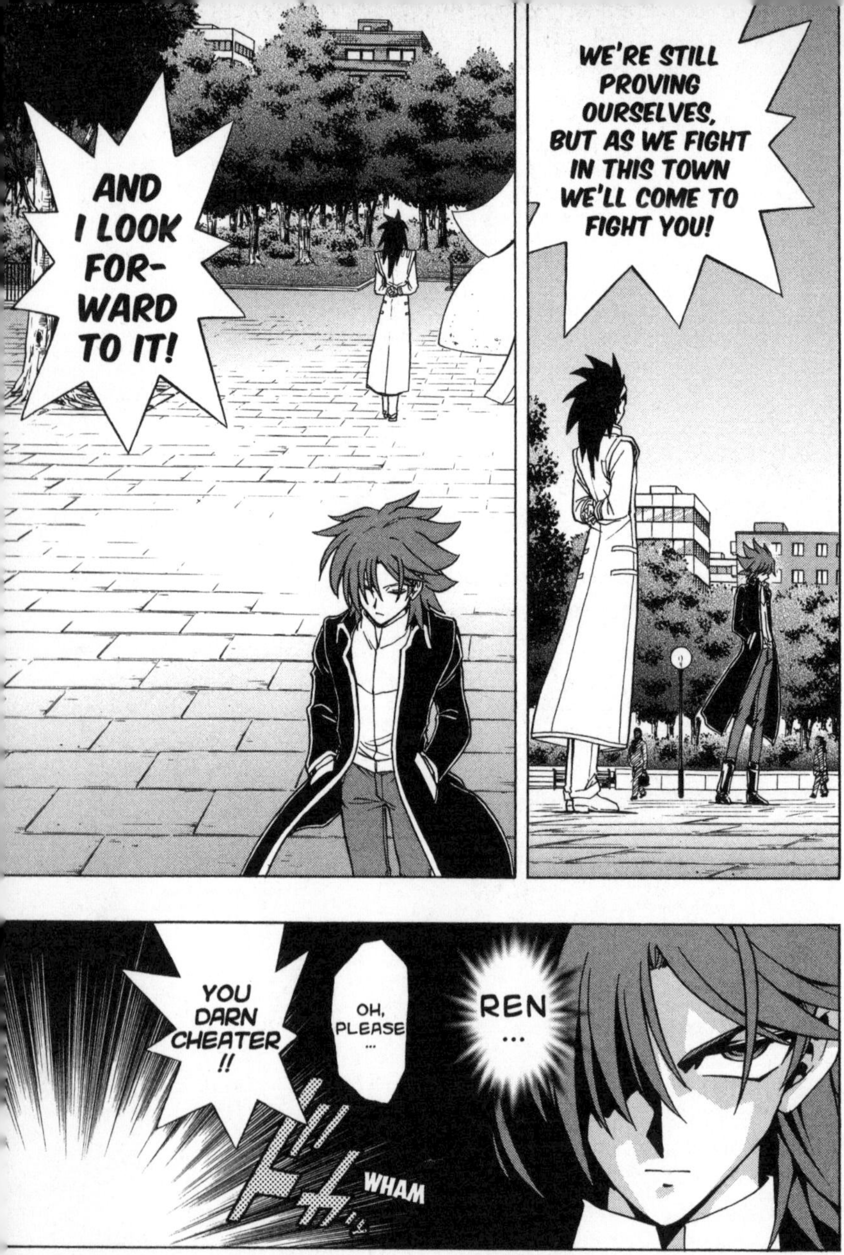
WE'RE STILL PROVING OURSELVES, BUT AS WE FIGHT IN THIS TOWN WE'LL COME TO FIGHT YOU!
AND I LOOK FOR-WARD TO IT!
REN ...
OH, PLEASE ...
YOU DARN CHEATER !!
WHAM

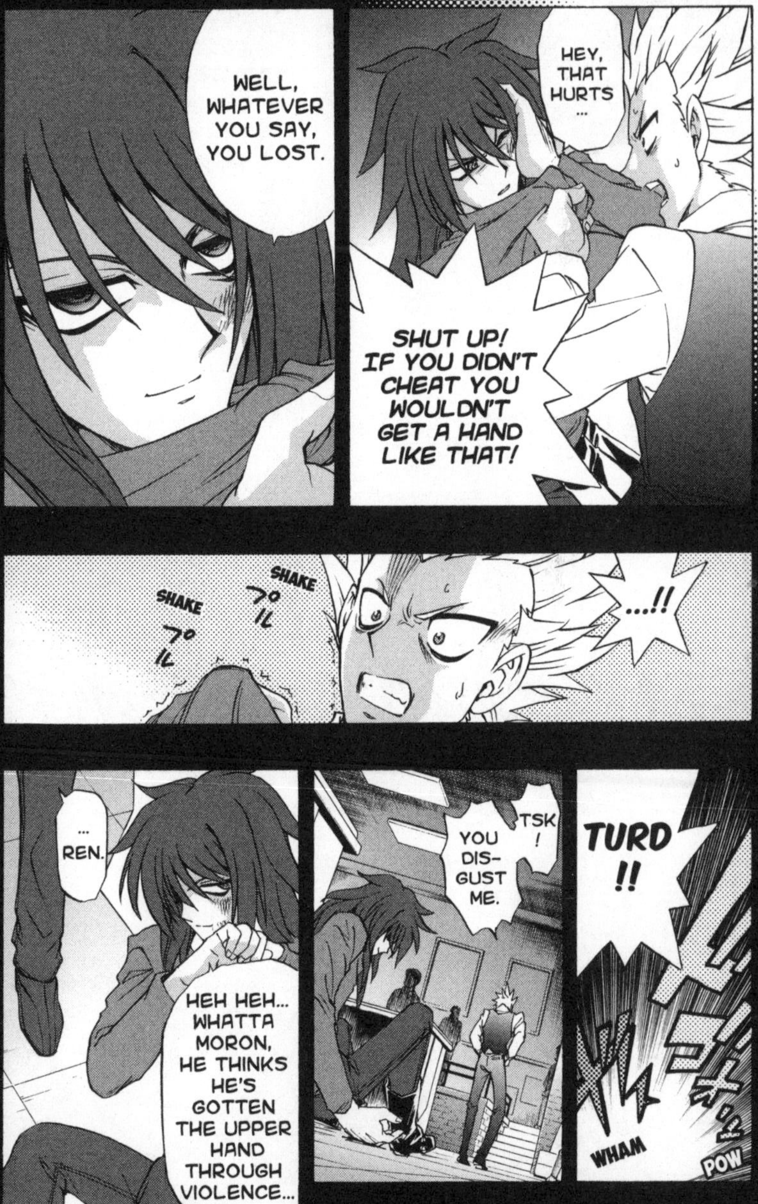
HEY, THAT HURTS ...
SHUT UP! IF YOU DIDN'T CHEAT YOU WOULDN'T GET A HAND LIKE THAT!
WELL, WHATEVER YOU SAY, YOU LOST.
...!!
SHAKE
プル
SHAKE
プル
TURD !!
POW
WHAM
TSK !
YOU DIS-GUST ME.
... REN.
HEH HEH... WHATTA MORON, HE THINKS HE'S GOTTEN THE UPPER HAND THROUGH VIOLENCE...

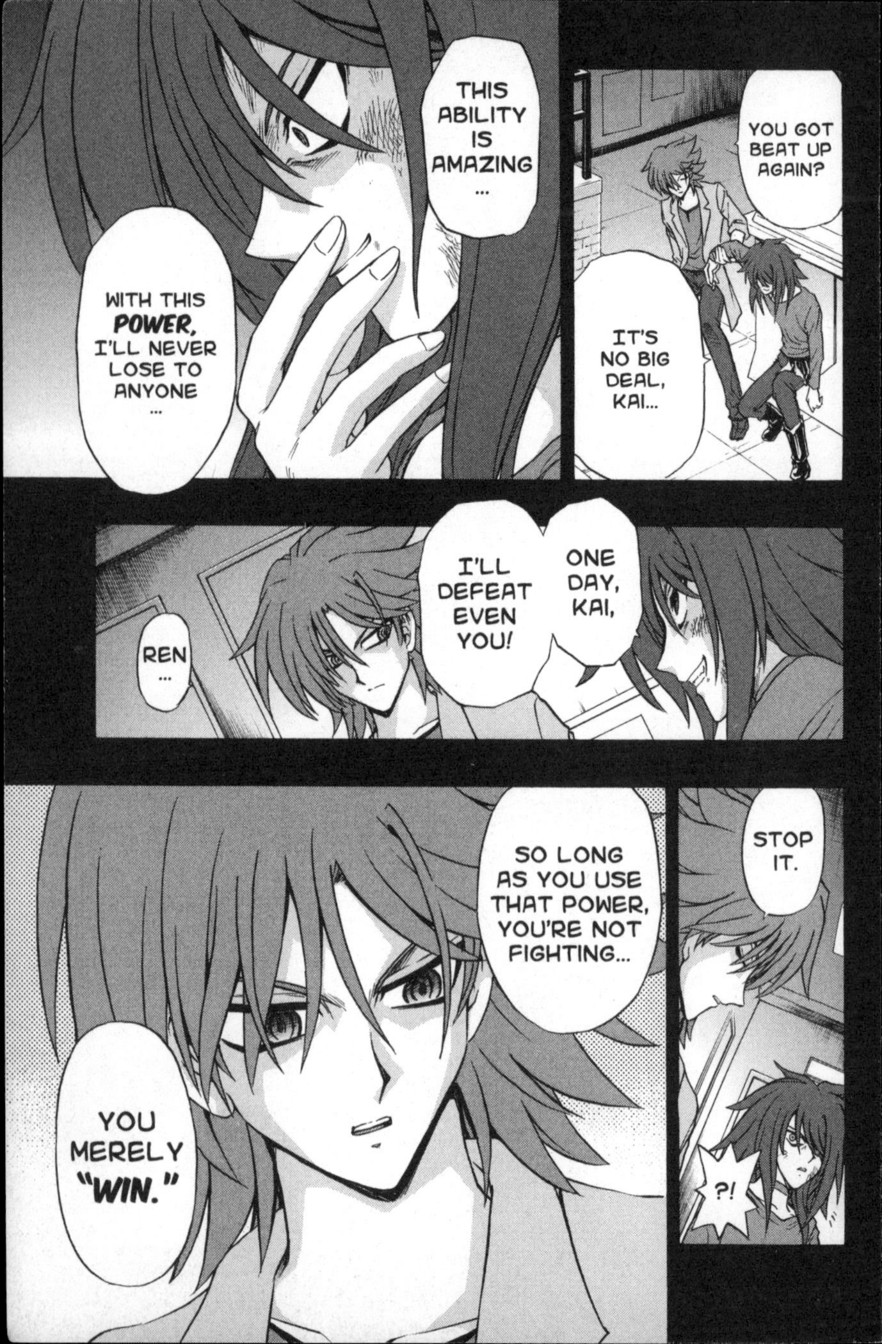
YOU GOT BEAT UP AGAIN?
IT'S NO BIG DEAL, KAI...
THIS ABILITY IS AMAZING...
WITH THIS **POWER,** I'LL NEVER LOSE TO ANYONE...
ONE DAY, KAI,
I'LL DEFEAT EVEN YOU!
REN...
STOP IT.
?!
SO LONG AS YOU USE THAT POWER, YOU'RE NOT FIGHTING...
YOU MERELY **"WIN."**

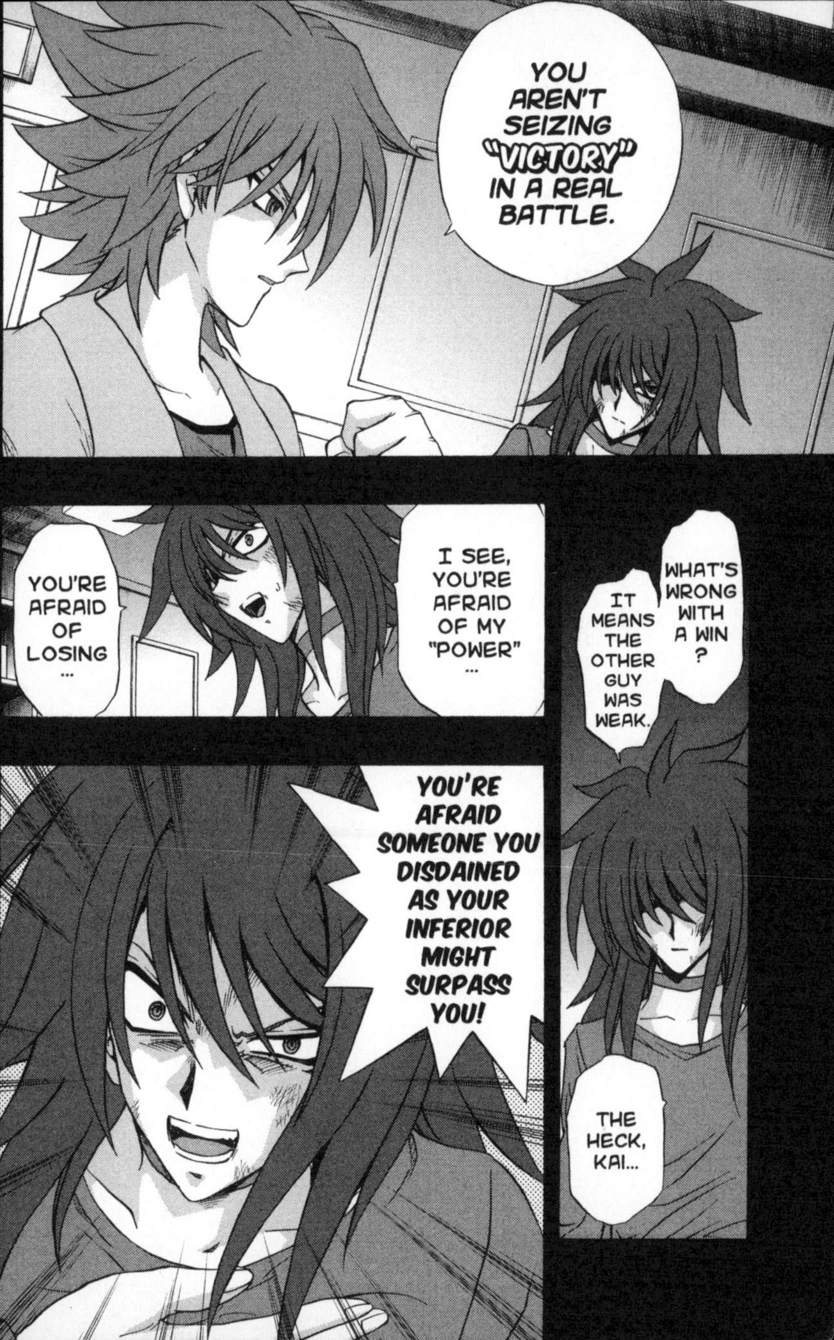
YOU AREN'T SEIZING "VICTORY" IN A REAL BATTLE.
WHAT'S WRONG WITH A WIN ?
IT MEANS THE OTHER GUY WAS WEAK.
THE HECK, KAI...
I SEE, YOU'RE AFRAID OF MY "POWER" ...
YOU'RE AFRAID OF LOSING ...
YOU'RE AFRAID SOMEONE YOU DISDAINED AS YOUR INFERIOR MIGHT SURPASS YOU!

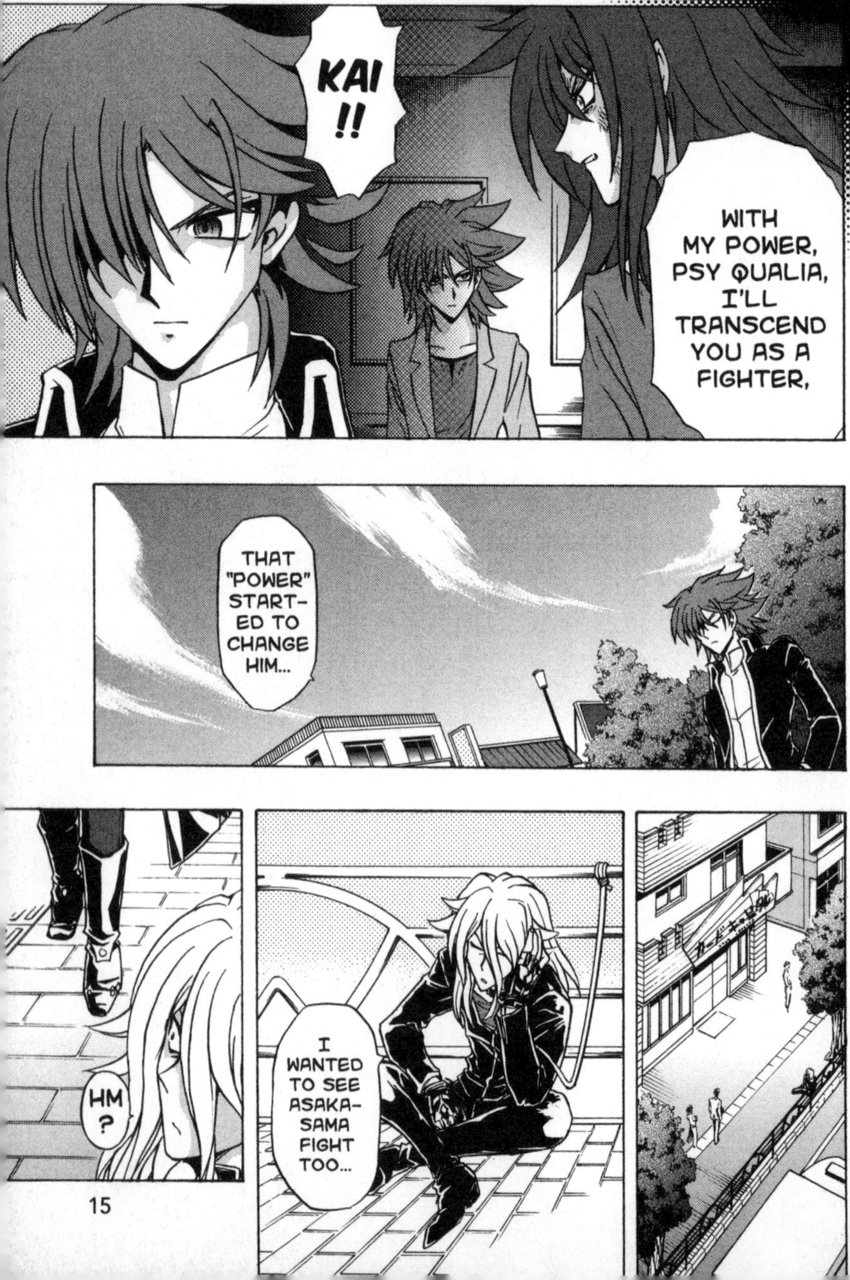
WITH MY POWER, PSY QUALIA, I'LL TRANSCEND YOU AS A FIGHTER,
KAI !!
THAT "POWER" STARTED TO CHANGE HIM...
I WANTED TO SEE ASAKA-SAMA FIGHT TOO...
HM ?

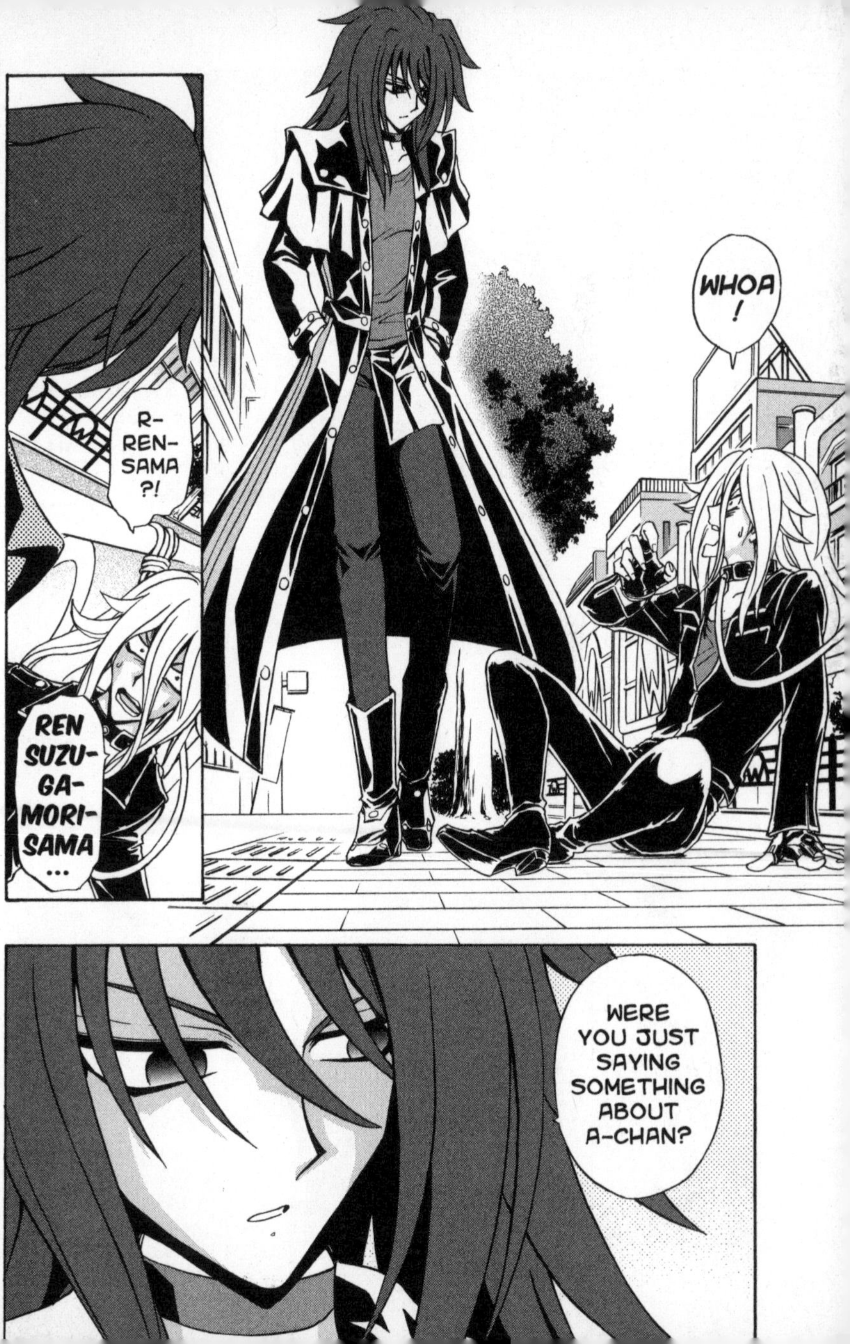
WHOA!
R-REN-SAMA?!
REN SUZUGAMORI-SAMA...
WERE YOU JUST SAYING SOMETHING ABOUT A-CHAN?

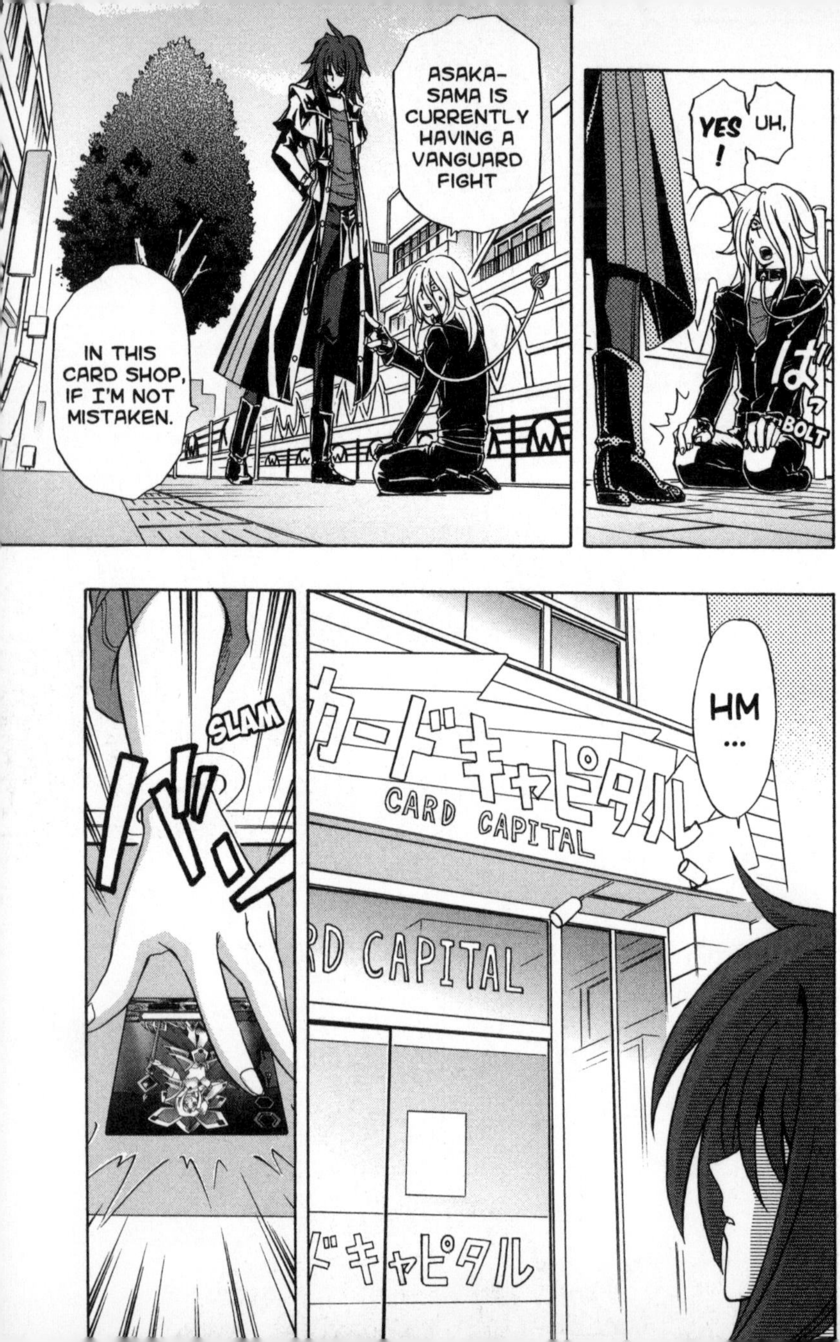
UH, YES!
ばっ
BOLT
ASAKA-SAMA IS CURRENTLY HAVING A VANGUARD FIGHT
IN THIS CARD SHOP, IF I'M NOT MISTAKEN.
HM ...
カードキャピタル
CARD CAPITAL
RD CAPITAL
ドキャピタル
SLAM
バンッ

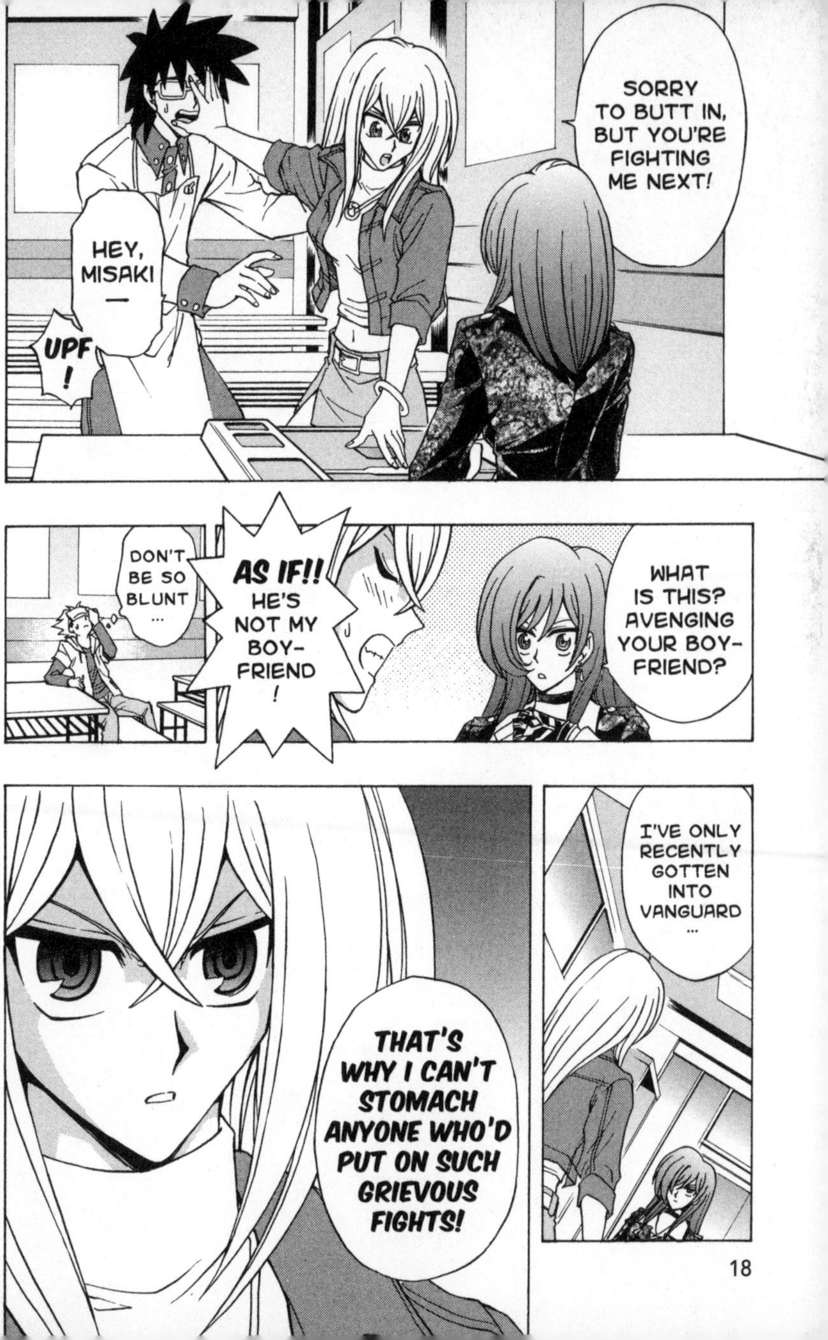
SORRY TO BUTT IN, BUT YOU'RE FIGHTING ME NEXT!
HEY, MISAKI —
UPF!
WHAT IS THIS? AVENGING YOUR BOY-FRIEND?
AS IF!! HE'S NOT MY BOY-FRIEND!
DON'T BE SO BLUNT ...
I'VE ONLY RECENTLY GOTTEN INTO VANGUARD ...
THAT'S WHY I CAN'T STOMACH ANYONE WHO'D PUT ON SUCH GRIEVOUS FIGHTS!

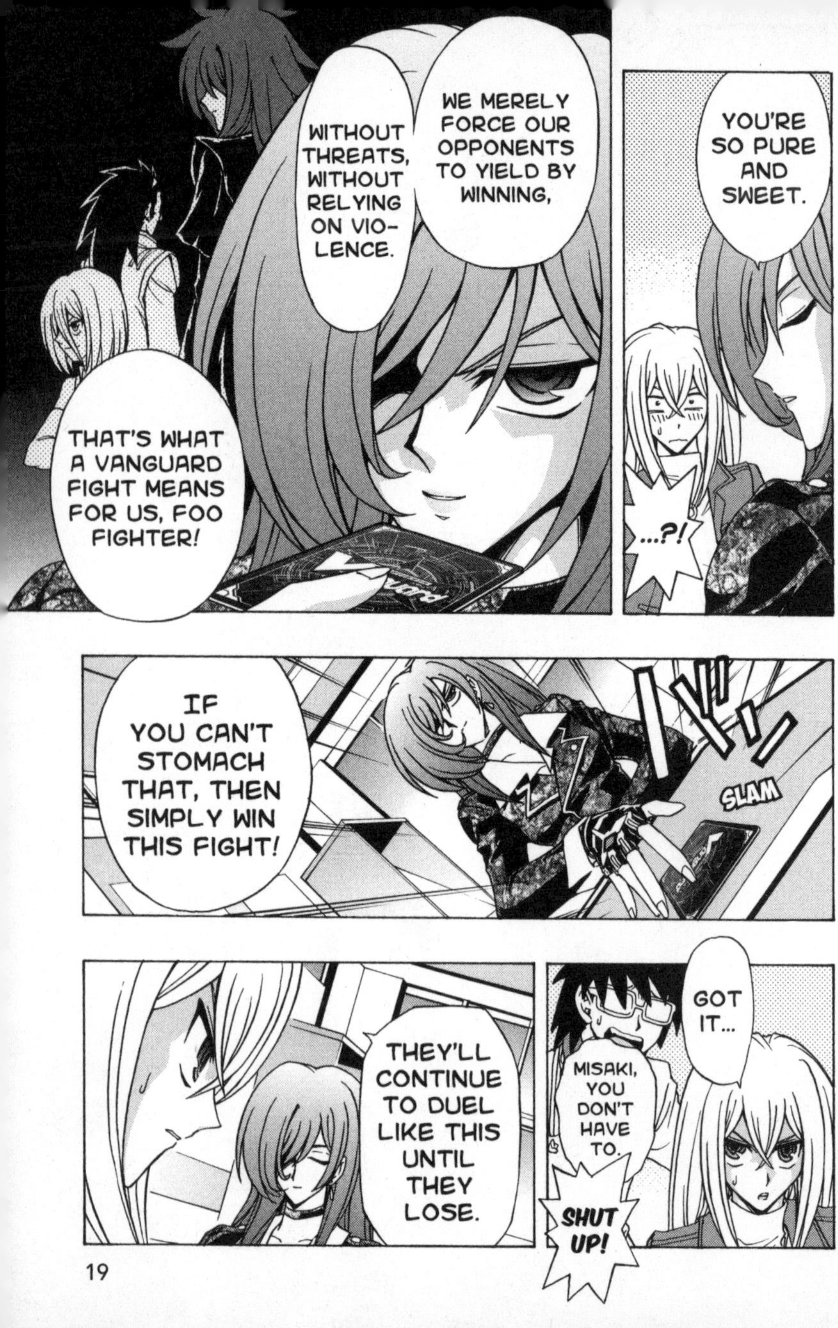
YOU'RE SO PURE AND SWEET.
...?!
WE MERELY FORCE OUR OPPONENTS TO YIELD BY WINNING,
WITHOUT THREATS, WITHOUT RELYING ON VIO-LENCE.
THAT'S WHAT A VANGUARD FIGHT MEANS FOR US, FOO FIGHTER!
IF YOU CAN'T STOMACH THAT, THEN SIMPLY WIN THIS FIGHT!
SLAM
GOT IT...
MISAKI, YOU DON'T HAVE TO.
SHUT UP!
THEY'LL CONTINUE TO DUEL LIKE THIS UNTIL THEY LOSE.

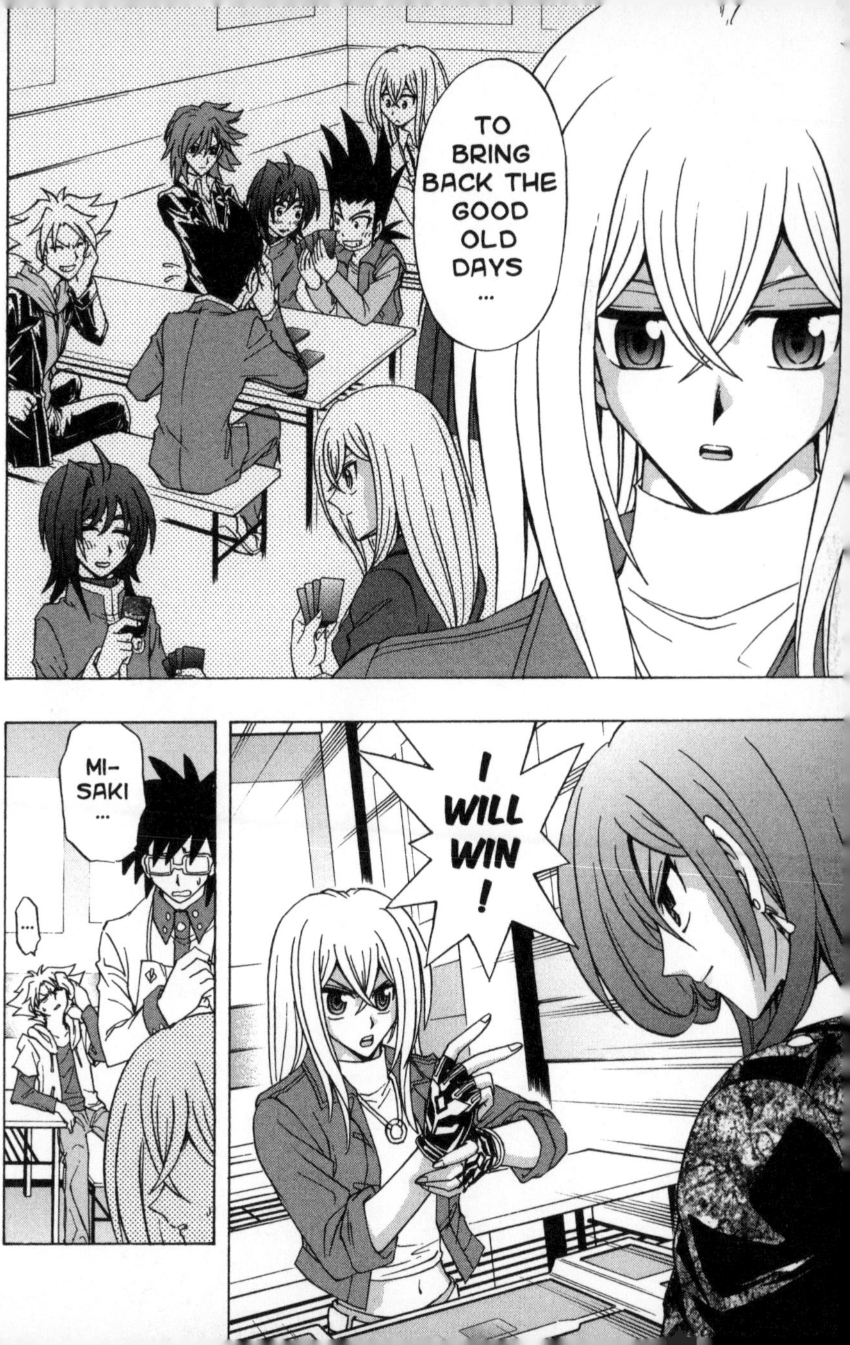
TO BRING BACK THE GOOD OLD DAYS ...
I WILL WIN!
MI-SAKI ...
...

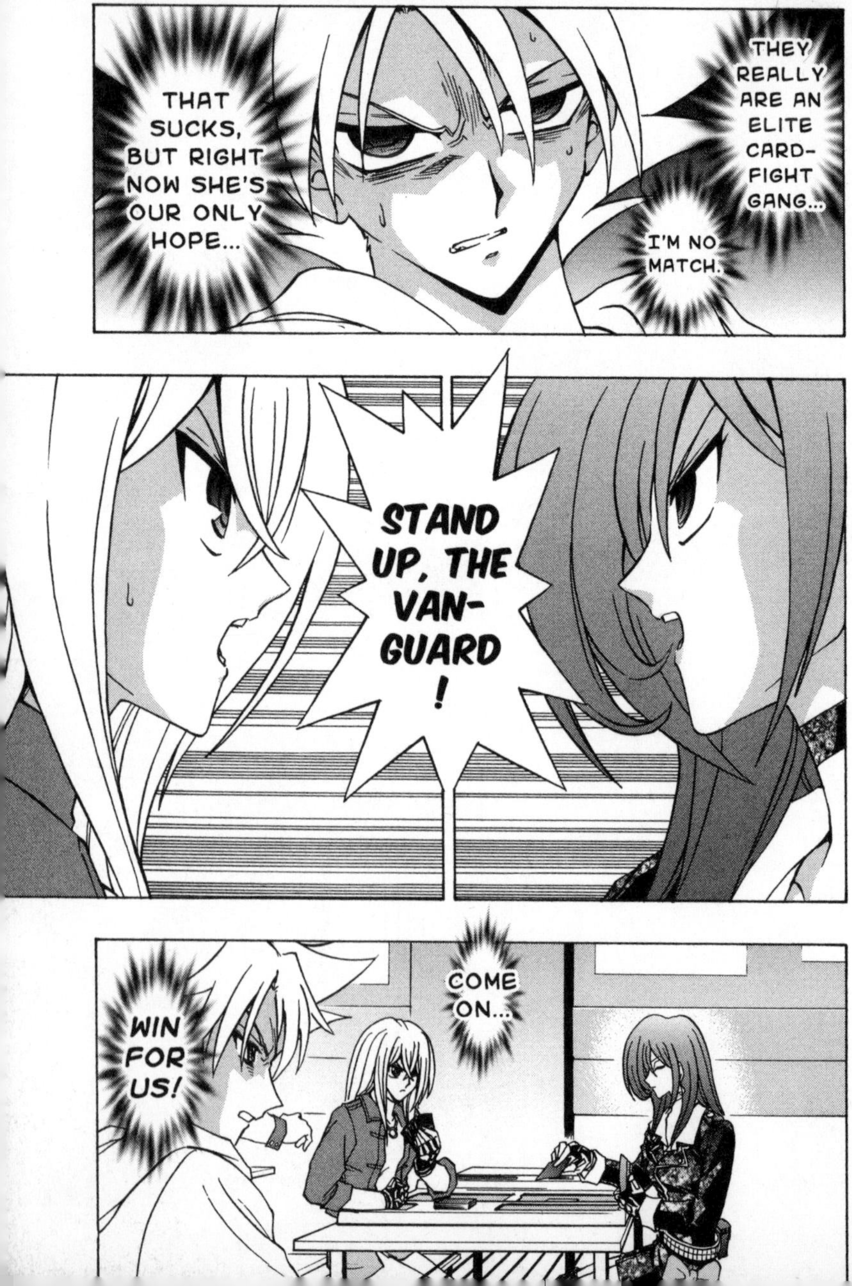
THEY REALLY ARE AN ELITE CARD-FIGHT GANG...
I'M NO MATCH.
THAT SUCKS, BUT RIGHT NOW SHE'S OUR ONLY HOPE...
STAND UP, THE VAN-GUARD!
COME ON...
WIN FOR US!

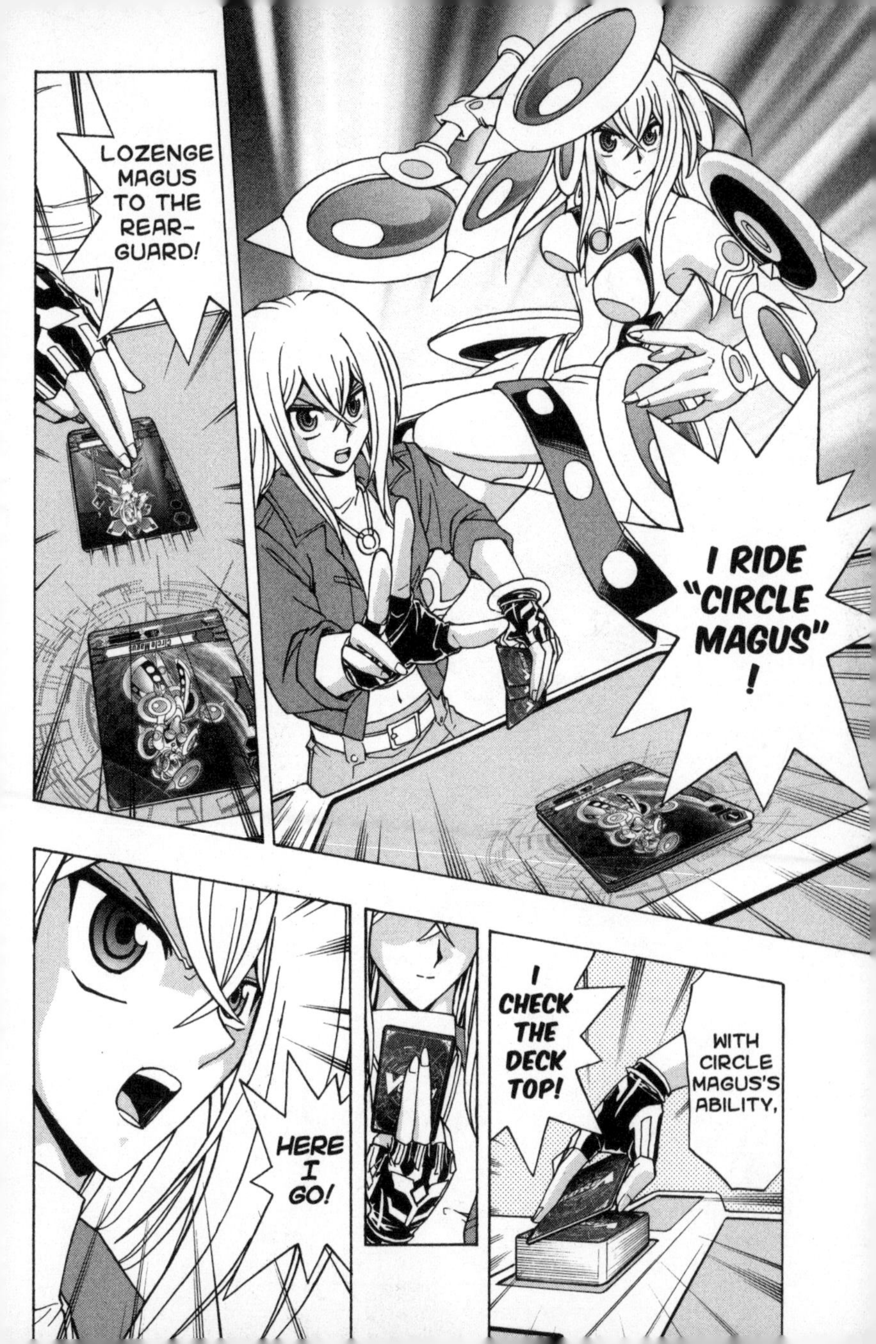
I RIDE "CIRCLE MAGUS"!
LOZENGE MAGUS TO THE REAR-GUARD!
WITH CIRCLE MAGUS'S ABILITY,
I CHECK THE DECK TOP!
HERE I GO!

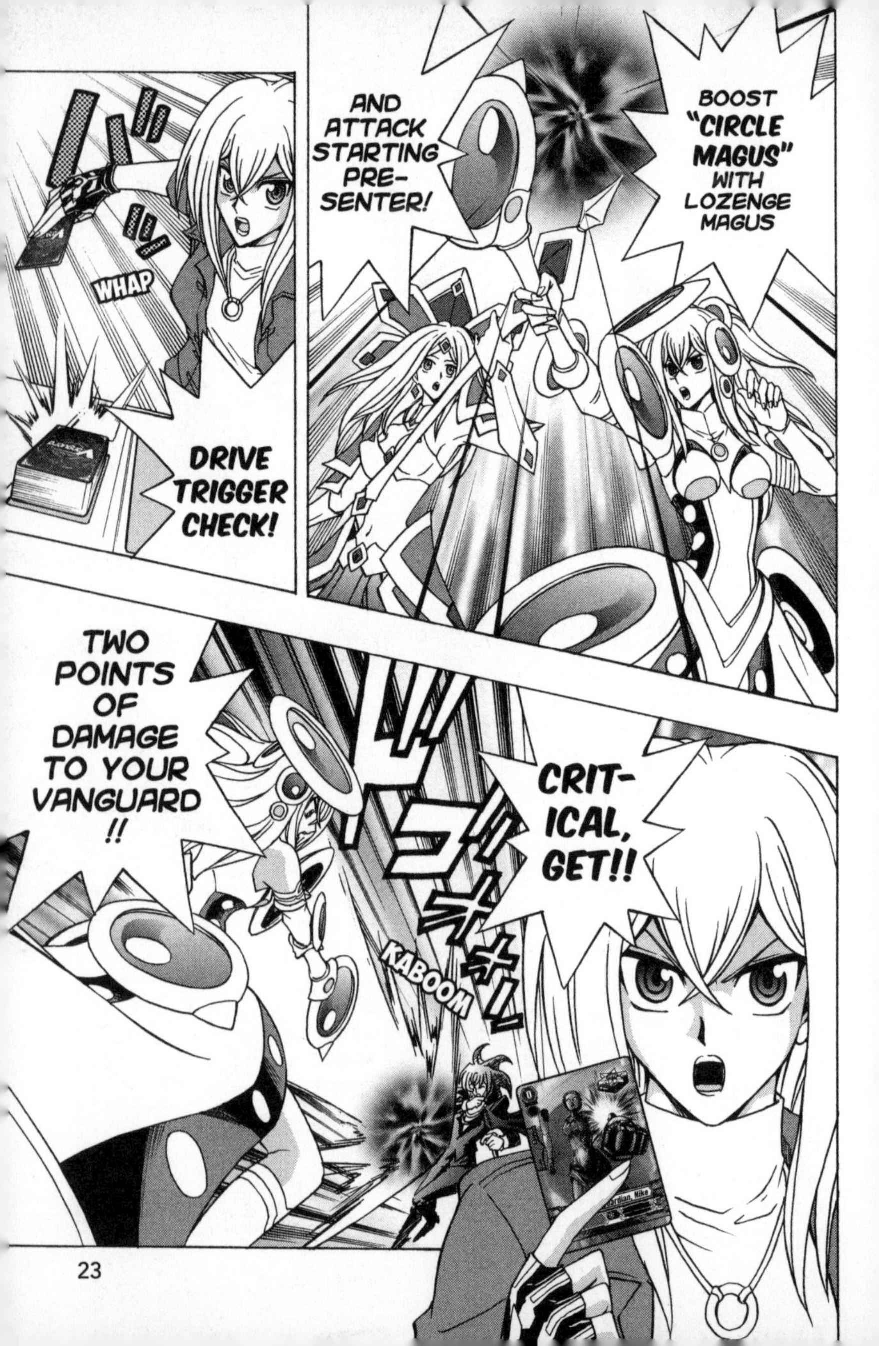
BOOST "CIRCLE MAGUS" WITH LOZENGE MAGUS
AND ATTACK STARTING PRE-SENTER!
WHAP
DRIVE TRIGGER CHECK!
CRIT-ICAL, GET!!
KABOOM
TWO POINTS OF DAMAGE TO YOUR VANGUARD !!

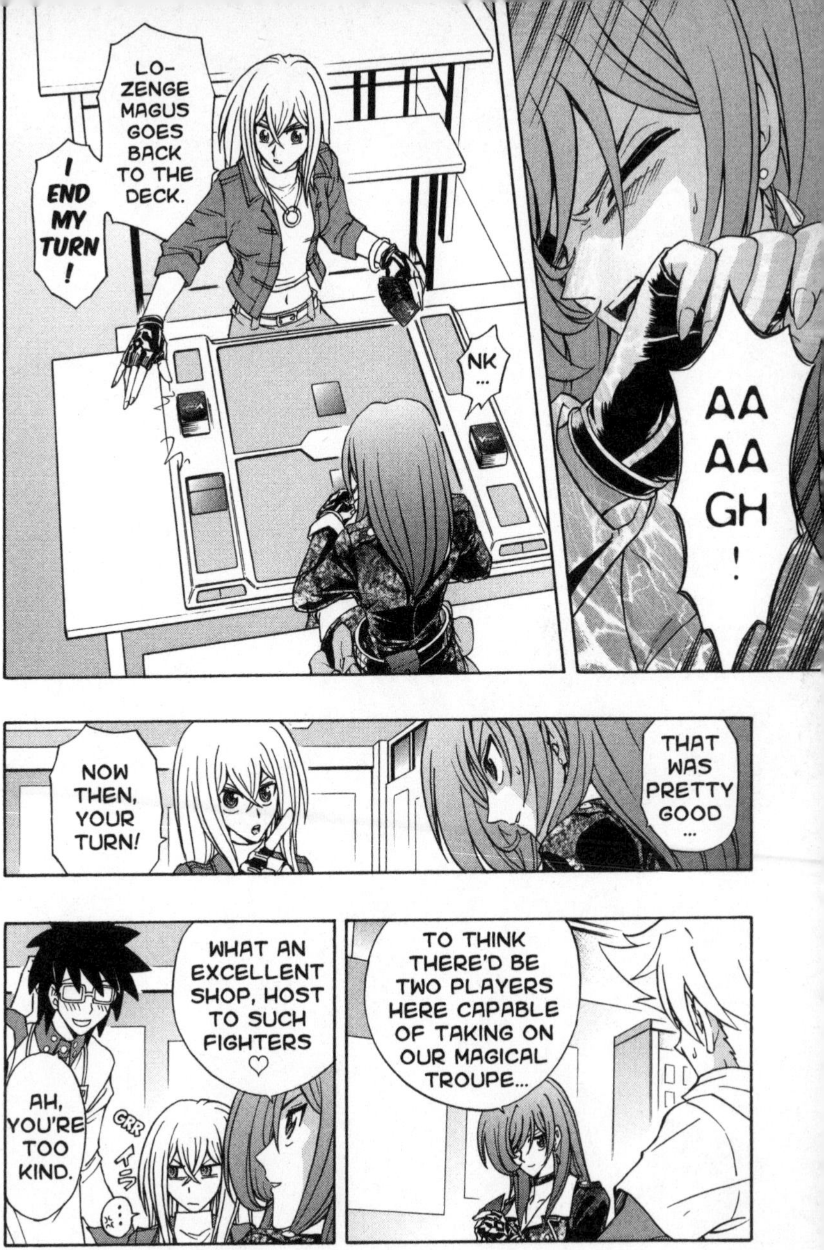
AAAAGH!
LO-ZENGE MAGUS GOES BACK TO THE DECK.
I END MY TURN!
NK...
THAT WAS PRETTY GOOD...
NOW THEN, YOUR TURN!
TO THINK THERE'D BE TWO PLAYERS HERE CAPABLE OF TAKING ON OUR MAGICAL TROUPE...
WHAT AN EXCELLENT SHOP, HOST TO SUCH FIGHTERS ♡
AH, YOU'RE TOO KIND.
GRR
...

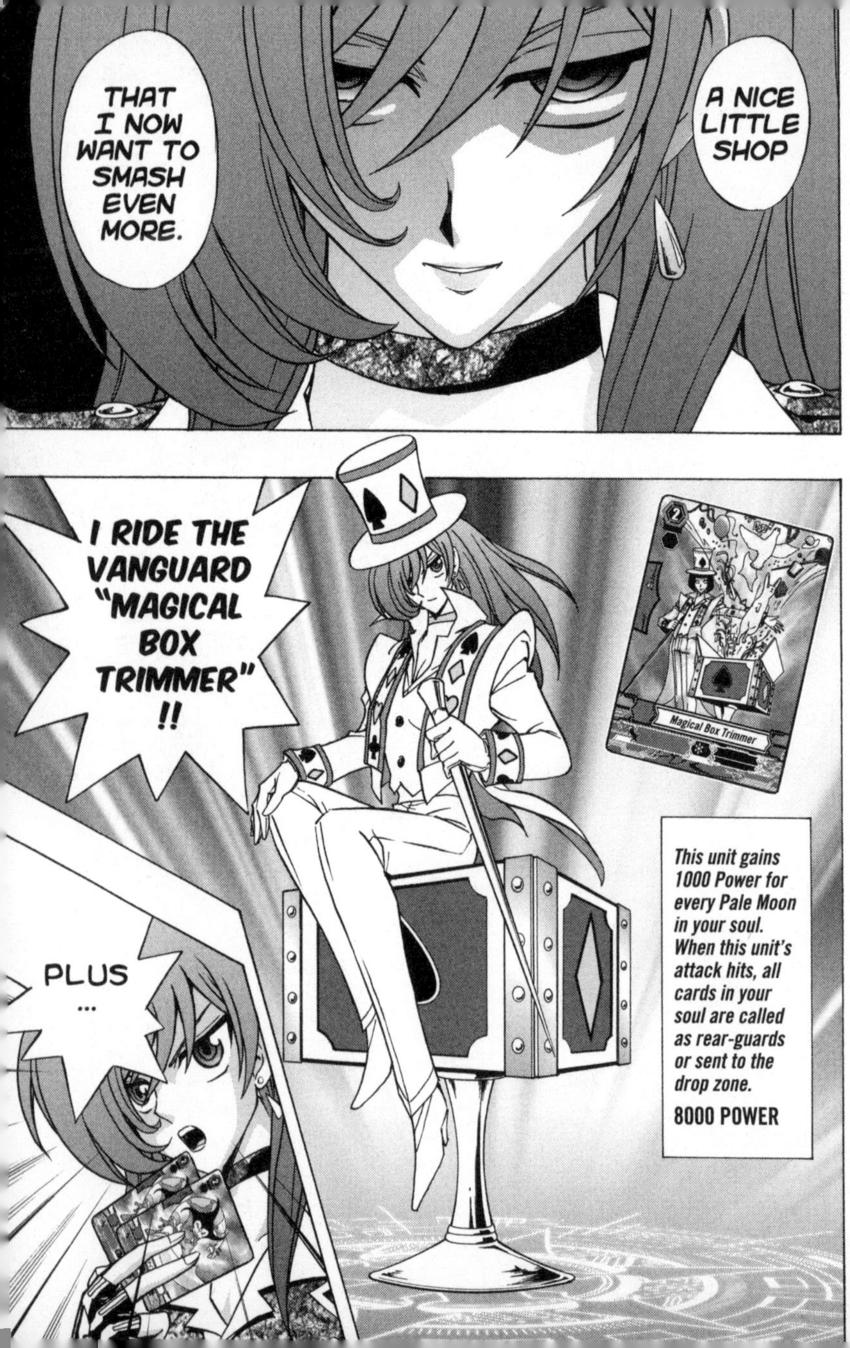
A NICE LITTLE SHOP
THAT I NOW WANT TO SMASH EVEN MORE.
Magical Box Trimmer
I RIDE THE VANGUARD "MAGICAL BOX TRIMMER" !!
This unit gains 1000 Power for every Pale Moon in your soul. When this unit's attack hits, all cards in your soul are called as rear-guards or sent to the drop zone.
8000 POWER
PLUS ...

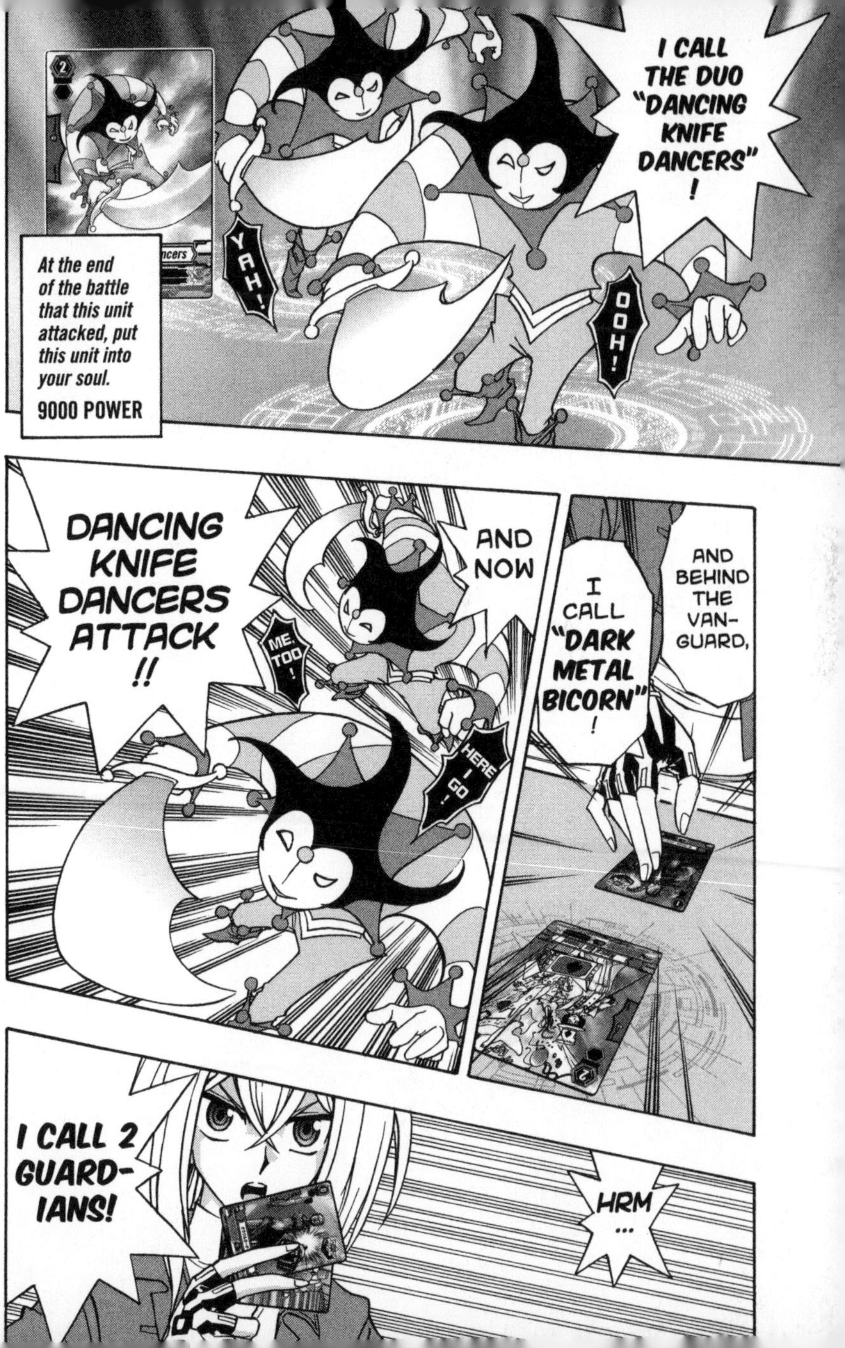
I CALL THE DUO "DANCING KNIFE DANCERS"!
OOH!
YAH!
At the end of the battle that this unit attacked, put this unit into your soul.
9000 POWER
AND BEHIND THE VAN-GUARD,
I CALL "DARK METAL BICORN"!
AND NOW
DANCING KNIFE DANCERS ATTACK!!
ME, TOO!
HERE I GO!
HRM...
I CALL 2 GUARD-IANS!

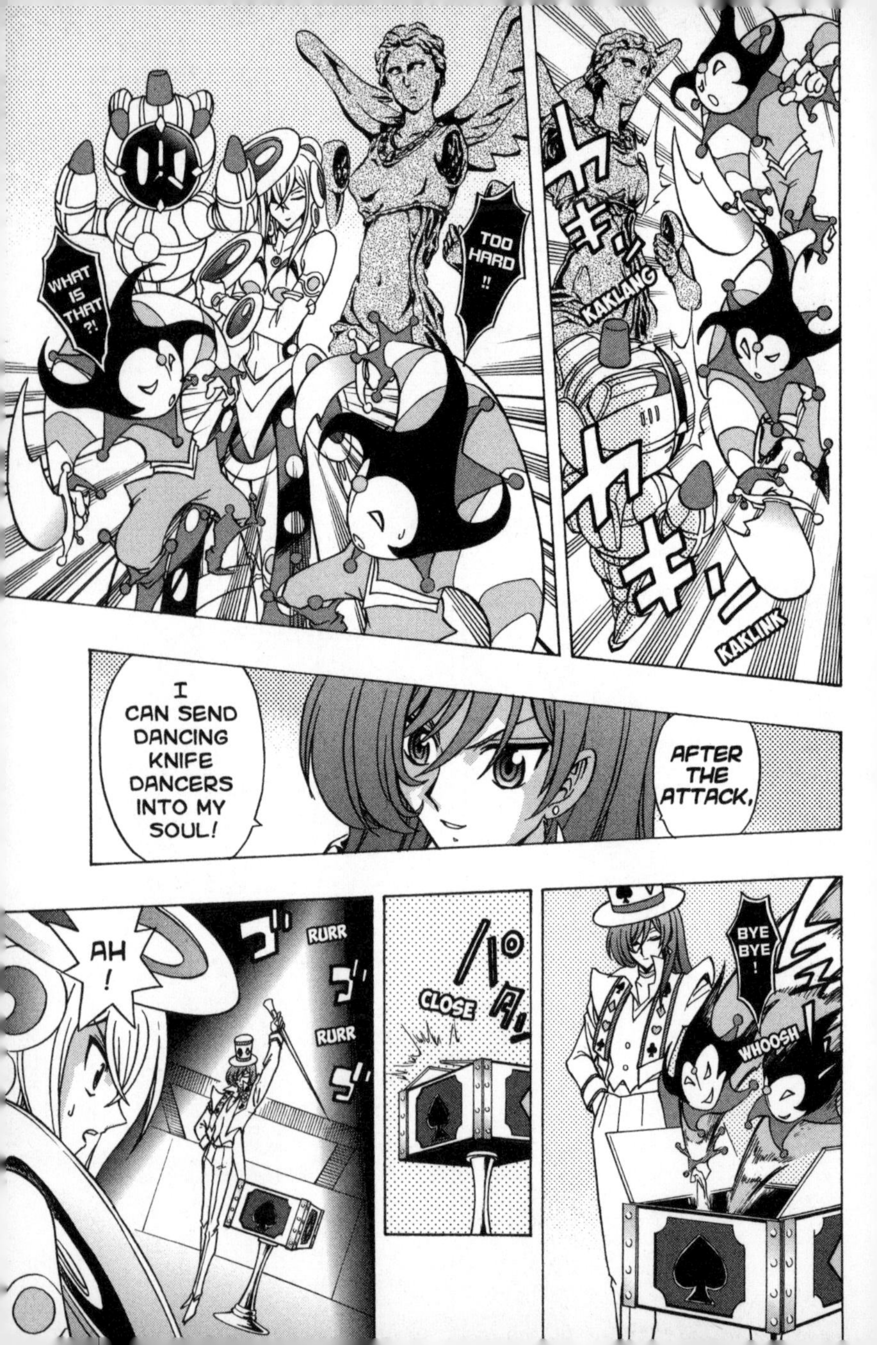
KAKLANG
KAKLINK
TOO HARD!!
WHAT IS THAT?!
AFTER THE ATTACK,
I CAN SEND DANCING KNIFE DANCERS INTO MY SOUL!
BYE BYE!
WHOOSH
CLOSE
AH!
RURR
RURR

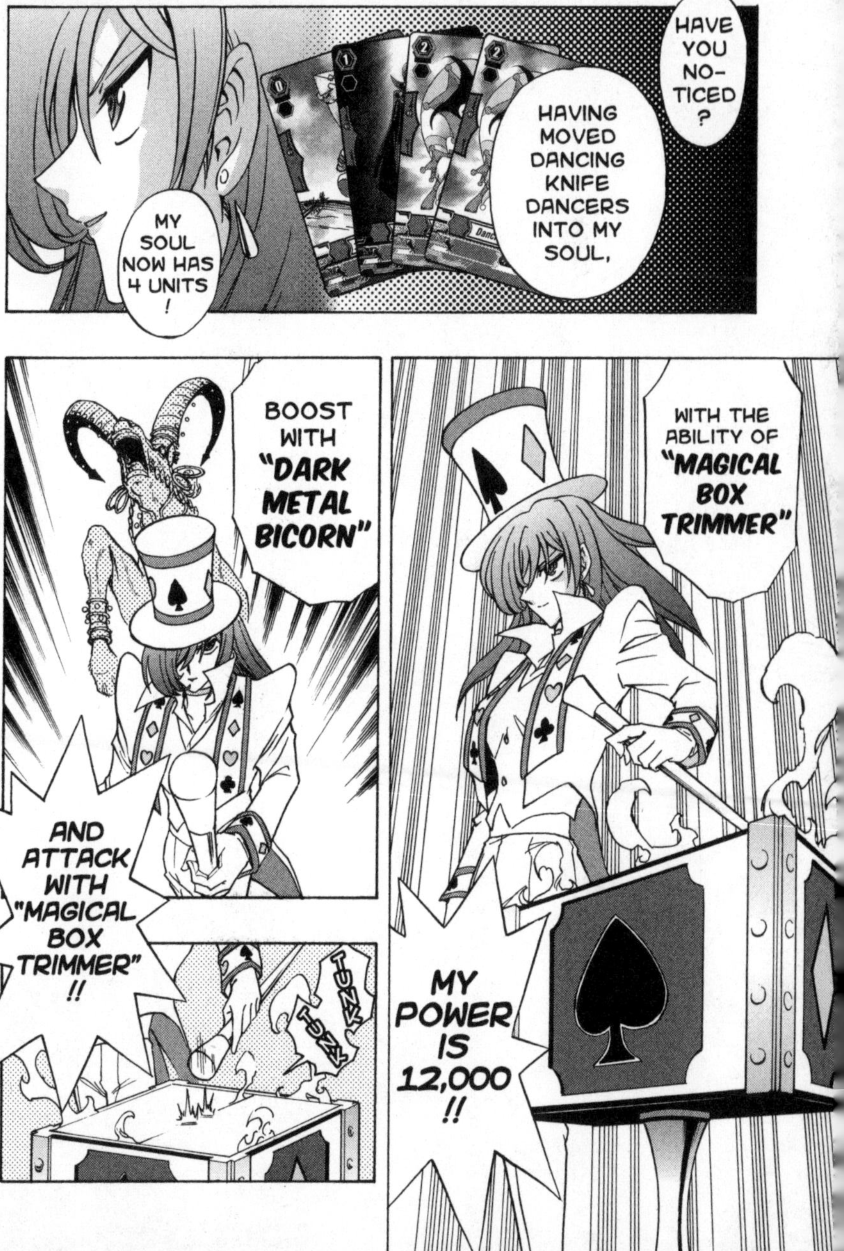
HAVE YOU NO-TICED?
HAVING MOVED DANCING KNIFE DANCERS INTO MY SOUL,
MY SOUL NOW HAS 4 UNITS!
WITH THE ABILITY OF "MAGICAL BOX TRIMMER"
MY POWER IS 12,000!!
BOOST WITH "DARK METAL BICORN"
AND ATTACK WITH "MAGICAL BOX TRIMMER"!!
TUNK
TUNK

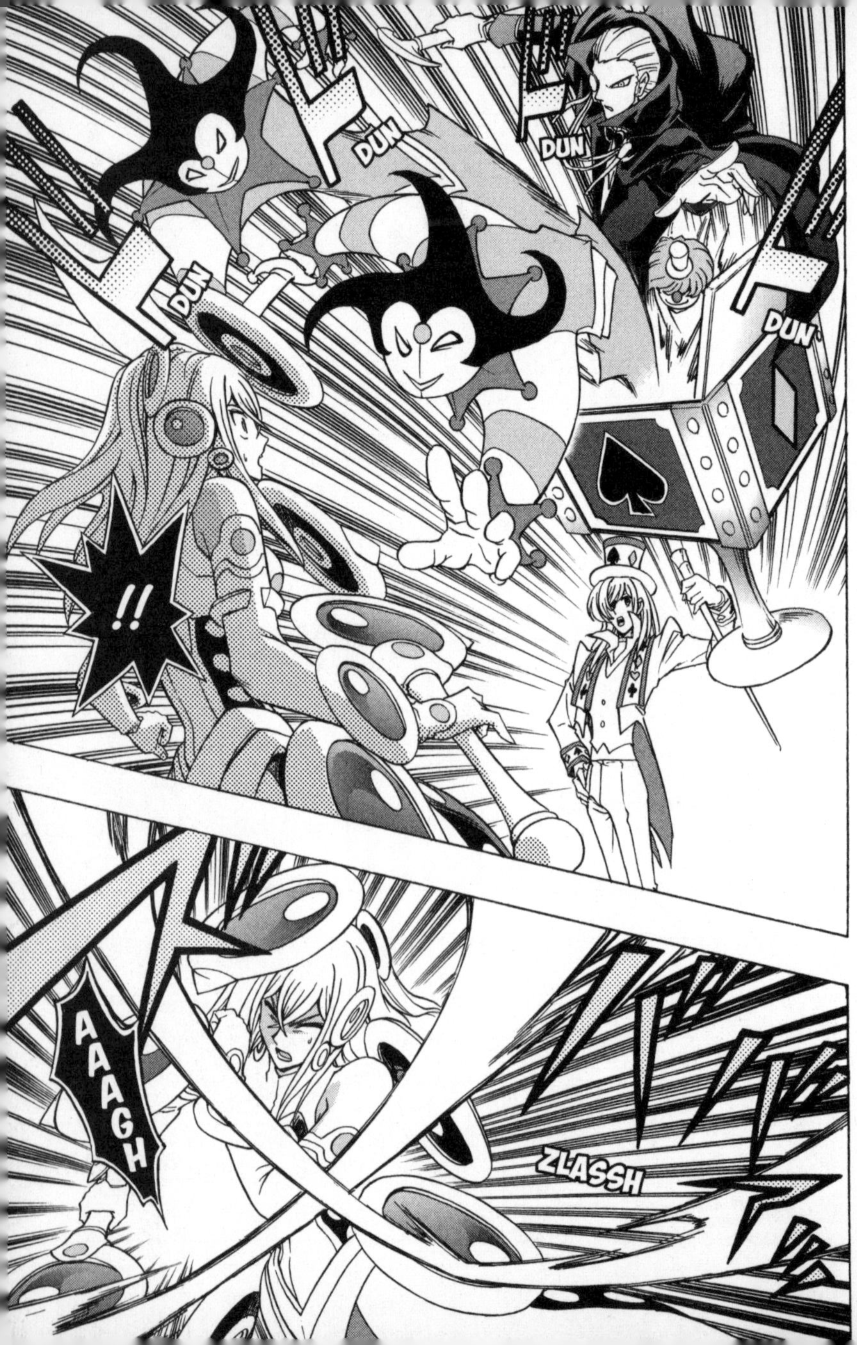
DUN
DUN
DUN
DUN
!!
ZLASSH
AAAGH

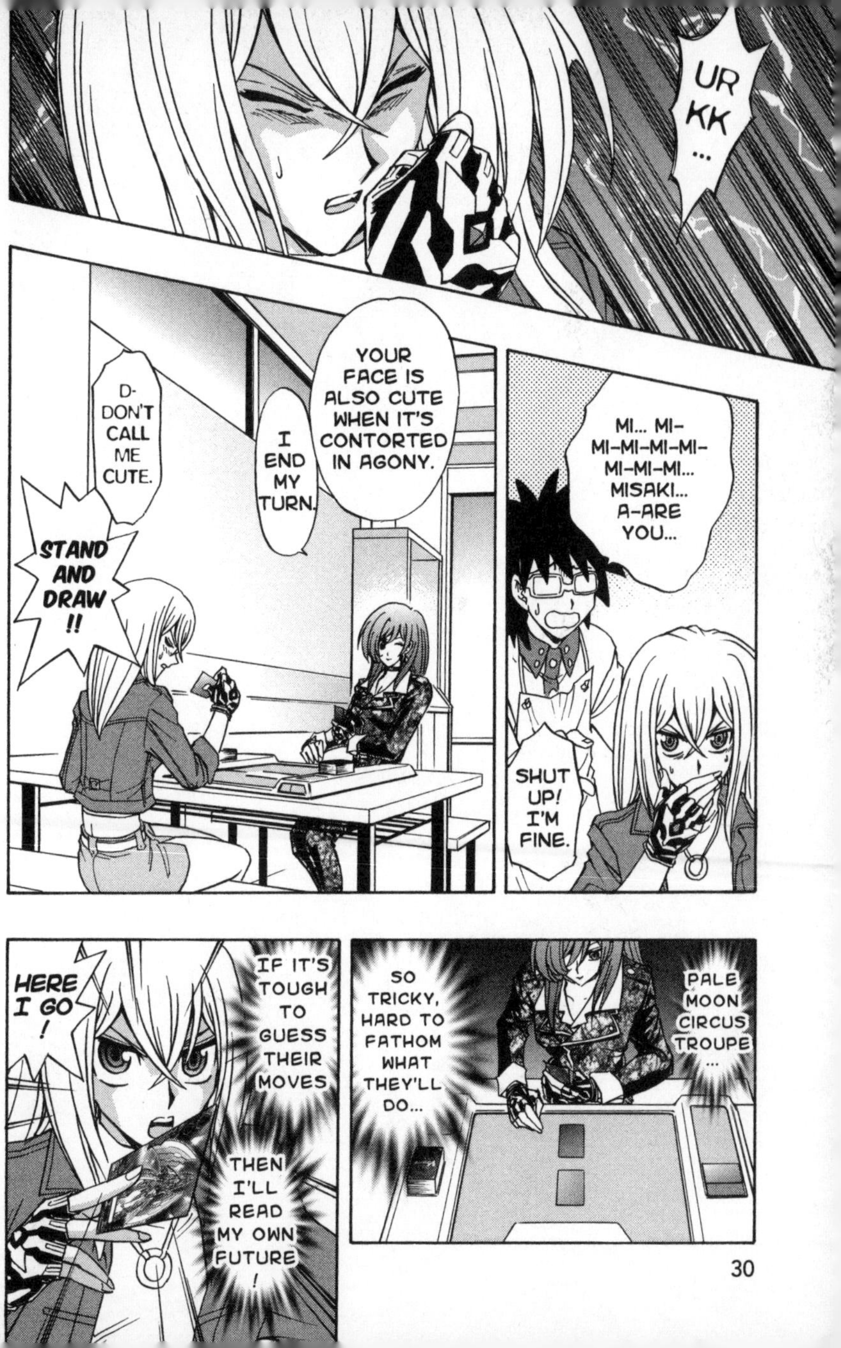
URKK...
MI... MI-MI-MI-MI-MI-MI-MI-MI... MISAKI... A-ARE YOU...
SHUT UP! I'M FINE.
YOUR FACE IS ALSO CUTE WHEN IT'S CONTORTED IN AGONY.
I END MY TURN.
D-DON'T CALL ME CUTE.
STAND AND DRAW!!
PALE MOON CIRCUS TROUPE...
SO TRICKY, HARD TO FATHOM WHAT THEY'LL DO...
IF IT'S TOUGH TO GUESS THEIR MOVES
HERE I GO!
THEN I'LL READ MY OWN FUTURE!

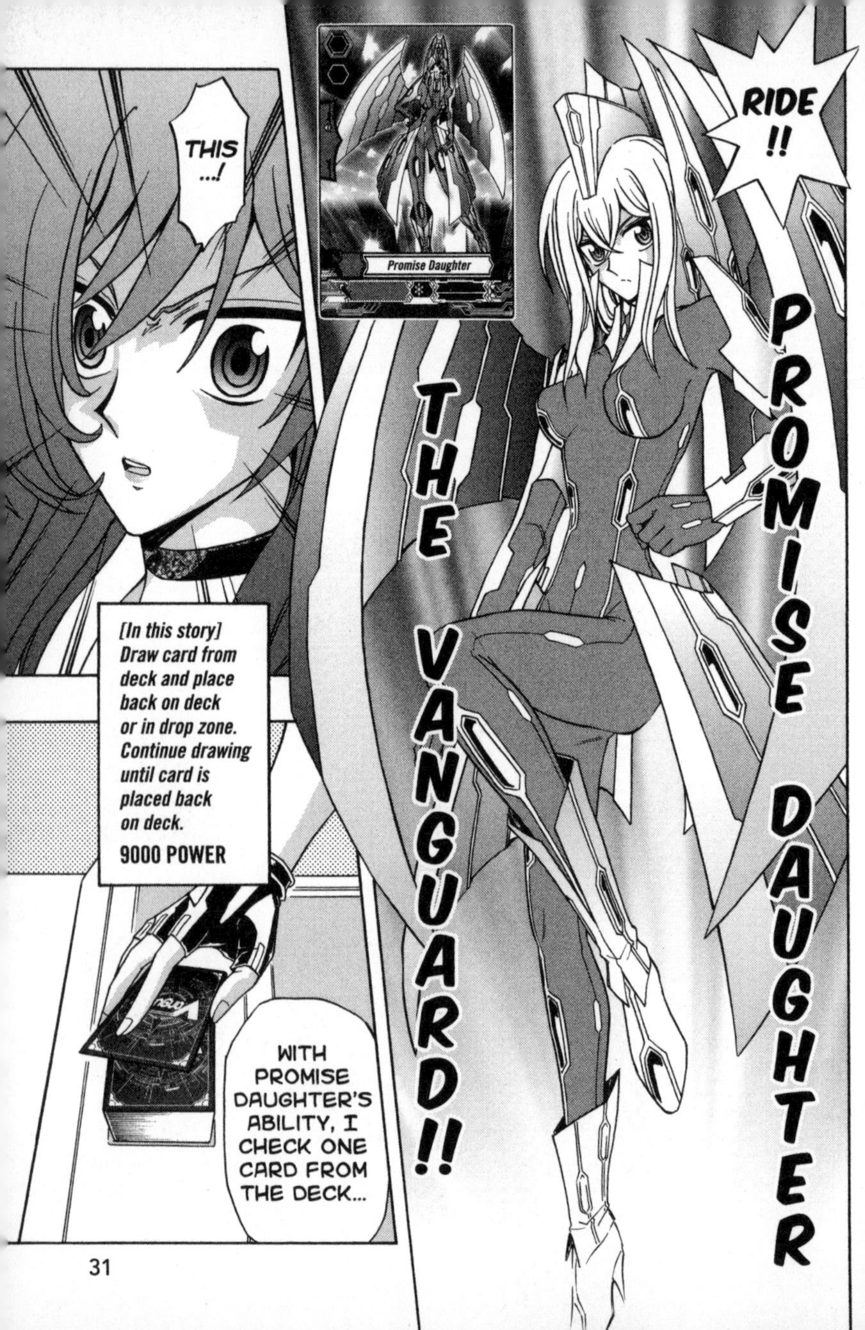
RIDE !!
Promise Daughter
PROMISE DAUGHTER
THE VANGUARD!!
THIS ...!
[In this story] Draw card from deck and place back on deck or in drop zone. Continue drawing until card is placed back on deck.
9000 POWER
WITH PROMISE DAUGHTER'S ABILITY, I CHECK ONE CARD FROM THE DECK...

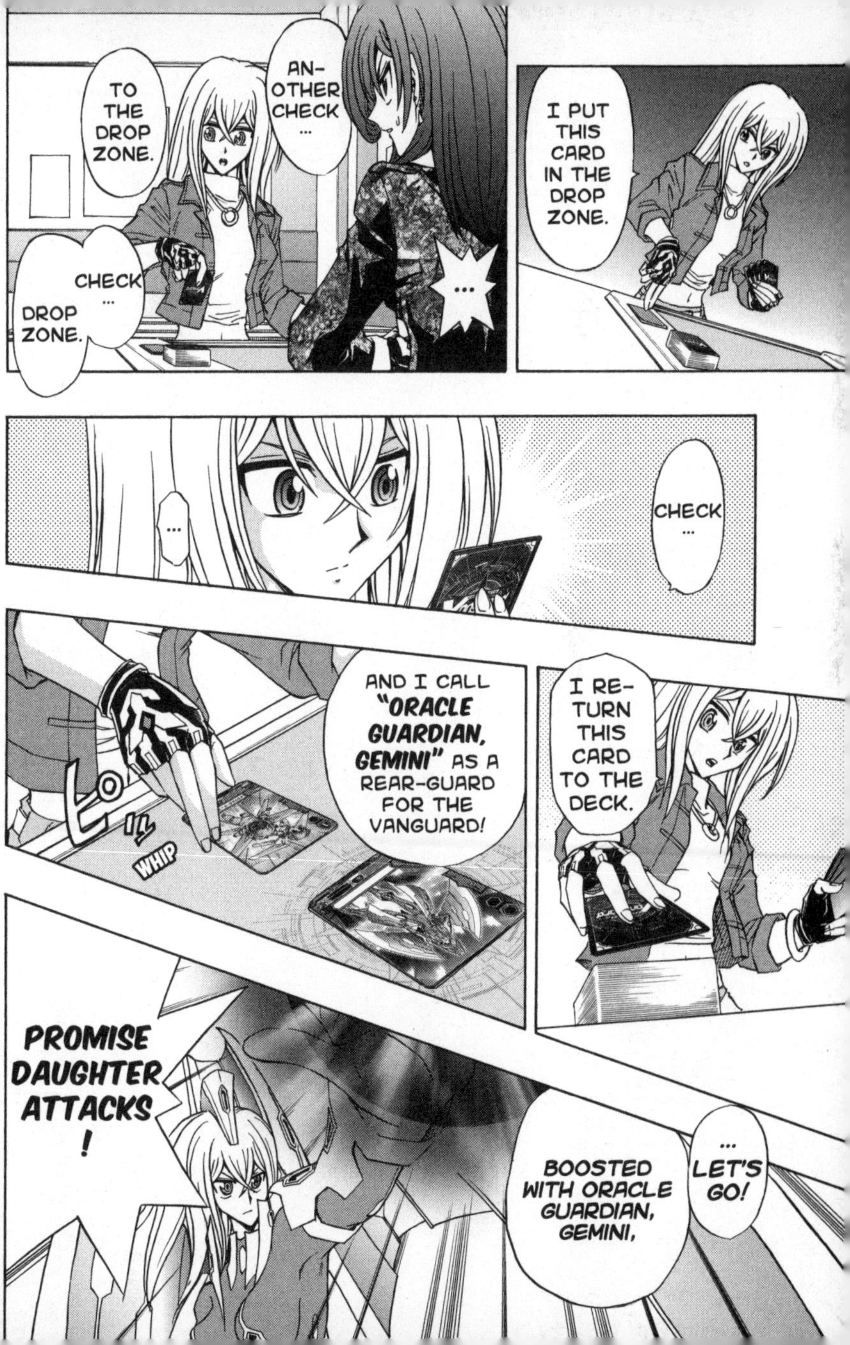
I PUT THIS CARD IN THE DROP ZONE.
AN-OTHER CHECK ...
TO THE DROP ZONE.
...
CHECK ... DROP ZONE.
CHECK ...
...
I RE-TURN THIS CARD TO THE DECK.
AND I CALL "ORACLE GUARDIAN, GEMINI" AS A REAR-GUARD FOR THE VANGUARD!
WHIP
... LET'S GO!
BOOSTED WITH ORACLE GUARDIAN, GEMINI,
PROMISE DAUGHTER ATTACKS!

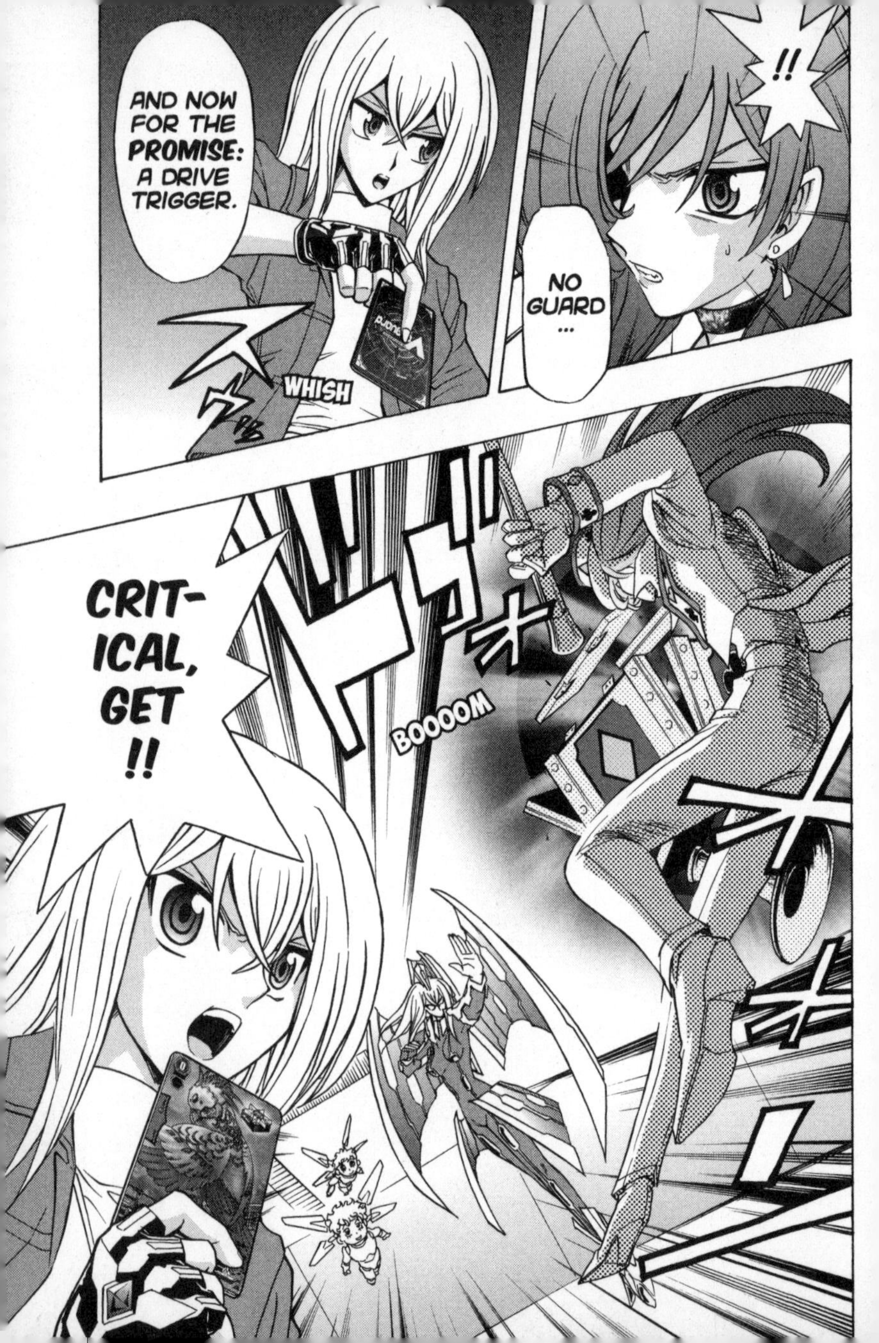
!!
NO GUARD ...
AND NOW FOR THE **PROMISE:** A DRIVE TRIGGER.
WHISH
CRIT-ICAL, GET !!
BOOOOM

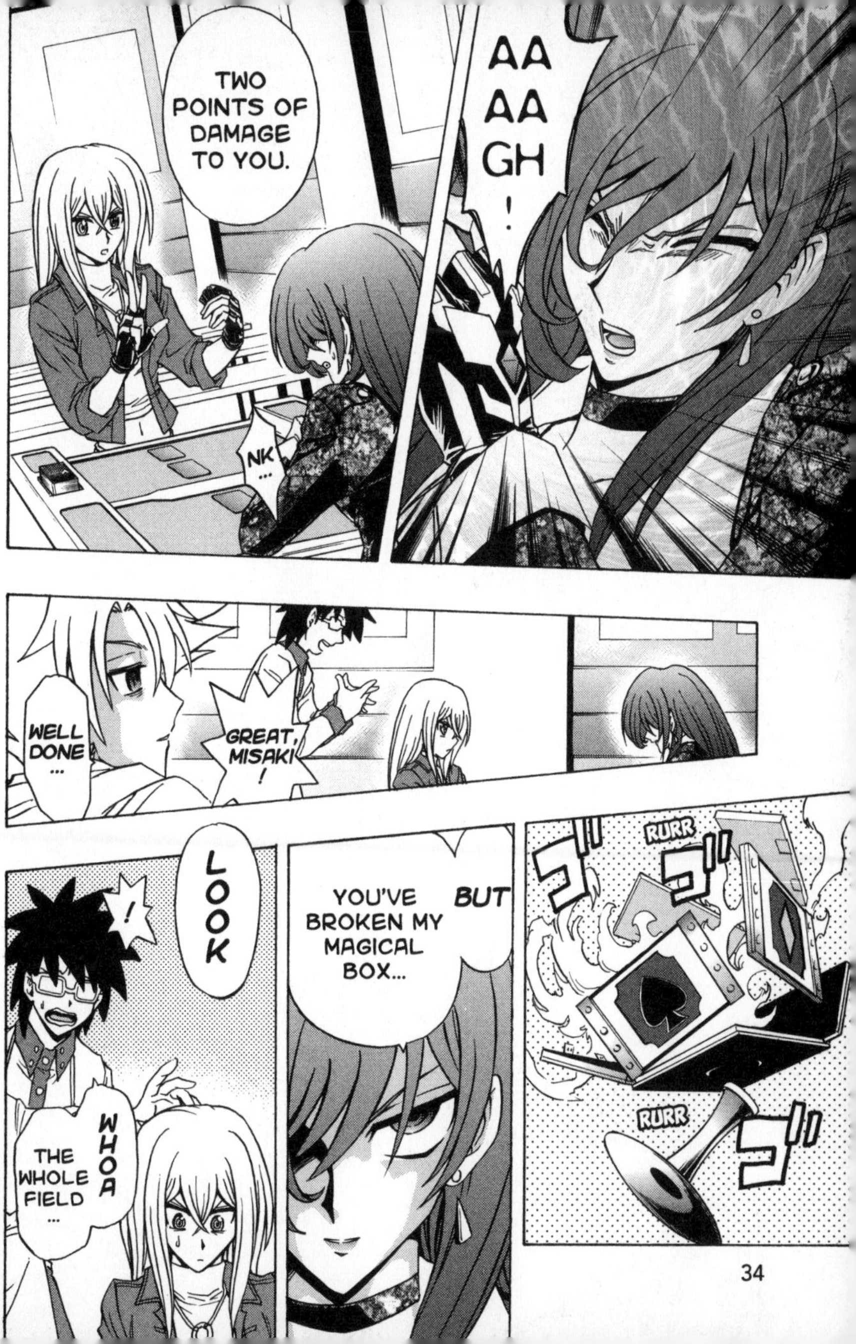
AAAAGH!
TWO POINTS OF DAMAGE TO YOU.
NK...
GREAT, MISAKI!
WELL DONE...
RURR
RURR
BUT
YOU'VE BROKEN MY MAGICAL BOX...
LOOK
!
WHOA
THE WHOLE FIELD...

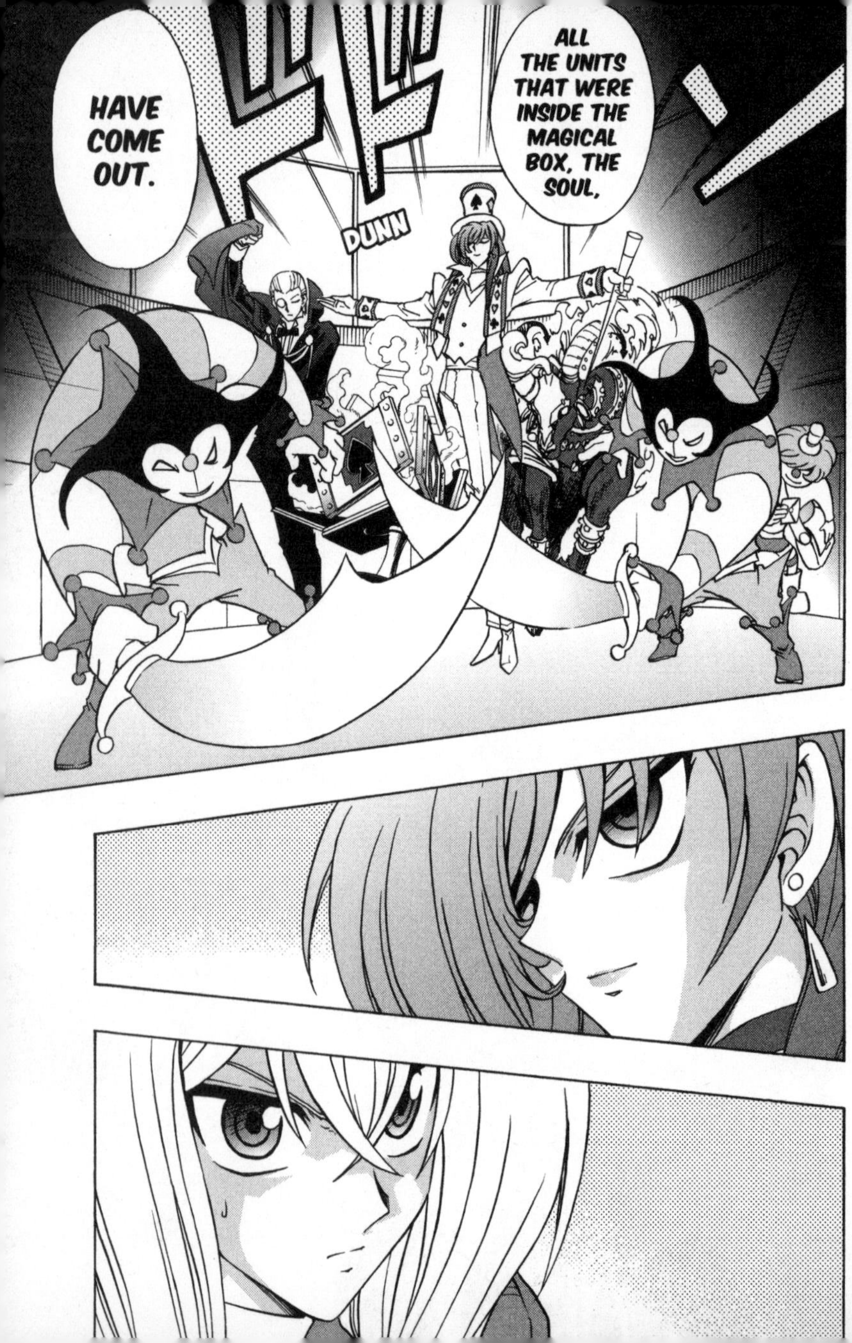
ALL THE UNITS THAT WERE INSIDE THE MAGICAL BOX, THE SOUL,
HAVE COME OUT.
DUNN

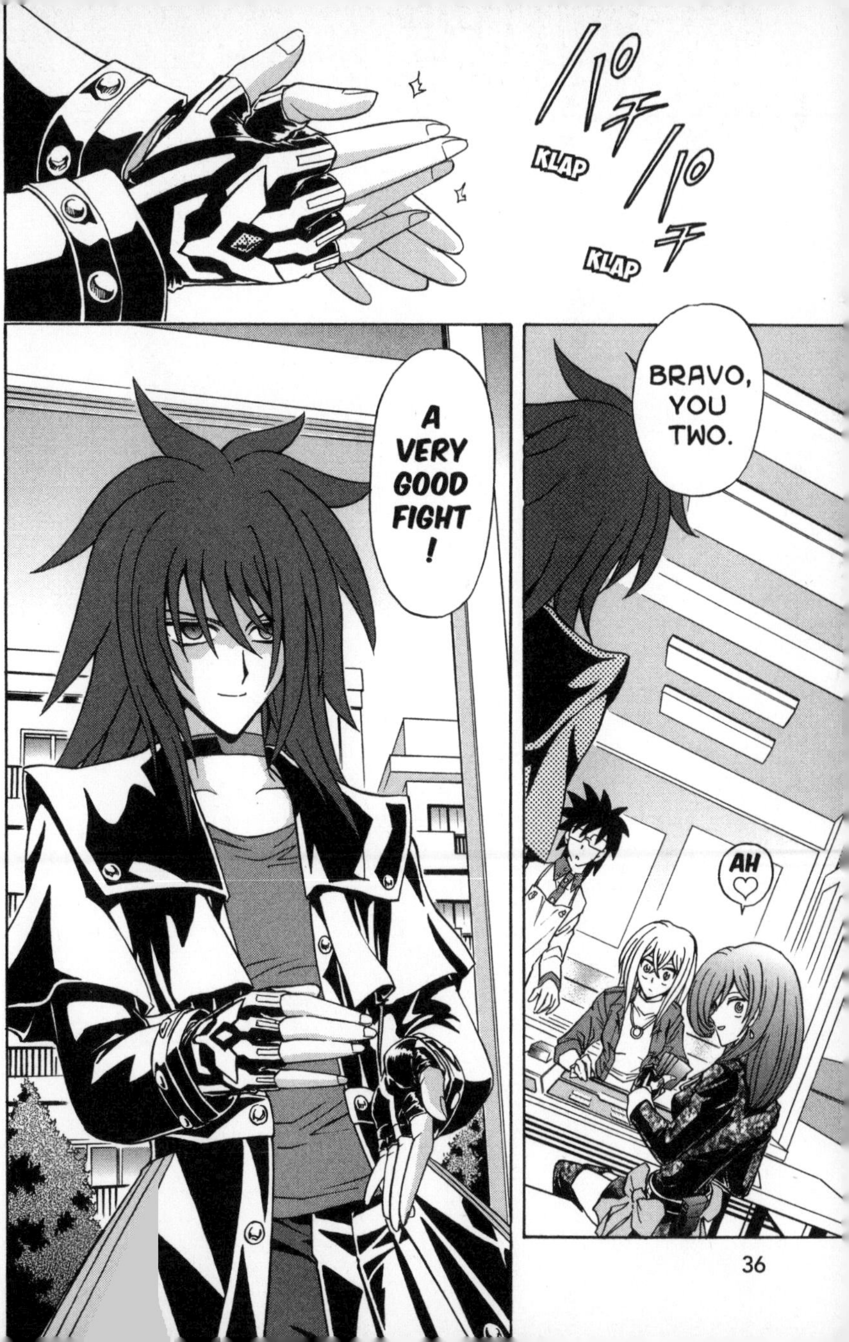

パチ
KLAP
パチ
KLAP
BRAVO, YOU TWO.
AH ♥
A VERY GOOD FIGHT!

BONUS! CARDFIGHT!! Vanguard NEVER-BEFORE-SEEN IMAGE BOARDS — CHARACTERS

These initial concept sketches that you can only check out in the comics are a huge hit! In volume 3, we'll show you concept sketches for "Foo Fighter AL4" and "Ultra Rare."

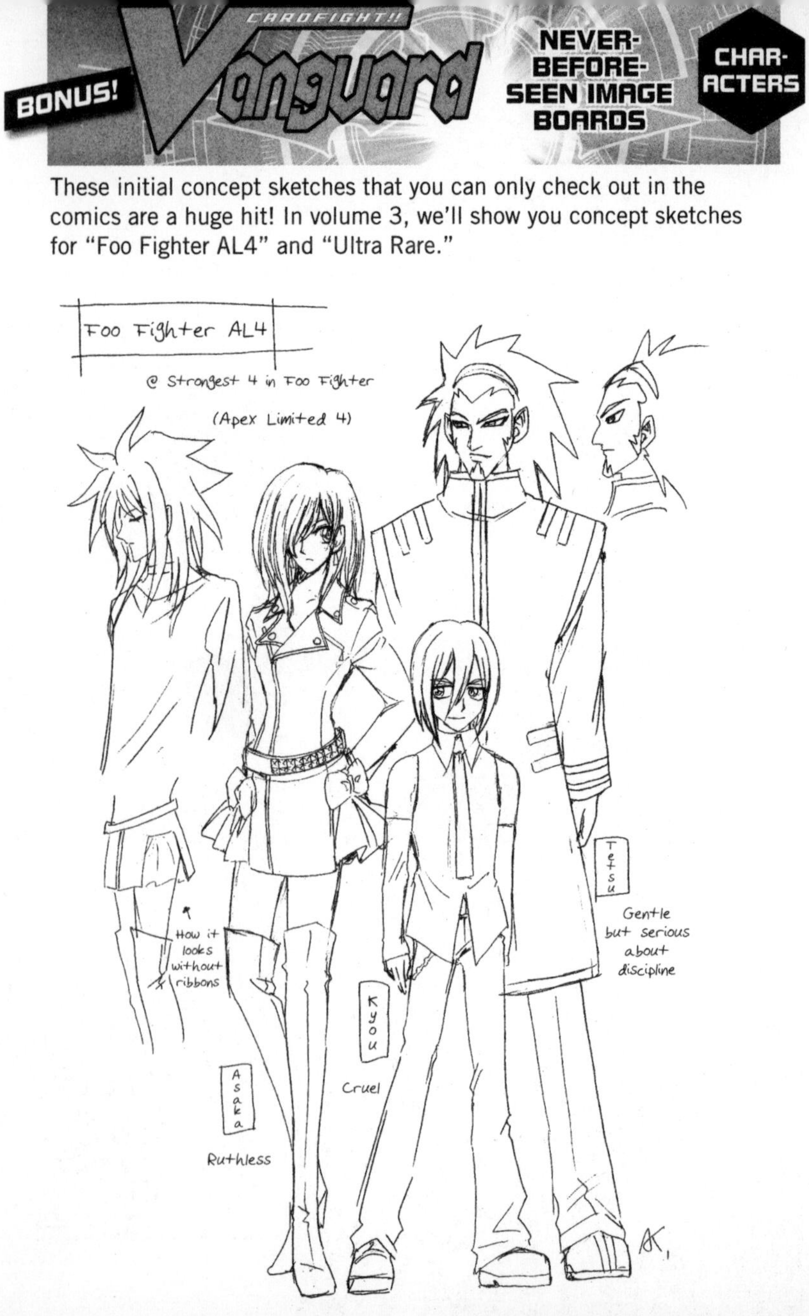

Foo Fighter AL4
@ Strongest 4 in Foo Fighter
(Apex Limited 4)
How it looks without ribbons
Tetsu
Gentle but serious about discipline
Kyou
Cruel
Asaka
Ruthless

BONUS! CARDFIGHT!! Vanguard

NEVER-BEFORE-SEEN IMAGE BOARDS

CHARACTERS

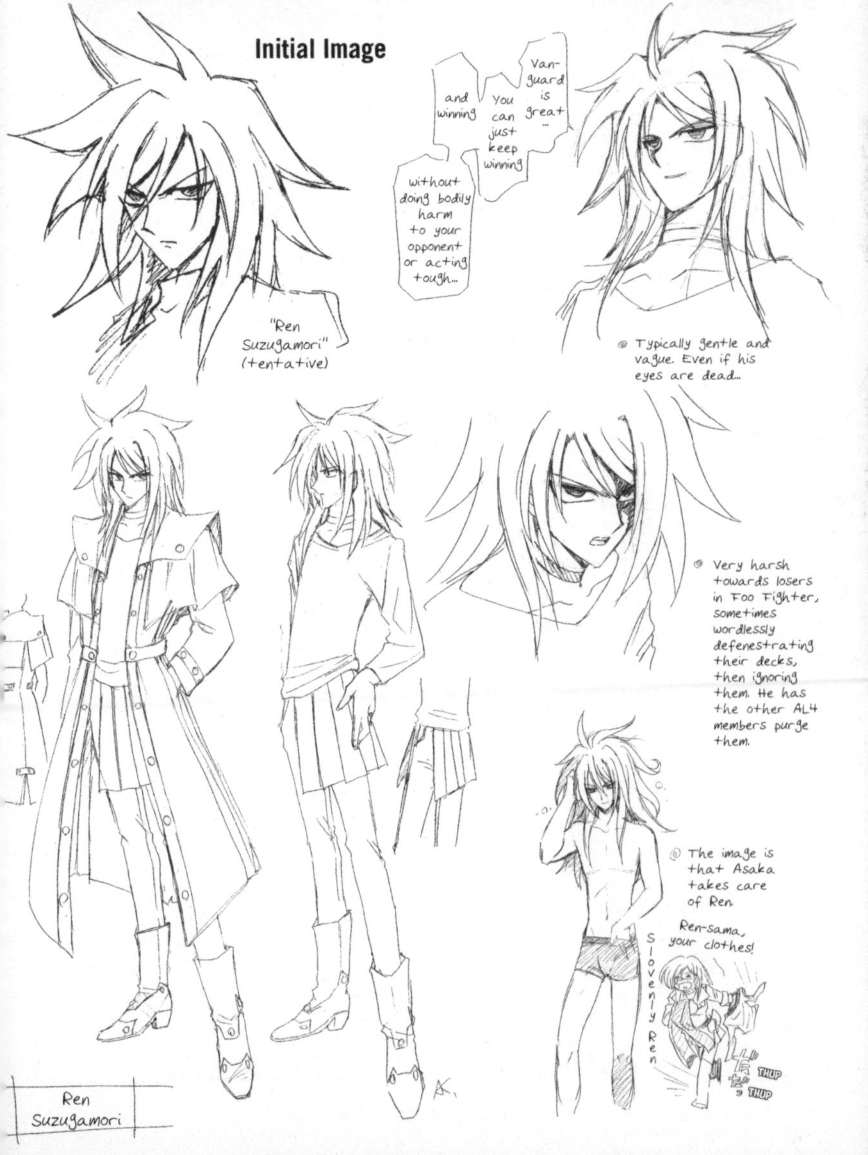

Initial Image
"Ren Suzugamori" (tentative)
Vanguard is great...
You can just keep winning
and winning
without doing bodily harm to your opponent or acting tough...
Typically gentle and vague. Even if his eyes are dead...
Very harsh towards losers in Foo Fighter, sometimes wordlessly defenestrating their decks, then ignoring them. He has the other AL4 members purge them.
The image is that Asaka takes care of Ren.
Ren-sama, your clothes!
Slovenly Ren
THUP
THUP
Ren Suzugamori

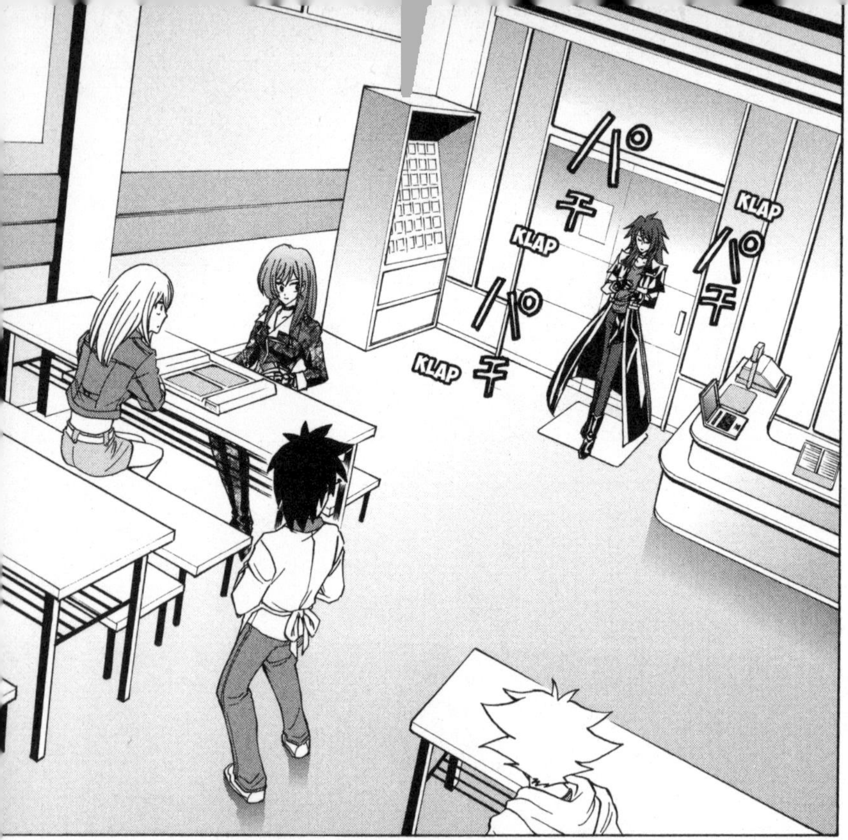
KLAP
パチ
パチ
KLAP
パチ
KLAP

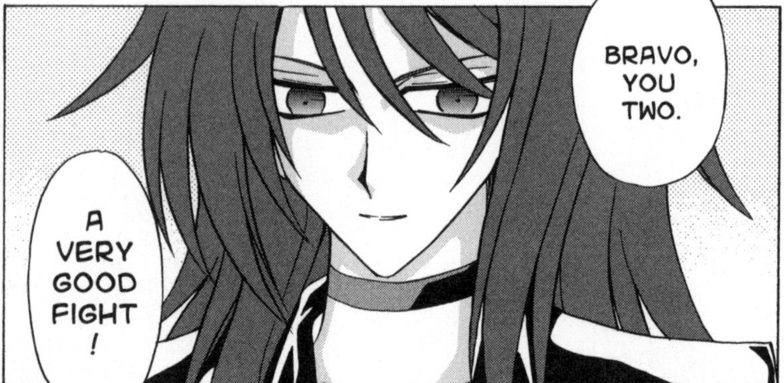
BRAVO, YOU TWO.
A VERY GOOD FIGHT!

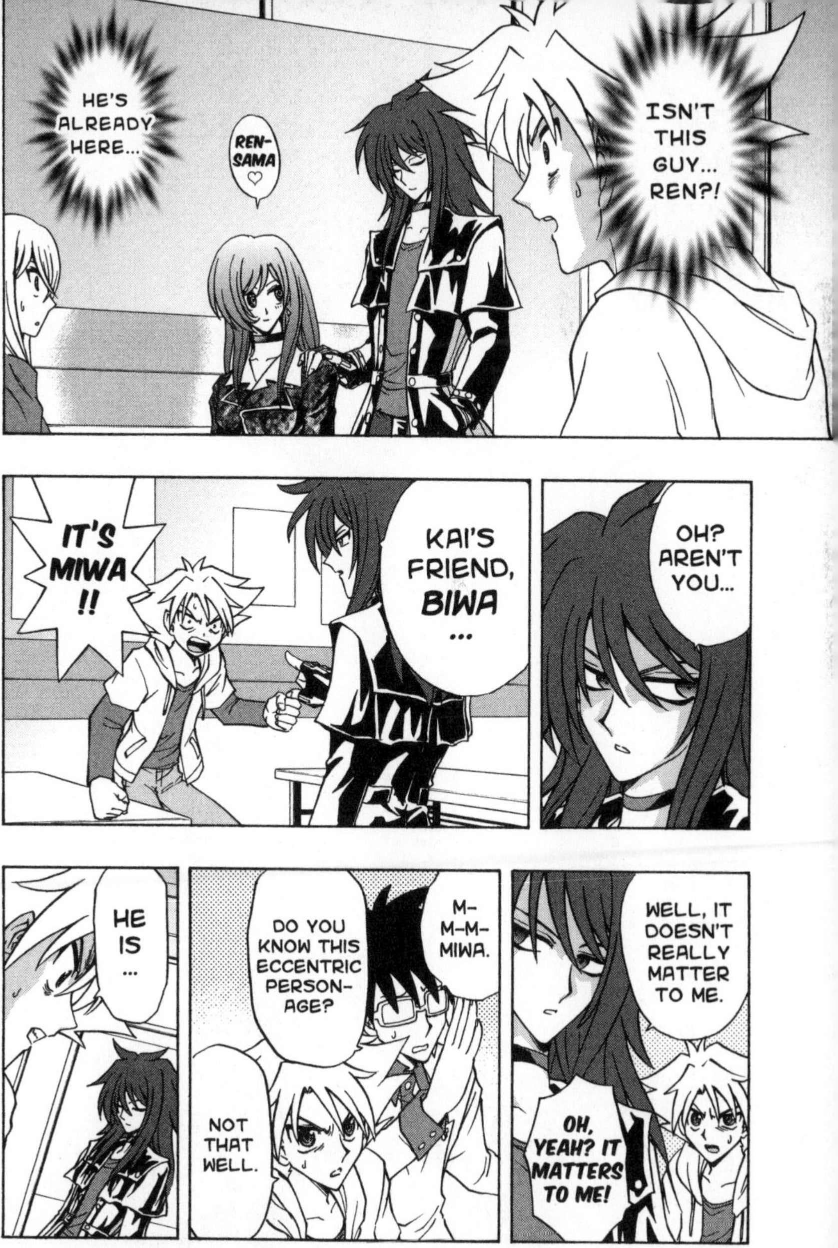

ISN'T THIS GUY... REN?!
REN-SAMA ♡
HE'S ALREADY HERE...
OH? AREN'T YOU...
KAI'S FRIEND, BIWA ...
IT'S MIWA !!
WELL, IT DOESN'T REALLY MATTER TO ME.
OH, YEAH? IT MATTERS TO ME!
M-M-M-MIWA.
DO YOU KNOW THIS ECCENTRIC PERSON-AGE?
NOT THAT WELL.
HE IS ...

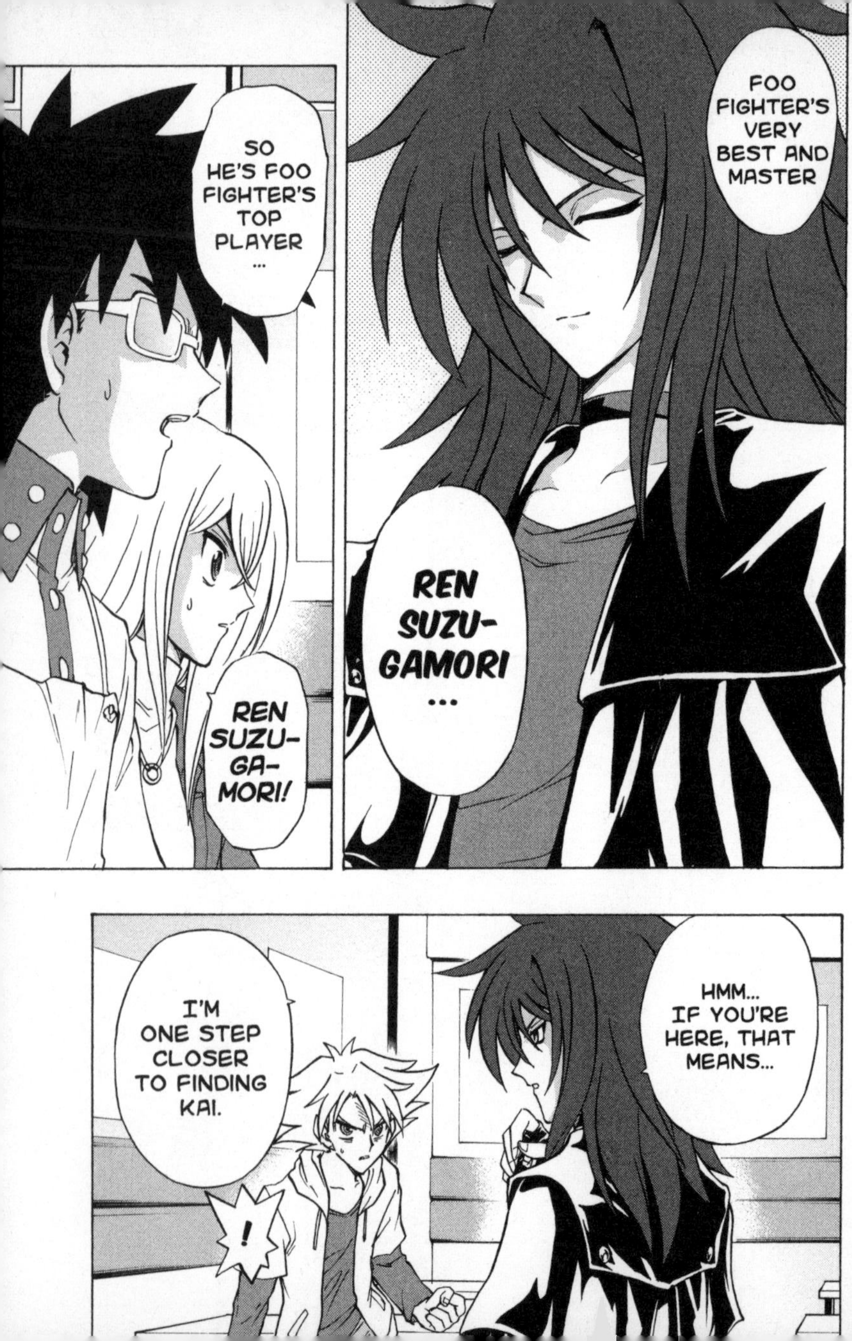
FOO FIGHTER'S VERY BEST AND MASTER
REN SUZU-GAMORI...
SO HE'S FOO FIGHTER'S TOP PLAYER...
REN SUZU-GA-MORI!
HMM... IF YOU'RE HERE, THAT MEANS...
I'M ONE STEP CLOSER TO FINDING KAI.
!

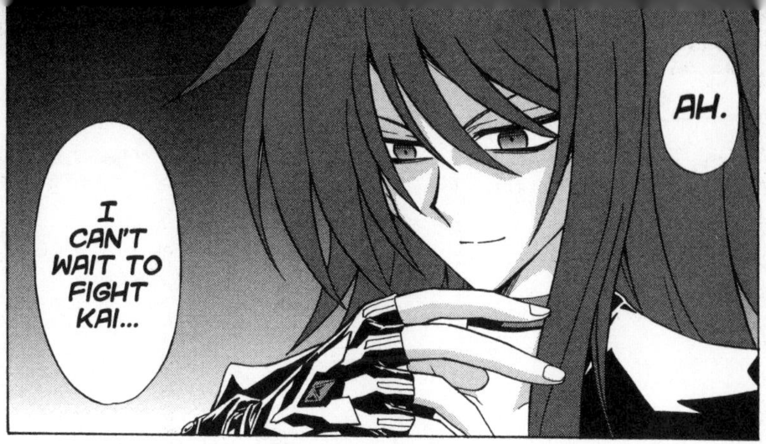
AH.
I CAN'T WAIT TO FIGHT KAI...
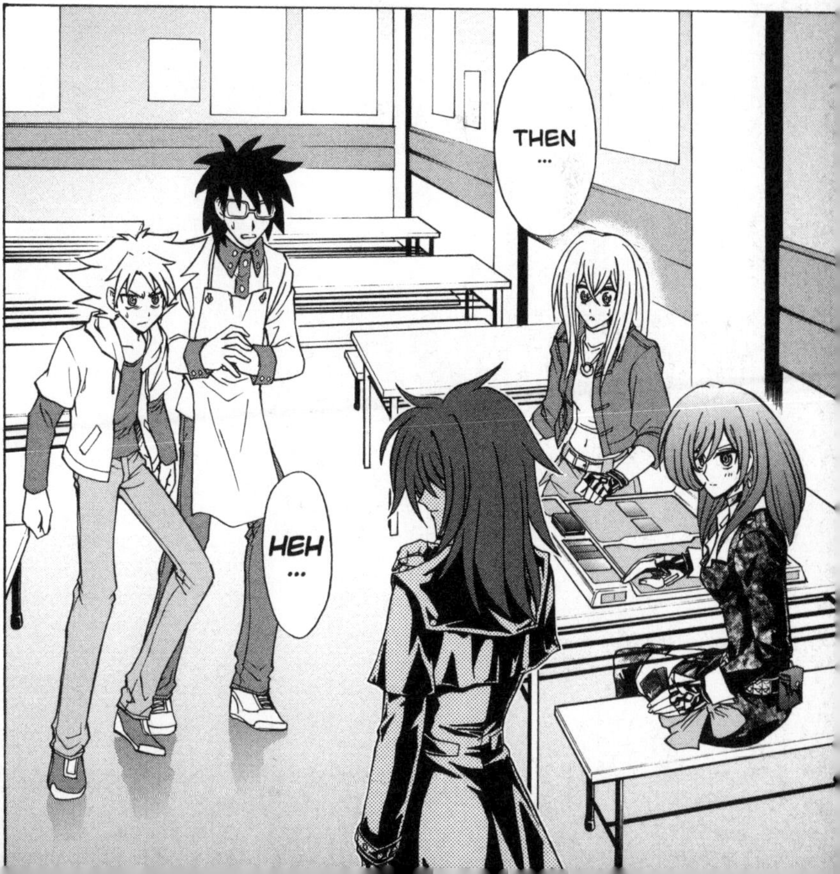
THEN ...
HEH ...

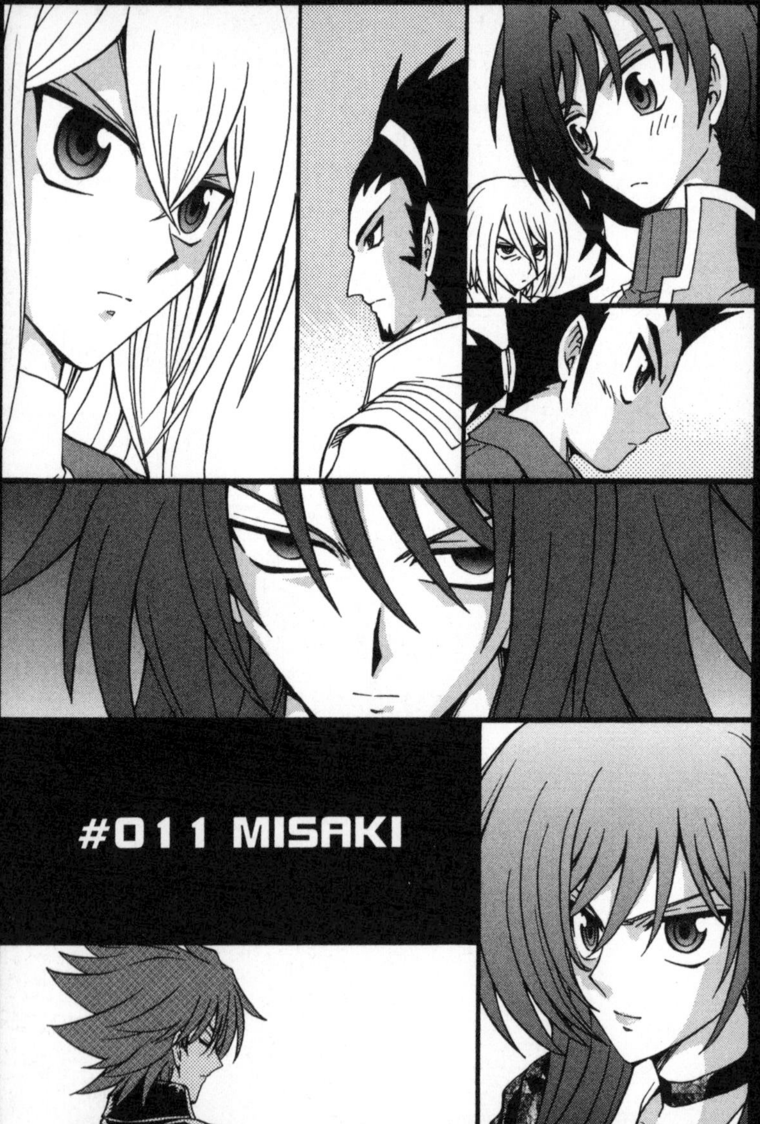
#011 MISAKI

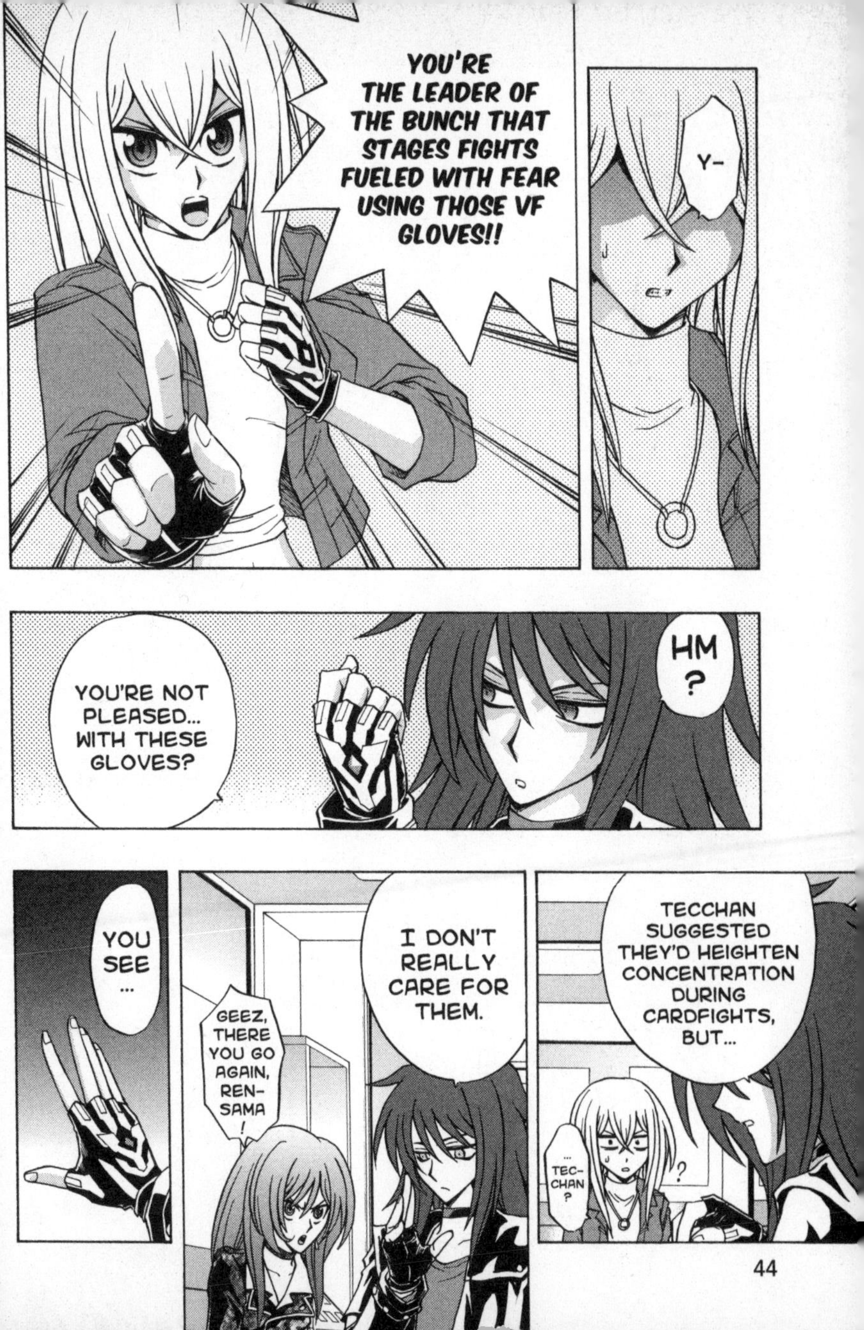
Y-
YOU'RE THE LEADER OF THE BUNCH THAT STAGES FIGHTS FUELED WITH FEAR USING THOSE VF GLOVES!!
HM?
YOU'RE NOT PLEASED... WITH THESE GLOVES?
TECCHAN SUGGESTED THEY'D HEIGHTEN CONCENTRATION DURING CARDFIGHTS, BUT...
...TEC-CHAN?
I DON'T REALLY CARE FOR THEM.
GEEZ, THERE YOU GO AGAIN, REN-SAMA!
YOU SEE...

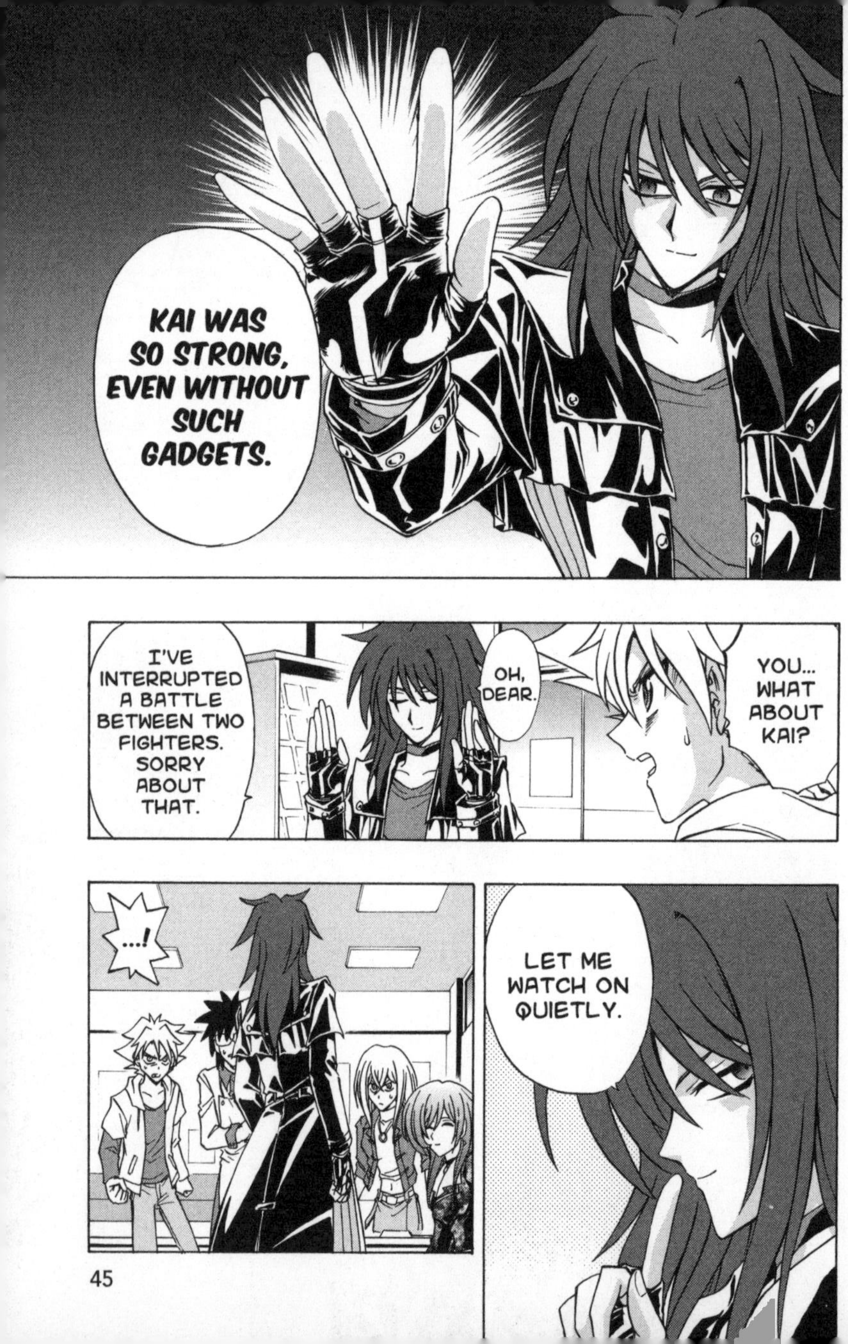
KAI WAS SO STRONG, EVEN WITHOUT SUCH GADGETS.
YOU... WHAT ABOUT KAI?
OH, DEAR.
I'VE INTERRUPTED A BATTLE BETWEEN TWO FIGHTERS. SORRY ABOUT THAT.
LET ME WATCH ON QUIETLY.
...!

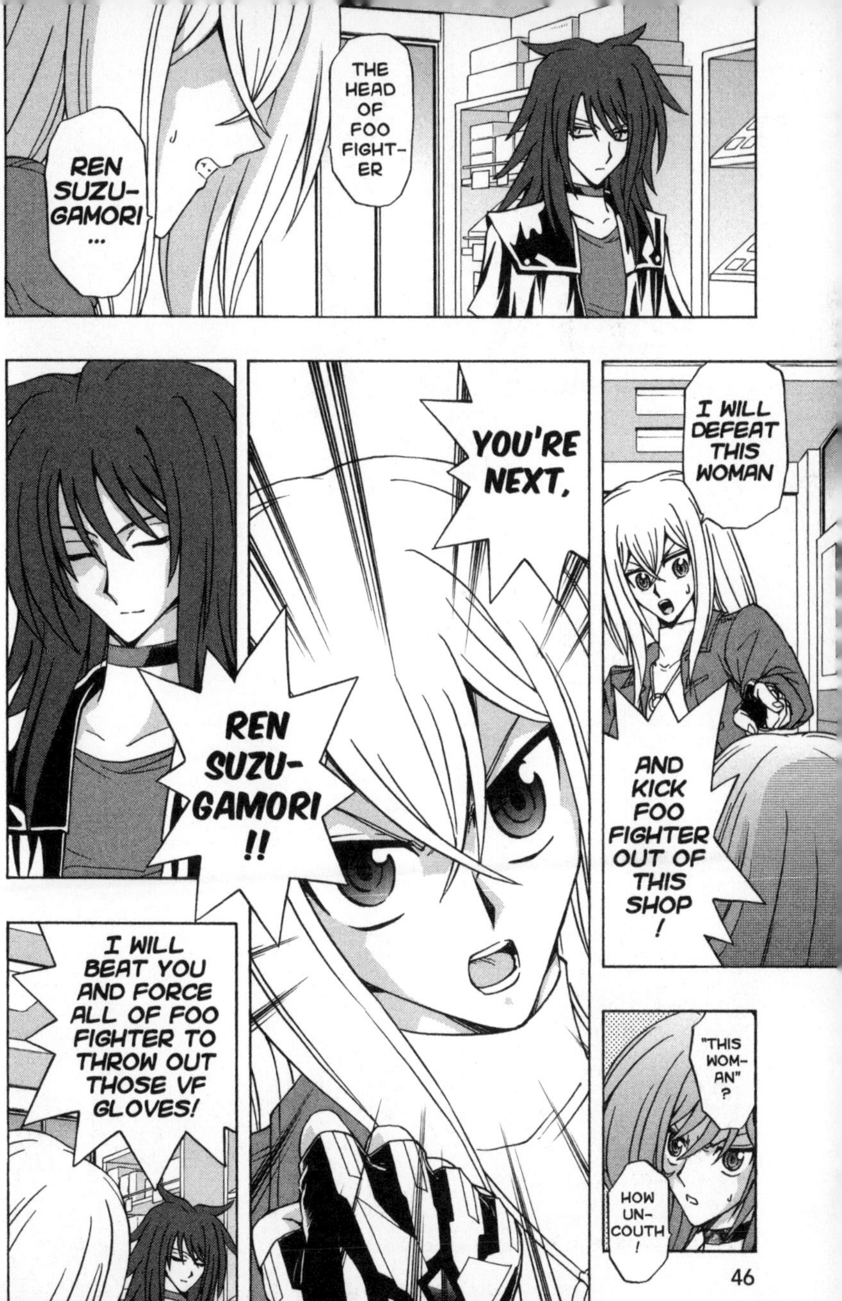
THE HEAD OF FOO FIGHTER
REN SUZUGAMORI...
I WILL DEFEAT THIS WOMAN
AND KICK FOO FIGHTER OUT OF THIS SHOP!
"THIS WOMAN"?
HOW UNCOUTH!
YOU'RE NEXT,
REN SUZUGAMORI!!
I WILL BEAT YOU AND FORCE ALL OF FOO FIGHTER TO THROW OUT THOSE VF GLOVES!

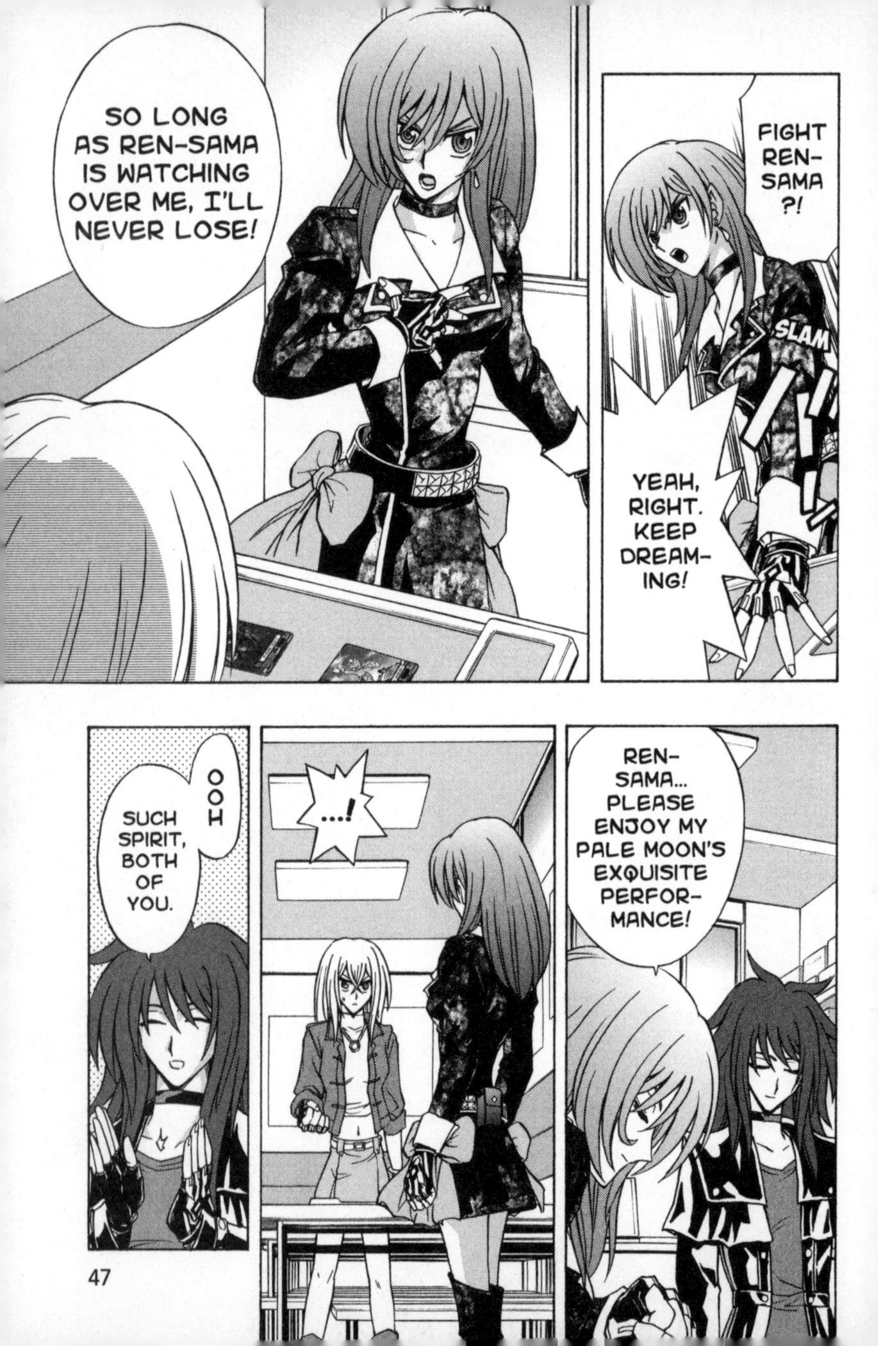
FIGHT REN-SAMA?!
SLAM
YEAH, RIGHT. KEEP DREAMING!
SO LONG AS REN-SAMA IS WATCHING OVER ME, I'LL NEVER LOSE!
REN-SAMA... PLEASE ENJOY MY PALE MOON'S EXQUISITE PERFORMANCE!
...!
OOH
SUCH SPIRIT, BOTH OF YOU.

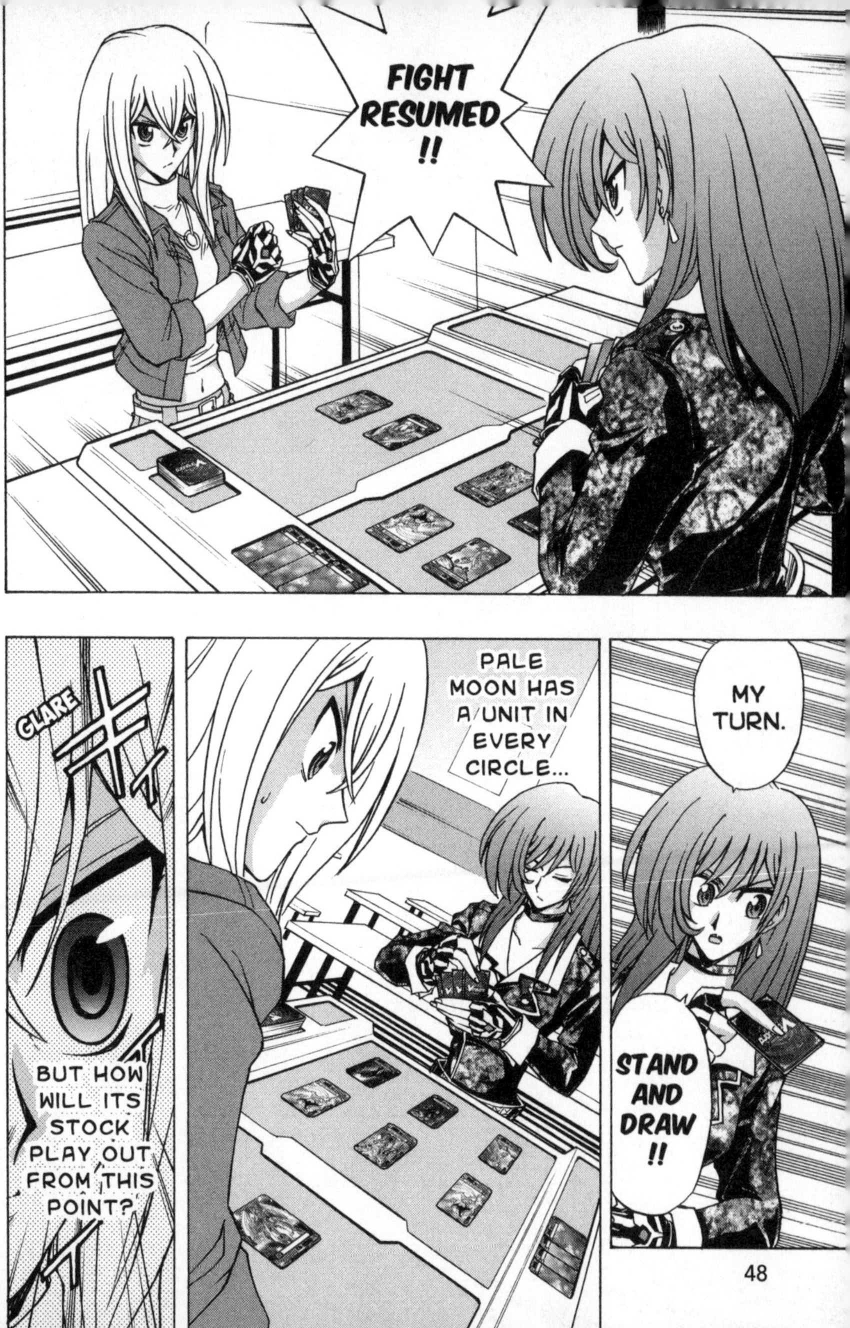
FIGHT RESUMED!!
MY TURN.
STAND AND DRAW!!
PALE MOON HAS A UNIT IN EVERY CIRCLE...
GLARE
BUT HOW WILL ITS STOCK PLAY OUT FROM THIS POINT?

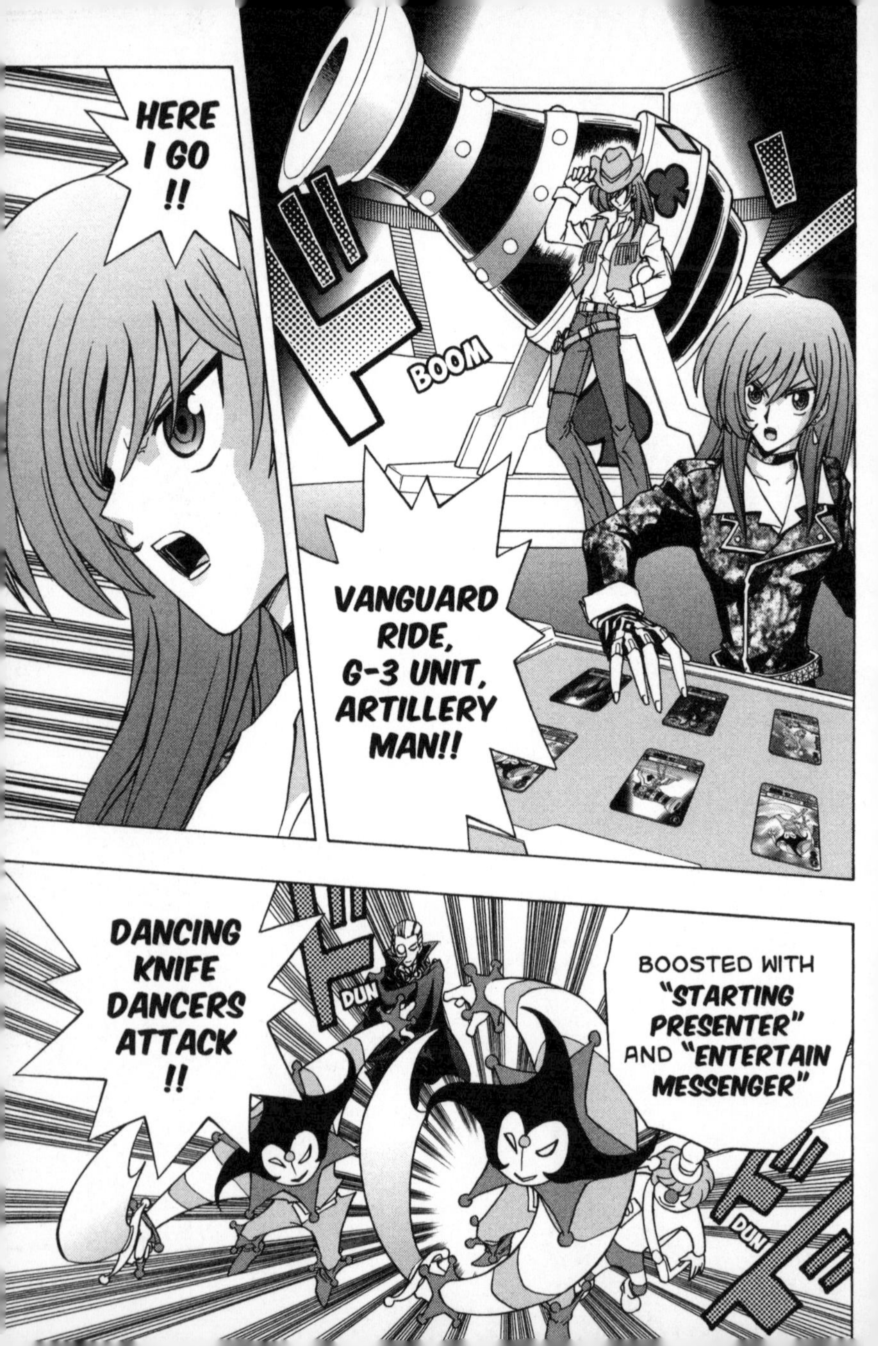
BOOM
VANGUARD RIDE, G-3 UNIT, ARTILLERY MAN!!
HERE I GO !!
BOOSTED WITH "STARTING PRESENTER" AND "ENTERTAIN MESSENGER"
DUN
DUN
DANCING KNIFE DANCERS ATTACK !!

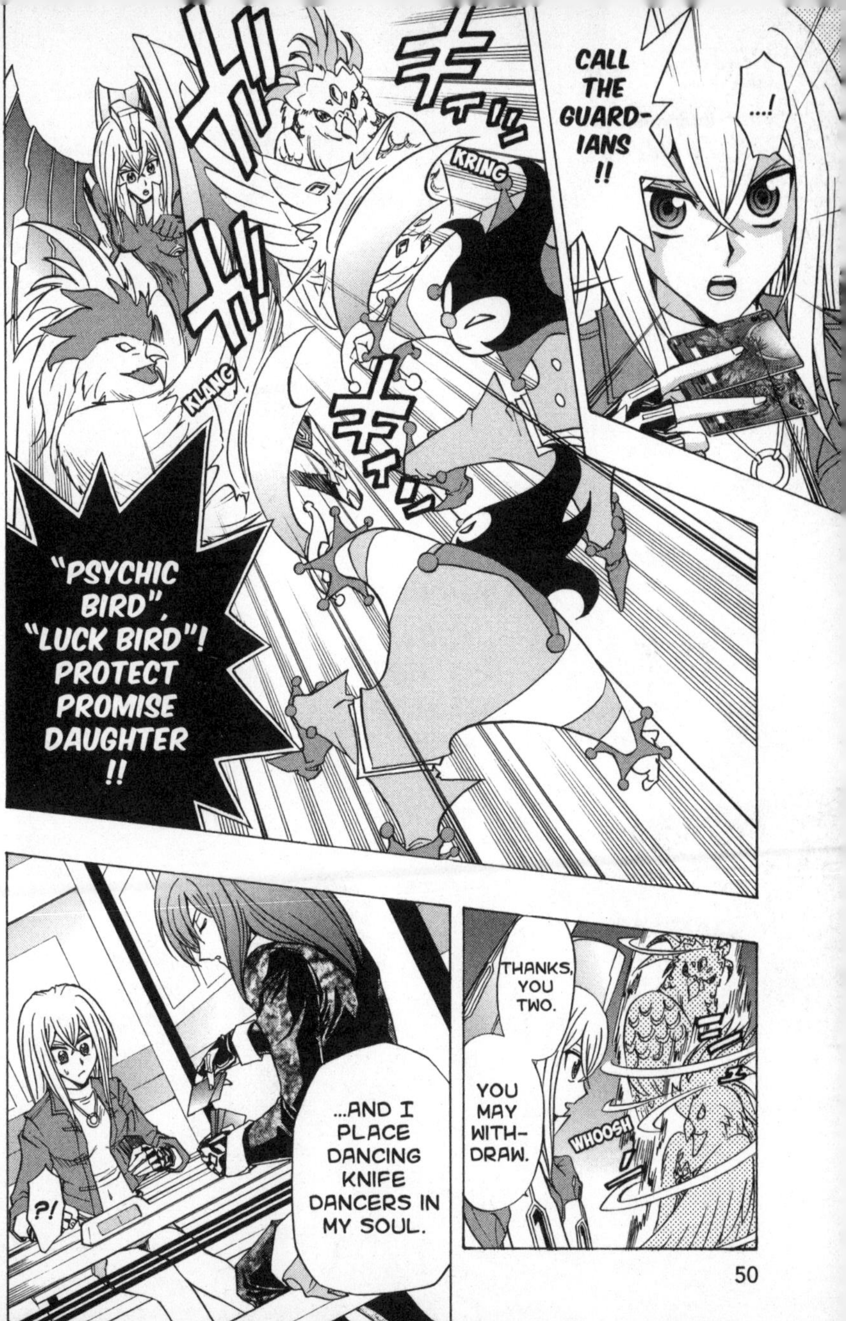
...!
CALL THE GUARDIANS !!
KRING
KLANG
"PSYCHIC BIRD", "LUCK BIRD"! PROTECT PROMISE DAUGHTER !!
THANKS, YOU TWO.
YOU MAY WITHDRAW.
WHOOSH
...AND I PLACE DANCING KNIFE DANCERS IN MY SOUL.
?!

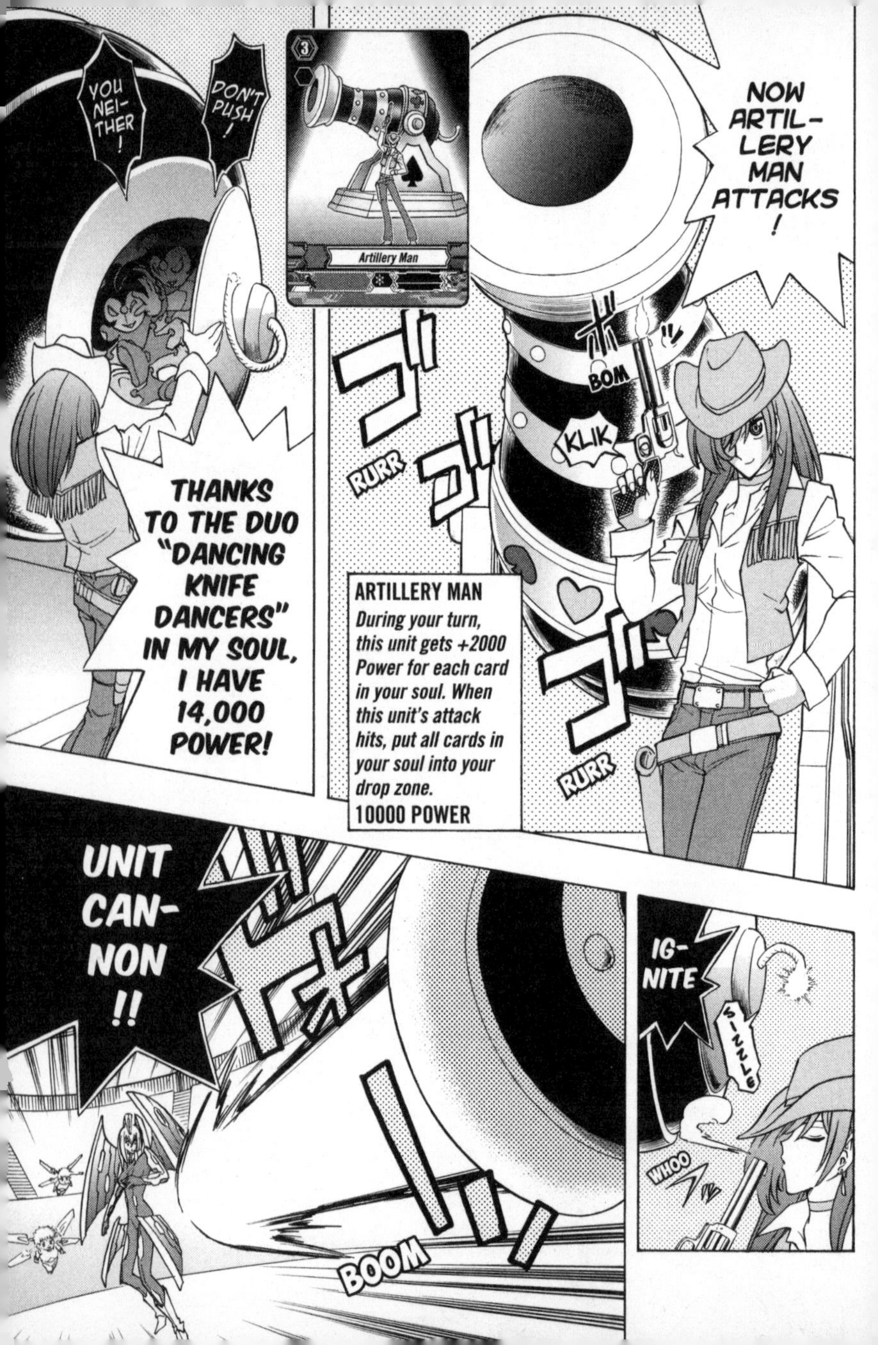
NOW ARTIL-LERY MAN ATTACKS!
Artillery Man
BOM
KLIK
RURR
ARTILLERY MAN
During your turn, this unit gets +2000 Power for each card in your soul. When this unit's attack hits, put all cards in your soul into your drop zone.
10000 POWER
RURR
DON'T PUSH!
YOU NEI-THER!
THANKS TO THE DUO "DANCING KNIFE DANCERS" IN MY SOUL, I HAVE 14,000 POWER!
IG-NITE
SIZZLE
WHOO
UNIT CAN-NON!!
BOOM

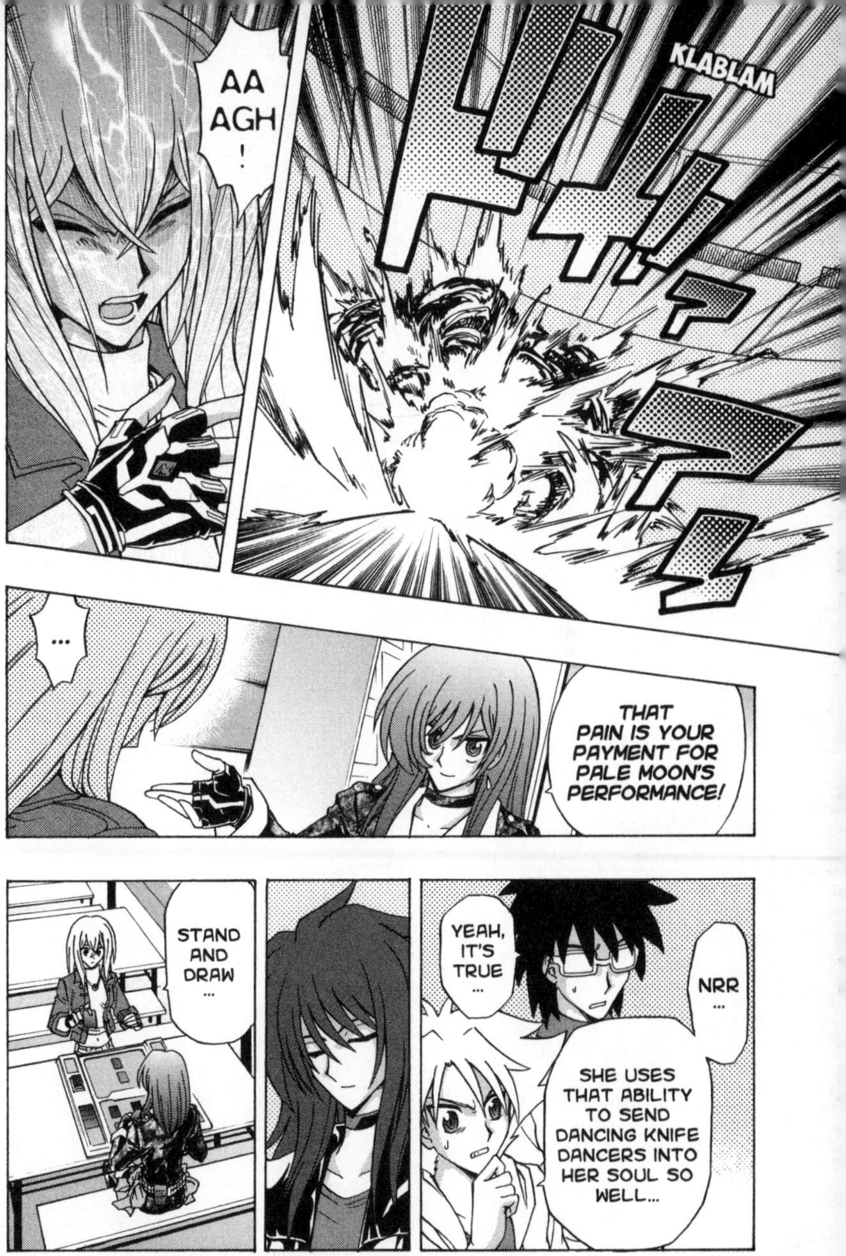
KLABLAM
AA AGH !
THAT PAIN IS YOUR PAYMENT FOR PALE MOON'S PERFORMANCE!
...
NRR ...
YEAH, IT'S TRUE ...
SHE USES THAT ABILITY TO SEND DANCING KNIFE DANCERS INTO HER SOUL SO WELL...
STAND AND DRAW ...

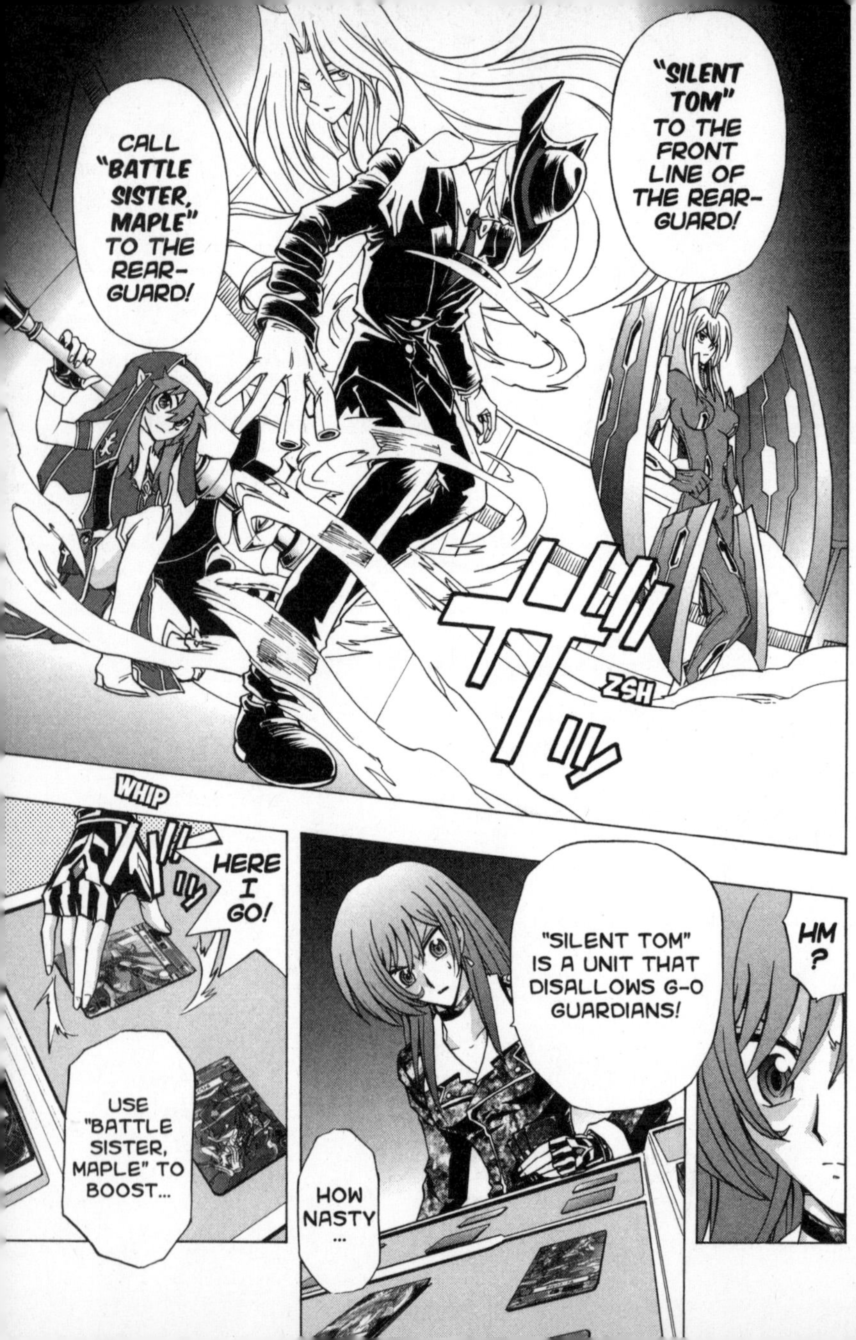
"SILENT TOM" TO THE FRONT LINE OF THE REAR-GUARD!
CALL "BATTLE SISTER, MAPLE" TO THE REAR-GUARD!
ZSH
HM ?
"SILENT TOM" IS A UNIT THAT DISALLOWS G-0 GUARDIANS!
HOW NASTY ...
WHIP
HERE I GO!
USE "BATTLE SISTER, MAPLE" TO BOOST...

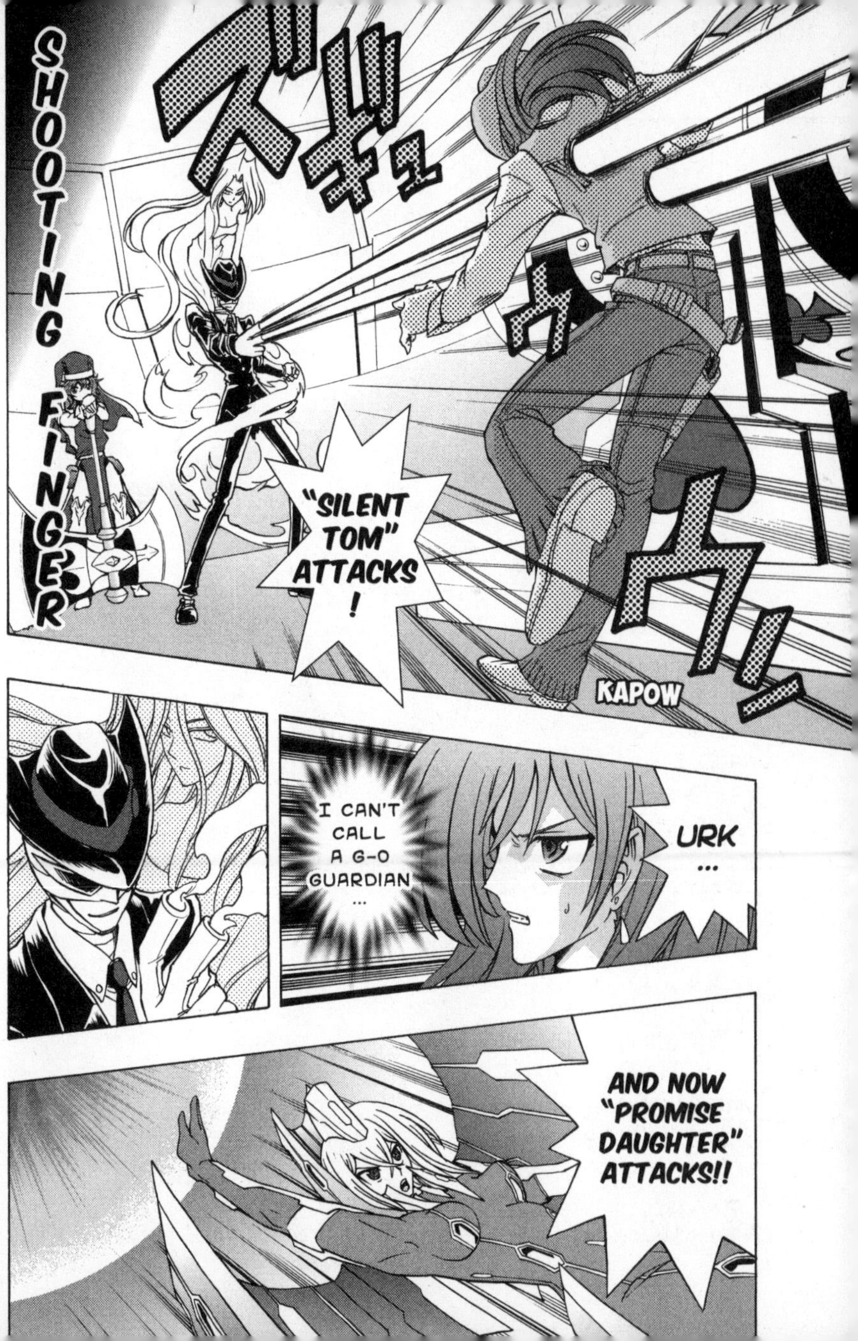
"SILENT TOM" ATTACKS !
KAPOW
SHOOTING FINGER
URK ...
I CAN'T CALL A G-0 GUARDIAN ...
AND NOW "PROMISE DAUGHTER" ATTACKS!!

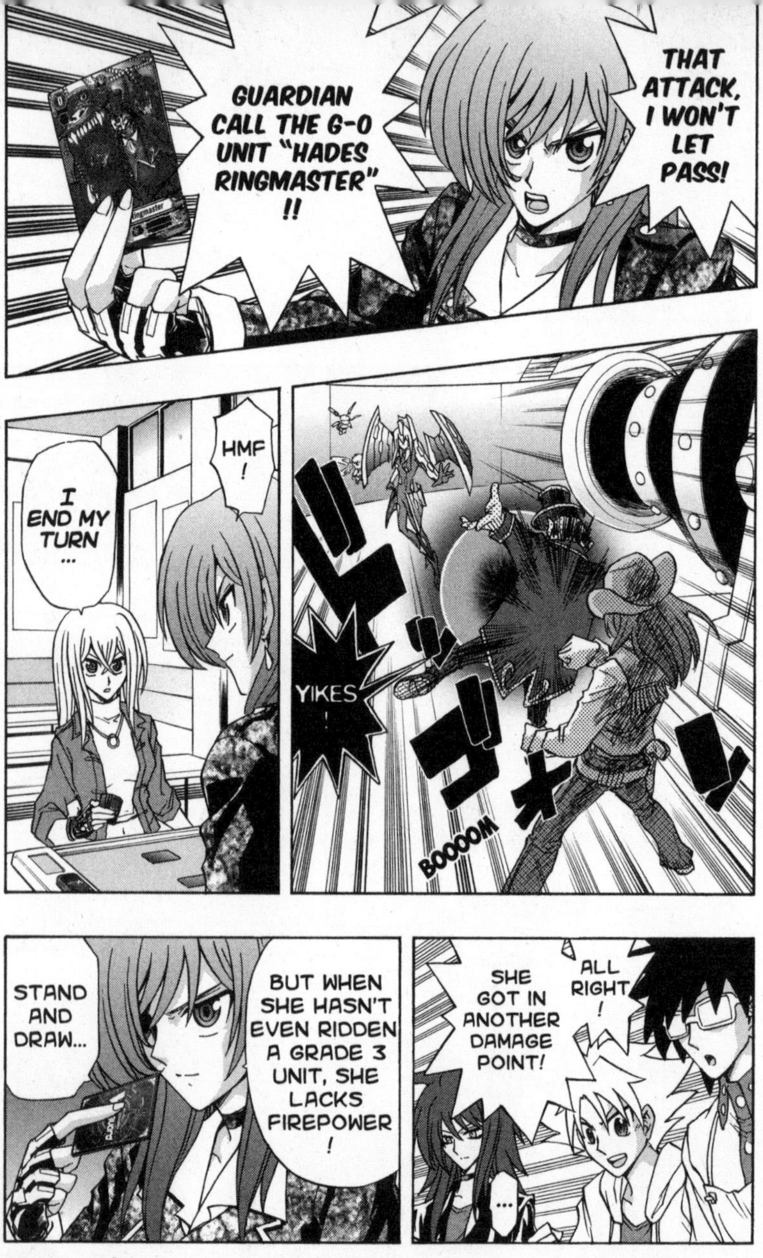
THAT ATTACK, I WON'T LET PASS!
GUARDIAN CALL THE G-0 UNIT "HADES RINGMASTER" !!
ringmaster
YIKES!
BOOOOM
HMF!
I END MY TURN ...
ALL RIGHT!
SHE GOT IN ANOTHER DAMAGE POINT!
...
STAND AND DRAW...
BUT WHEN SHE HASN'T EVEN RIDDEN A GRADE 3 UNIT, SHE LACKS FIREPOWER!

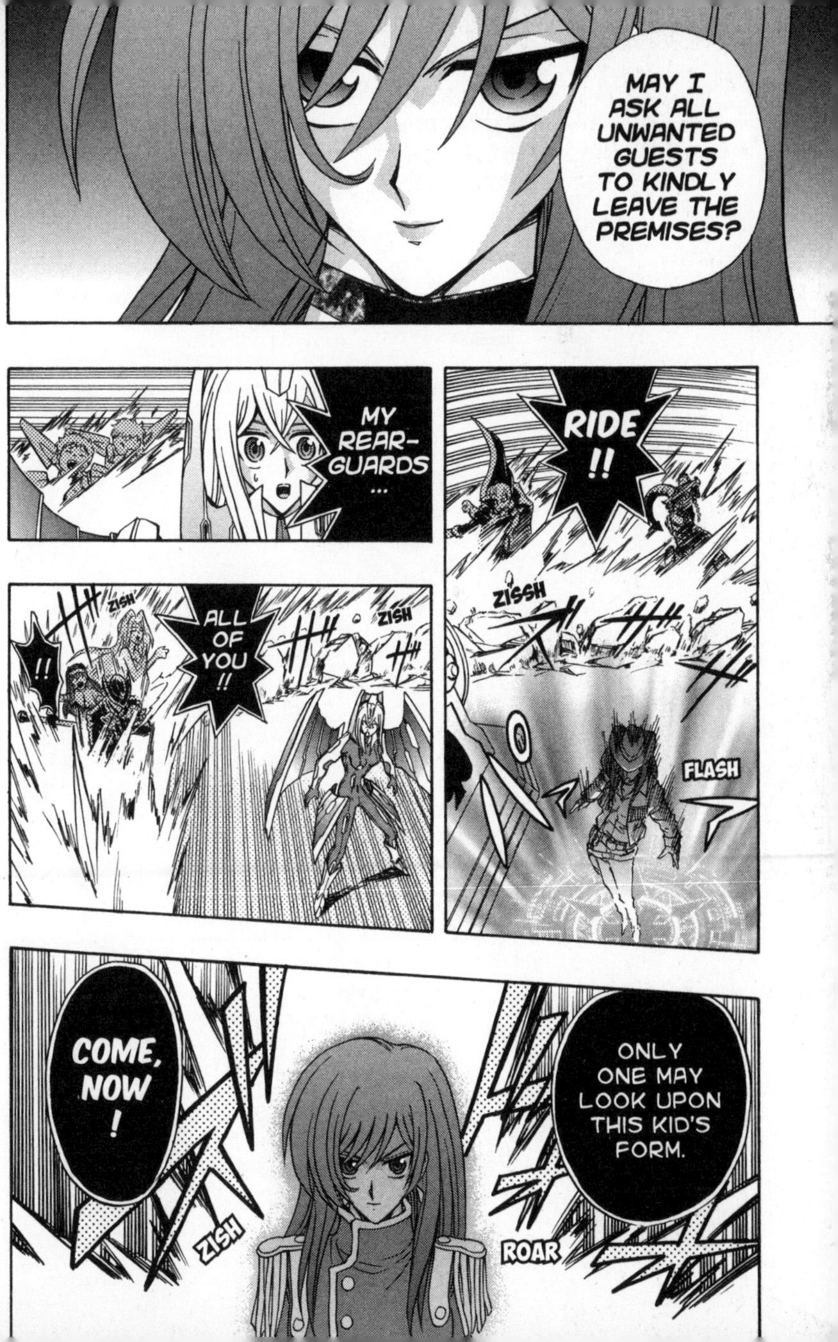
MAY I ASK ALL UNWANTED GUESTS TO KINDLY LEAVE THE PREMISES?
RIDE !!
ZISSH
FLASH
MY REAR-GUARDS ...
ZISH
ALL OF YOU !!
ZISH
!!
ONLY ONE MAY LOOK UPON THIS KID'S FORM.
COME, NOW !
ROAR
ZISH

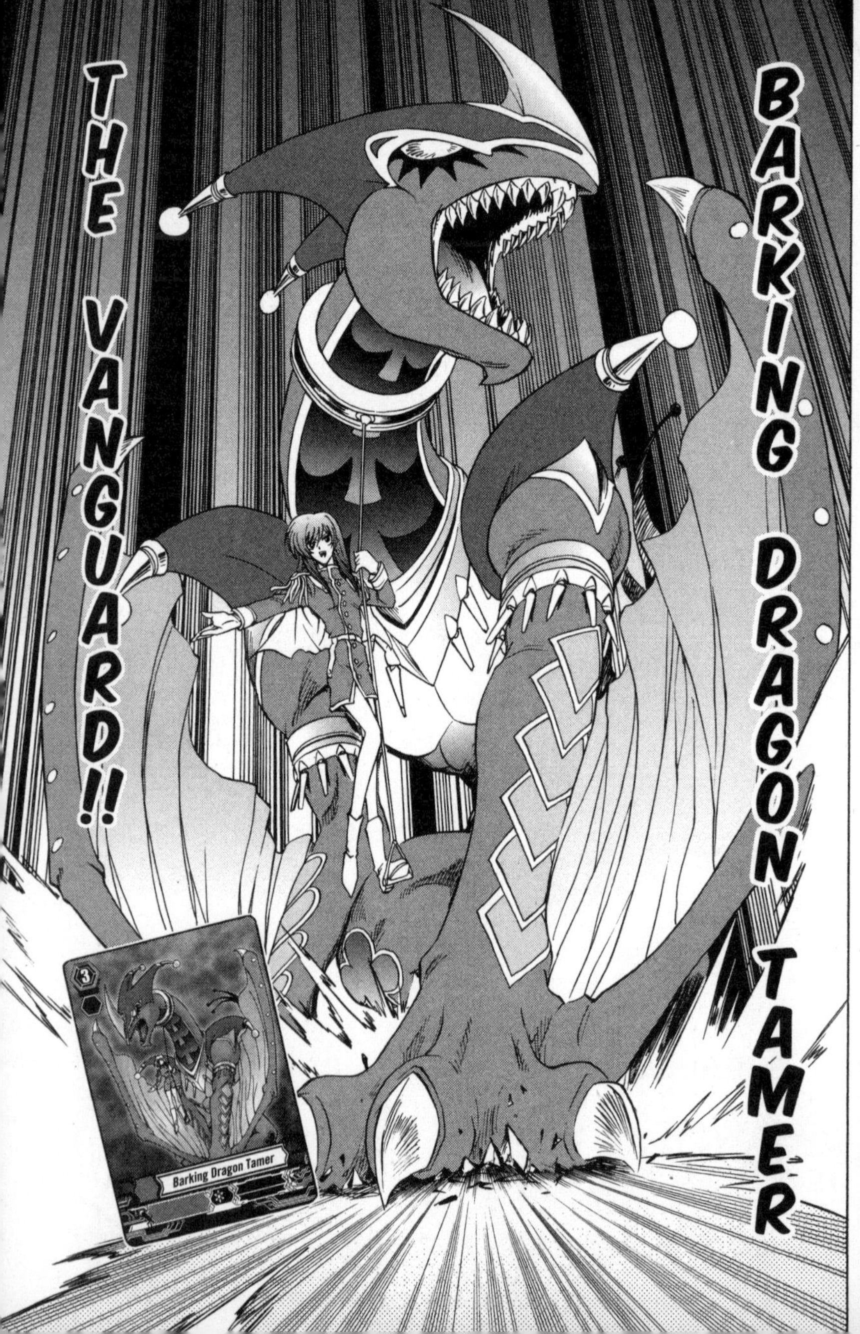
BARKING DRAGON TAMER
THE VANGUARD!!
3
Barking Dragon Tamer

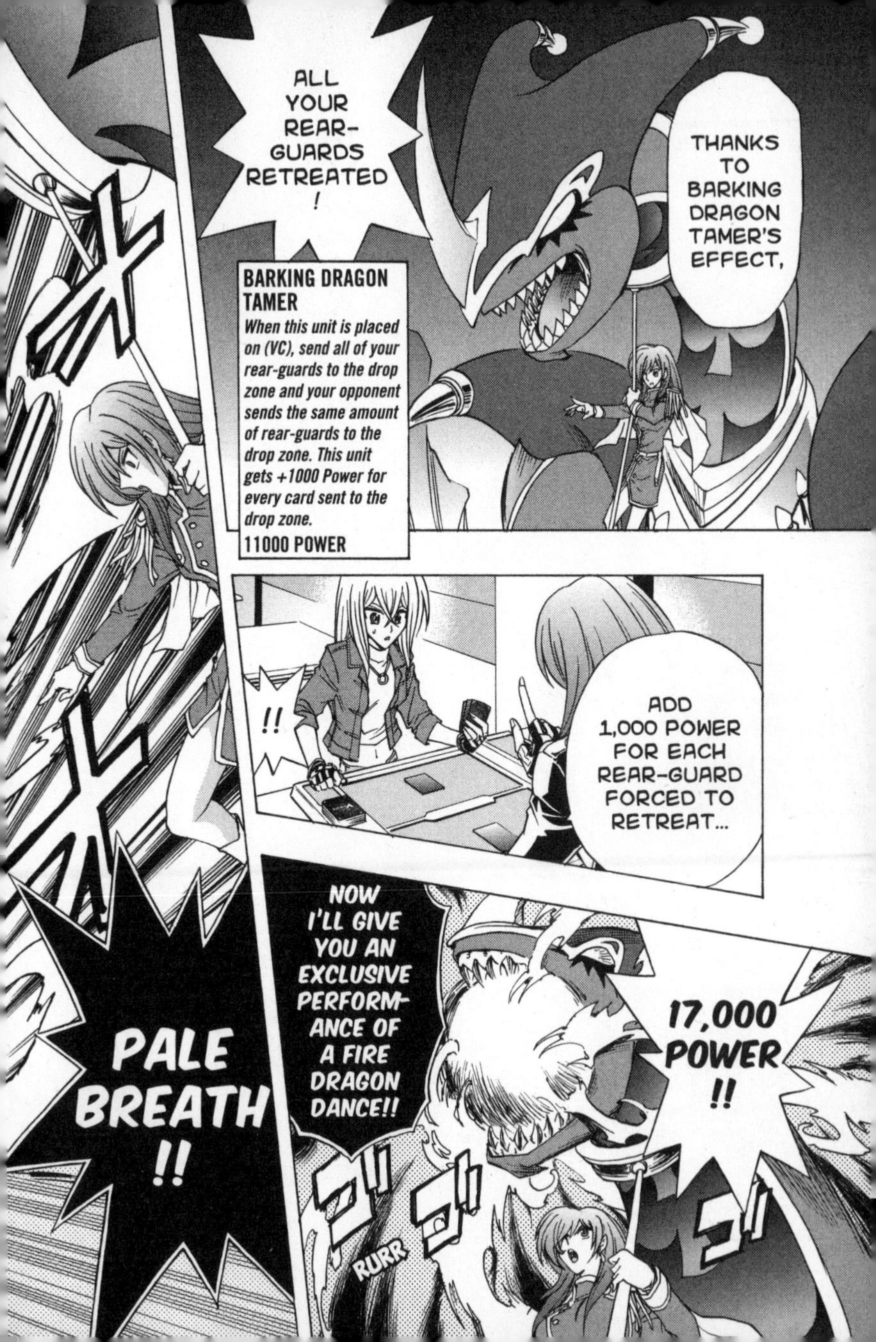
THANKS TO BARKING DRAGON TAMER'S EFFECT,
ALL YOUR REAR-GUARDS RETREATED!
BARKING DRAGON TAMER
When this unit is placed on (VC), send all of your rear-guards to the drop zone and your opponent sends the same amount of rear-guards to the drop zone. This unit gets +1000 Power for every card sent to the drop zone.
11000 POWER
ADD 1,000 POWER FOR EACH REAR-GUARD FORCED TO RETREAT...
!!
17,000 POWER!!
NOW I'LL GIVE YOU AN EXCLUSIVE PERFORMANCE OF A FIRE DRAGON DANCE!!
RURR
PALE BREATH!!

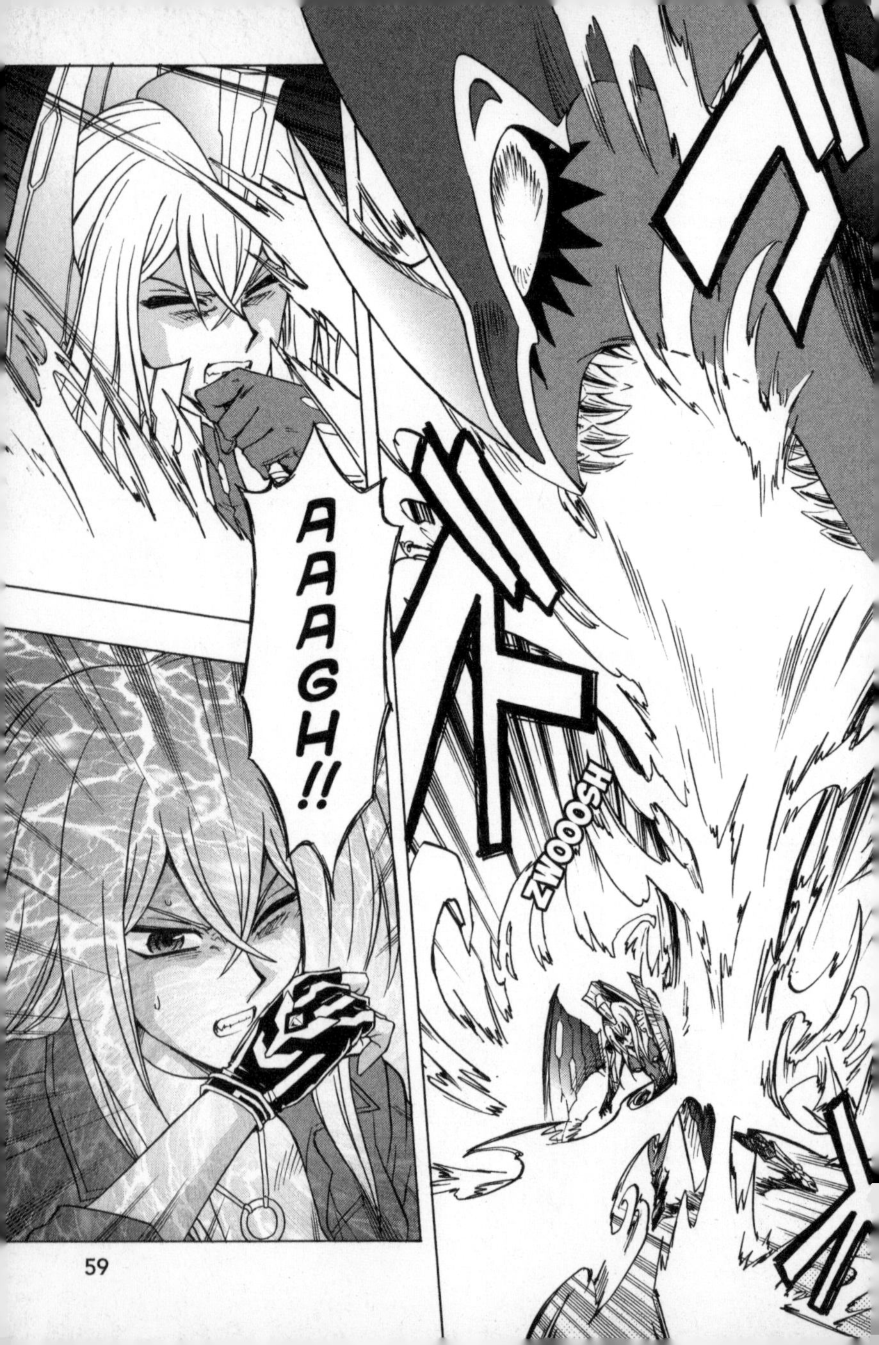
AAAAGH!!
ZWOOOSH

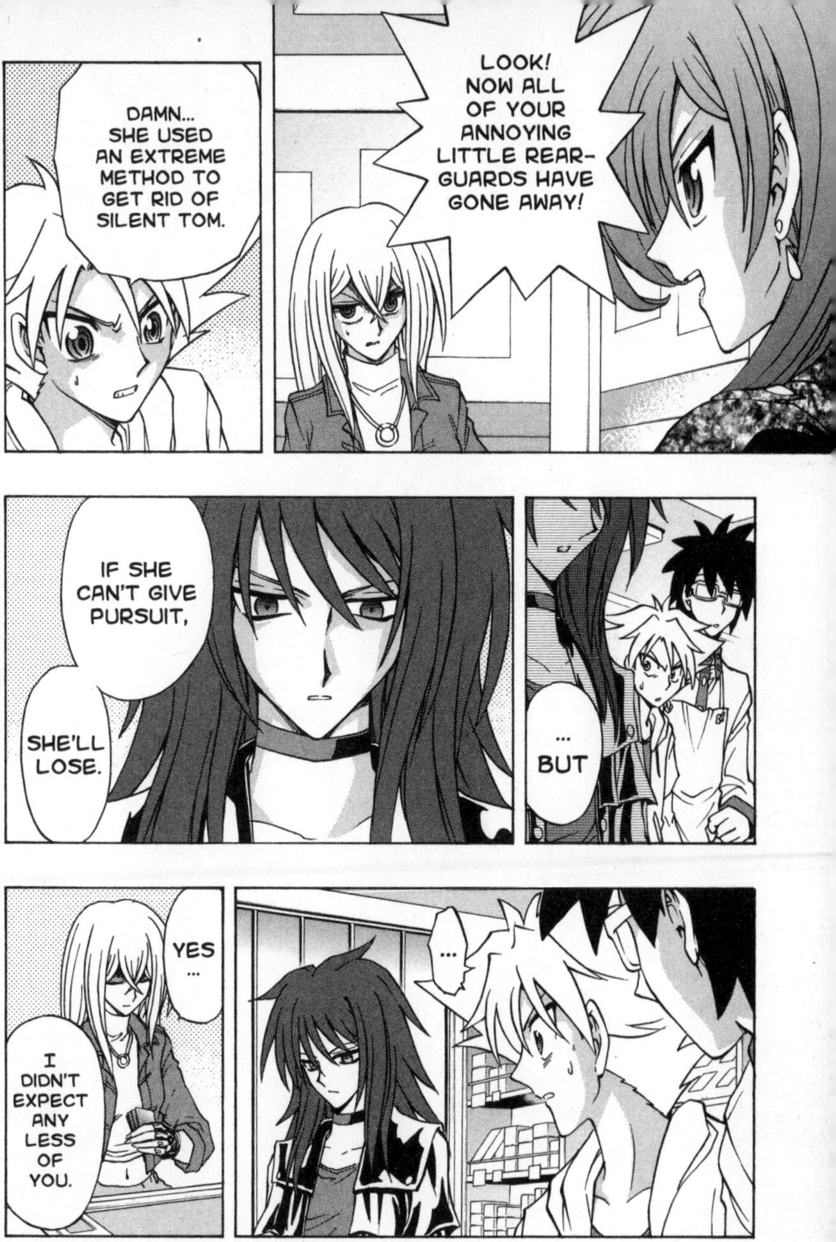

LOOK! NOW ALL OF YOUR ANNOYING LITTLE REAR-GUARDS HAVE GONE AWAY!
DAMN... SHE USED AN EXTREME METHOD TO GET RID OF SILENT TOM.
... BUT
IF SHE CAN'T GIVE PURSUIT,
SHE'LL LOSE.
...
YES ...
I DIDN'T EXPECT ANY LESS OF YOU.

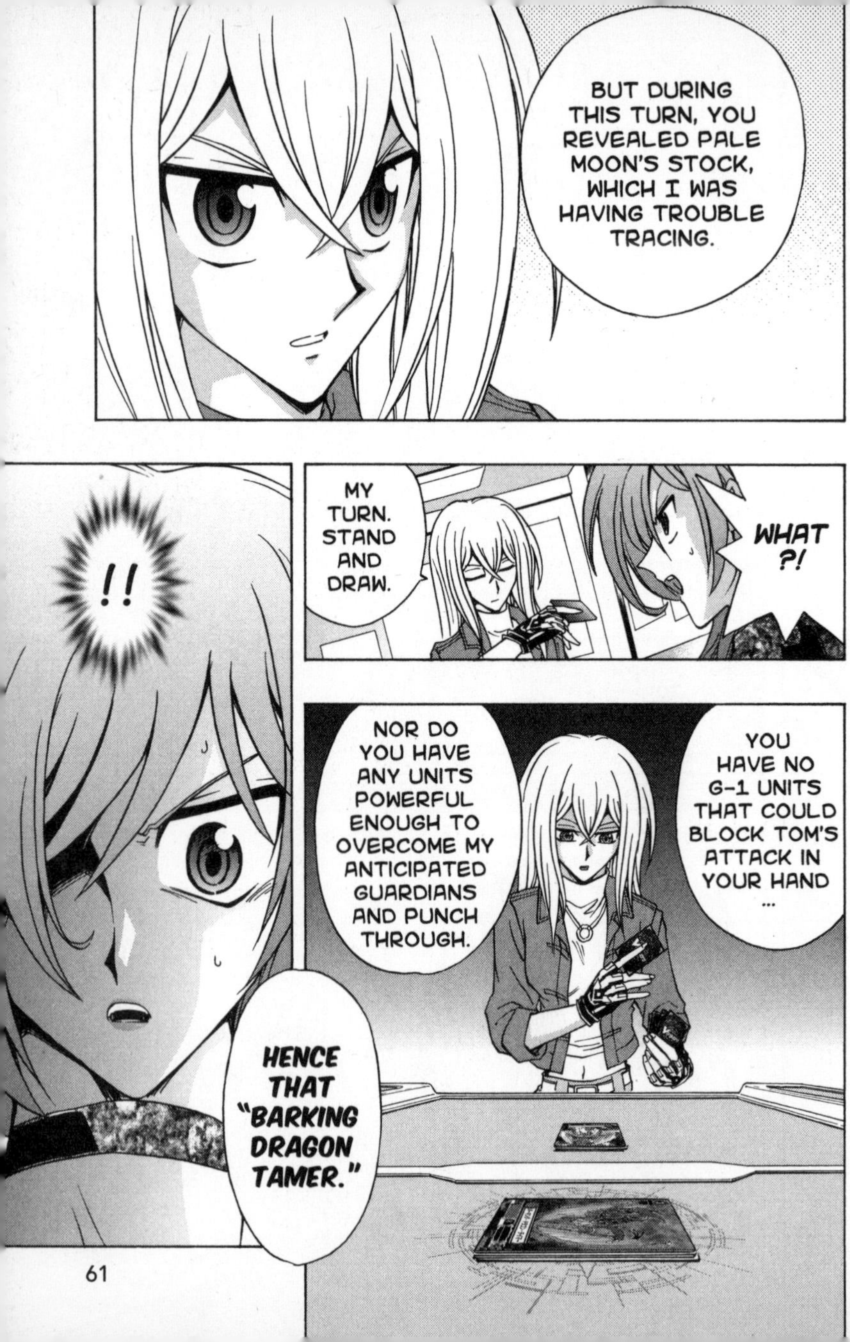
BUT DURING THIS TURN, YOU REVEALED PALE MOON'S STOCK, WHICH I WAS HAVING TROUBLE TRACING.
MY TURN. STAND AND DRAW.
WHAT?!
YOU HAVE NO G-1 UNITS THAT COULD BLOCK TOM'S ATTACK IN YOUR HAND ...
NOR DO YOU HAVE ANY UNITS POWERFUL ENOUGH TO OVERCOME MY ANTICIPATED GUARDIANS AND PUNCH THROUGH.
!!
HENCE THAT "BARKING DRAGON TAMER."

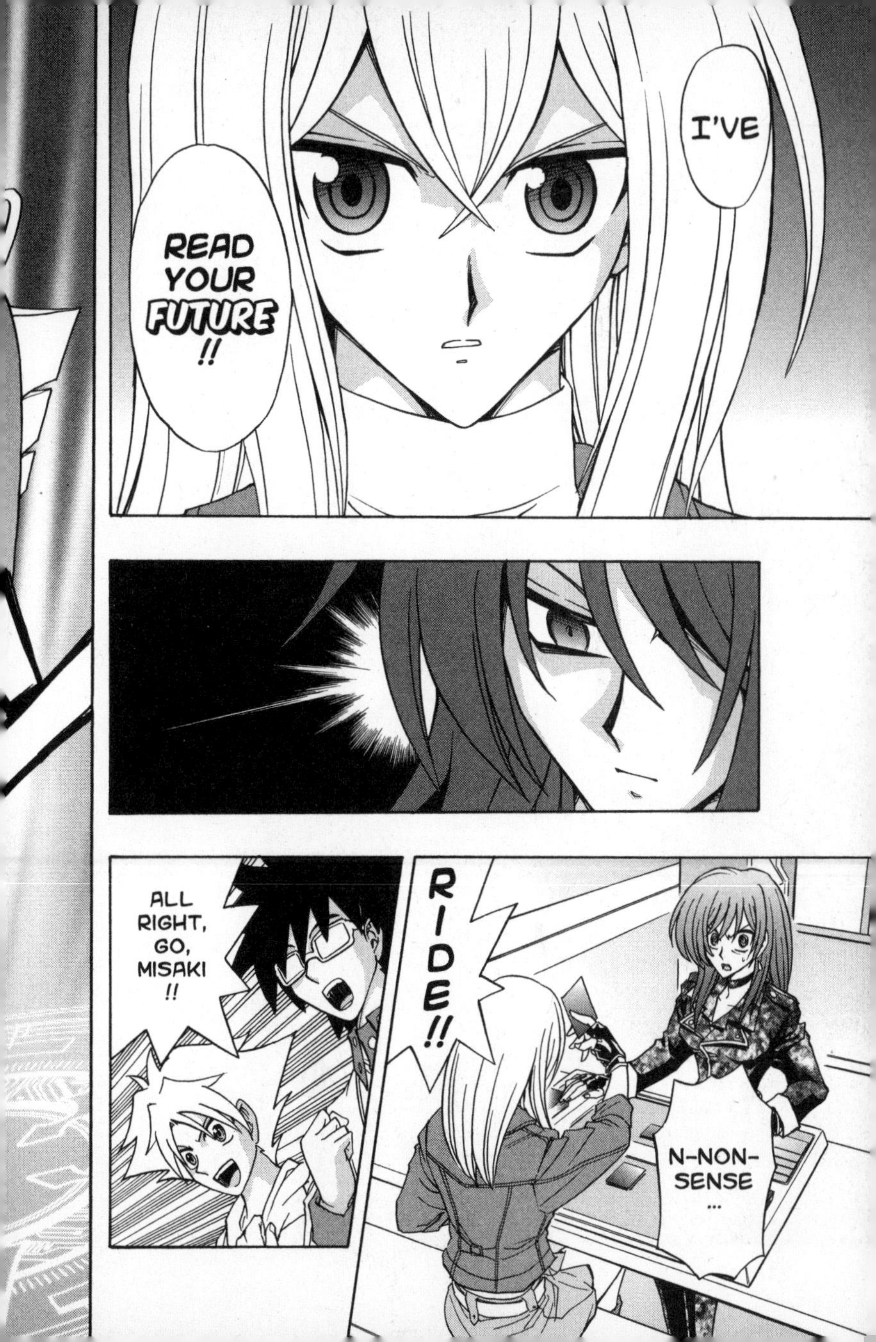
I'VE
READ YOUR FUTURE !!
RIDE!!
N-NON-SENSE ...
ALL RIGHT, GO, MISAKI !!

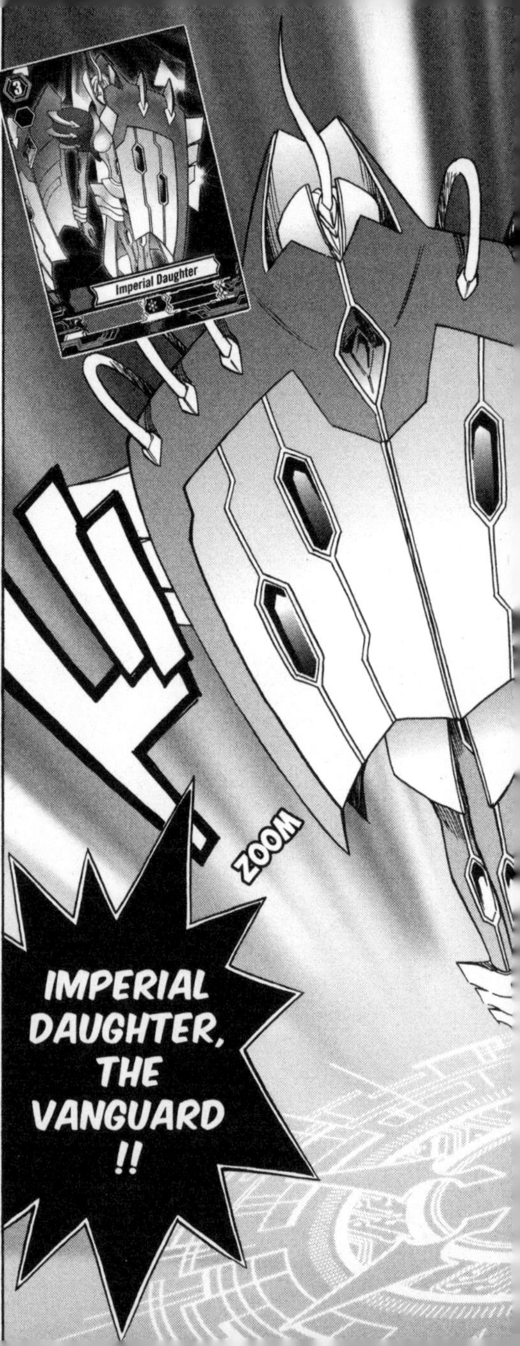
Imperial Daughter
ZOOM
IMPERIAL DAUGHTER, THE VANGUARD !!

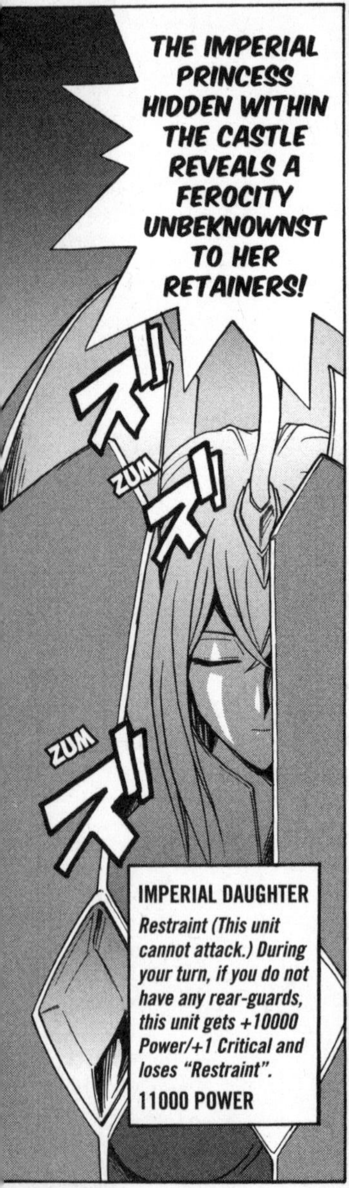
THE IMPERIAL PRINCESS HIDDEN WITHIN THE CASTLE REVEALS A FEROCITY UNBEKNOWNST TO HER RETAINERS!
ZUM
ZUM
IMPERIAL DAUGHTER
Restraint (This unit cannot attack.) During your turn, if you do not have any rear-guards, this unit gets +10000 Power/+1 Critical and loses "Restraint".
11000 POWER

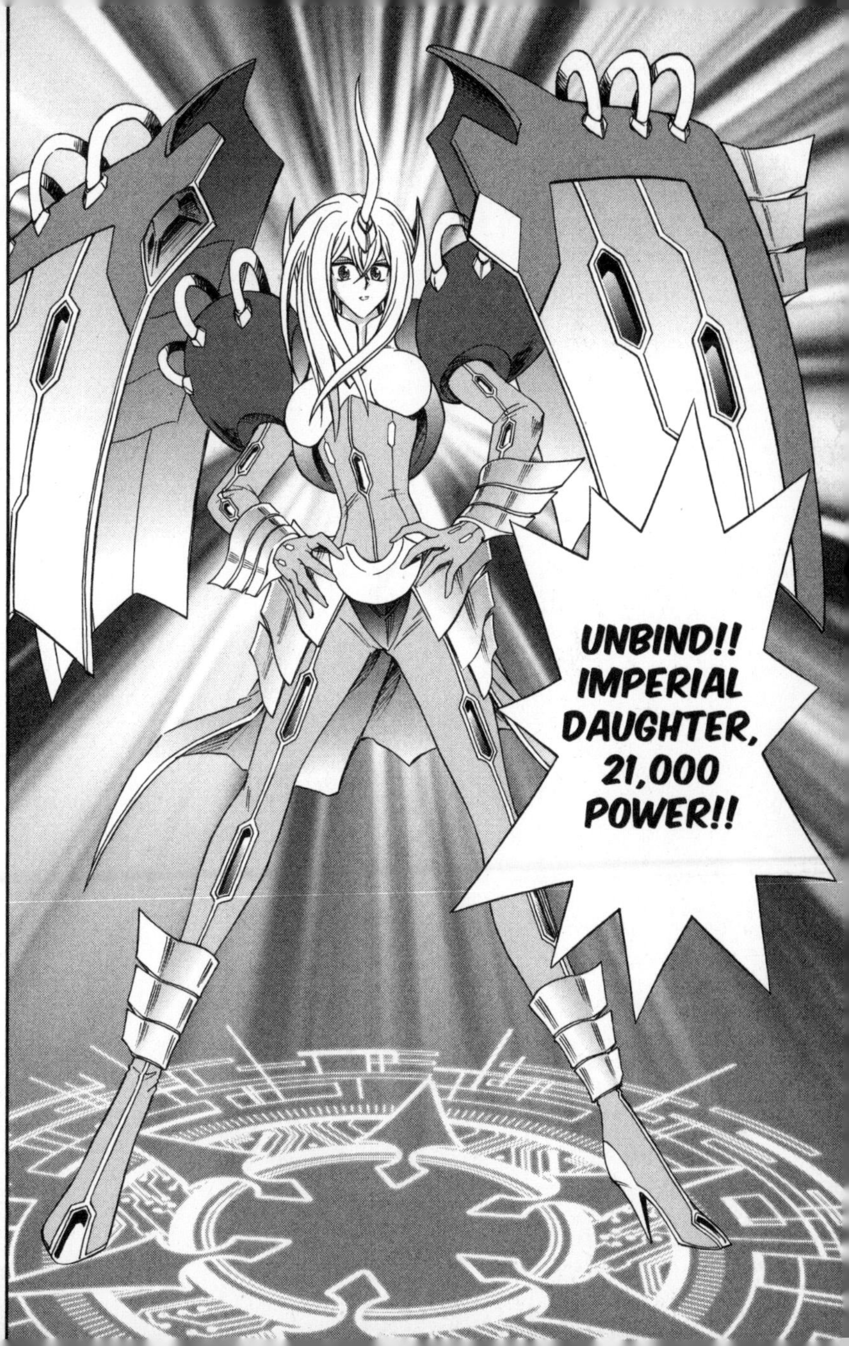
UNBIND!! IMPERIAL DAUGHTER, 21,000 POWER!!

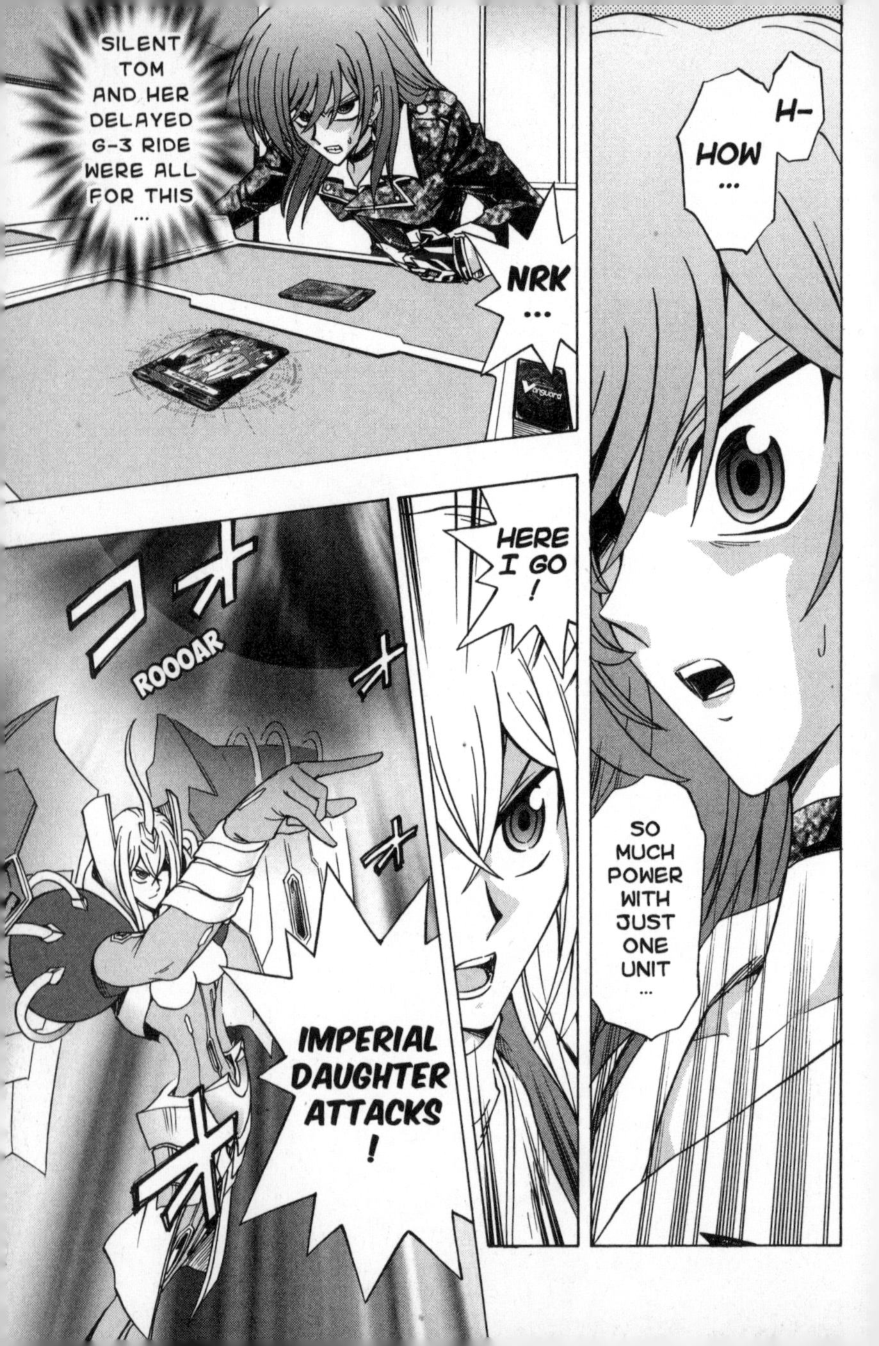
H-HOW ...
SO MUCH POWER WITH JUST ONE UNIT ...
NRK ...
SILENT TOM AND HER DELAYED G-3 RIDE WERE ALL FOR THIS ...
HERE I GO!
ROOOAR
IMPERIAL DAUGHTER ATTACKS!

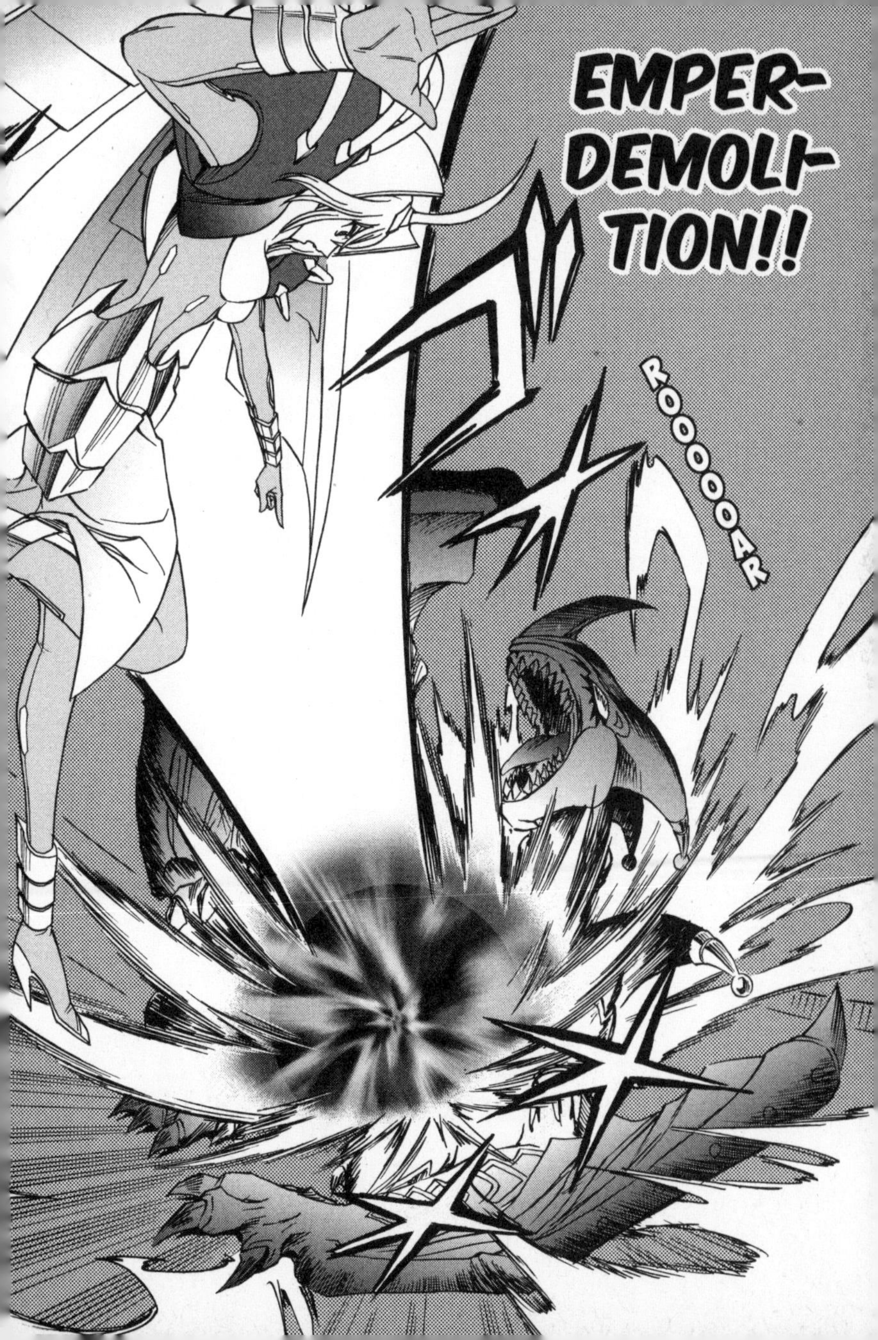
EMPER-DEMOLI-TION!!
ROOOOOOAR

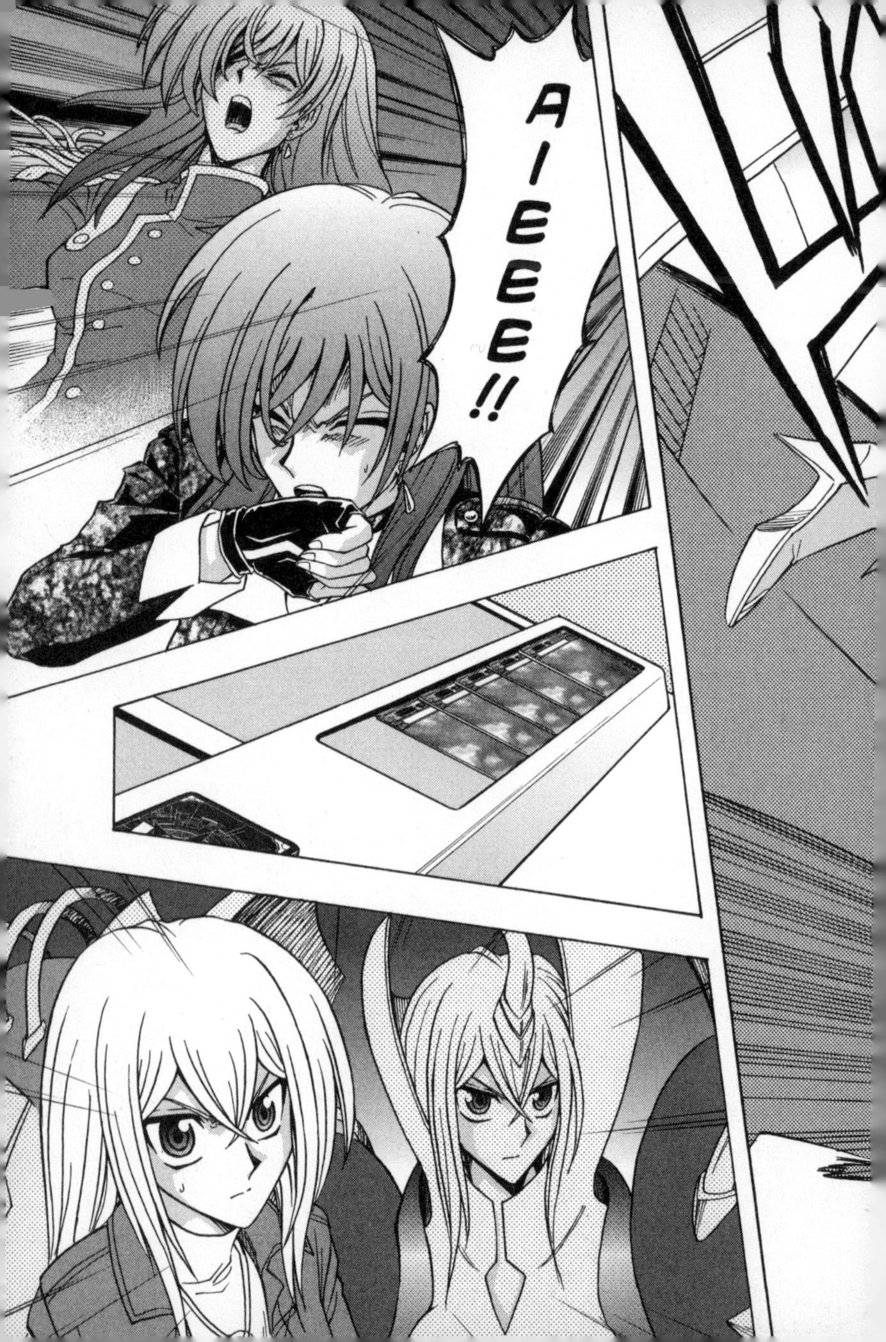
AIEEEE!!

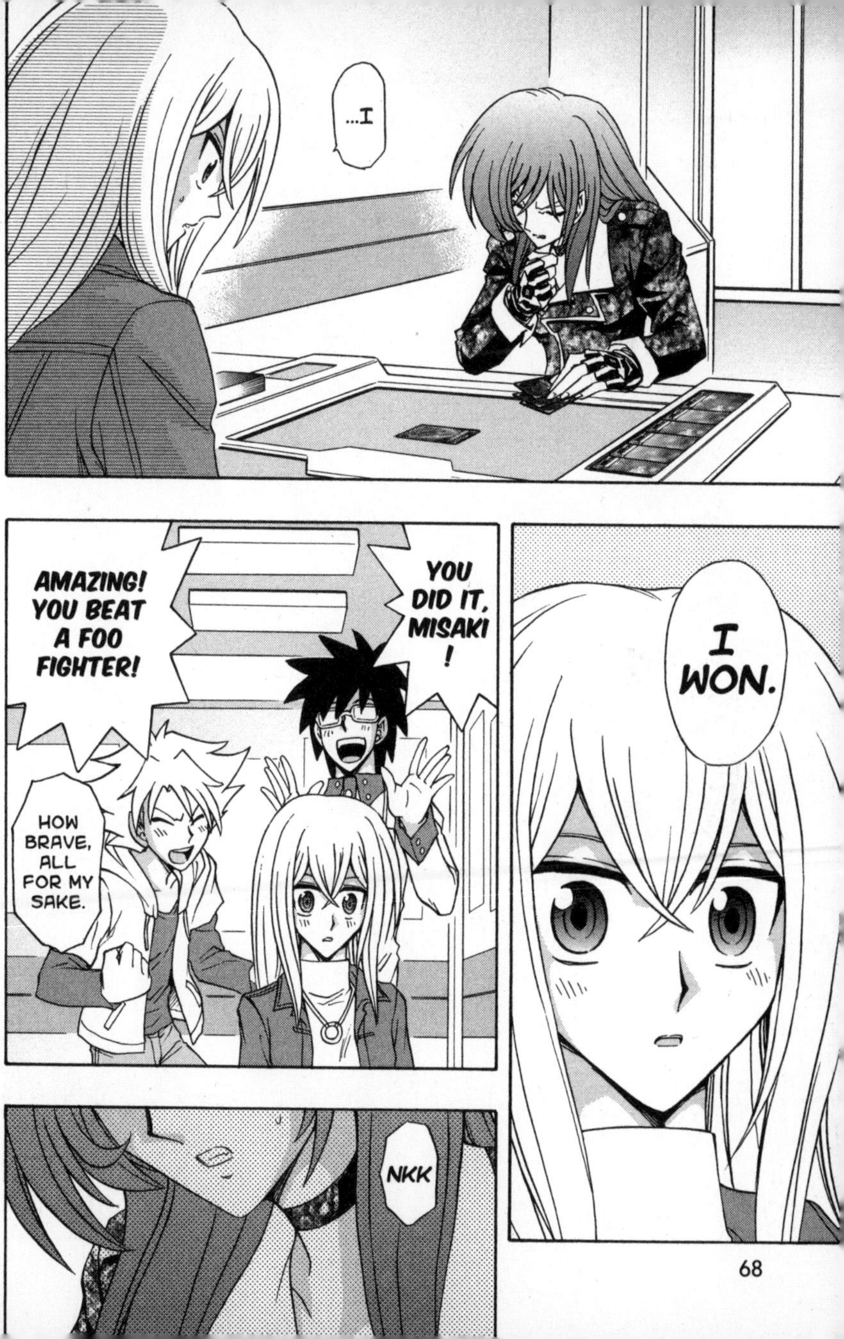
...I
I WON.
YOU DID IT, MISAKI!
AMAZING! YOU BEAT A FOO FIGHTER!
HOW BRAVE, ALL FOR MY SAKE.
NKK

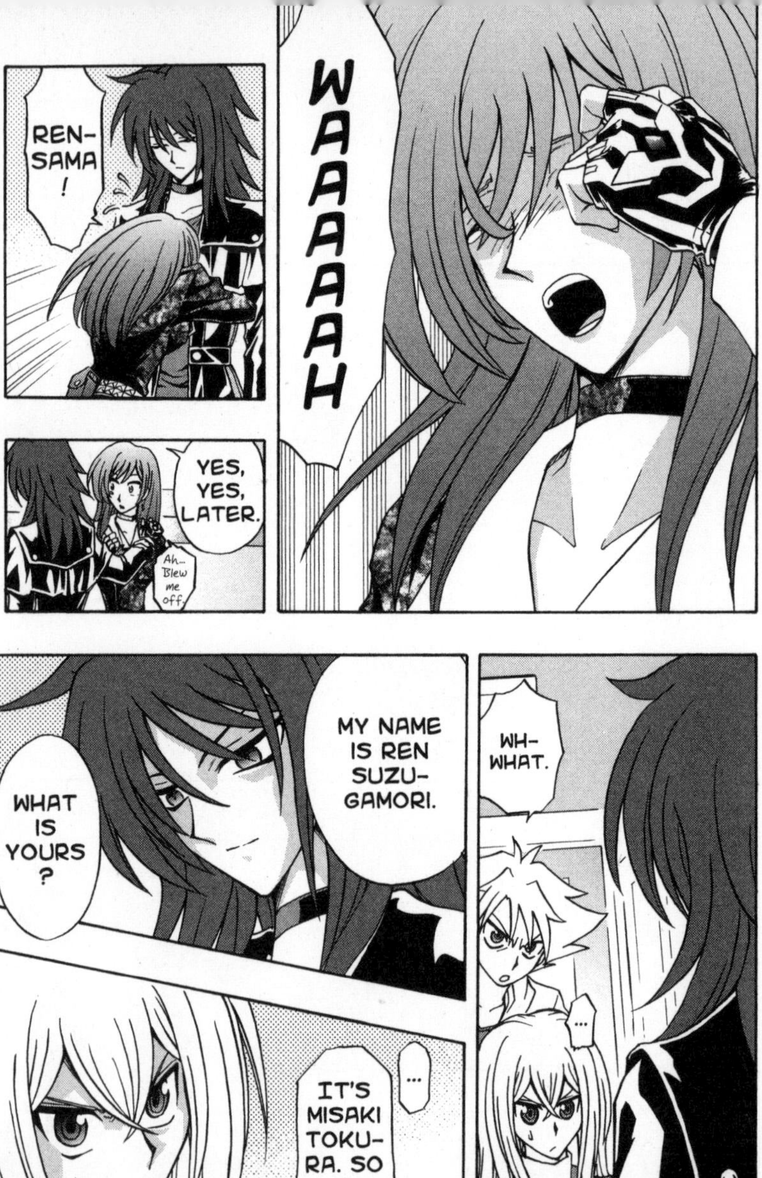
WAAAAAAH
REN-SAMA!
YES, YES, LATER.
Ah... Blew me off.
WH-WHAT.
...
MY NAME IS REN SUZU-GAMORI.
WHAT IS YOURS?
...
IT'S MISAKI TOKU-RA. SO?

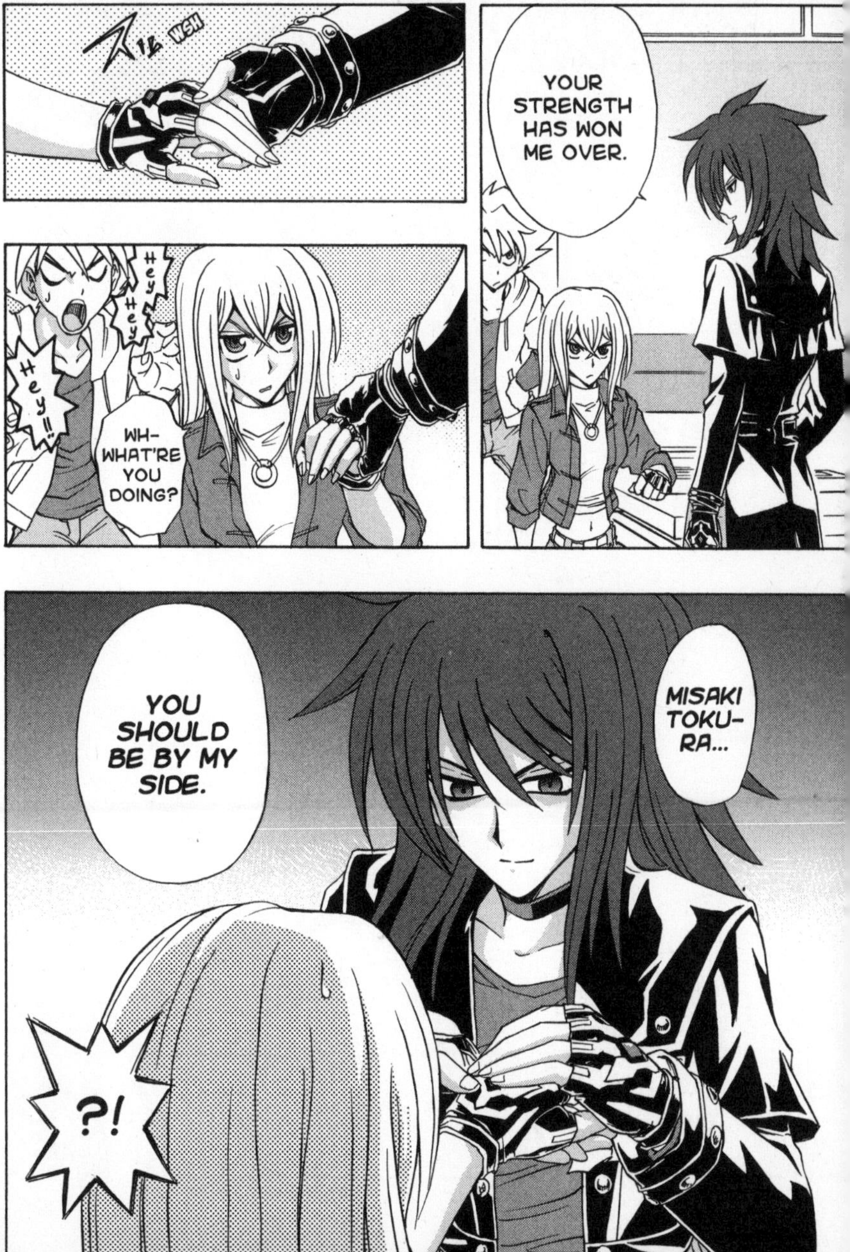
YOUR STRENGTH HAS WON ME OVER.
WSH
Hey Hey
Hey!!
WH-WHAT'RE YOU DOING?
MISAKI TOKU-RA...
YOU SHOULD BE BY MY SIDE.
?!

BONUS! CARDFIGHT!! Vanguard NEVER-BEFORE-SEEN IMAGE BOARDS

UNITS

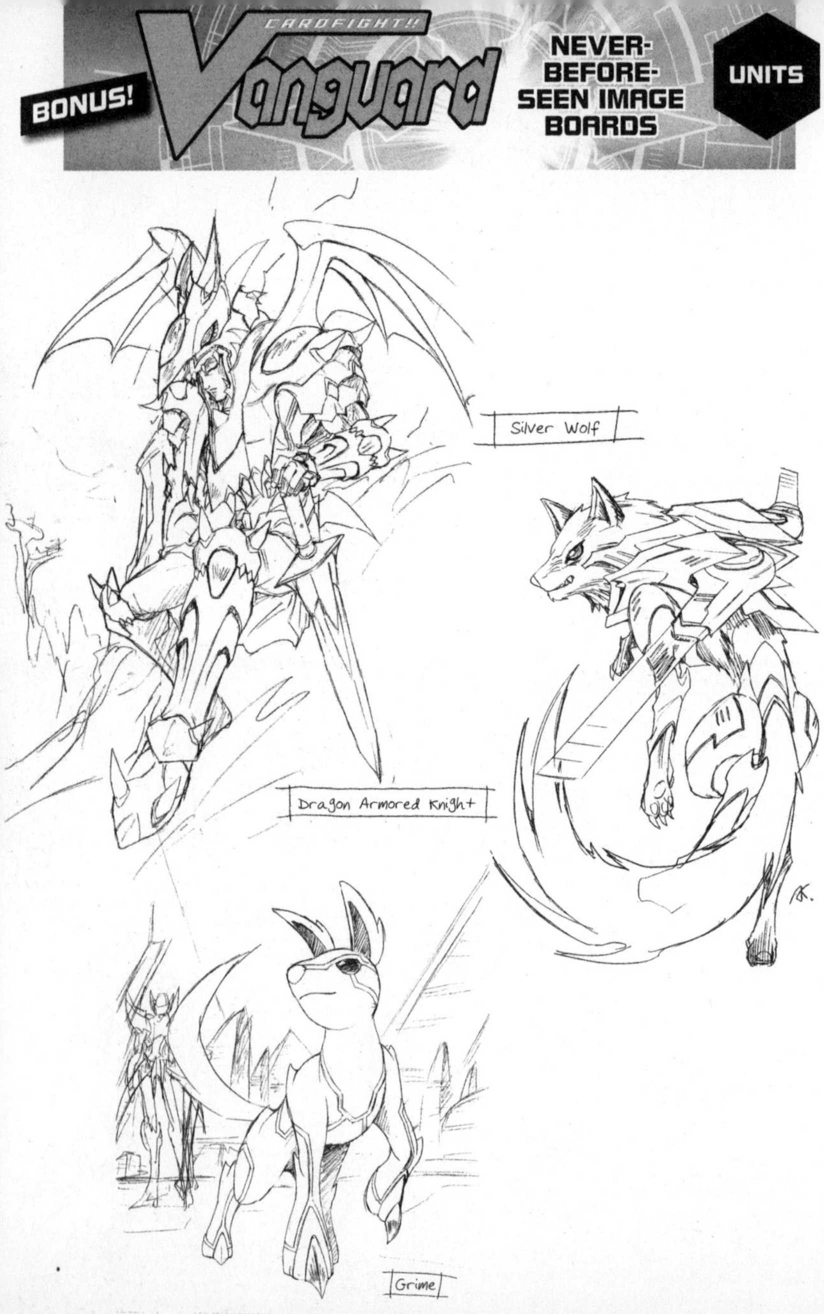

Silver Wolf
Dragon Armored Knight
Grime

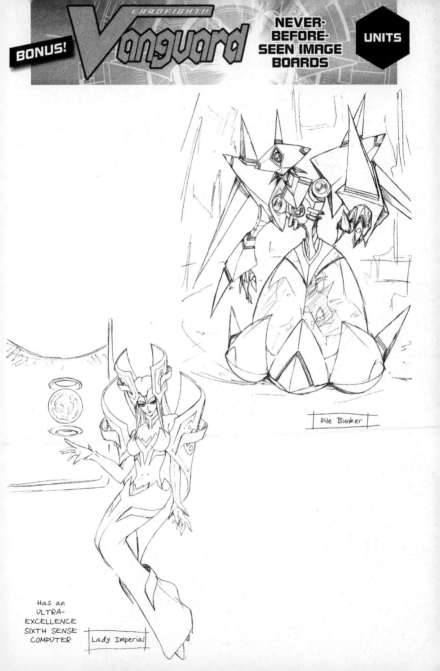

BONUS! CARDFIGHT!! Vanguard

NEVER-BEFORE-SEEN IMAGE BOARDS

UNITS

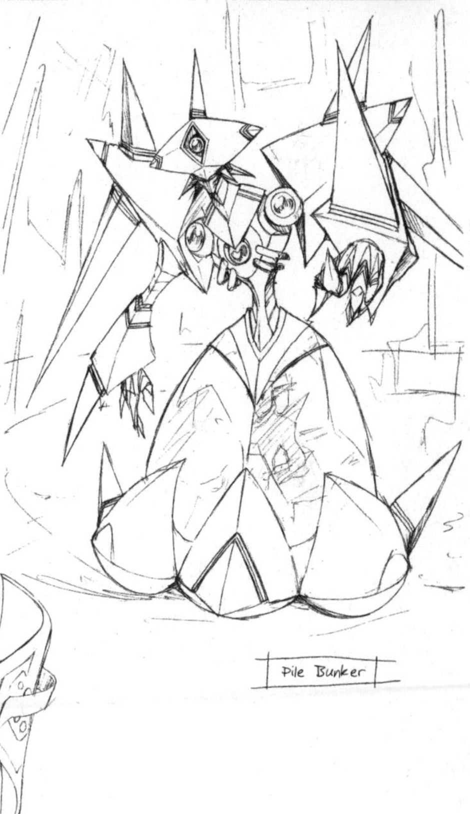

Pile Bunker

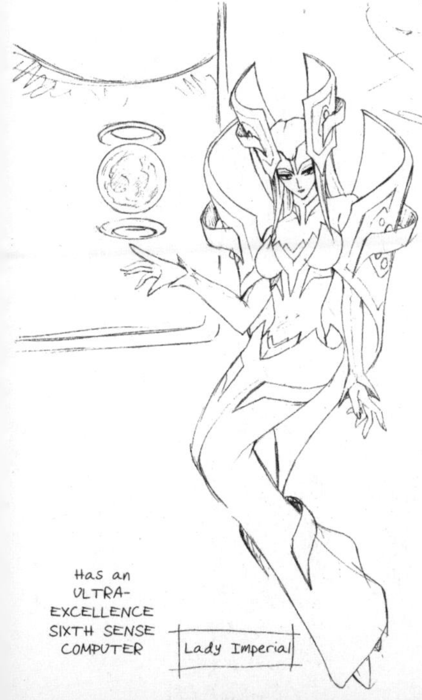

Has an ULTRA-EXCELLENCE SIXTH SENSE COMPUTER

Lady Imperial

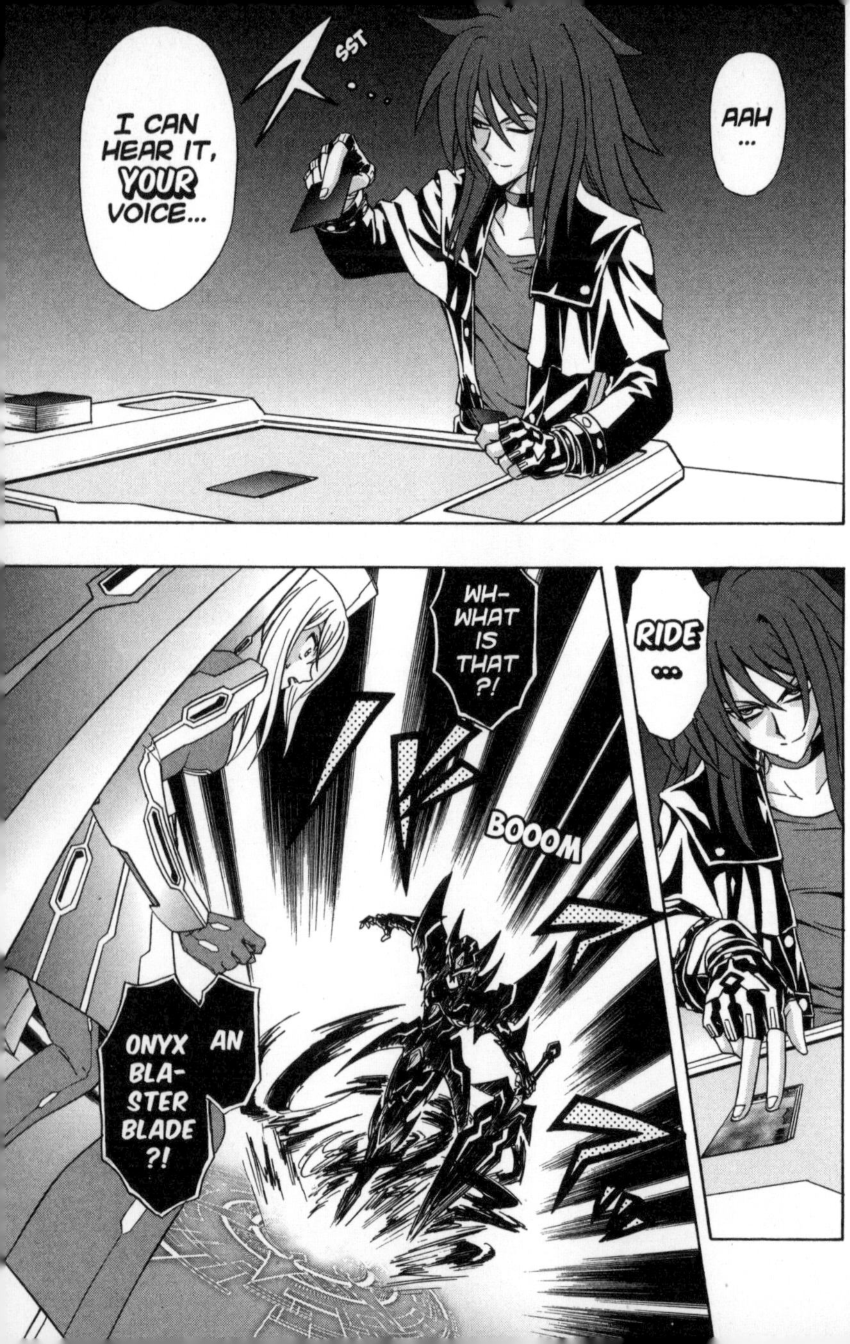
AAH ...
SST
I CAN HEAR IT, YOUR VOICE...
RIDE ...
WH-WHAT IS THAT?!
BOOOM
AN ONYX BLA-STER BLADE?!

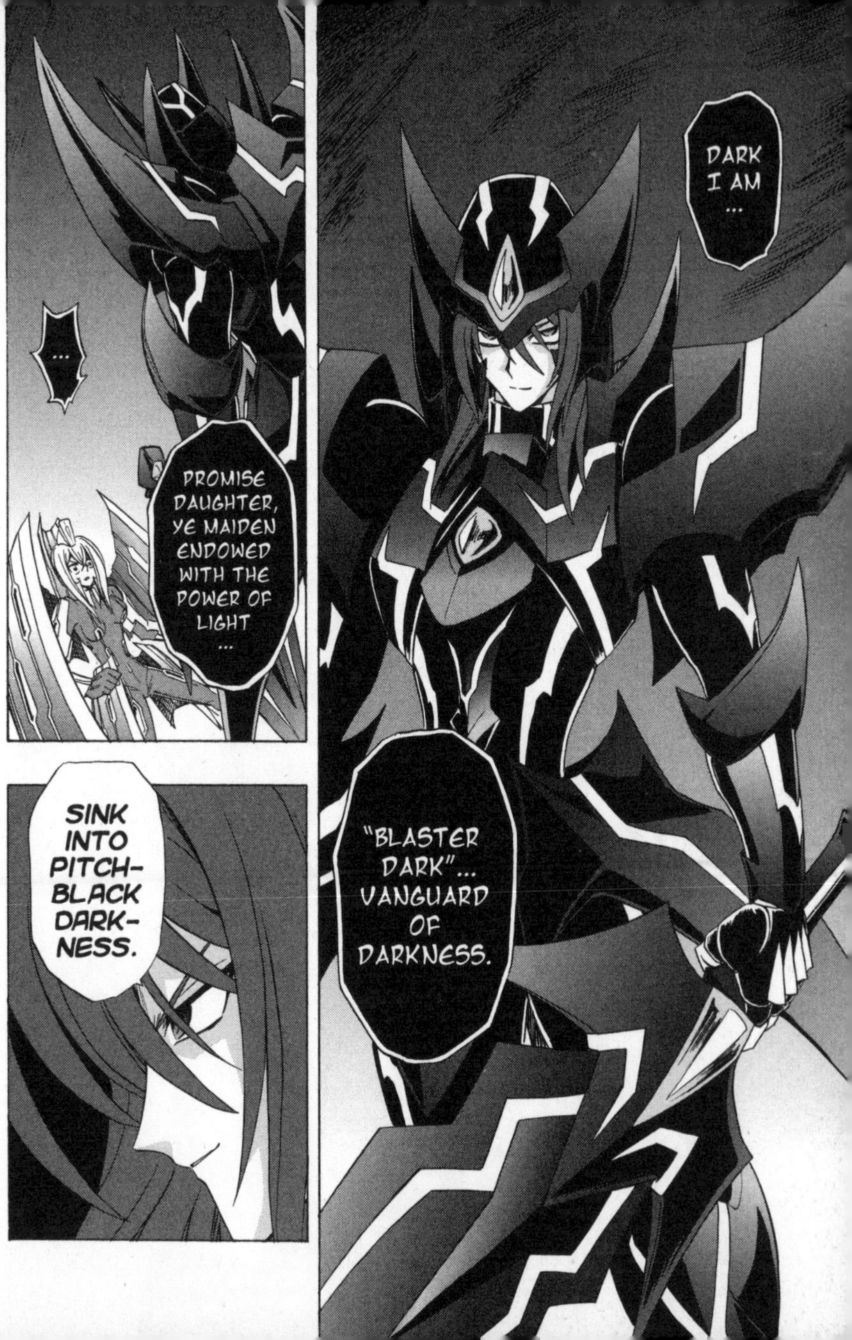
DARK I AM ...
"BLASTER DARK"... VANGUARD OF DARKNESS.
...
PROMISE DAUGHTER, YE MAIDEN ENDOWED WITH THE POWER OF LIGHT ...
SINK INTO PITCH-BLACK DARK-NESS.

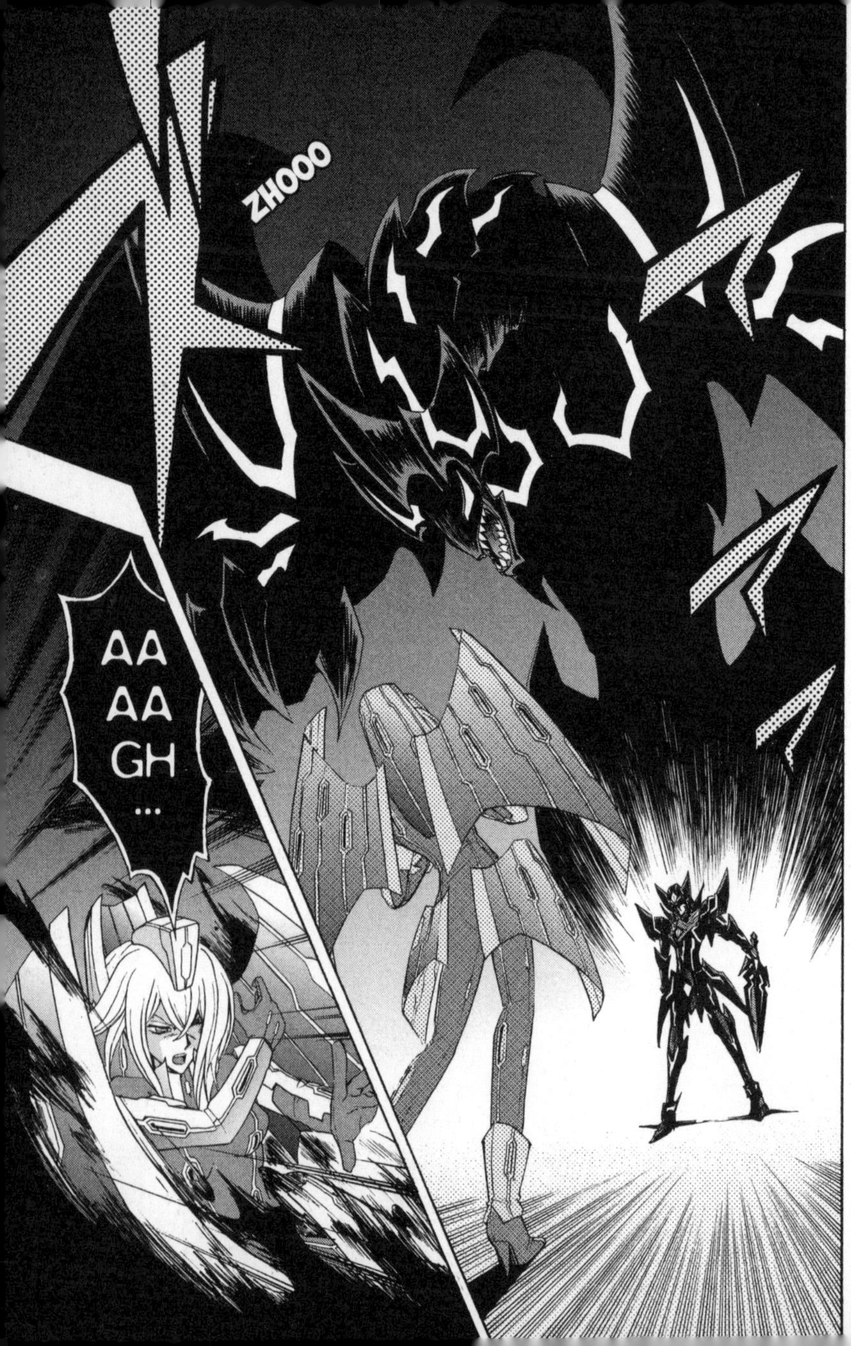
ZHOOO
AAAAGH...

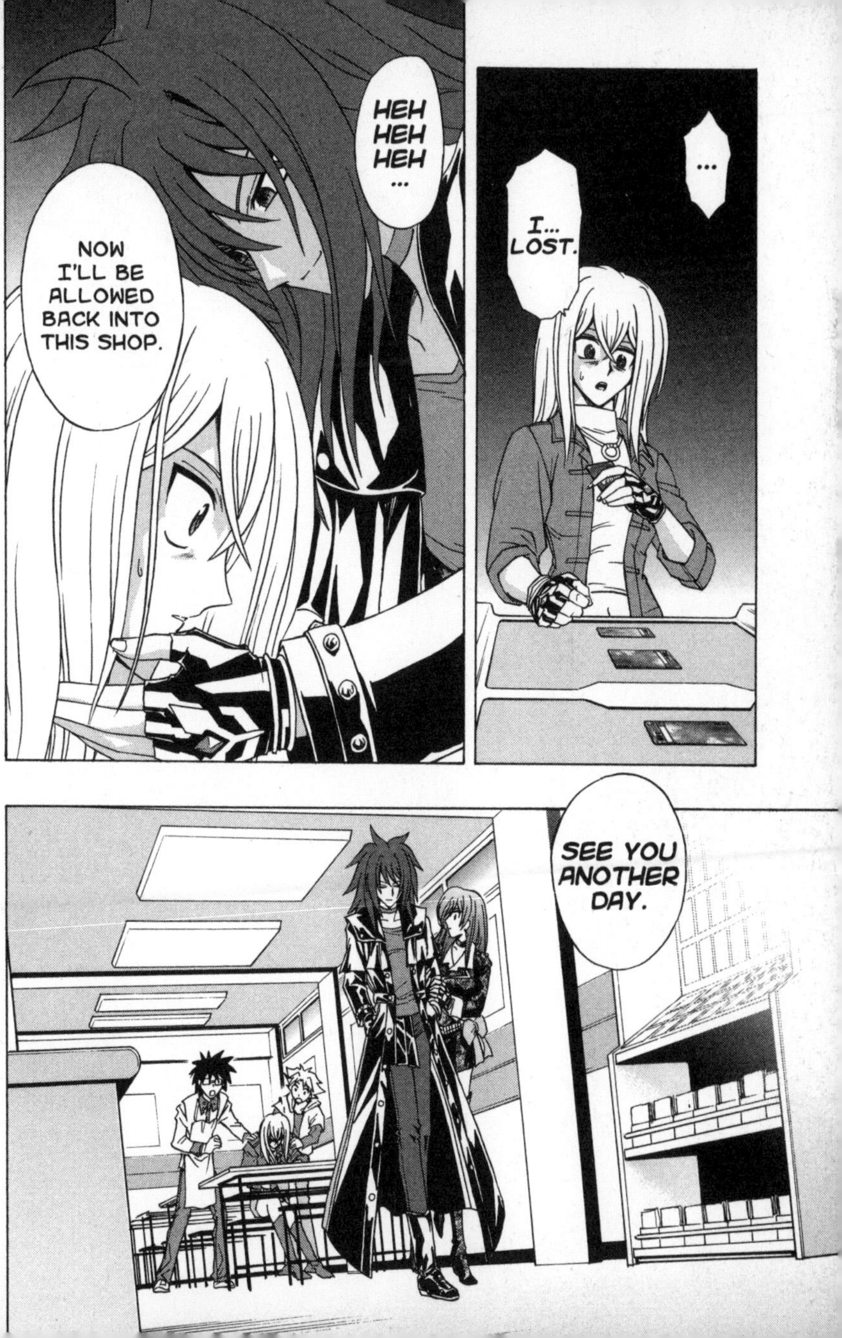
...
I... LOST.
HEH HEH HEH ...
NOW I'LL BE ALLOWED BACK INTO THIS SHOP.
SEE YOU ANOTHER DAY.

#012 TETSU

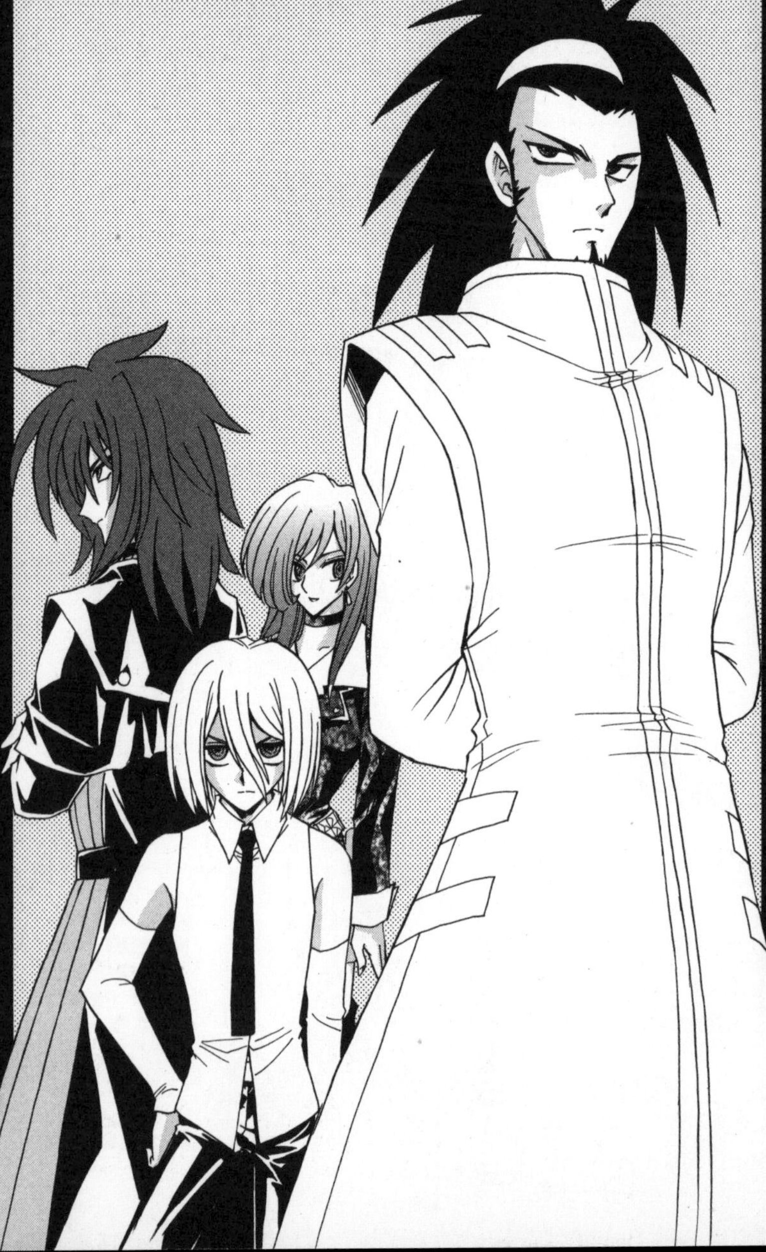

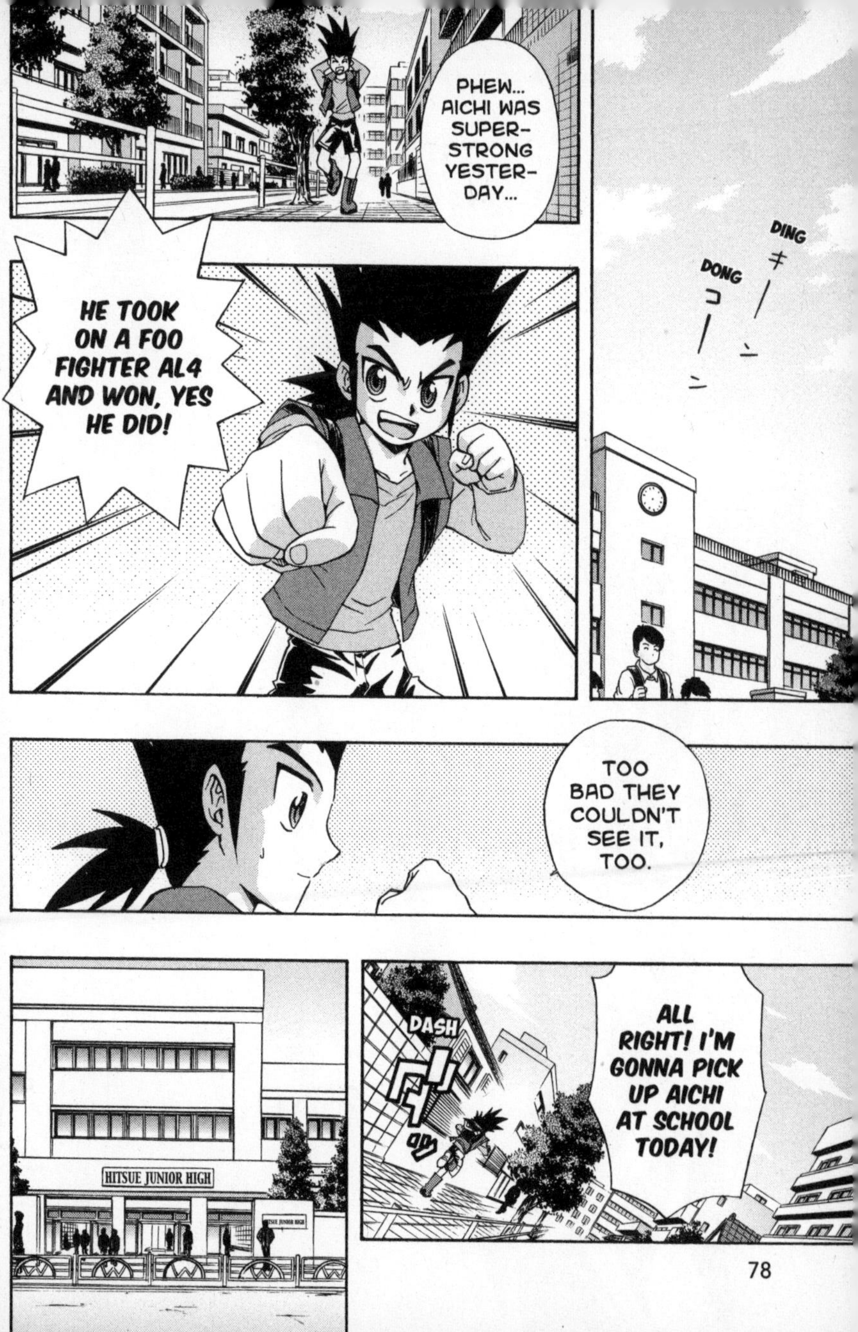
DING
キーン
DONG
コーン
PHEW... AICHI WAS SUPER-STRONG YESTER-DAY...
HE TOOK ON A FOO FIGHTER AL4 AND WON, YES HE DID!
TOO BAD THEY COULDN'T SEE IT, TOO.
DASH
ALL RIGHT! I'M GONNA PICK UP AICHI AT SCHOOL TODAY!
HITSUE JUNIOR HIGH

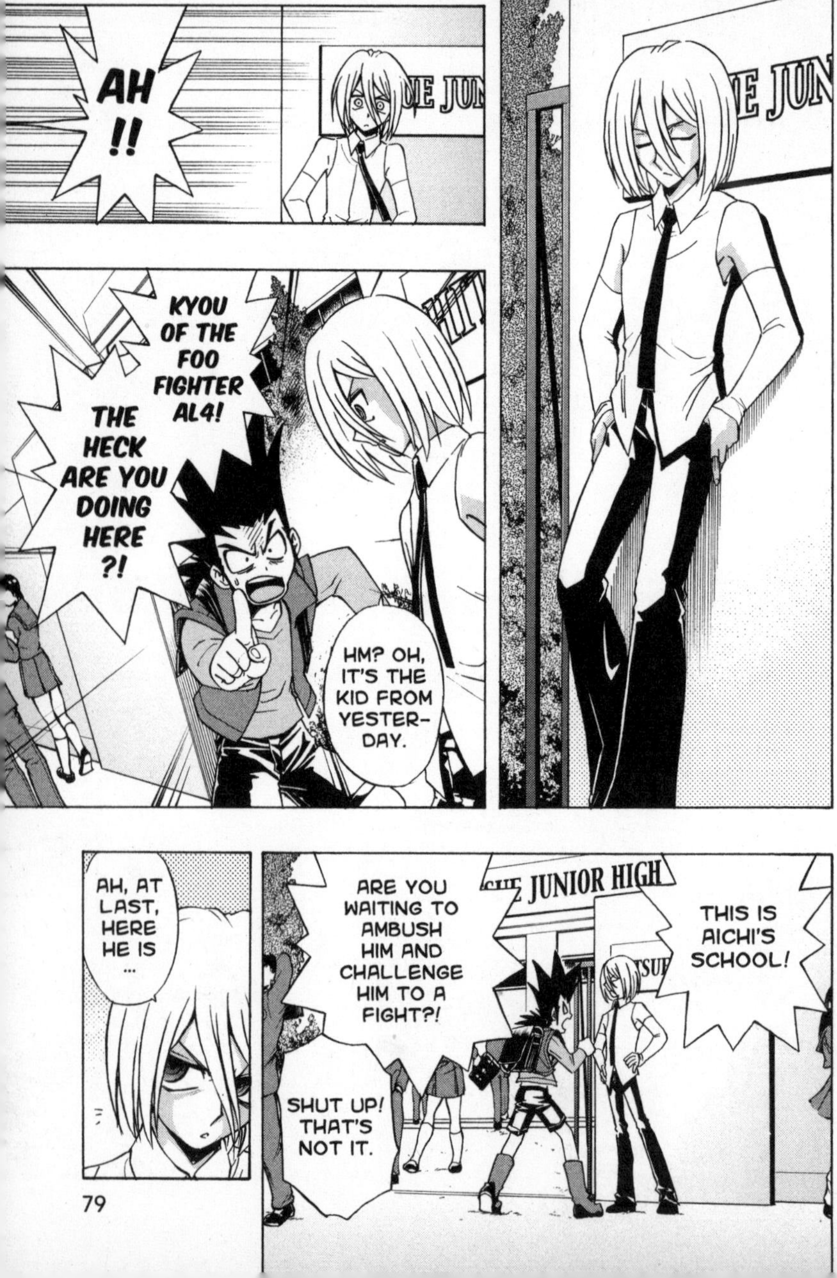

AH!!
KYOU OF THE FOO FIGHTER AL4!
THE HECK ARE YOU DOING HERE?!
HM? OH, IT'S THE KID FROM YESTER-DAY.
THIS IS AICHI'S SCHOOL!
JUNIOR HIGH
ARE YOU WAITING TO AMBUSH HIM AND CHALLENGE HIM TO A FIGHT?!
SHUT UP! THAT'S NOT IT.
AH, AT LAST, HERE HE IS ...

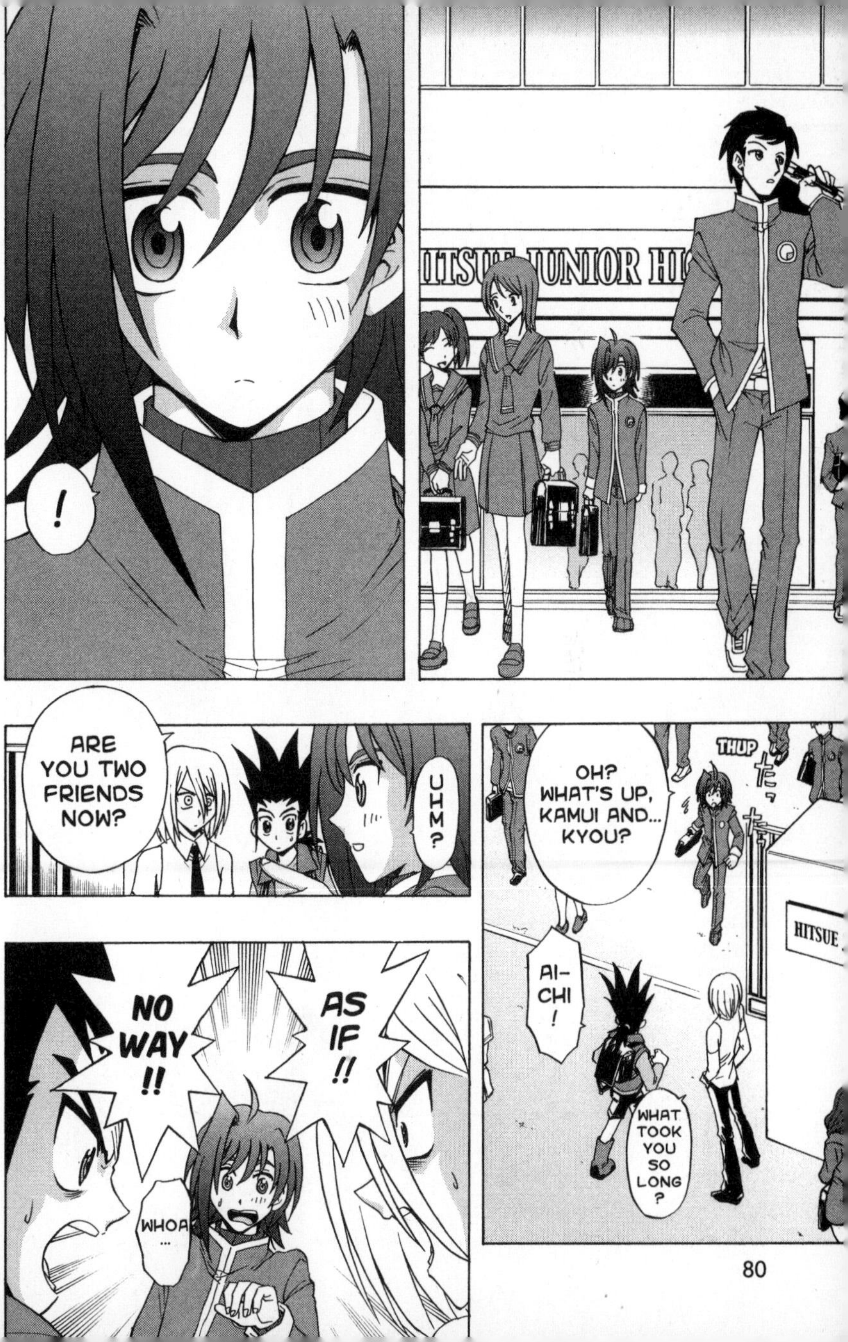
ITSUE JUNIOR HI
!
THUP
OH? WHAT'S UP, KAMUI AND... KYOU?
HITSUE
AI-CHI!
WHAT TOOK YOU SO LONG?
UHM?
ARE YOU TWO FRIENDS NOW?
AS IF!!
NO WAY!!
WHOA...

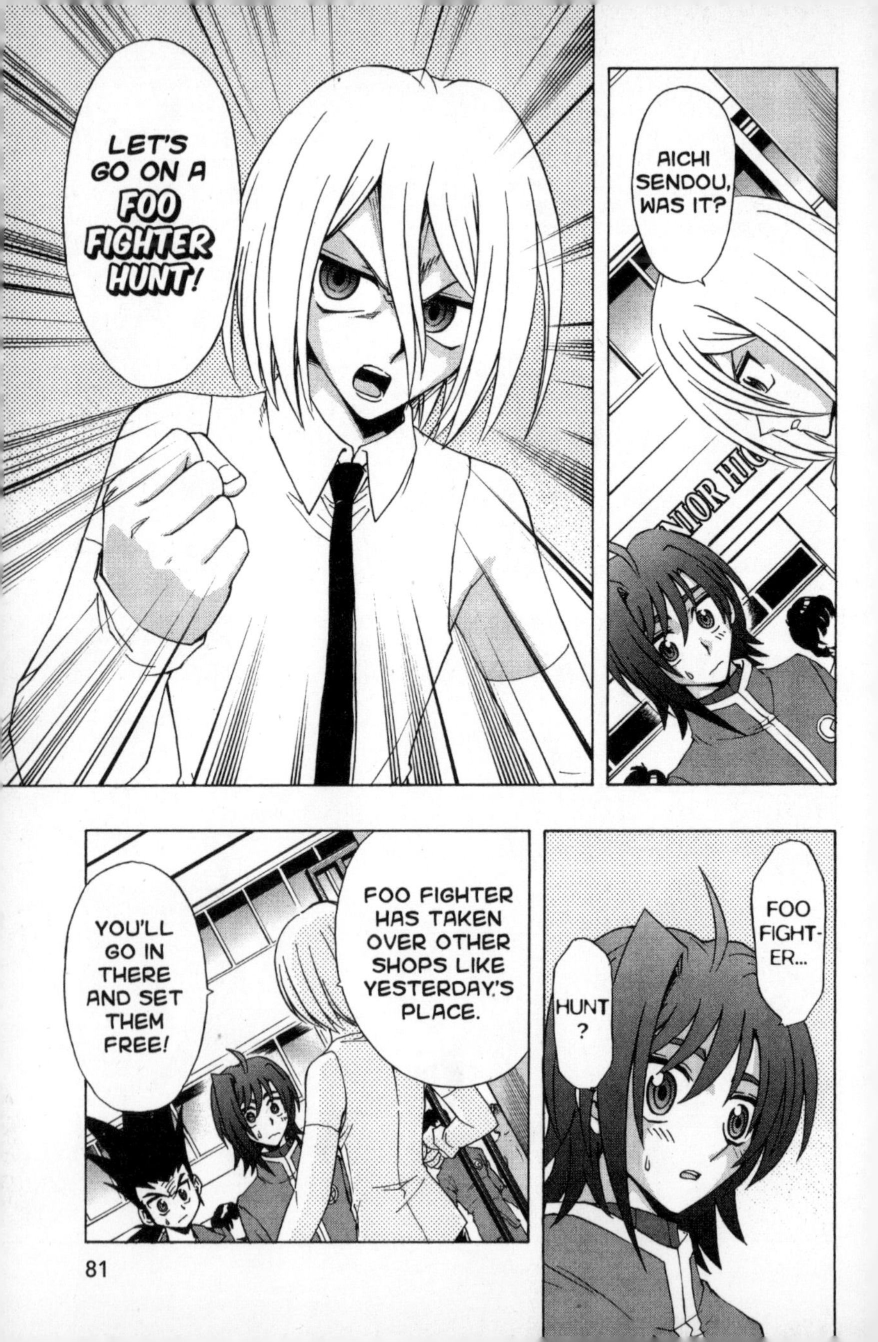
AICHI SENDOU, WAS IT?
LET'S GO ON A FOO FIGHTER HUNT!
FOO FIGHT-ER...
HUNT?
FOO FIGHTER HAS TAKEN OVER OTHER SHOPS LIKE YESTERDAY'S PLACE.
YOU'LL GO IN THERE AND SET THEM FREE!

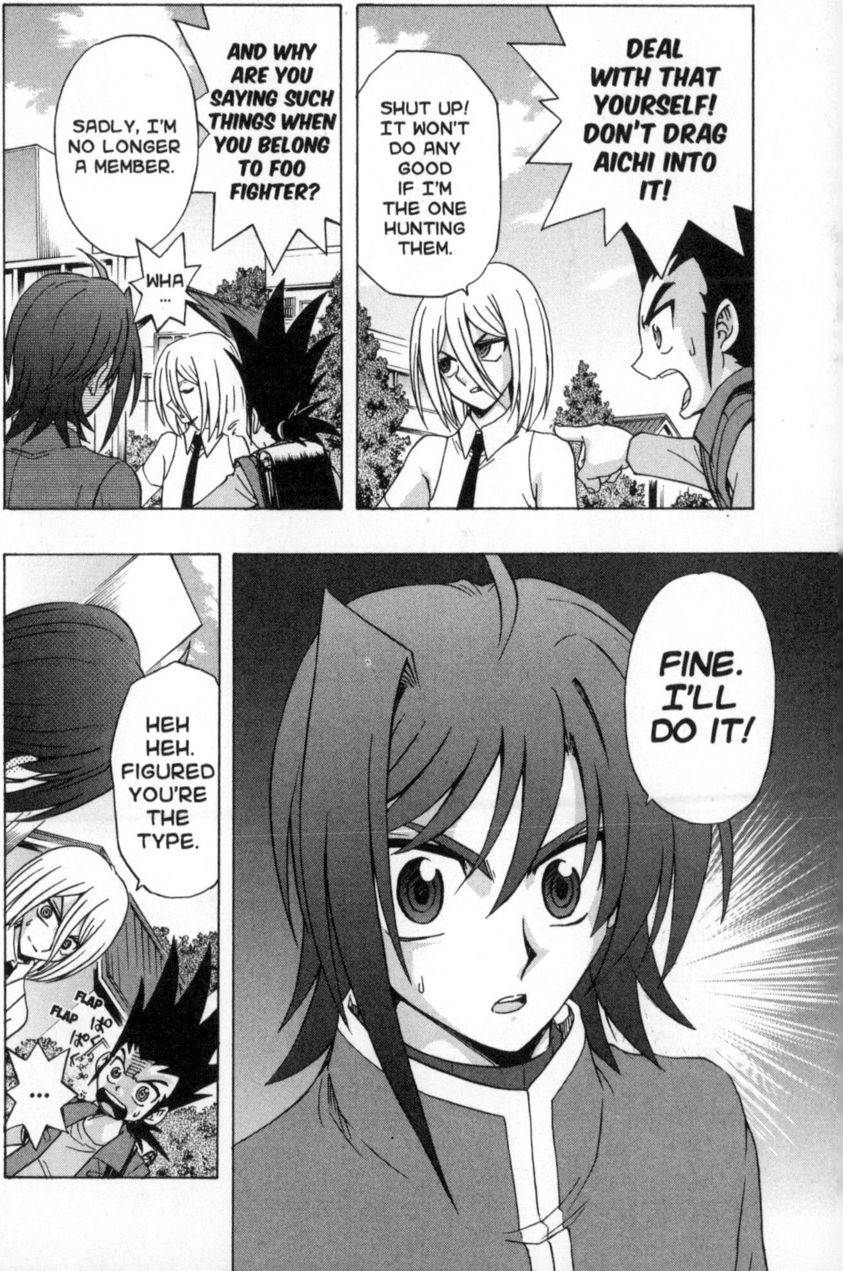
DEAL WITH THAT YOURSELF! DON'T DRAG AICHI INTO IT!
SHUT UP! IT WON'T DO ANY GOOD IF I'M THE ONE HUNTING THEM.
AND WHY ARE YOU SAYING SUCH THINGS WHEN YOU BELONG TO FOO FIGHTER?
SADLY, I'M NO LONGER A MEMBER.
WHA...
FINE. I'LL DO IT!
HEH HEH. FIGURED YOU'RE THE TYPE.
FLAP FLAP
...

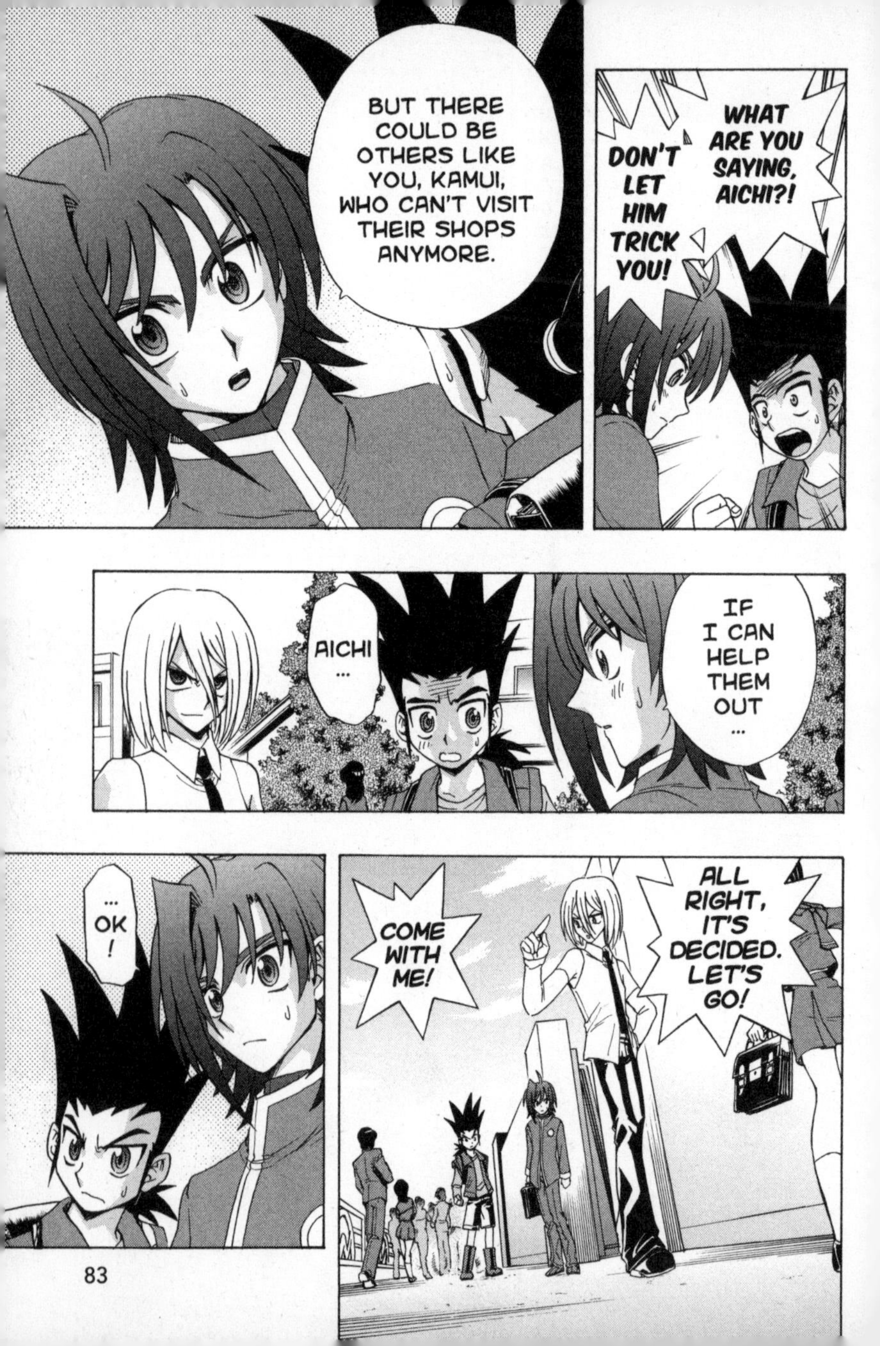
WHAT ARE YOU SAYING, AICHI?!
DON'T LET HIM TRICK YOU!
BUT THERE COULD BE OTHERS LIKE YOU, KAMUI, WHO CAN'T VISIT THEIR SHOPS ANYMORE.
IF I CAN HELP THEM OUT ...
AICHI ...
ALL RIGHT, IT'S DECIDED. LET'S GO!
COME WITH ME!
... OK!

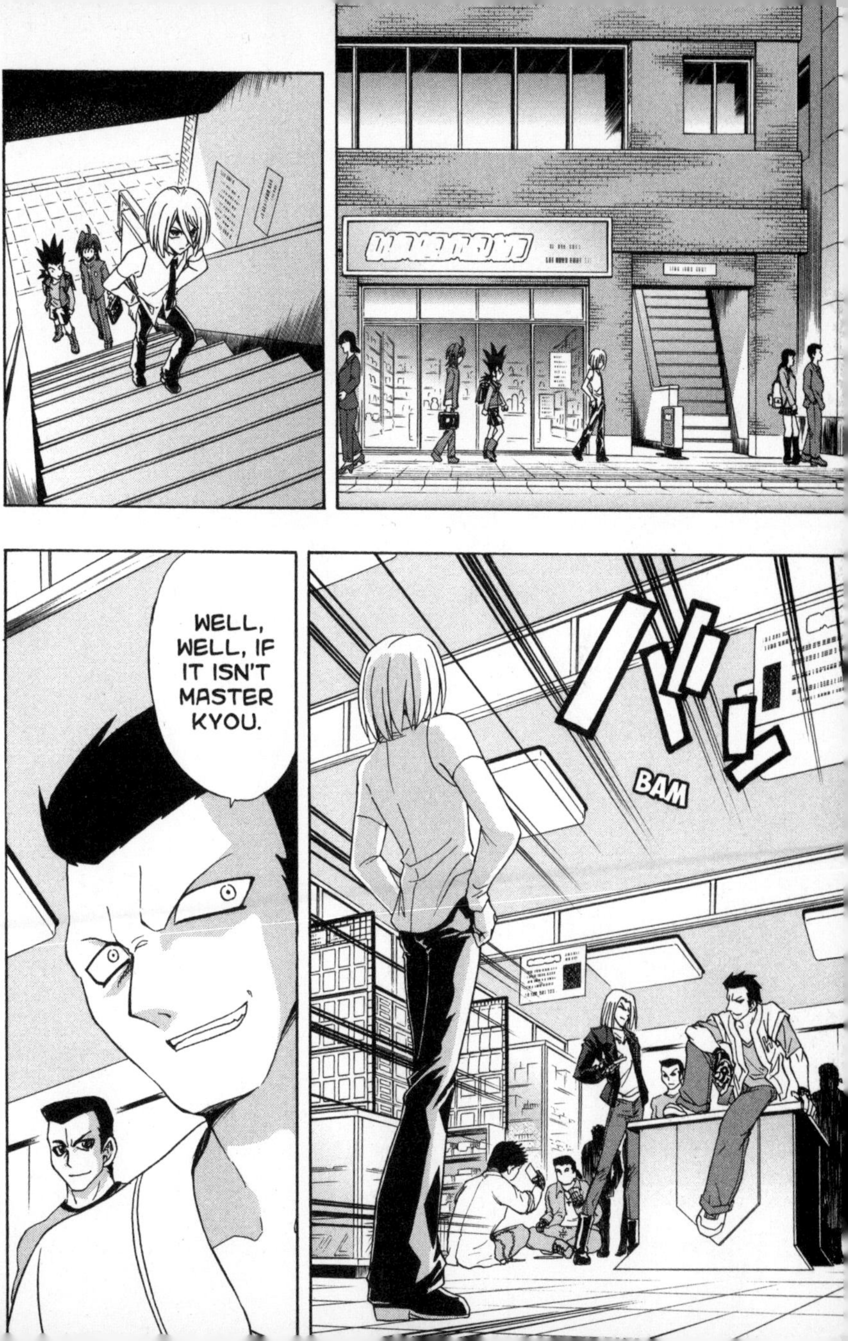
BAM
WELL, WELL, IF IT ISN'T MASTER KYOU.

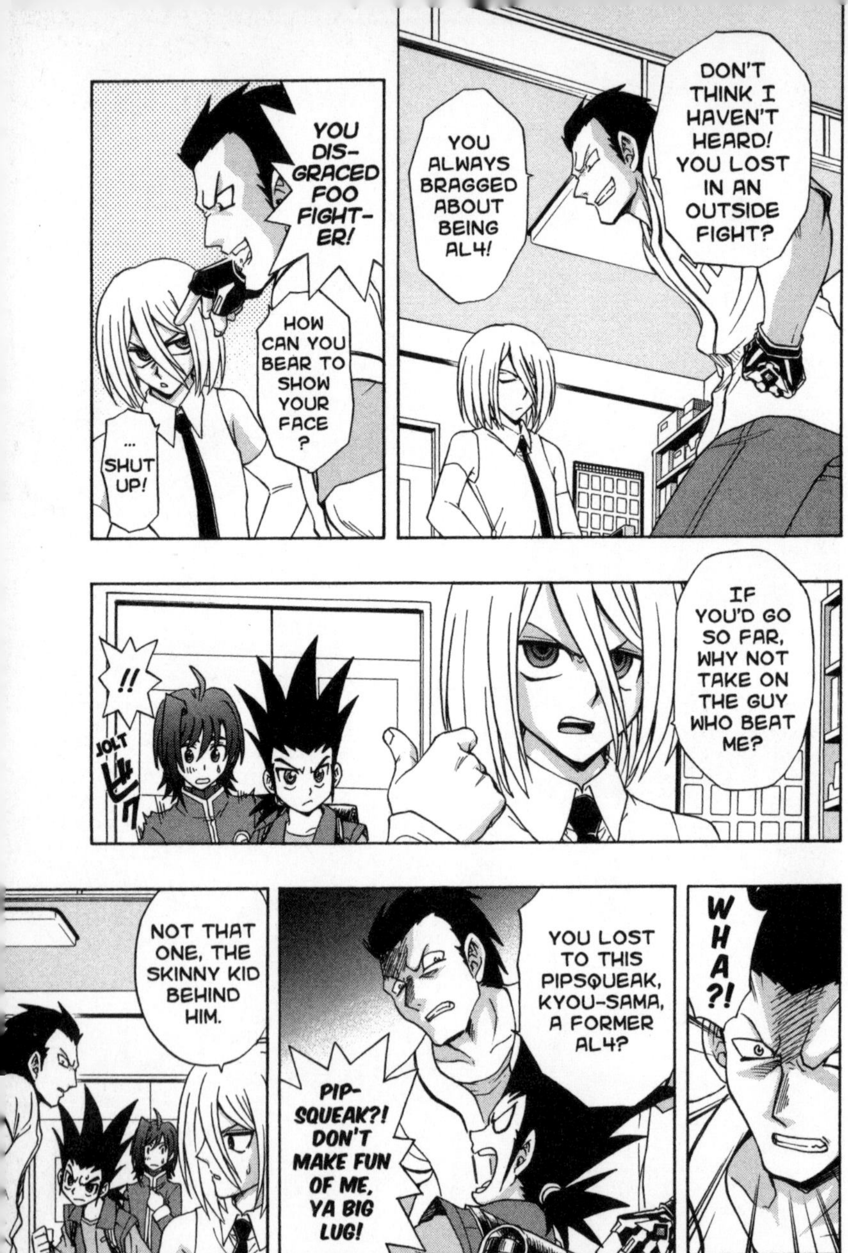
YOU DIS-GRACED FOO FIGHT-ER!
HOW CAN YOU BEAR TO SHOW YOUR FACE?
... SHUT UP!
YOU ALWAYS BRAGGED ABOUT BEING AL4!
DON'T THINK I HAVEN'T HEARD! YOU LOST IN AN OUTSIDE FIGHT?
!!
JOLT
IF YOU'D GO SO FAR, WHY NOT TAKE ON THE GUY WHO BEAT ME?
NOT THAT ONE, THE SKINNY KID BEHIND HIM.
YOU LOST TO THIS PIPSQUEAK, KYOU-SAMA, A FORMER AL4?
PIP-SQUEAK?! DON'T MAKE FUN OF ME, YA BIG LUG!
WHA?!

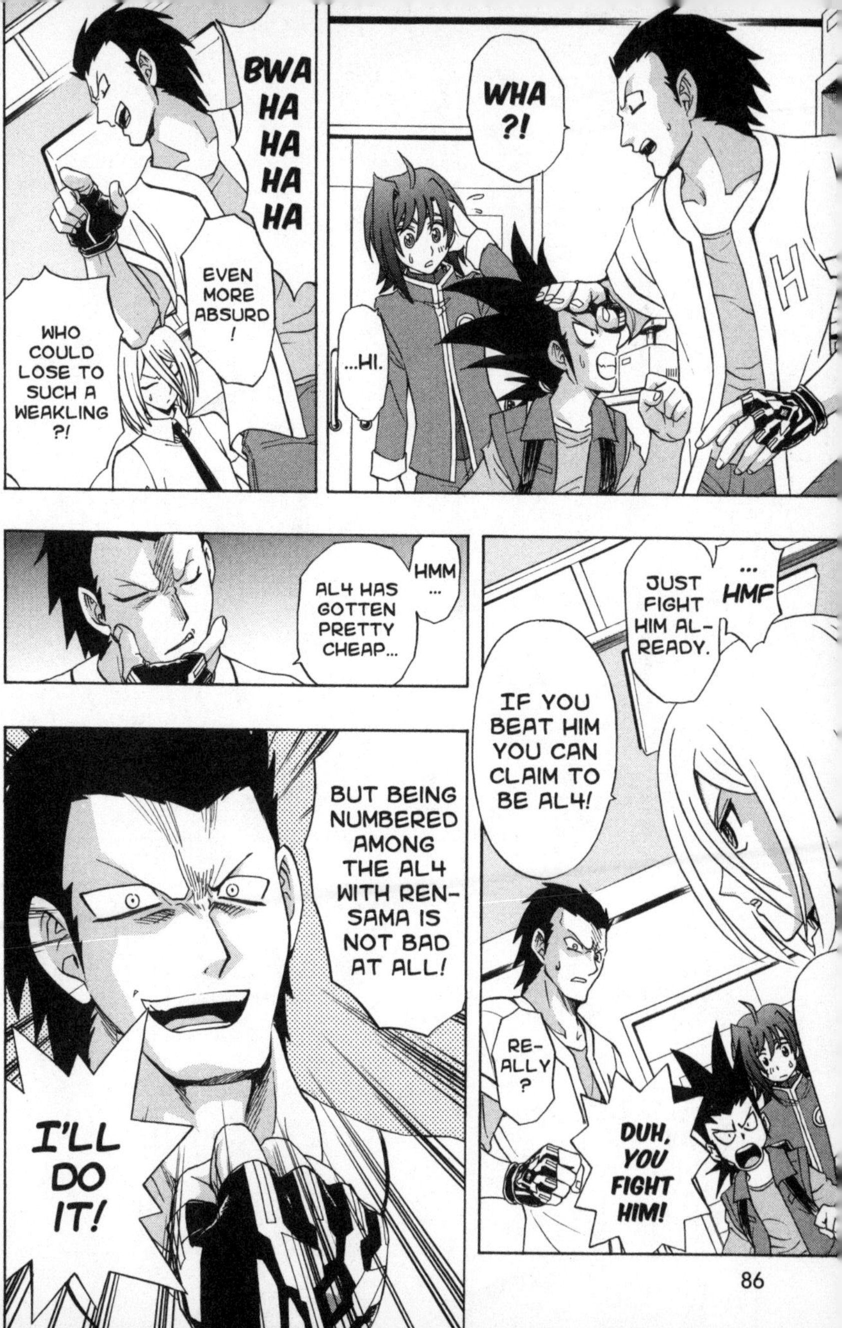
WHA ?!
...HI.
BWA HA HA HA HA
EVEN MORE ABSURD!
WHO COULD LOSE TO SUCH A WEAKLING?!
... HMF
JUST FIGHT HIM AL-READY.
IF YOU BEAT HIM YOU CAN CLAIM TO BE AL4!
RE-ALLY?
DUH, YOU FIGHT HIM!
HMM...
AL4 HAS GOTTEN PRETTY CHEAP...
BUT BEING NUMBERED AMONG THE AL4 WITH REN-SAMA IS NOT BAD AT ALL!
I'LL DO IT!

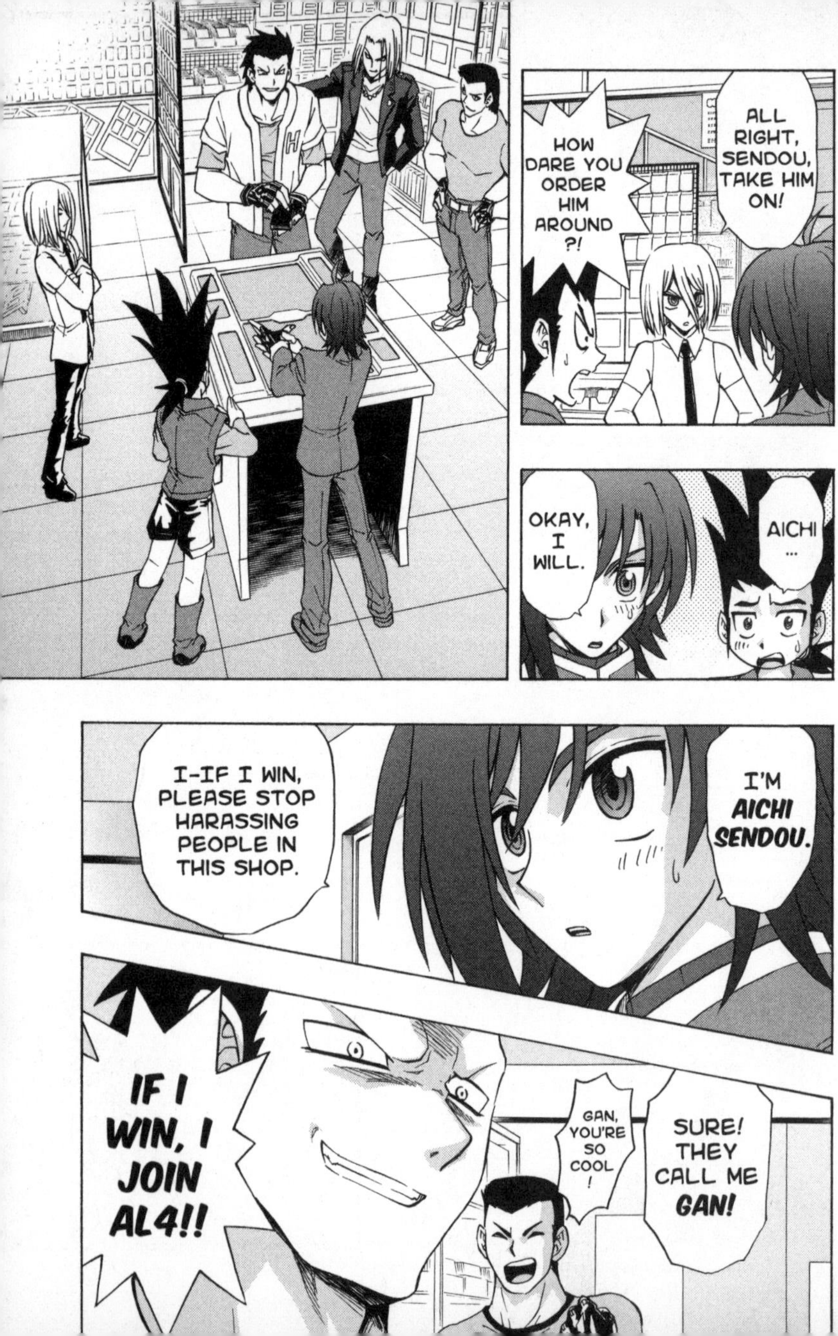
ALL RIGHT, SENDOU, TAKE HIM ON!
HOW DARE YOU ORDER HIM AROUND?!
AICHI...
OKAY, I WILL.
I'M **AICHI SENDOU.**
I-IF I WIN, PLEASE STOP HARASSING PEOPLE IN THIS SHOP.
SURE! THEY CALL ME **GAN!**
GAN, YOU'RE SO COOL!
IF I WIN, I JOIN AL4!!

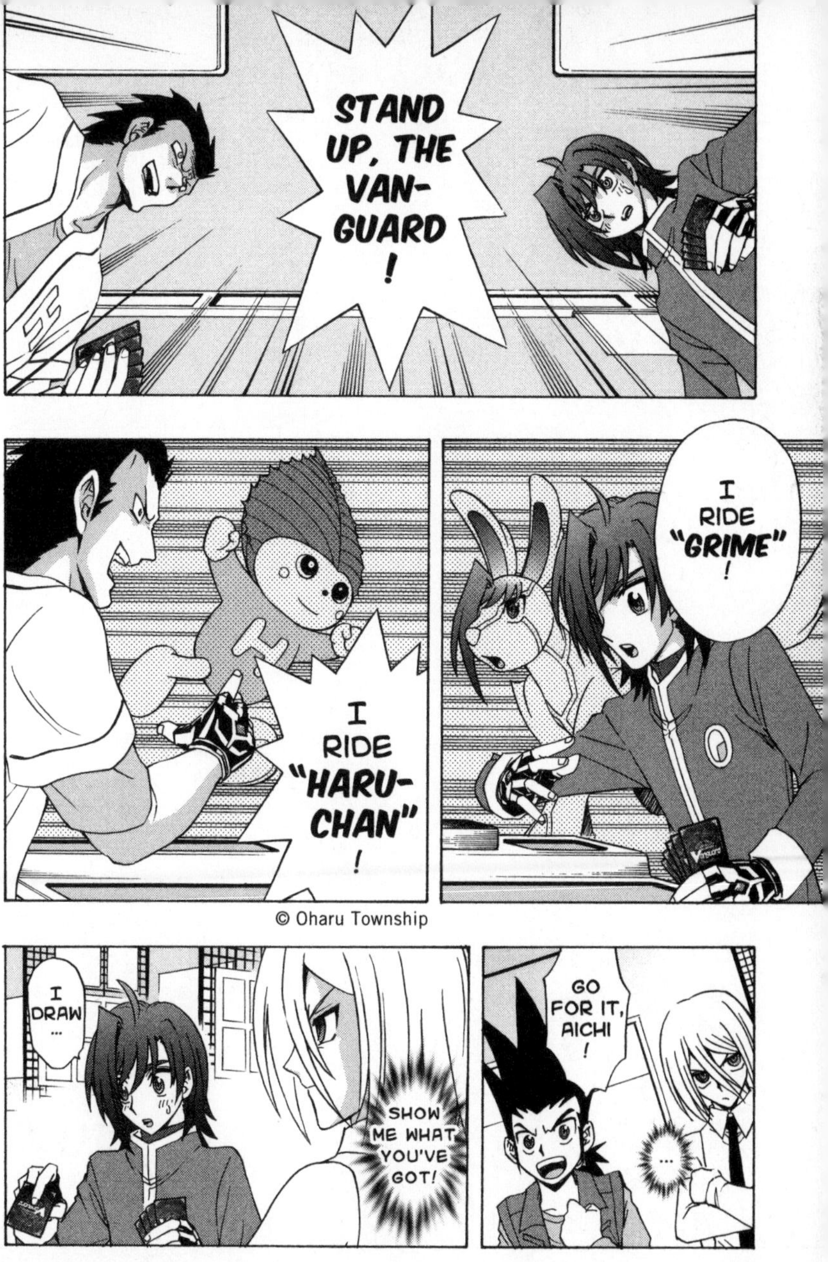
STAND UP, THE VAN-GUARD!
I RIDE "GRIME"!
I RIDE "HARU-CHAN"!
GO FOR IT, AICHI!
...
I DRAW...
SHOW ME WHAT YOU'VE GOT!

© Oharu Township

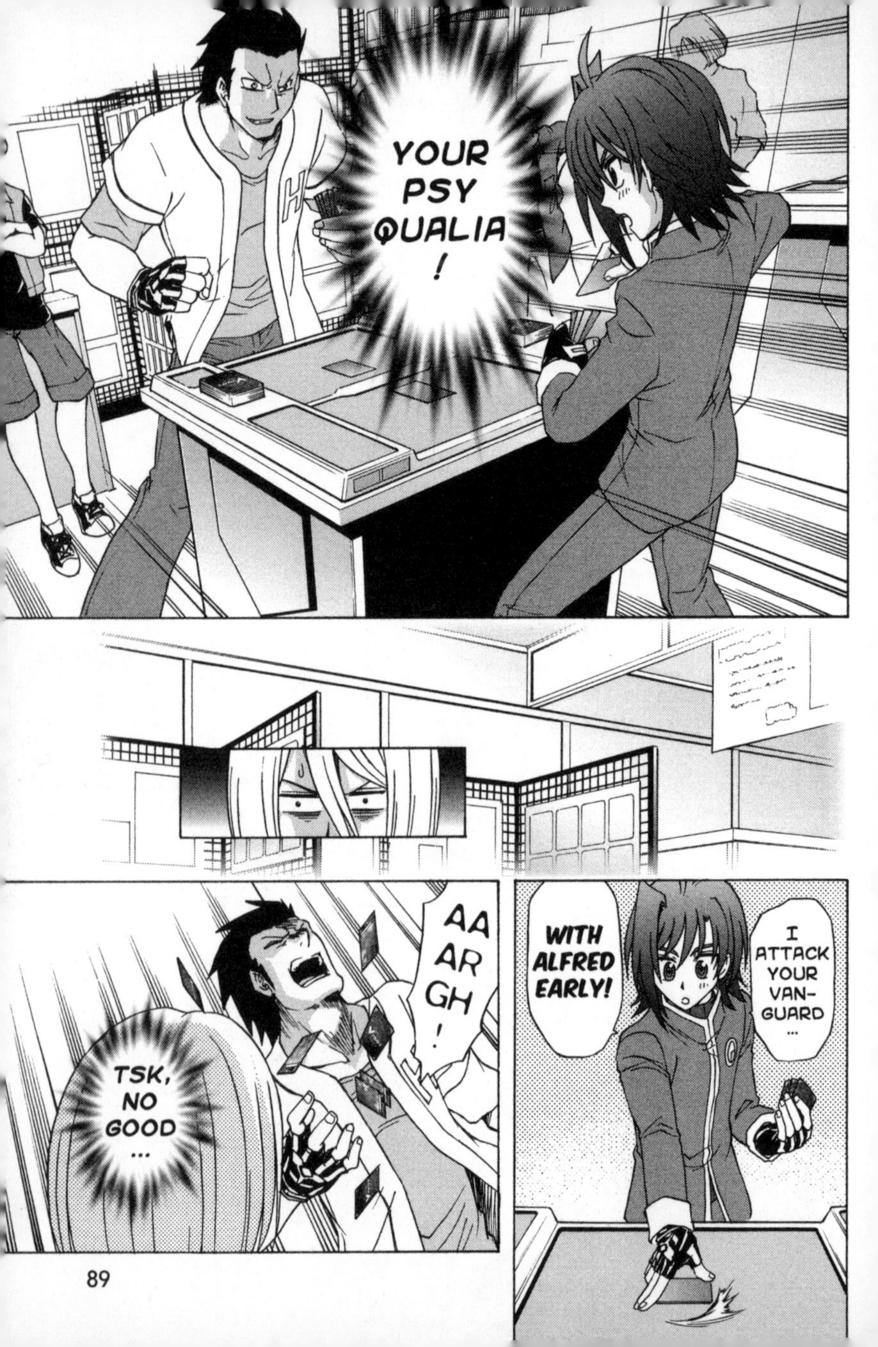
YOUR PSY QUALIA !
I ATTACK YOUR VAN-GUARD ...
WITH ALFRED EARLY!
AAARGH !
TSK, NO GOOD ...

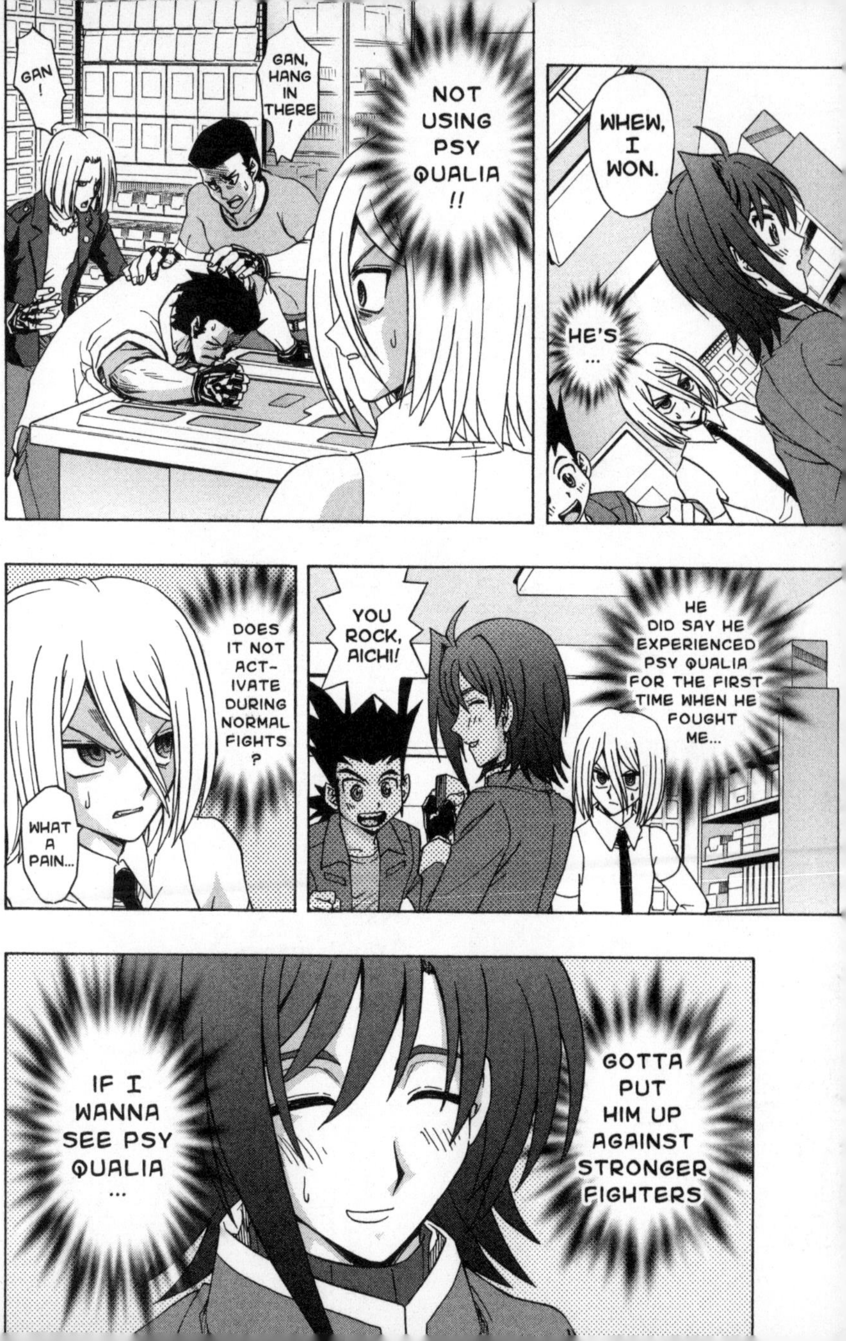

WHEW, I WON.
HE'S...
NOT USING PSY QUALIA!!
GAN, HANG IN THERE!
GAN!
HE DID SAY HE EXPERIENCED PSY QUALIA FOR THE FIRST TIME WHEN HE FOUGHT ME...
YOU ROCK, AICHI!
DOES IT NOT ACT-IVATE DURING NORMAL FIGHTS?
WHAT A PAIN...
GOTTA PUT HIM UP AGAINST STRONGER FIGHTERS
IF I WANNA SEE PSY QUALIA...

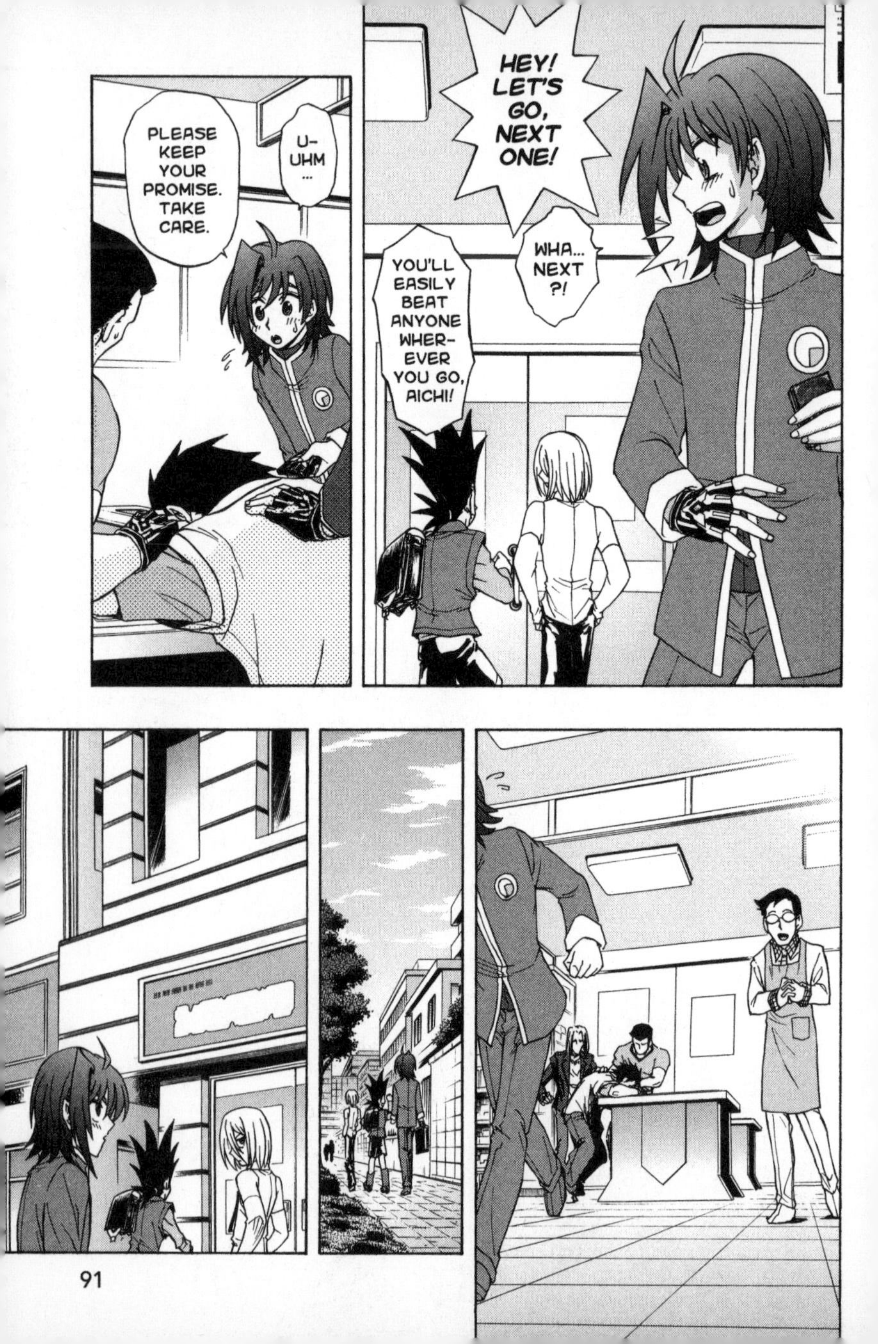
HEY! LET'S GO, NEXT ONE!
WHA... NEXT?!
YOU'LL EASILY BEAT ANYONE WHEREVER YOU GO, AICHI!
PLEASE KEEP YOUR PROMISE. TAKE CARE.
U-UHM...

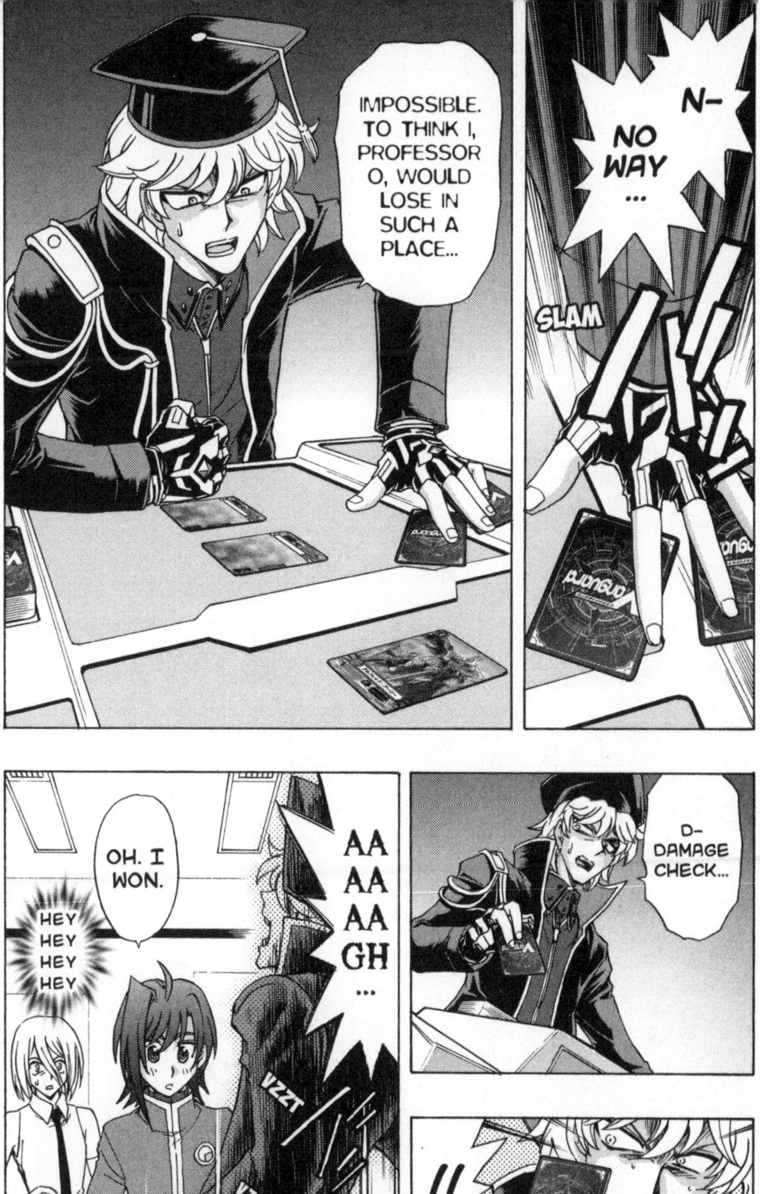
N-
NO WAY ...
SLAM
IMPOSSIBLE. TO THINK I, PROFESSOR O, WOULD LOSE IN SUCH A PLACE...
D-DAMAGE CHECK...
!!
AAAAAAGH ...
VZZT
VZZT
OH. I WON.
HEY HEY HEY HEY

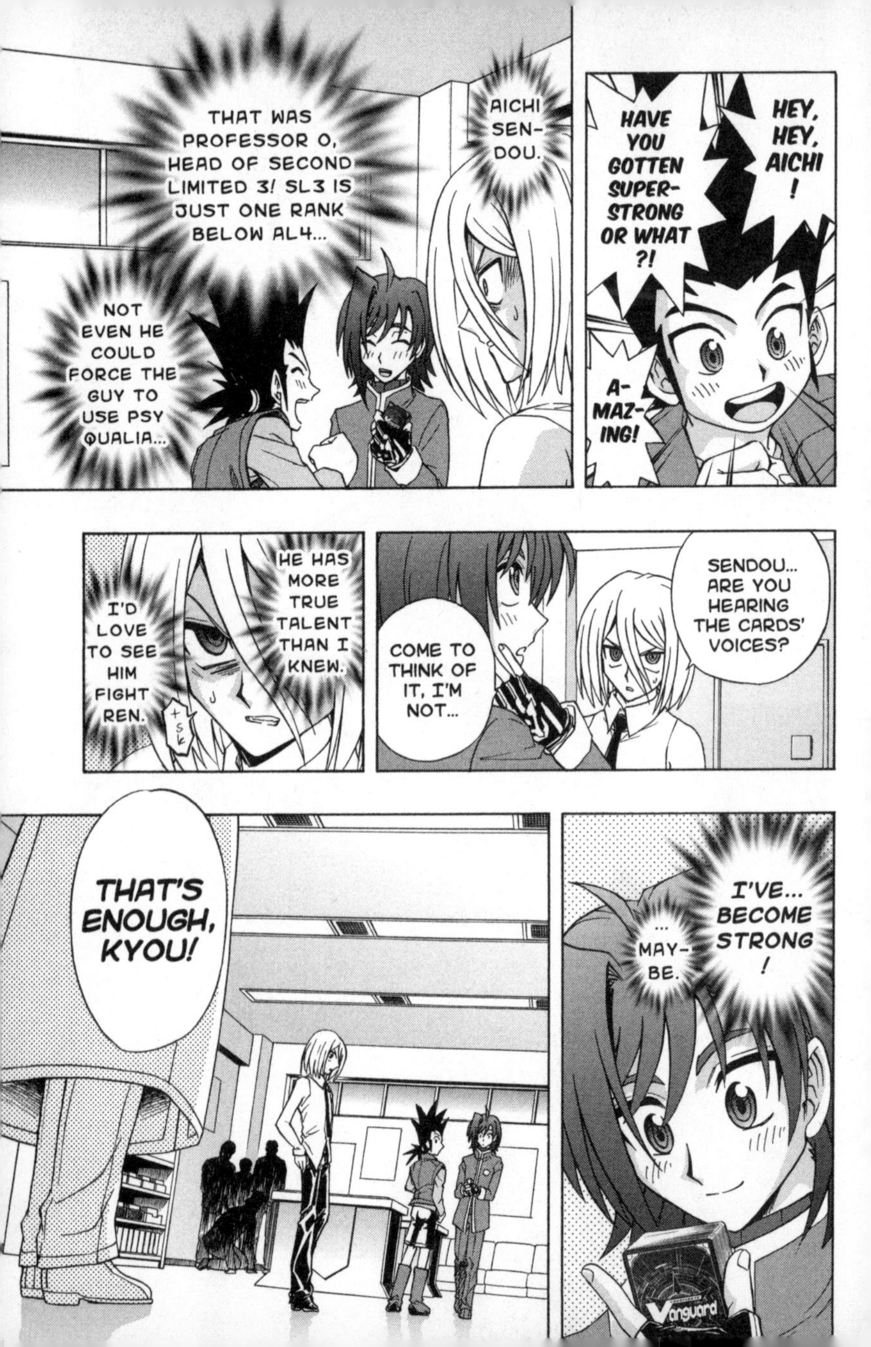
HEY, HEY, AICHI!
HAVE YOU GOTTEN SUPER-STRONG OR WHAT?!
A-MAZ-ING!
AICHI SENDOU.
THAT WAS PROFESSOR O, HEAD OF SECOND LIMITED 3! SL3 IS JUST ONE RANK BELOW AL4...
NOT EVEN HE COULD FORCE THE GUY TO USE PSY QUALIA...
SENDOU... ARE YOU HEARING THE CARDS' VOICES?
COME TO THINK OF IT, I'M NOT...
HE HAS MORE TRUE TALENT THAN I KNEW.
I'D LOVE TO SEE HIM FIGHT REN.
TSK
I'VE... BECOME STRONG!
...MAYBE.
Vanguard
THAT'S ENOUGH, KYOU!

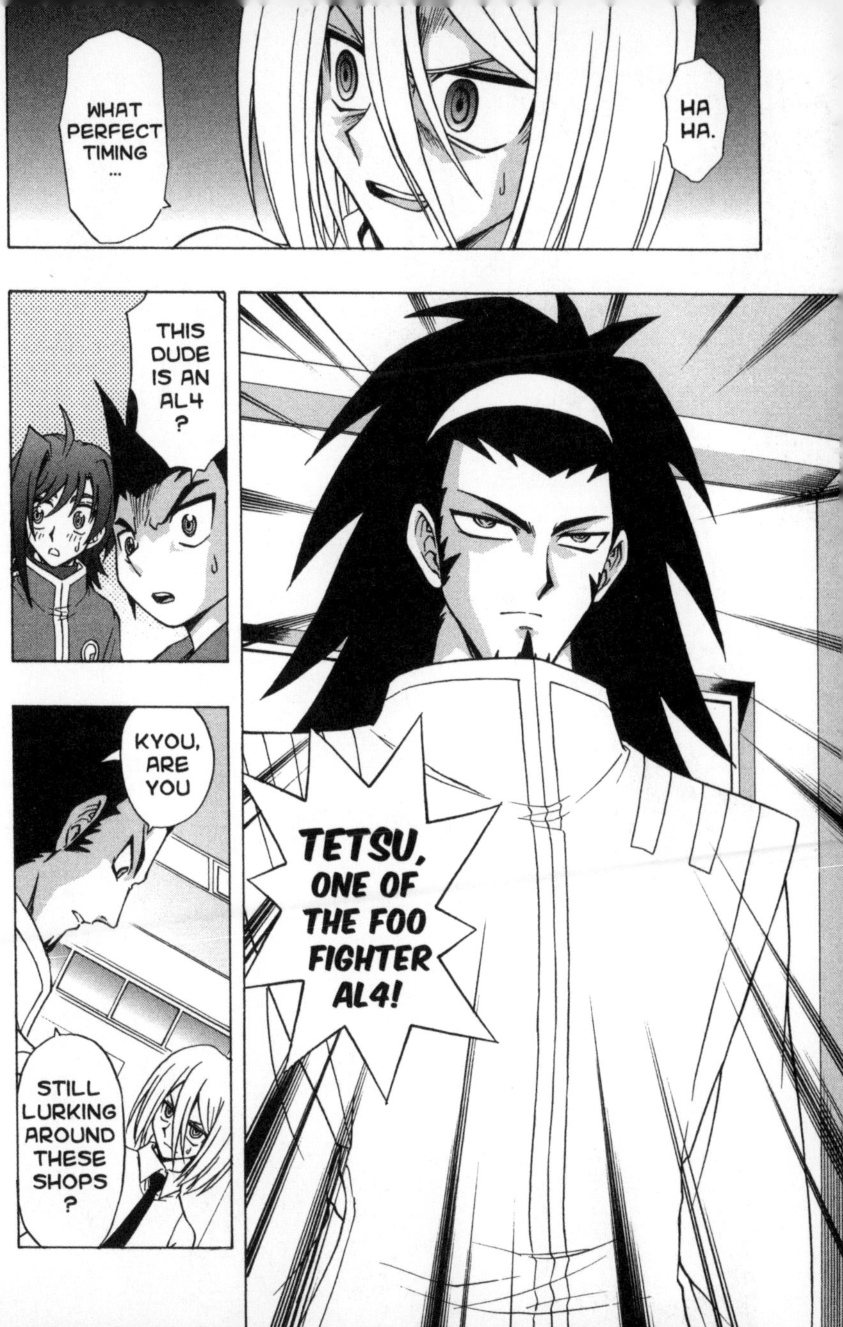
HA HA.
WHAT PERFECT TIMING ...
TETSU, ONE OF THE FOO FIGHTER AL4!
THIS DUDE IS AN AL4 ?
KYOU, ARE YOU
STILL LURKING AROUND THESE SHOPS ?

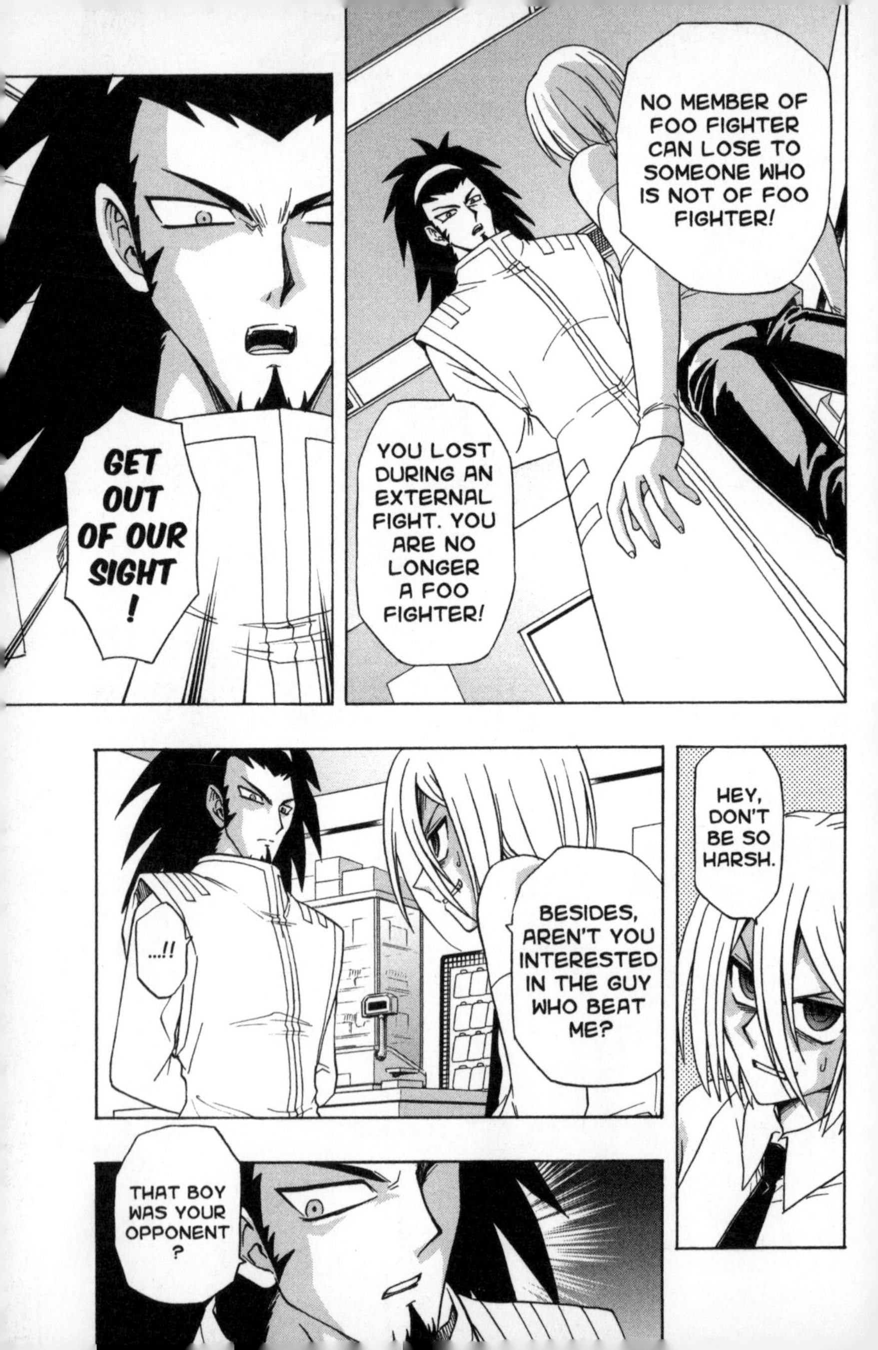
NO MEMBER OF FOO FIGHTER CAN LOSE TO SOMEONE WHO IS NOT OF FOO FIGHTER!
YOU LOST DURING AN EXTERNAL FIGHT. YOU ARE NO LONGER A FOO FIGHTER!
GET OUT OF OUR SIGHT!
HEY, DON'T BE SO HARSH.
BESIDES, AREN'T YOU INTERESTED IN THE GUY WHO BEAT ME?
...!!
THAT BOY WAS YOUR OPPONENT?

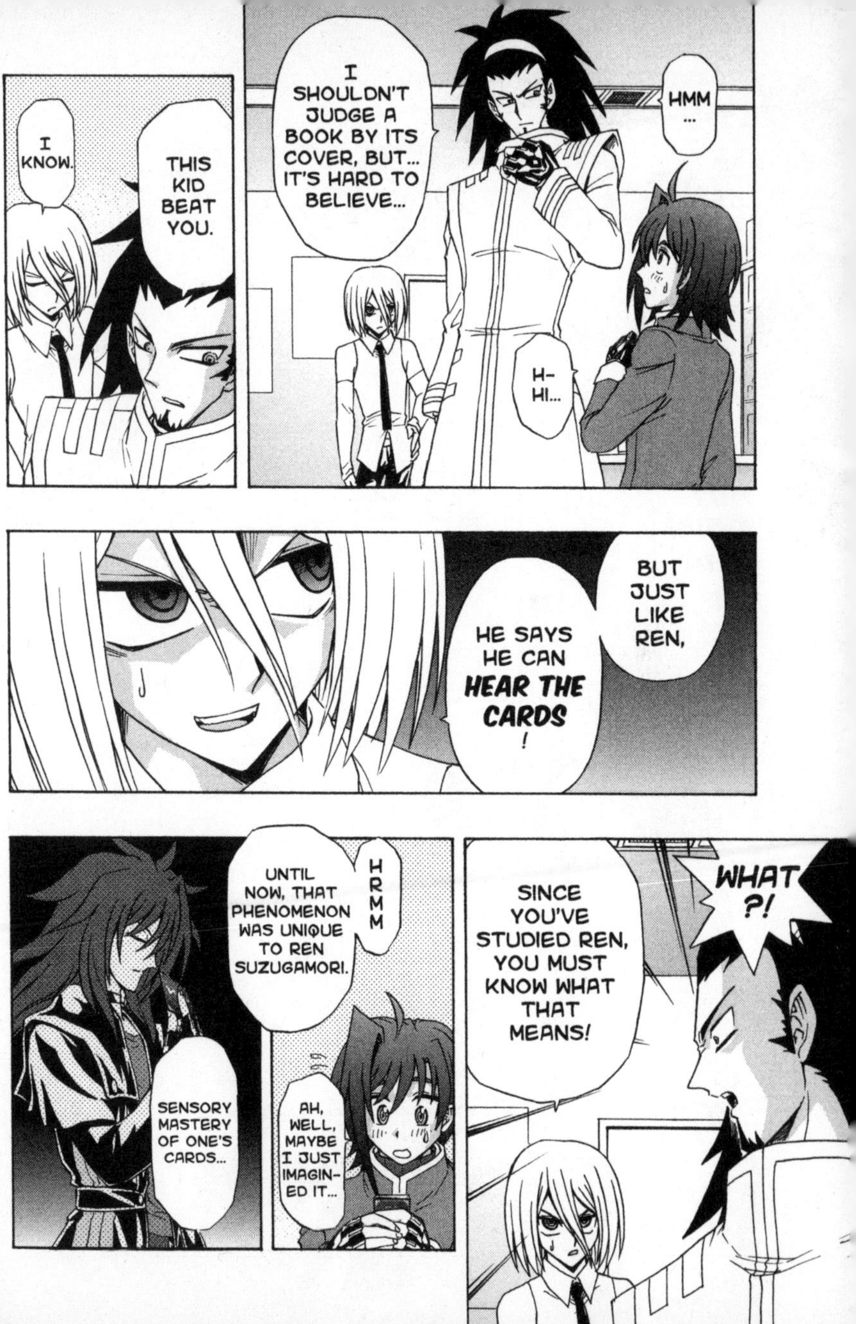
HMM...
I SHOULDN'T JUDGE A BOOK BY ITS COVER, BUT... IT'S HARD TO BELIEVE...
H-HI...
THIS KID BEAT YOU.
I KNOW.
BUT JUST LIKE REN,
HE SAYS HE CAN **HEAR THE CARDS**!
WHAT?!
SINCE YOU'VE STUDIED REN, YOU MUST KNOW WHAT THAT MEANS!
HRMM
UNTIL NOW, THAT PHENOMENON WAS UNIQUE TO REN SUZUGAMORI.
AH, WELL, MAYBE I JUST IMAGINED IT...
SENSORY MASTERY OF ONE'S CARDS...

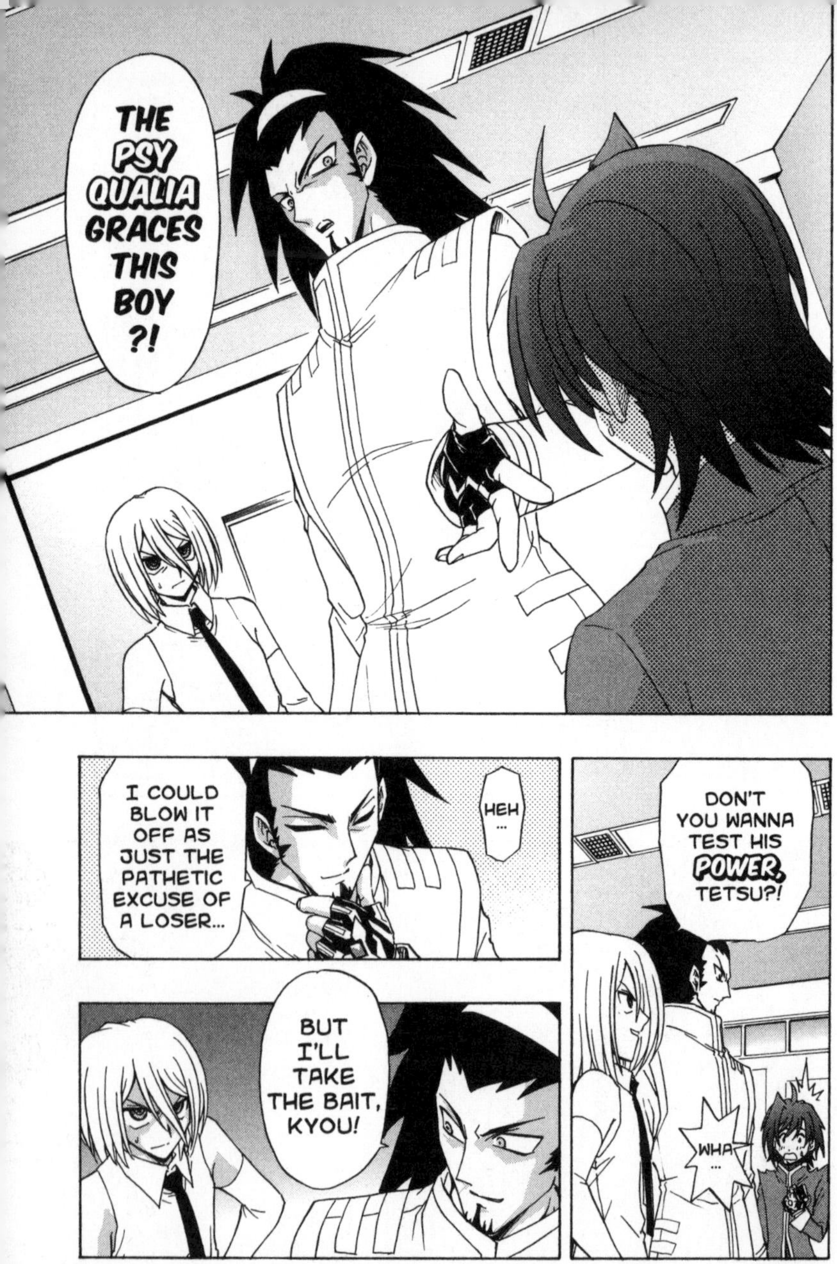
THE PSY QUALIA GRACES THIS BOY?!
DON'T YOU WANNA TEST HIS POWER, TETSU?!
WHA...
HEH...
I COULD BLOW IT OFF AS JUST THE PATHETIC EXCUSE OF A LOSER...
BUT I'LL TAKE THE BAIT, KYOU!

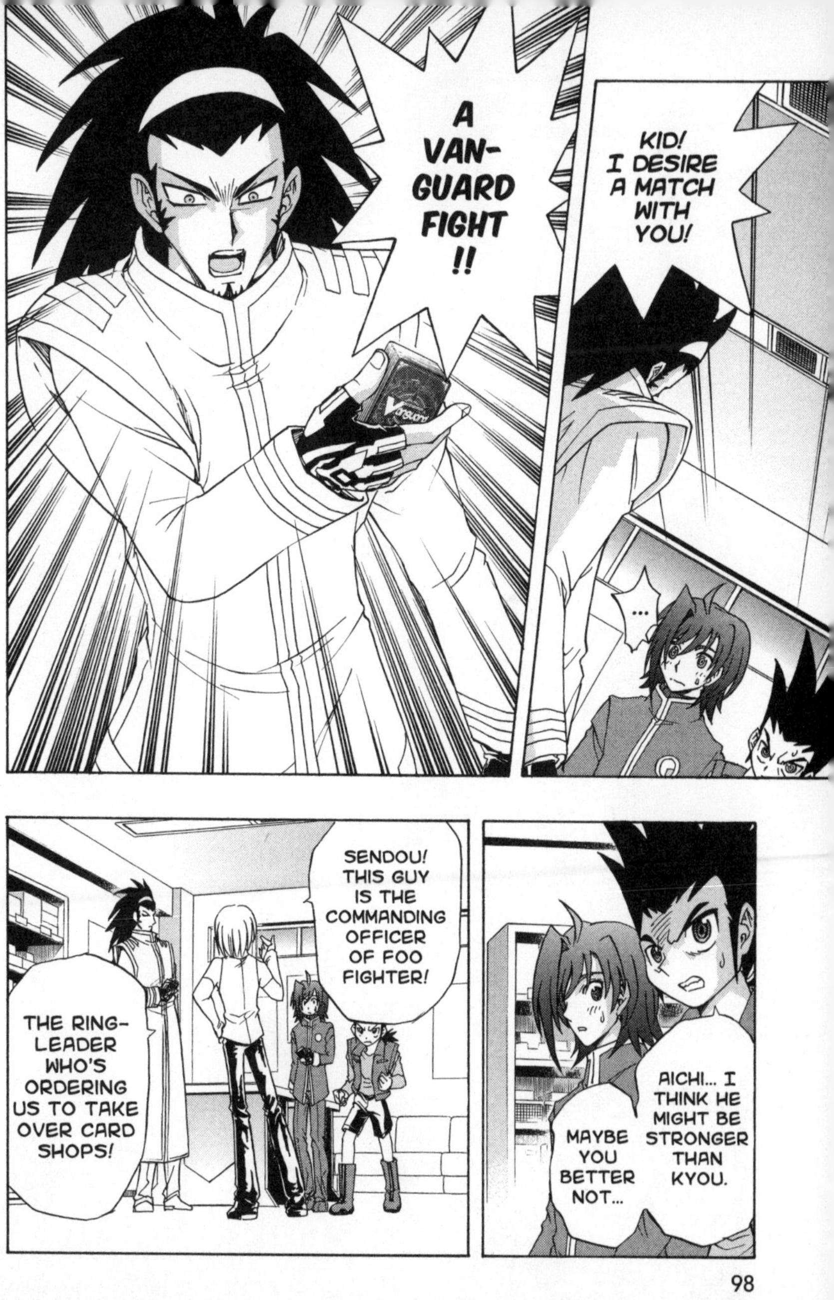
KID! I DESIRE A MATCH WITH YOU!
...
A VAN-GUARD FIGHT !!
AICHI... I THINK HE MIGHT BE STRONGER THAN KYOU.
MAYBE YOU BETTER NOT...
SENDOU! THIS GUY IS THE COMMANDING OFFICER OF FOO FIGHTER!
THE RING-LEADER WHO'S ORDERING US TO TAKE OVER CARD SHOPS!

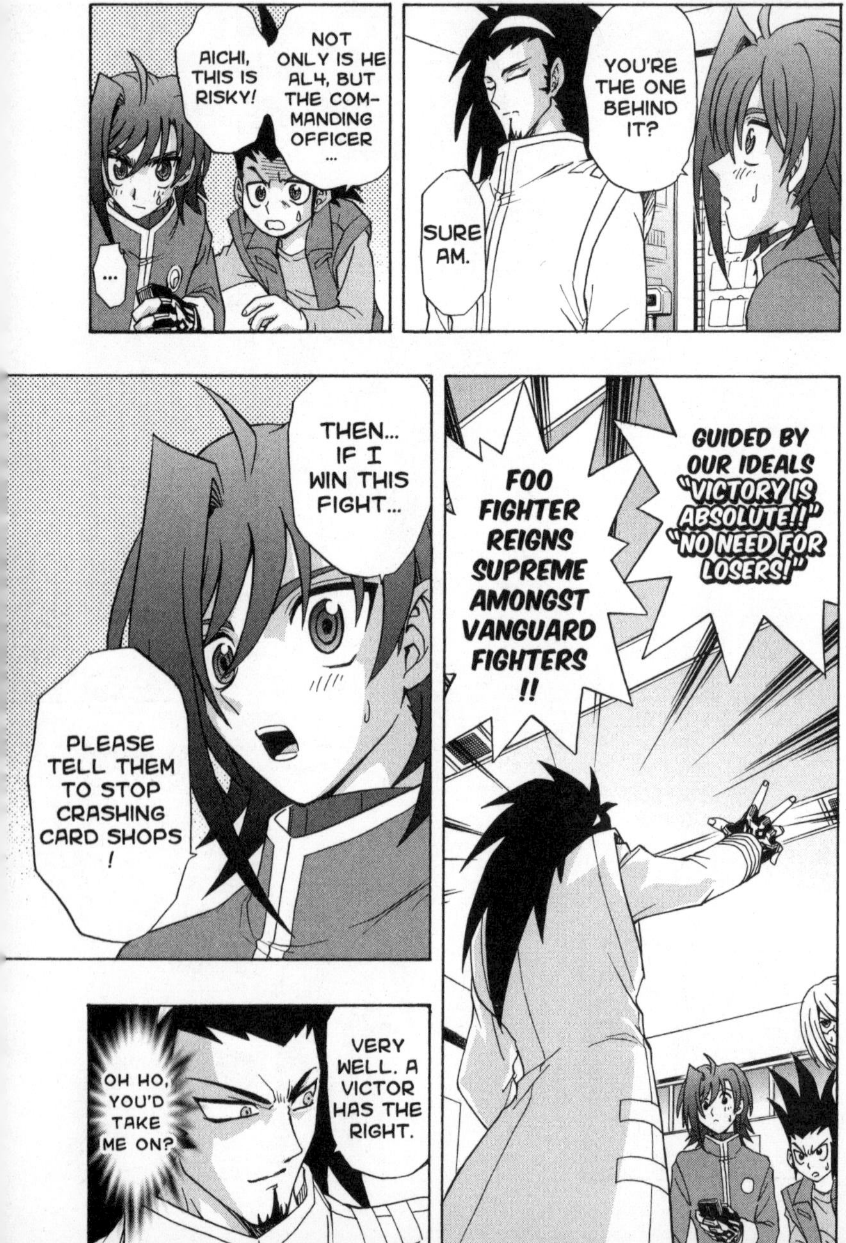
YOU'RE THE ONE BEHIND IT?
SURE AM.
NOT ONLY IS HE AL4, BUT THE COM-MANDING OFFICER ...
AICHI, THIS IS RISKY!
...
GUIDED BY OUR IDEALS "VICTORY IS ABSOLUTE!!" "NO NEED FOR LOSERS!"
FOO FIGHTER REIGNS SUPREME AMONGST VANGUARD FIGHTERS !!
THEN... IF I WIN THIS FIGHT...
PLEASE TELL THEM TO STOP CRASHING CARD SHOPS !
VERY WELL. A VICTOR HAS THE RIGHT.
OH HO, YOU'D TAKE ME ON?

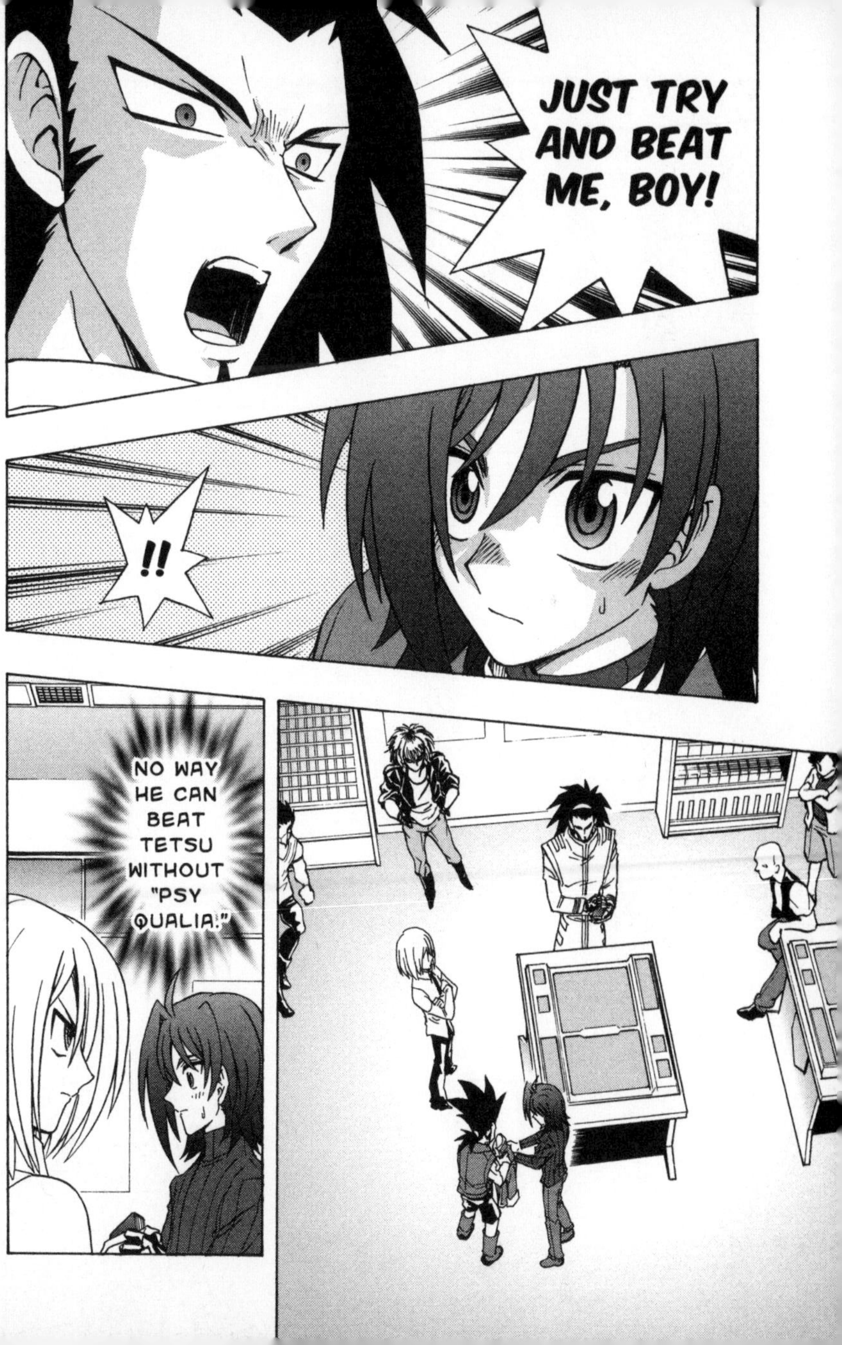
JUST TRY AND BEAT ME, BOY!
!!
NO WAY HE CAN BEAT TETSU WITHOUT "PSY QUALIA."

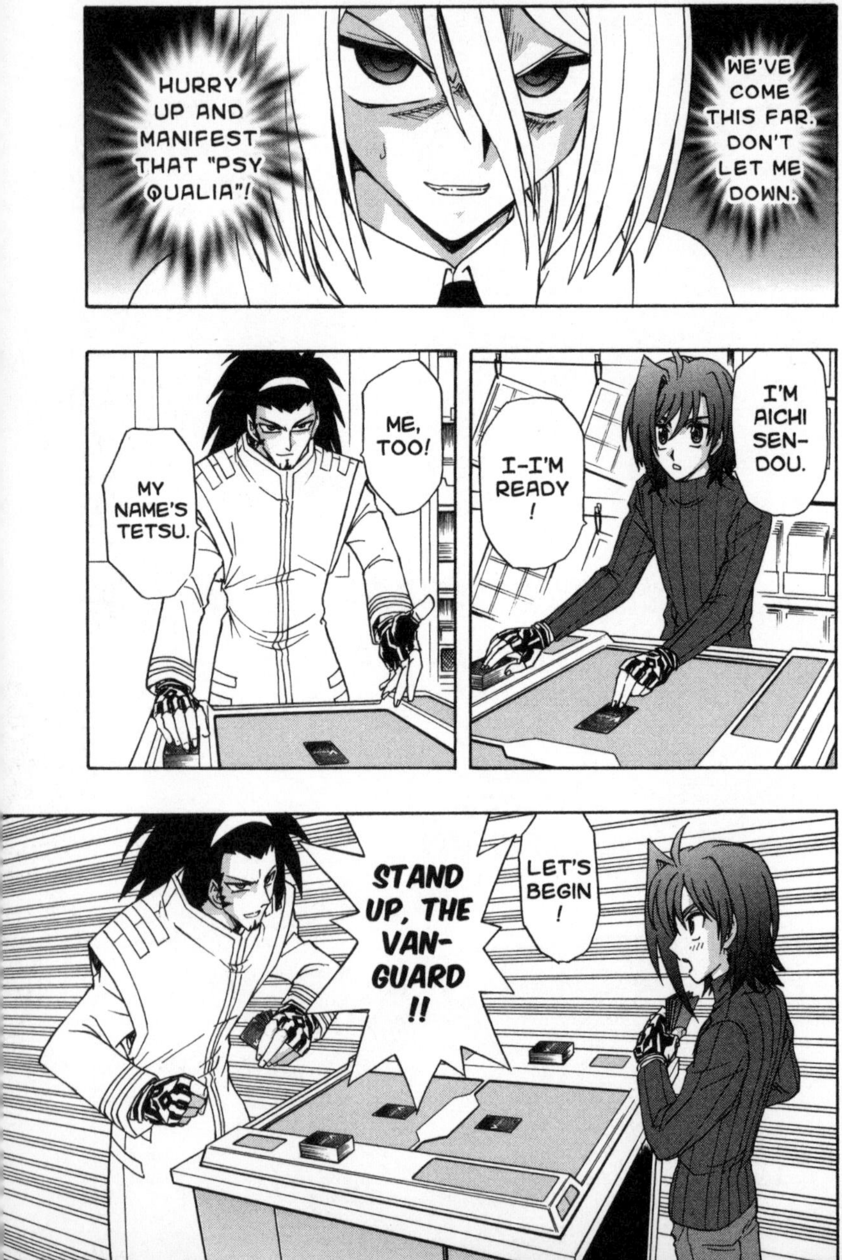
WE'VE COME THIS FAR. DON'T LET ME DOWN.
HURRY UP AND MANIFEST THAT "PSY QUALIA"!
I'M AICHI SEN-DOU.
I-I'M READY!
ME, TOO!
MY NAME'S TETSU.
LET'S BEGIN!
STAND UP, THE VAN-GUARD!!

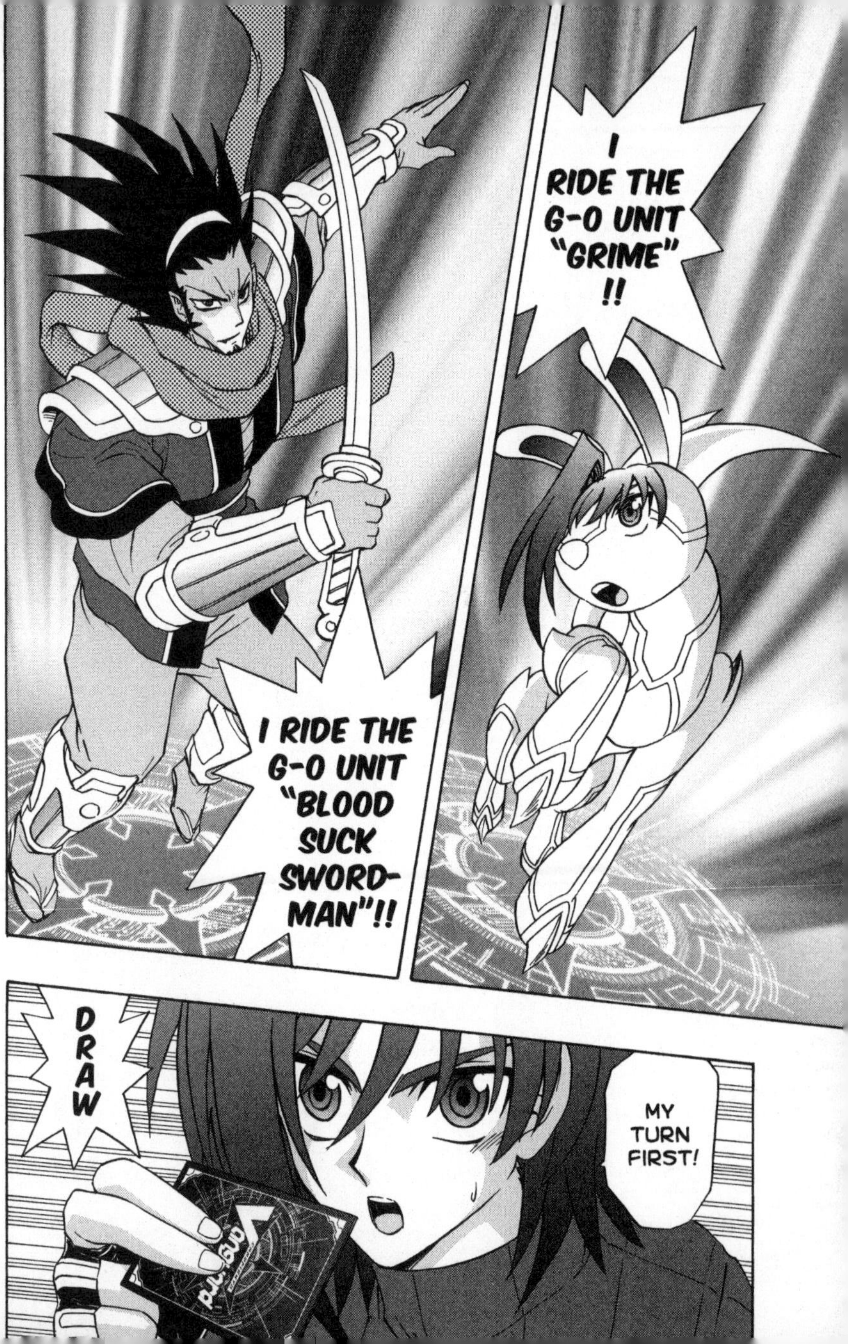
I RIDE THE G-O UNIT "GRIME" !!
I RIDE THE G-O UNIT "BLOOD SUCK SWORD-MAN"!!
MY TURN FIRST!
DRAW

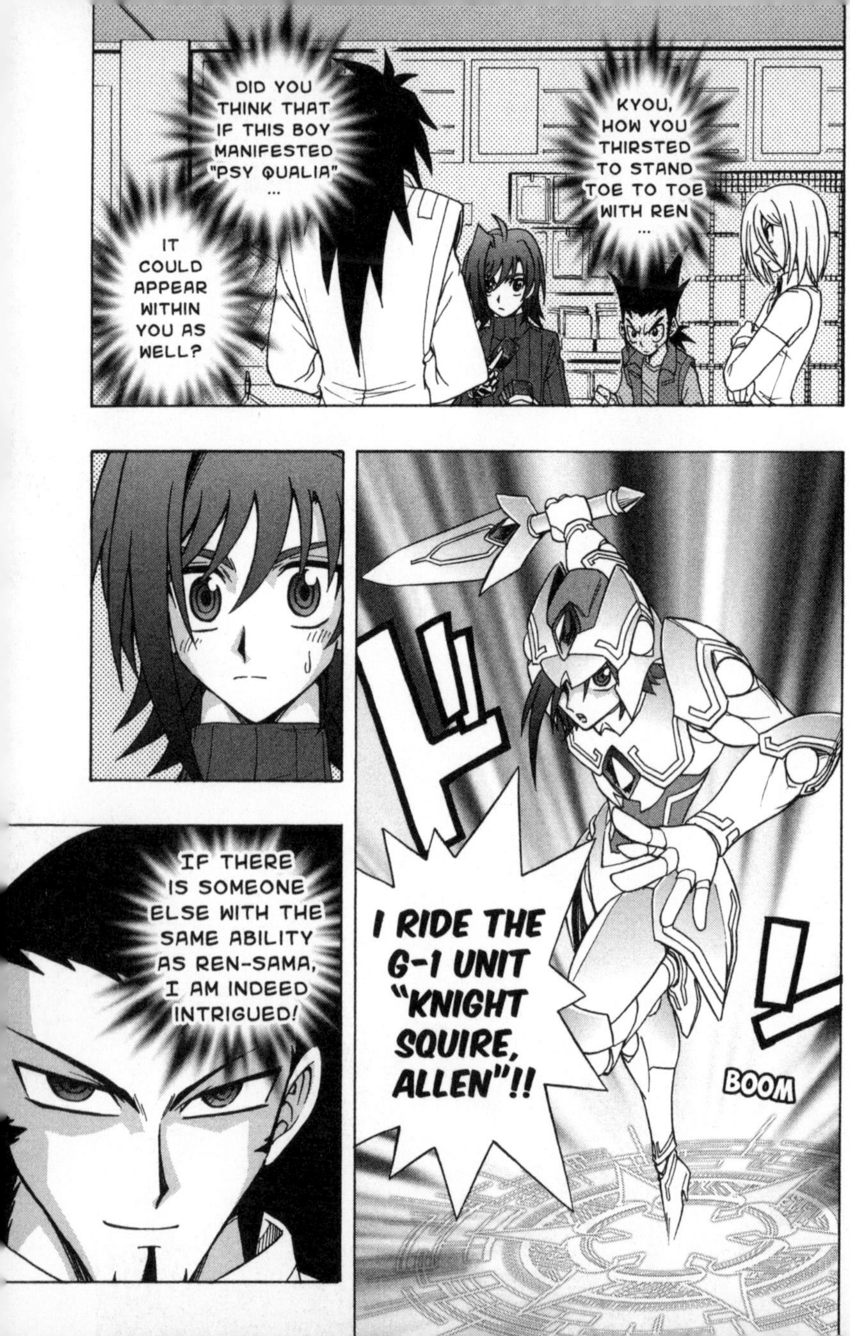
KYOU, HOW YOU THIRSTED TO STAND TOE TO TOE WITH REN ...
DID YOU THINK THAT IF THIS BOY MANIFESTED "PSY QUALIA" ...
IT COULD APPEAR WITHIN YOU AS WELL?
I RIDE THE G-1 UNIT "KNIGHT SQUIRE, ALLEN"!!
BOOM
IF THERE IS SOMEONE ELSE WITH THE SAME ABILITY AS REN-SAMA, I AM INDEED INTRIGUED!

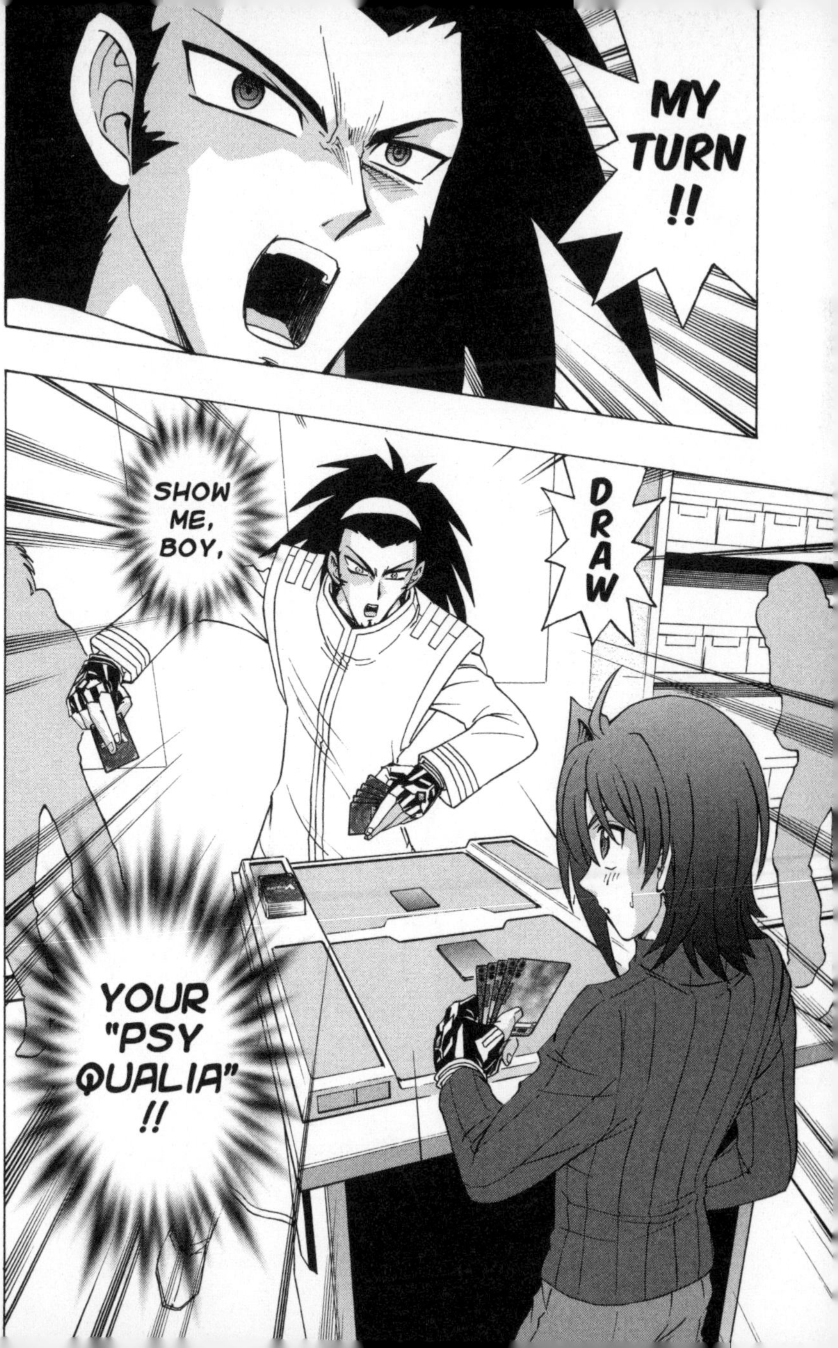

MY TURN !!
DRAW
SHOW ME, BOY,
YOUR "PSY QUALIA" !!

BONUS! CARDFIGHT!! Vanguard

NEVER-BEFORE-SEEN IMAGE BOARDS

CHARACTERS

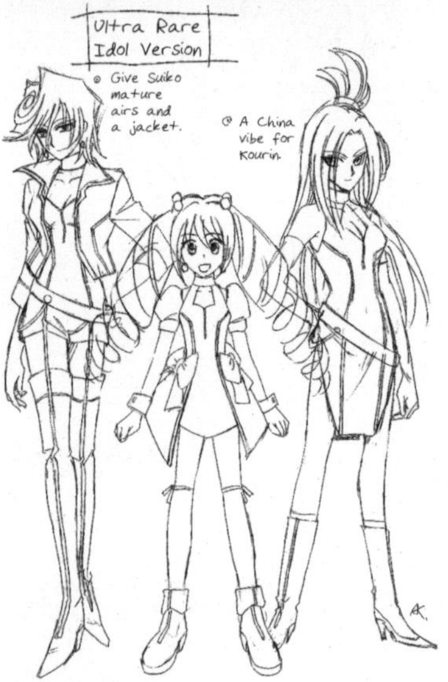
Ultra Rare
Idol Version
Give Suiko mature airs and a jacket.
A China vibe for Kourin.
AK.

Initial Sketches

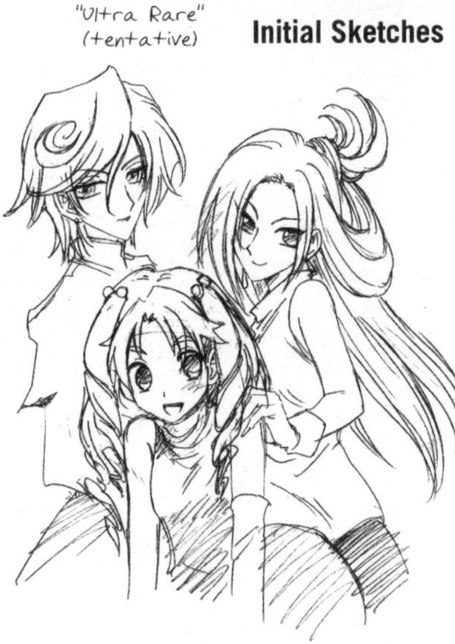
"Ultra Rare"
(tentative)

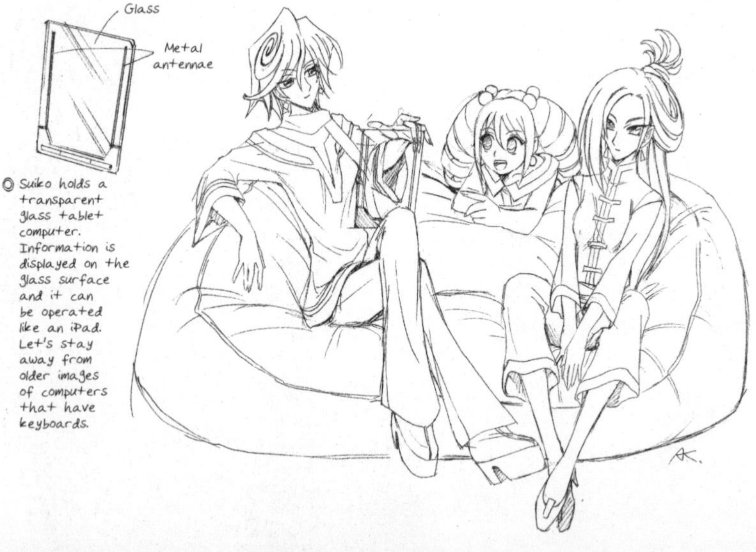
Glass
Metal antennae
Suiko holds a transparent glass tablet computer. Information is displayed on the glass surface and it can be operated like an iPad. Let's stay away from older images of computers that have keyboards.
AK.

BONUS! CARDFIGHT!! Vanguard NEVER-BEFORE-SEEN IMAGE BOARDS

CHAR-ACTERS

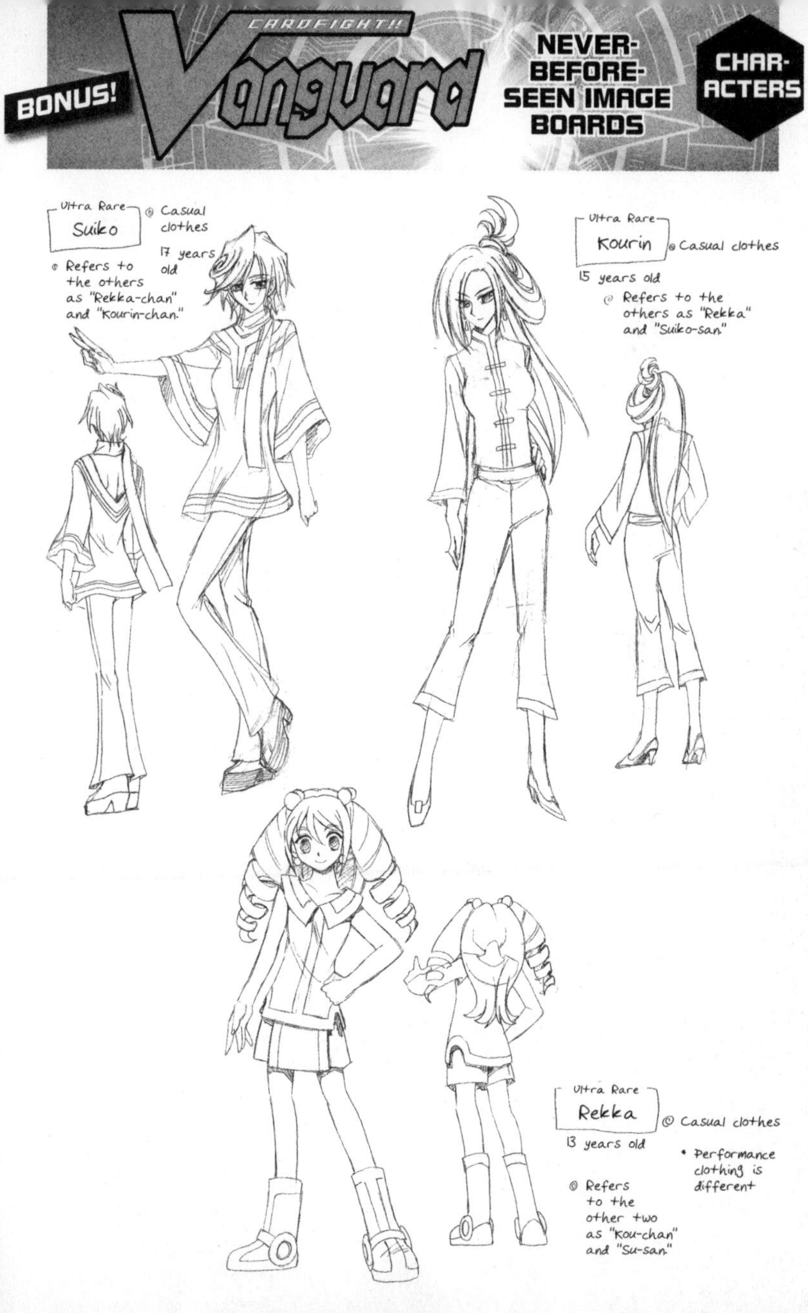
Ultra Rare
Suiko
◎ Casual clothes
17 years old
◎ Refers to the others as "Rekka-chan" and "Kourin-chan."
Ultra Rare
Kourin
◎ Casual clothes
15 years old
◎ Refers to the others as "Rekka" and "Suiko-san."
Ultra Rare
Rekka
◎ Casual clothes
13 years old
• Performance clothing is different
◎ Refers to the other two as "Kou-chan" and "Su-san."

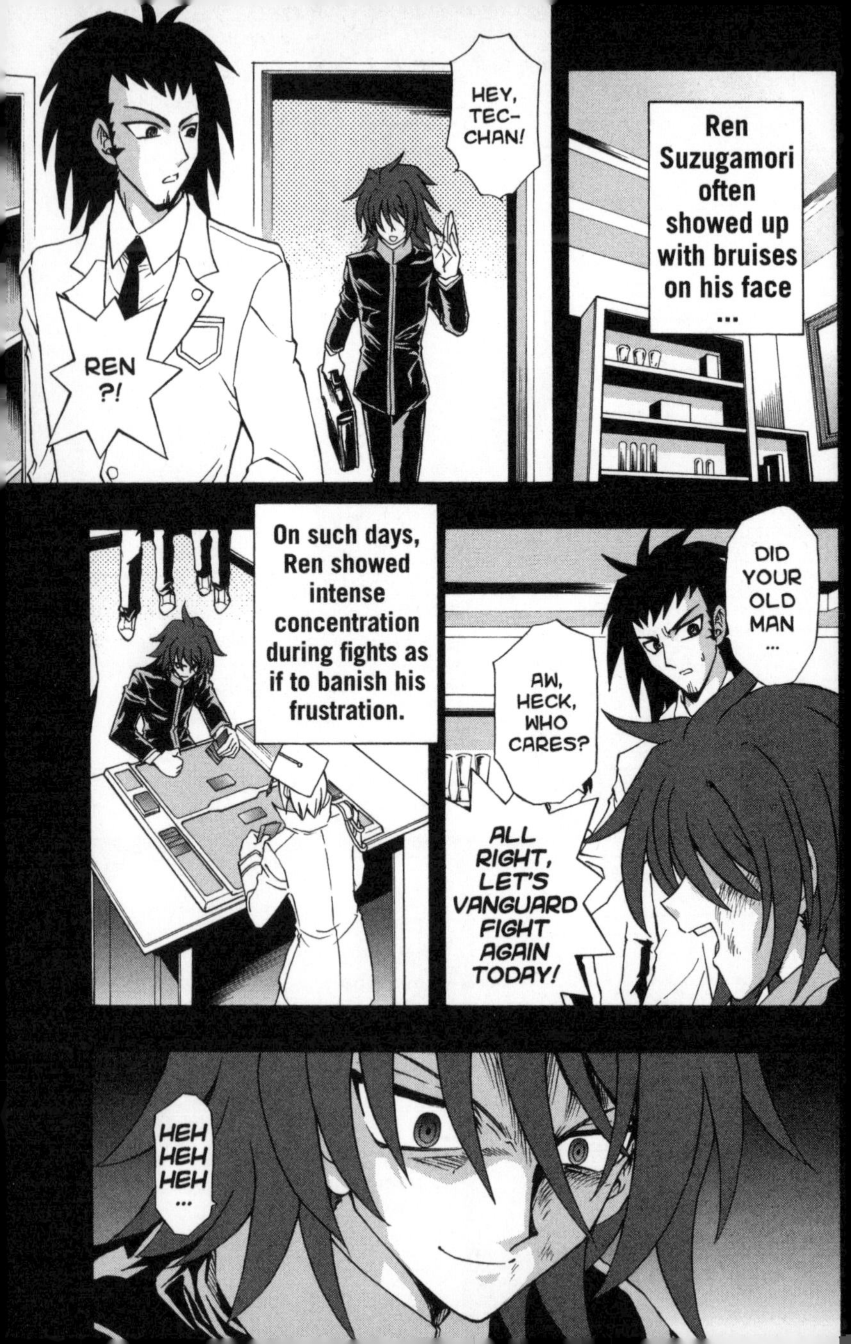
Ren Suzugamori often showed up with bruises on his face ...
HEY, TEC-CHAN!
REN ?!
DID YOUR OLD MAN ...
AW, HECK, WHO CARES?
ALL RIGHT, LET'S VANGUARD FIGHT AGAIN TODAY!
On such days, Ren showed intense concentration during fights as if to banish his frustration.
HEH HEH HEH ...

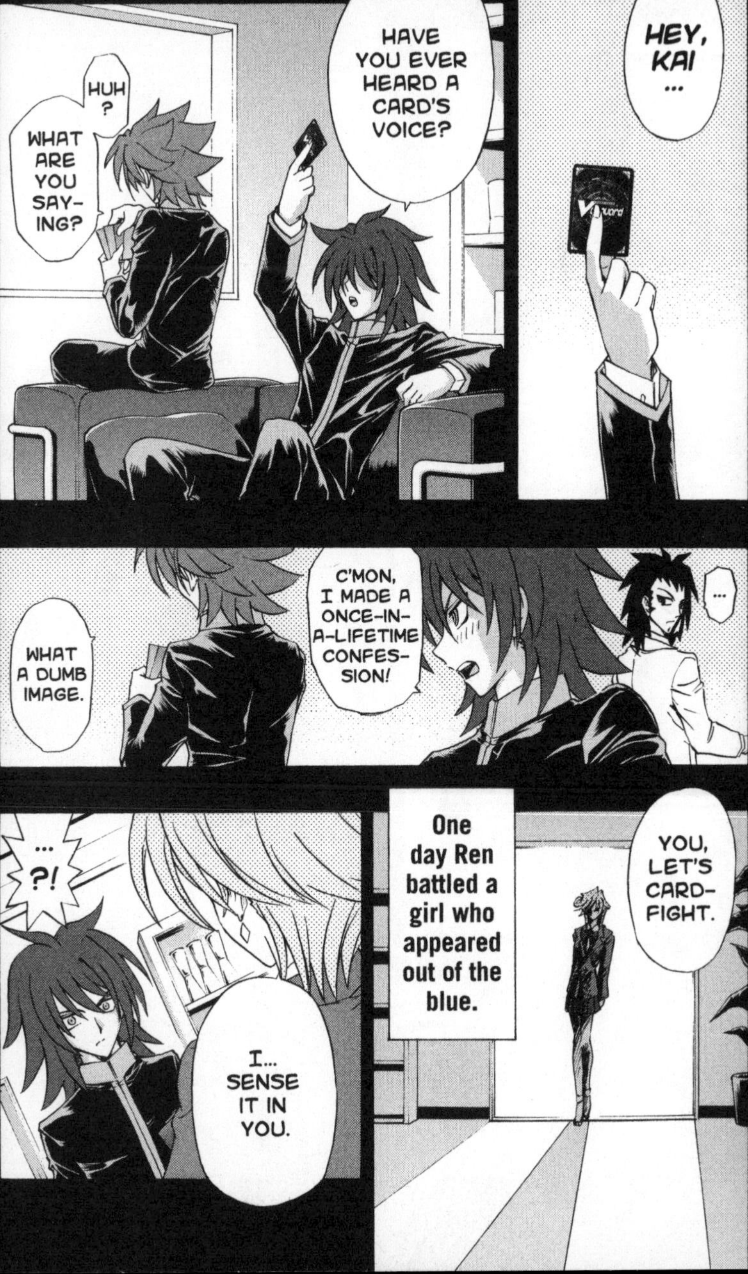
HEY, KAI ...
HAVE YOU EVER HEARD A CARD'S VOICE?
HUH ?
WHAT ARE YOU SAY-ING?
...
C'MON, I MADE A ONCE-IN-A-LIFETIME CONFES-SION!
WHAT A DUMB IMAGE.
YOU, LET'S CARD-FIGHT.
One day Ren battled a girl who appeared out of the blue.
... ?!
I... SENSE IT IN YOU.

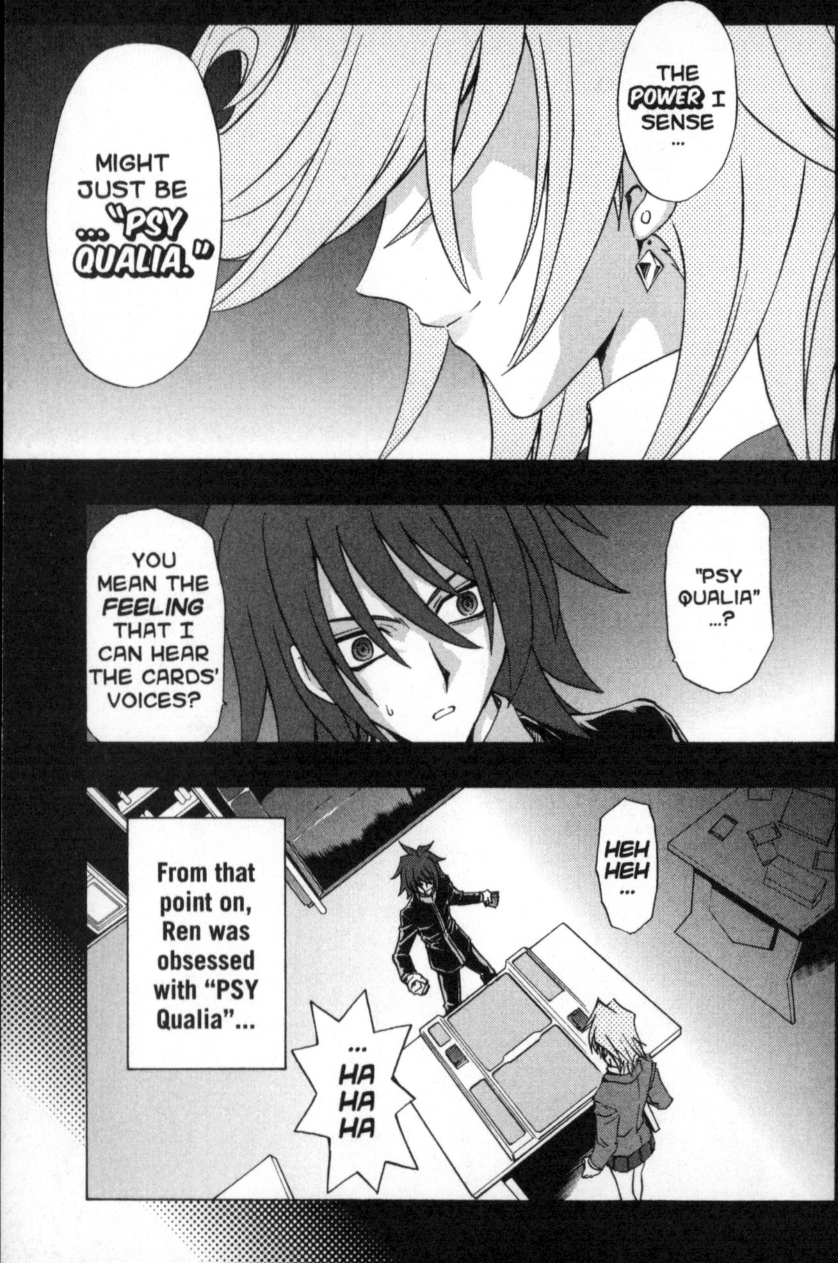
THE POWER I SENSE ...
MIGHT JUST BE ... "PSY QUALIA."
"PSY QUALIA" ...?
YOU MEAN THE FEELING THAT I CAN HEAR THE CARDS' VOICES?
HEH HEH ...
From that point on, Ren was obsessed with "PSY Qualia"...
... HA HA HA

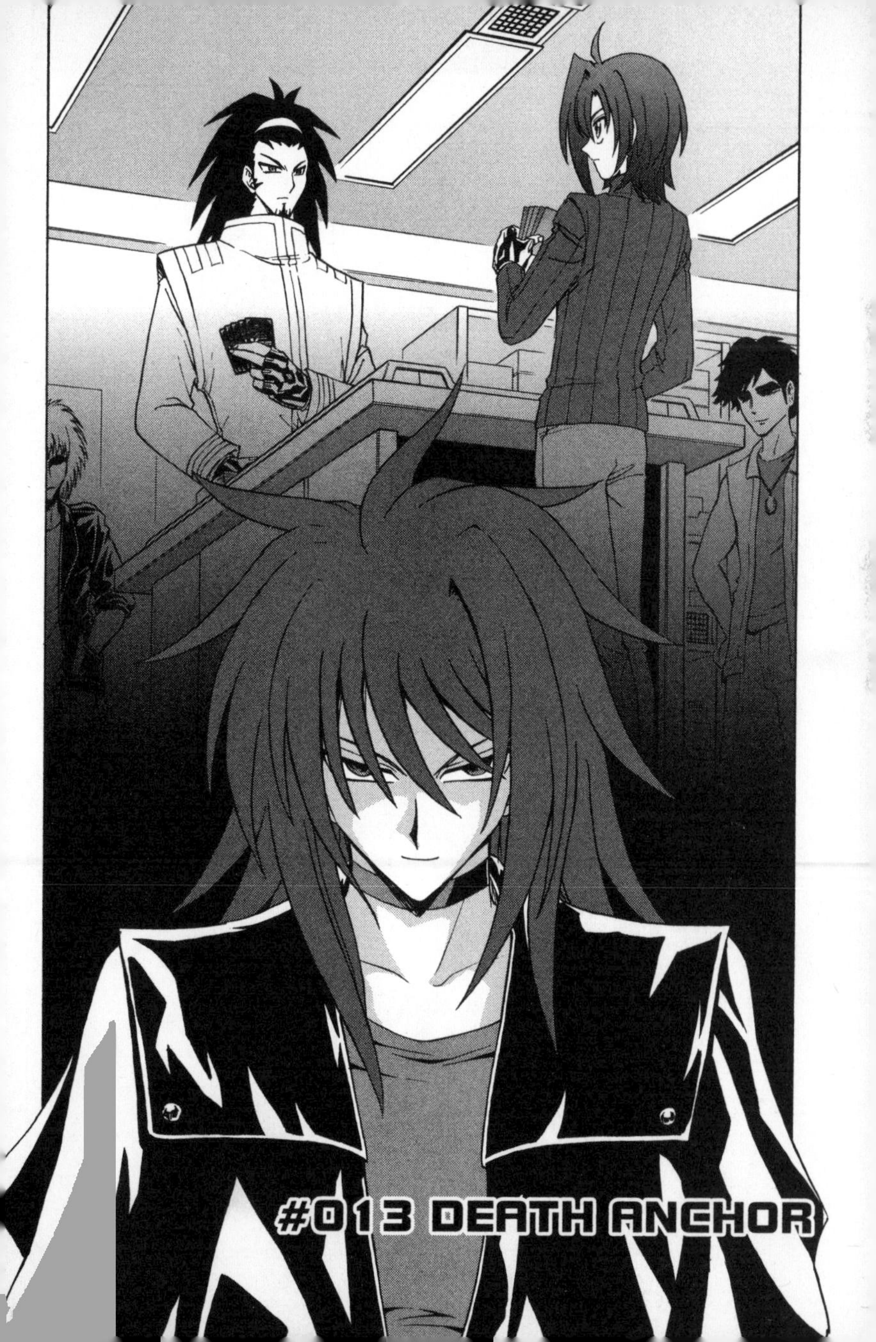
#013 DEATH ANCHOR

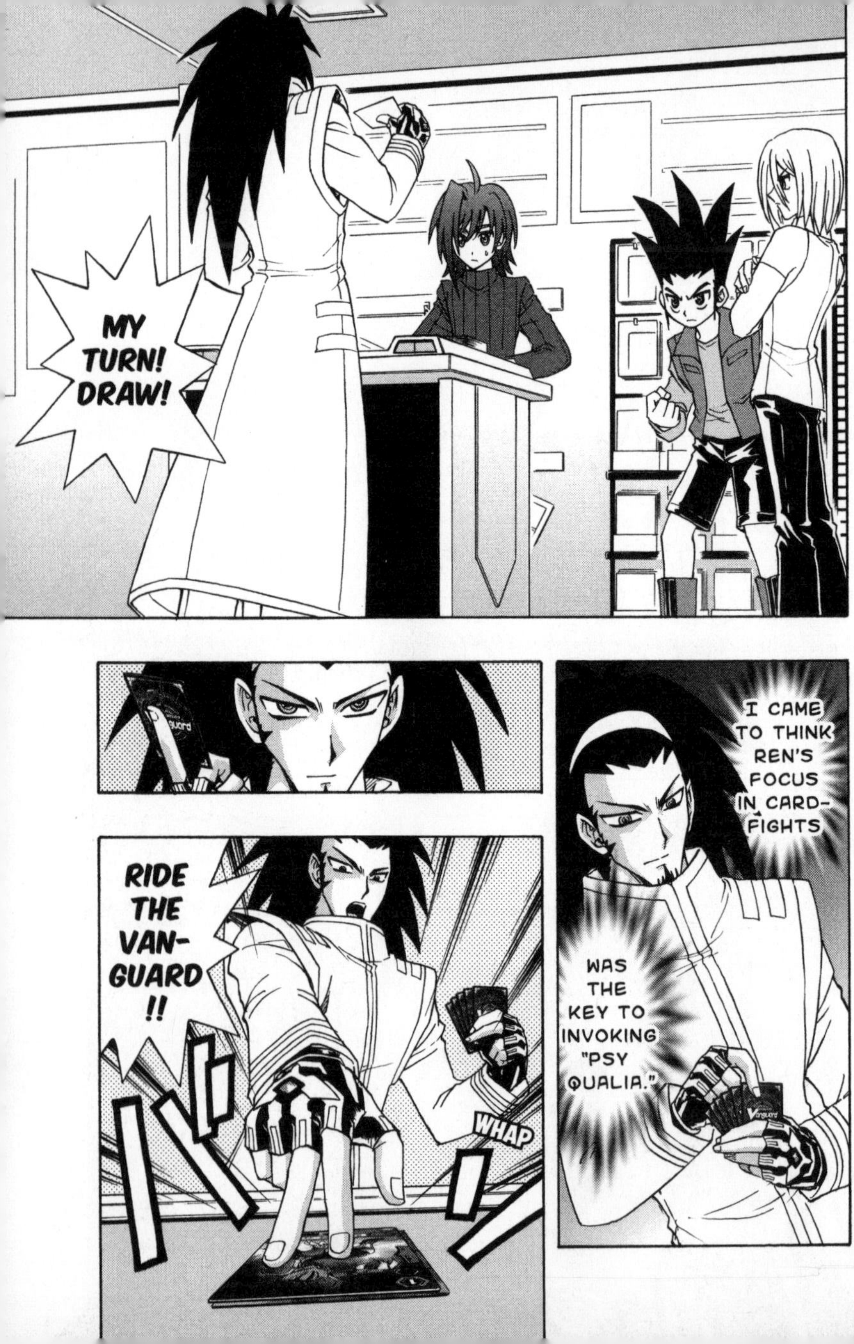
MY TURN! DRAW!
I CAME TO THINK REN'S FOCUS IN CARD-FIGHTS
WAS THE KEY TO INVOKING "PSY QUALIA."
RIDE THE VAN-GUARD!!
WHAP

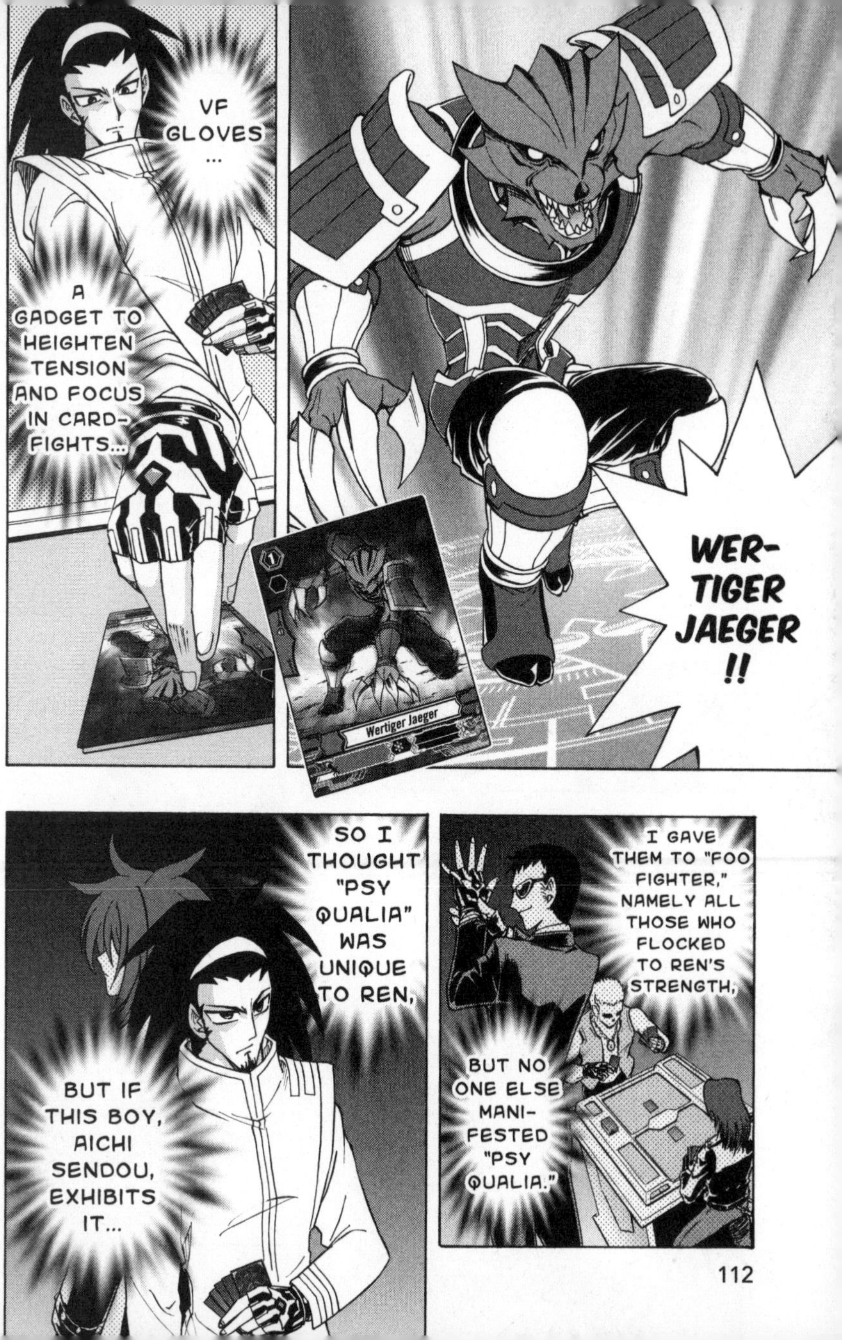
WER-TIGER JAEGER!!
Wertiger Jaeger
VF GLOVES...
A GADGET TO HEIGHTEN TENSION AND FOCUS IN CARD-FIGHTS...
I GAVE THEM TO "FOO FIGHTER," NAMELY ALL THOSE WHO FLOCKED TO REN'S STRENGTH,
BUT NO ONE ELSE MANI-FESTED "PSY QUALIA."
SO I THOUGHT "PSY QUALIA" WAS UNIQUE TO REN,
BUT IF THIS BOY, AICHI SENDOU, EXHIBITS IT...

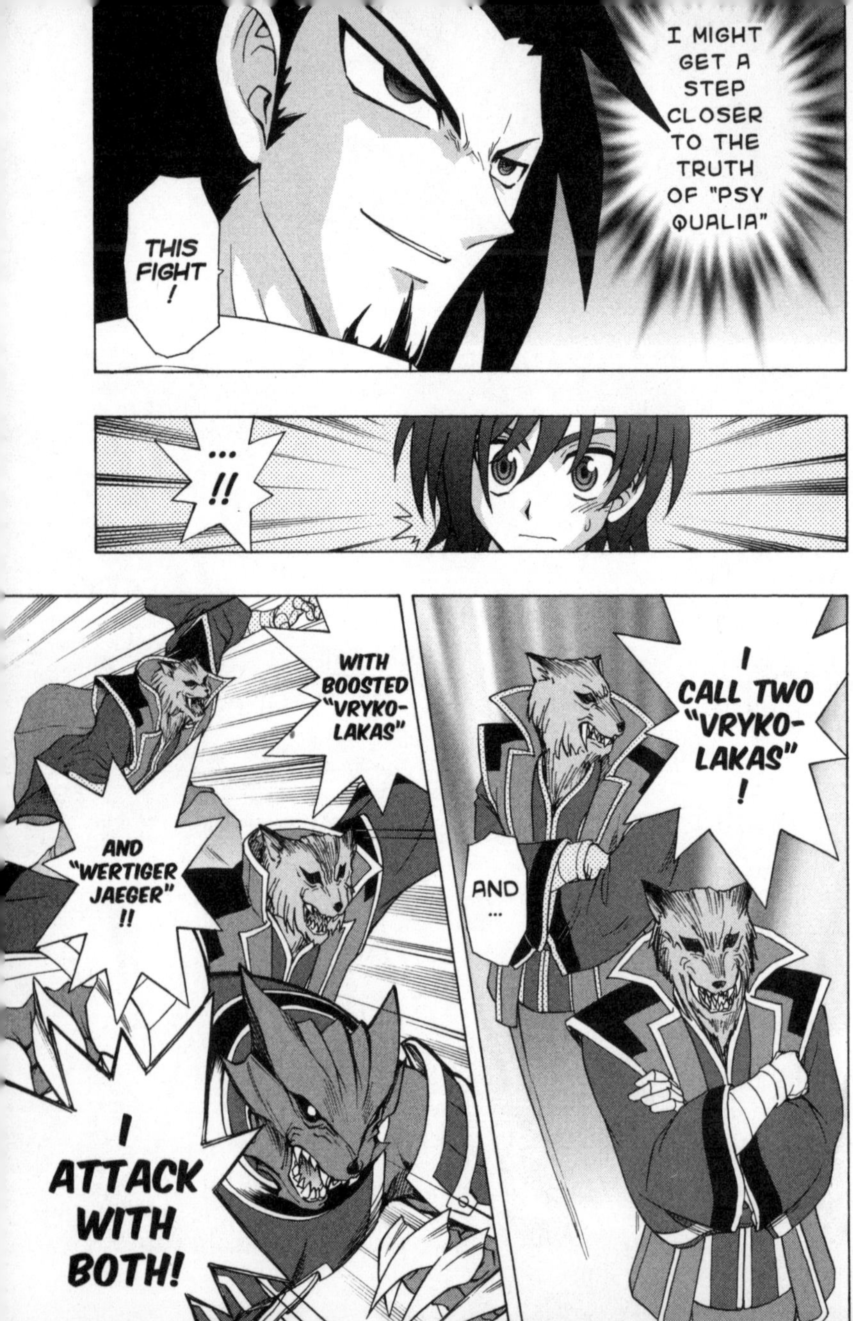
I MIGHT GET A STEP CLOSER TO THE TRUTH OF "PSY QUALIA"
THIS FIGHT !
... !!
I CALL TWO "VRYKO-LAKAS" !
AND ...
WITH BOOSTED "VRYKO-LAKAS"
AND "WERTIGER JAEGER" !!
I ATTACK WITH BOTH!

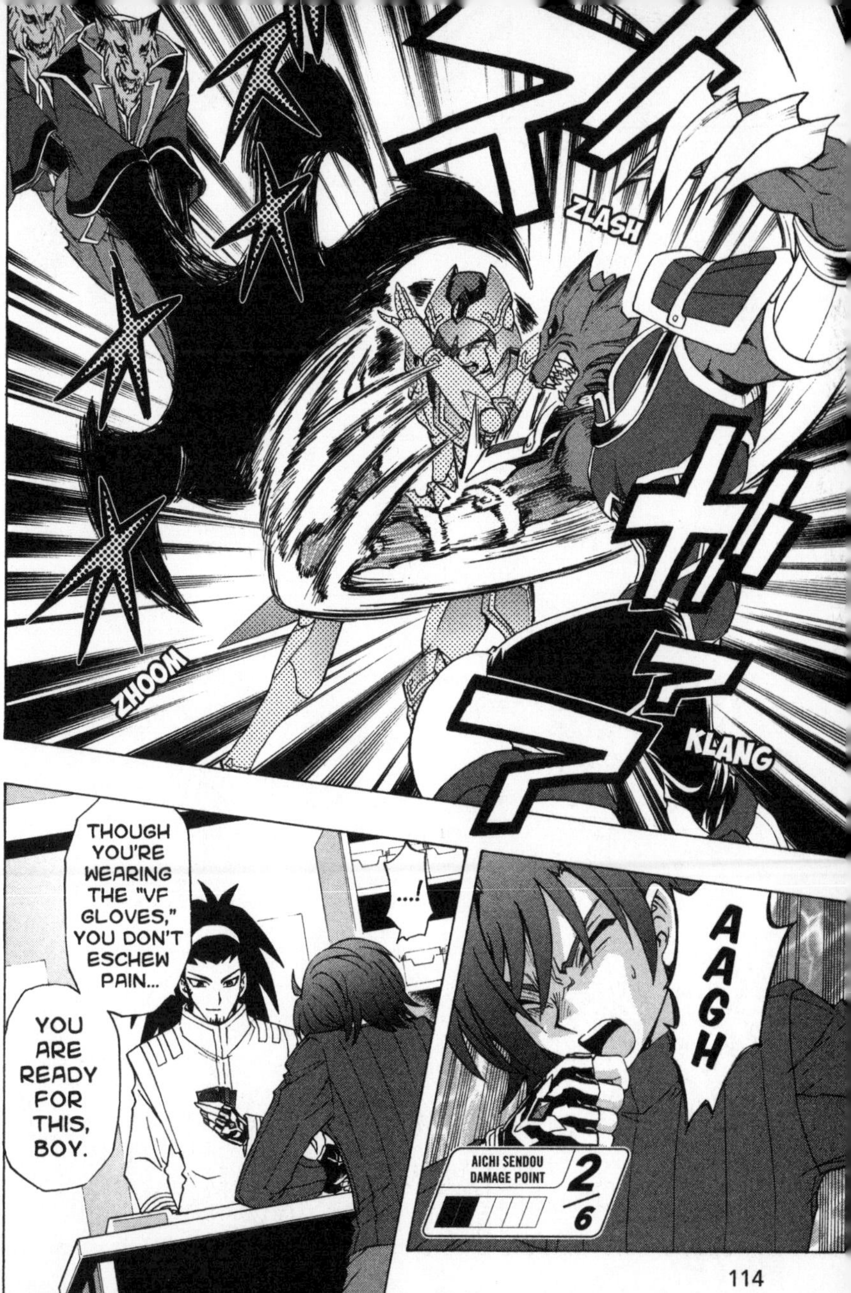
ZLASH
KLANG
ZHOOM
AAGH
AICHI SENDOU
DAMAGE POINT
2/6
....!
THOUGH YOU'RE WEARING THE "VF GLOVES," YOU DON'T ESCHEW PAIN...
YOU ARE READY FOR THIS, BOY.

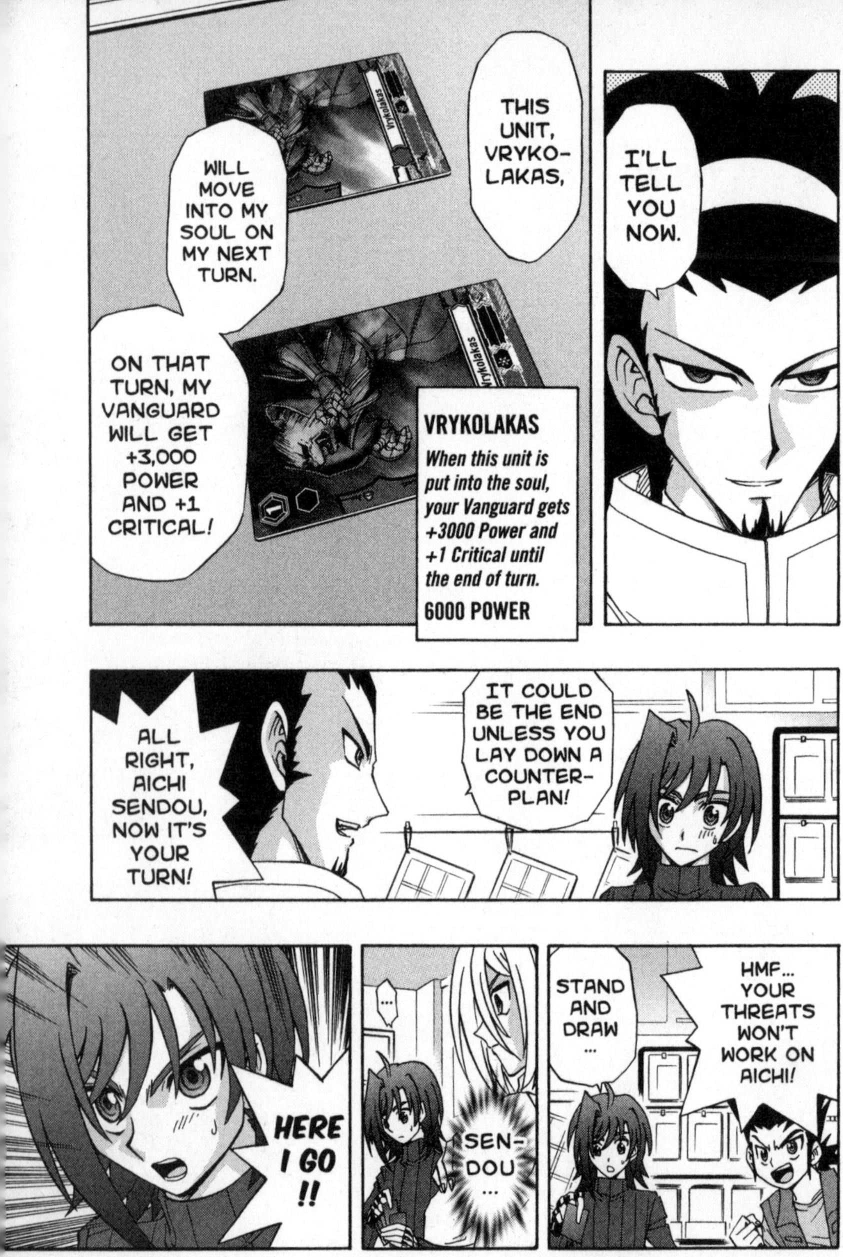
I'LL TELL YOU NOW.
THIS UNIT, VRYKO-LAKAS,
WILL MOVE INTO MY SOUL ON MY NEXT TURN.
Vrykolakas
Vrykolakas
ON THAT TURN, MY VANGUARD WILL GET +3,000 POWER AND +1 CRITICAL!
VRYKOLAKAS
When this unit is put into the soul, your Vanguard gets +3000 Power and +1 Critical until the end of turn.
6000 POWER
IT COULD BE THE END UNLESS YOU LAY DOWN A COUNTER-PLAN!
ALL RIGHT, AICHI SENDOU, NOW IT'S YOUR TURN!
HMF... YOUR THREATS WON'T WORK ON AICHI!
STAND AND DRAW ...
...
SEN-DOU ...
HERE I GO !!

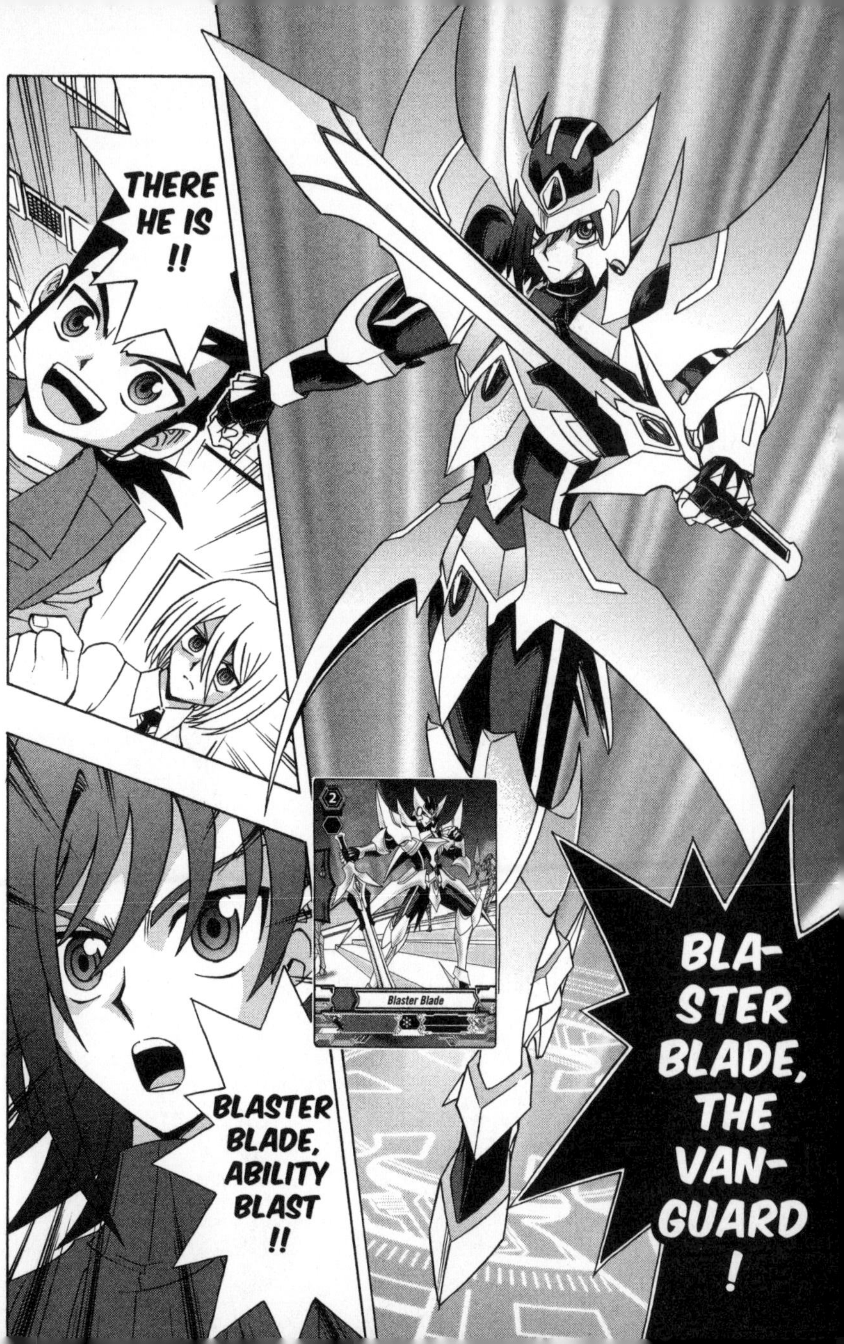
2
Blaster Blade
BLA-STER BLADE, THE VAN-GUARD!
THERE HE IS!!
BLASTER BLADE, ABILITY BLAST!!

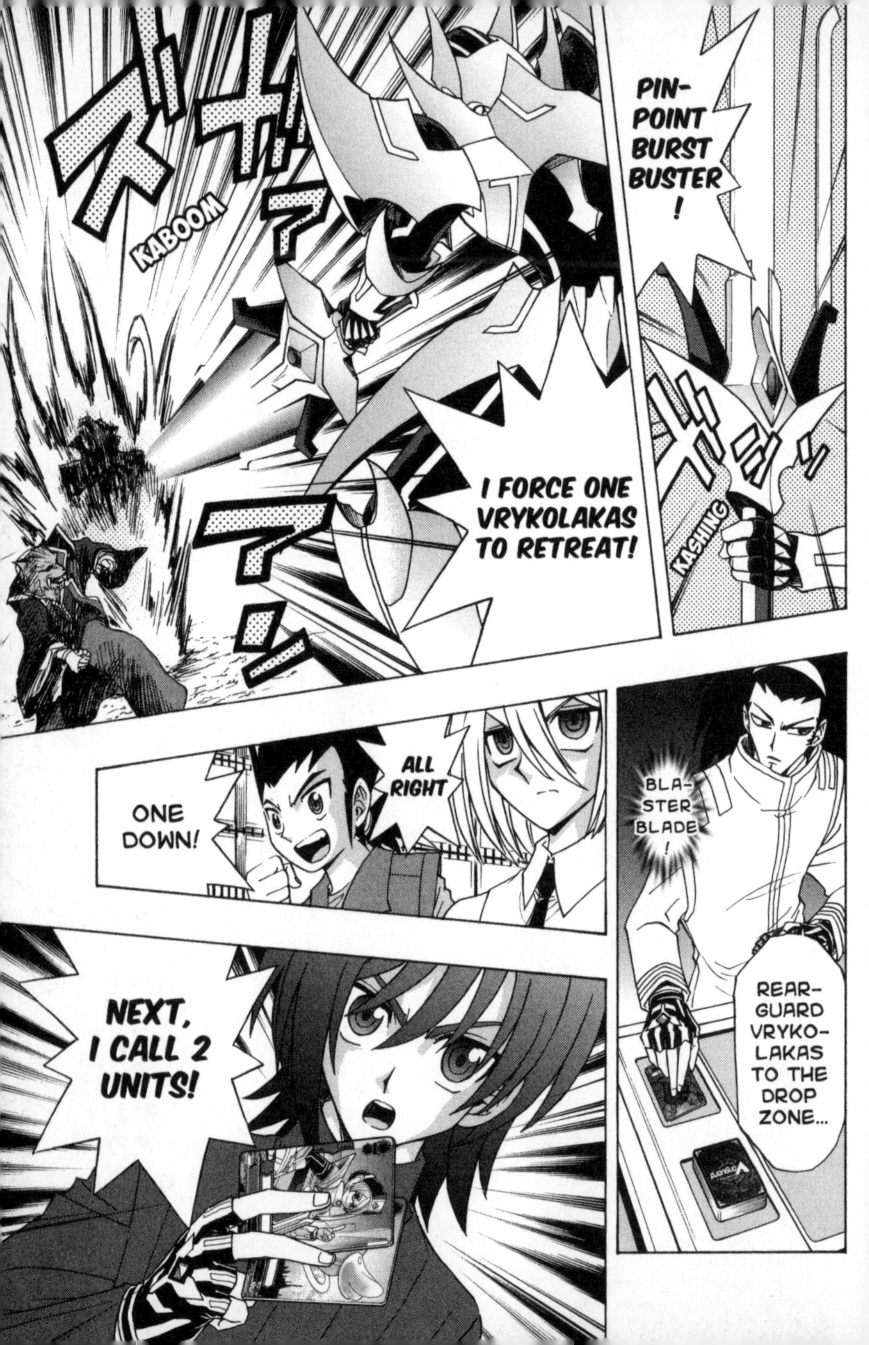
PIN-POINT BURST BUSTER !
KASHING
I FORCE ONE VRYKOLAKAS TO RETREAT!
KABOOM
BLASTER BLADE !
REAR-GUARD VRYKOLAKAS TO THE DROP ZONE...
ALL RIGHT
ONE DOWN!
NEXT, I CALL 2 UNITS!

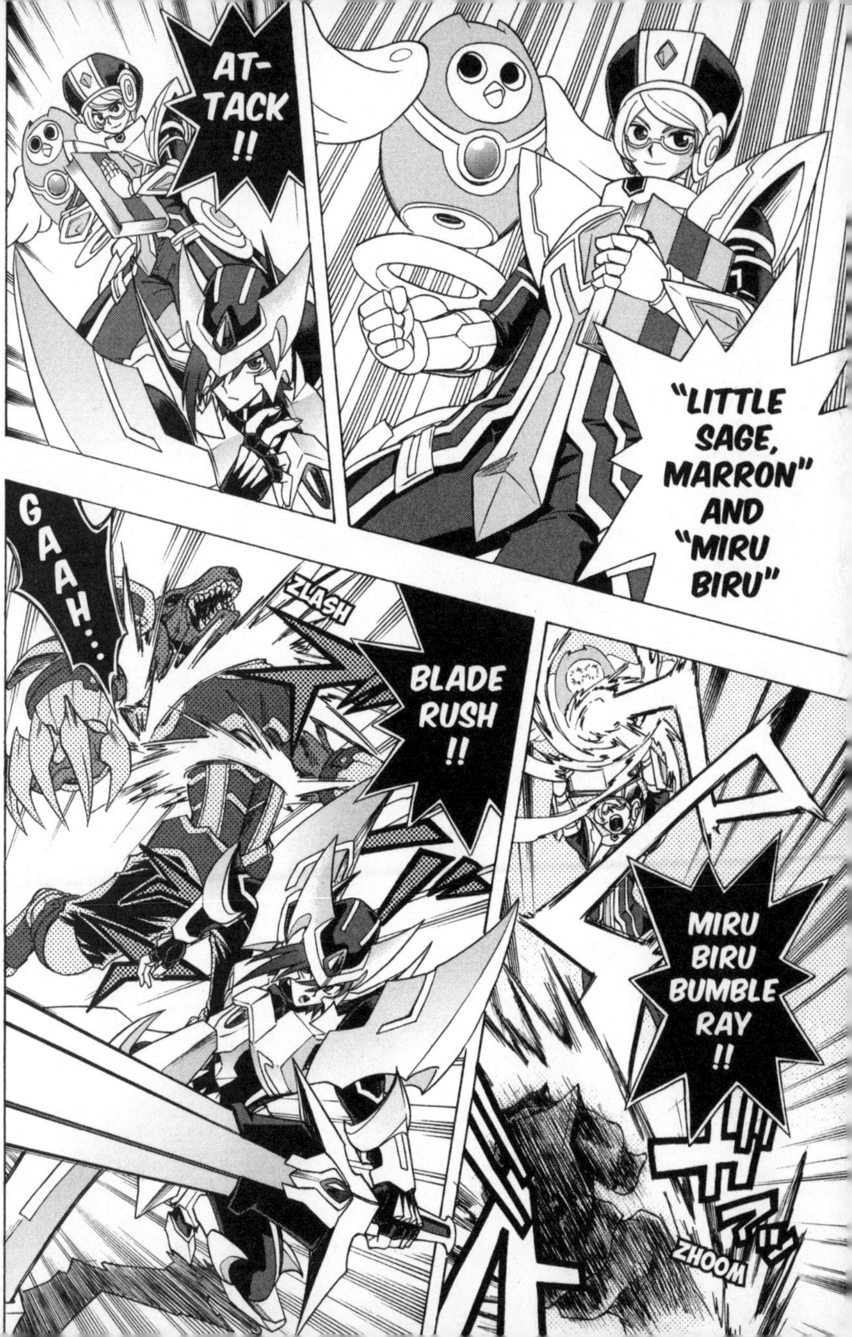
"LITTLE SAGE, MARRON" AND "MIRU BIRU"
AT-TACK !!
MIRU BIRU BUMBLE RAY !!
ZHOOM
GAAH...
ZLASH
BLADE RUSH !!

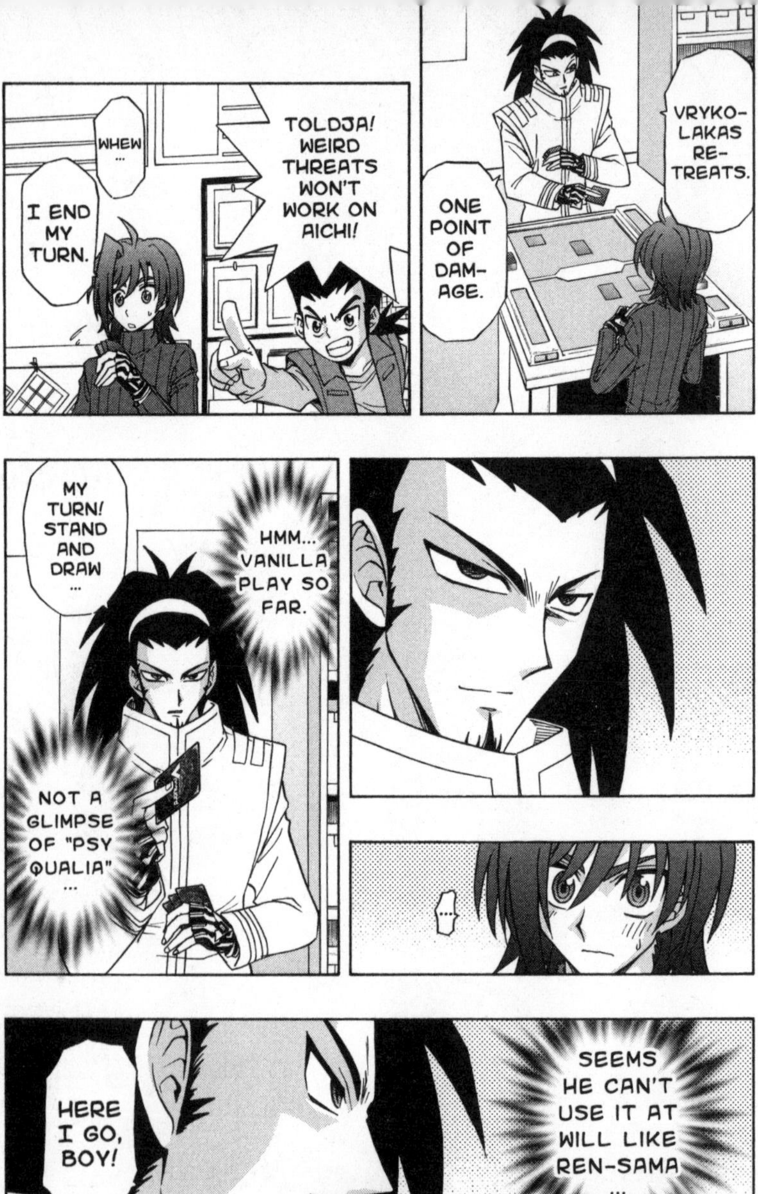
VRYKO-LAKAS RE-TREATS.
ONE POINT OF DAM-AGE.
TOLDJA! WEIRD THREATS WON'T WORK ON AICHI!
WHEW ...
I END MY TURN.
...
MY TURN! STAND AND DRAW ...
HMM... VANILLA PLAY SO FAR.
NOT A GLIMPSE OF "PSY QUALIA" ...
SEEMS HE CAN'T USE IT AT WILL LIKE REN-SAMA ...
HERE I GO, BOY!

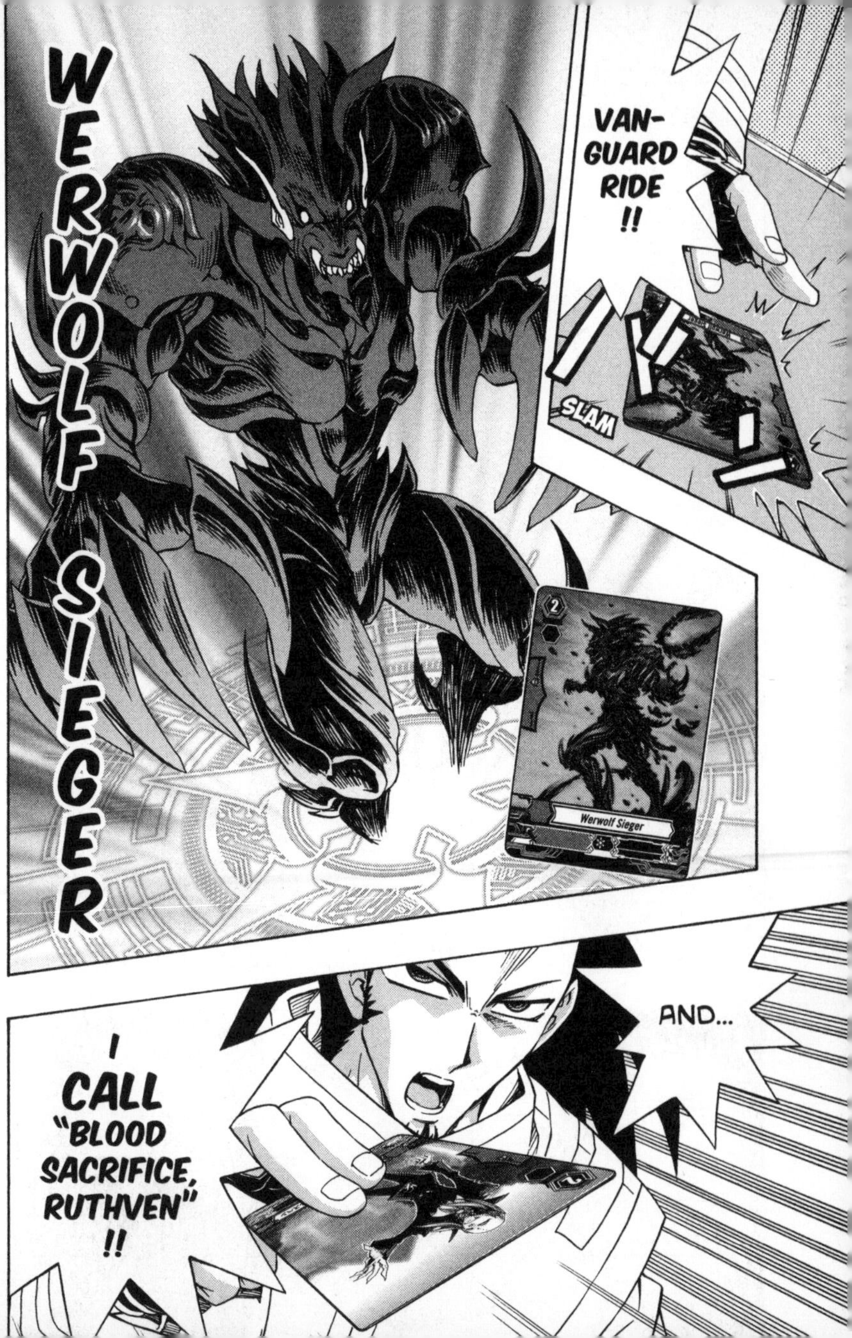
VAN-GUARD RIDE !!
SLAM
WERWOLF SIEGER
2
Werwolf Sieger
AND...
I CALL "BLOOD SACRIFICE, RUTHVEN" !!

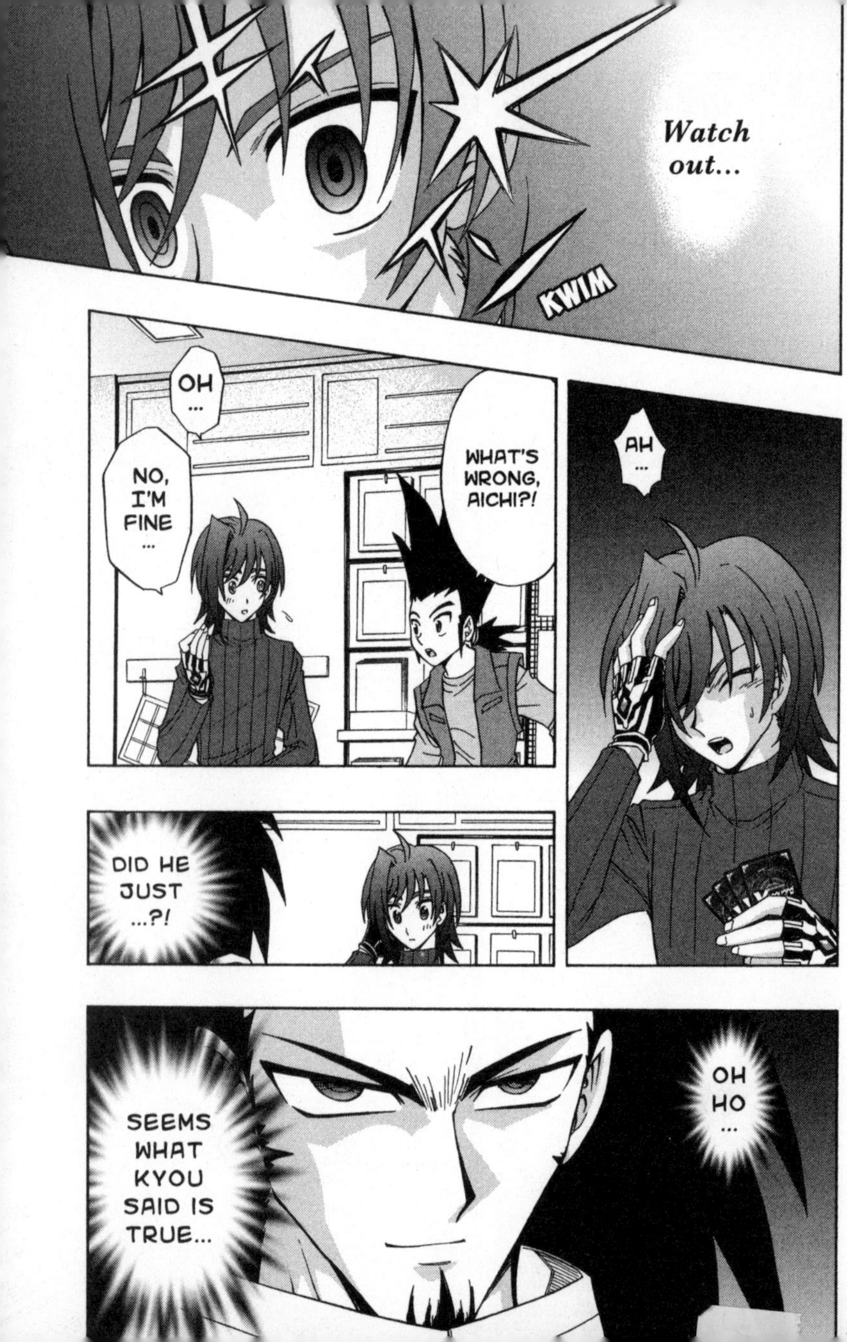
Watch out...
KWIM
AH ...
WHAT'S WRONG, AICHI?!
OH ...
NO, I'M FINE ...
DID HE JUST ...?!
OH HO ...
SEEMS WHAT KYOU SAID IS TRUE...

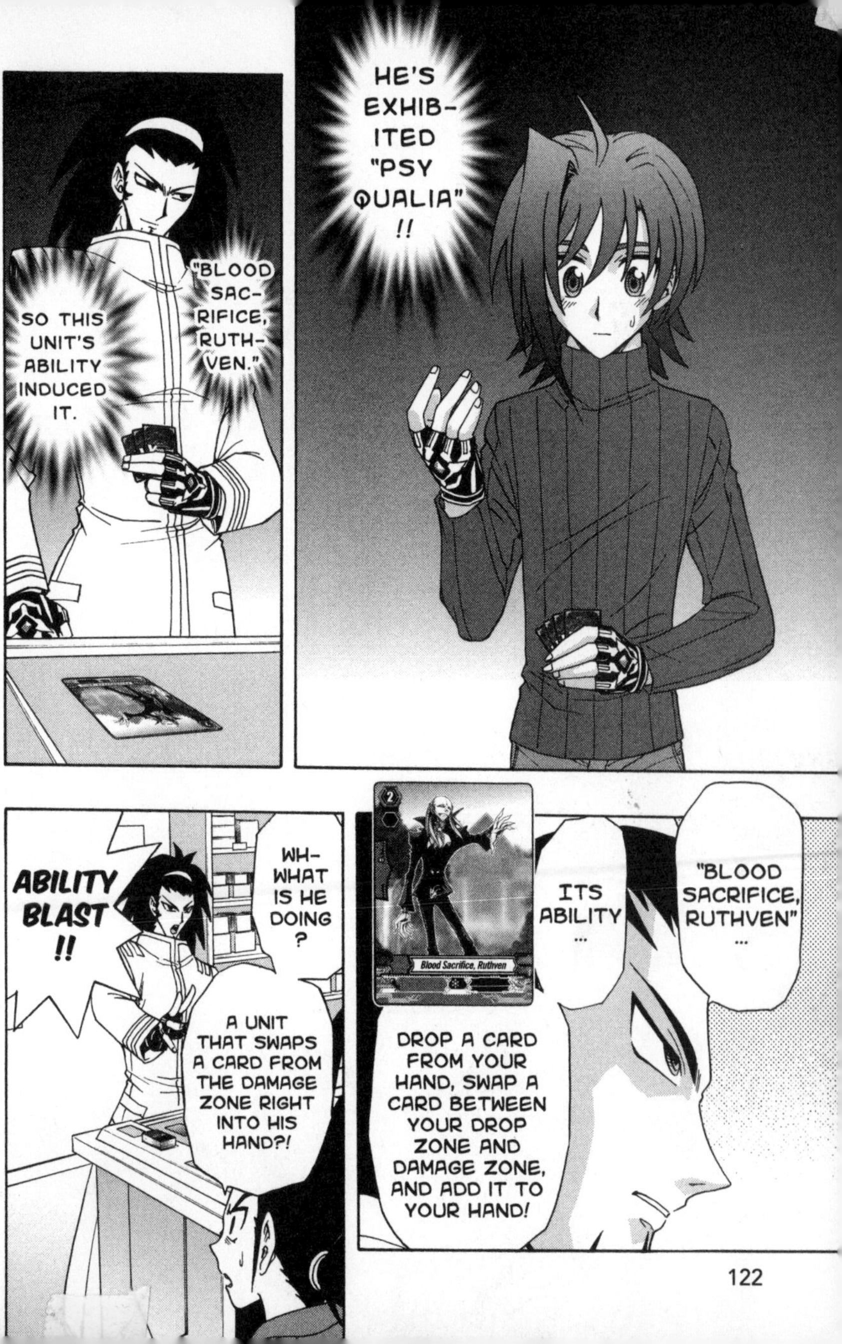
HE'S EXHIBITED "PSY QUALIA"!!
"BLOOD SACRIFICE, RUTHVEN."
SO THIS UNIT'S ABILITY INDUCED IT.
"BLOOD SACRIFICE, RUTHVEN"...
ITS ABILITY...
Blood Sacrifice, Ruthven
DROP A CARD FROM YOUR HAND, SWAP A CARD BETWEEN YOUR DROP ZONE AND DAMAGE ZONE, AND ADD IT TO YOUR HAND!
WH-WHAT IS HE DOING?
ABILITY BLAST!!
A UNIT THAT SWAPS A CARD FROM THE DAMAGE ZONE RIGHT INTO HIS HAND?!

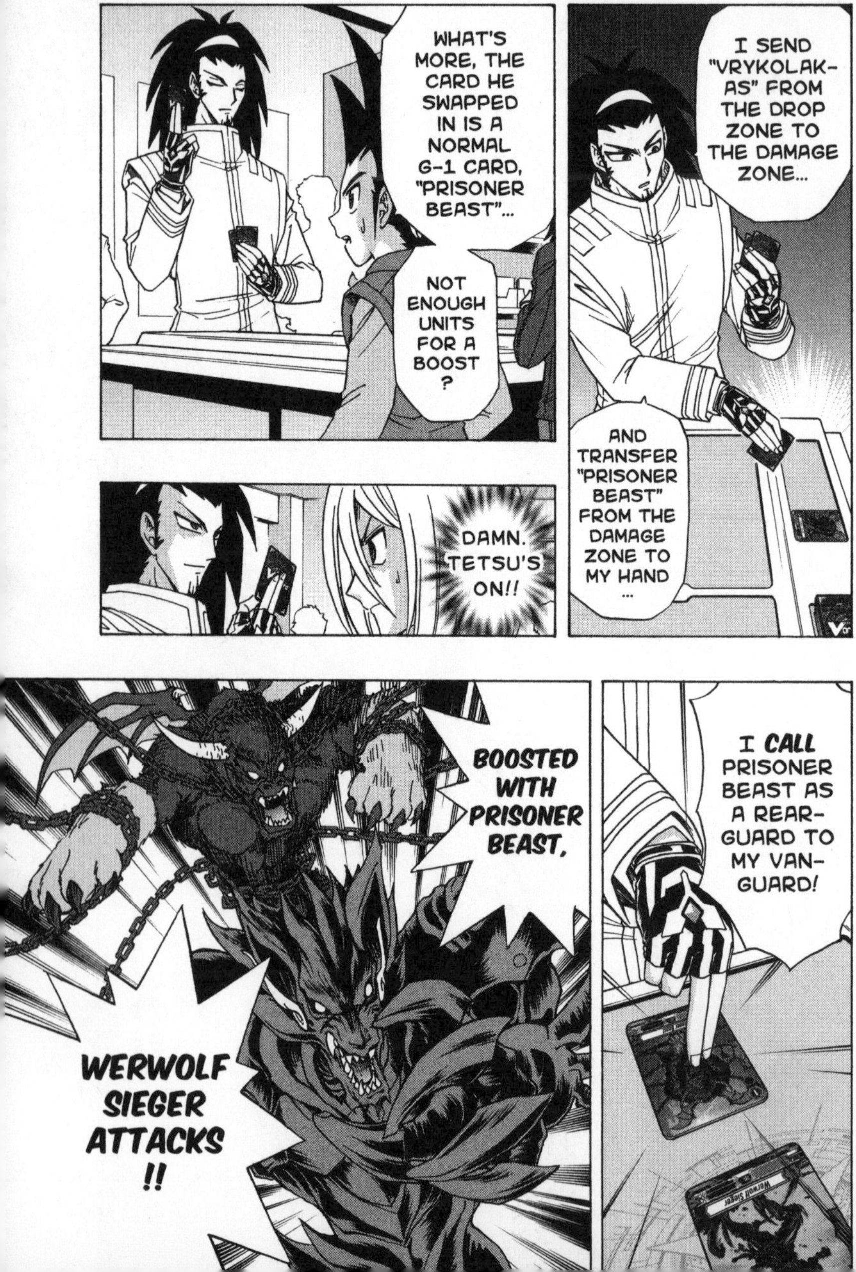
I SEND "VRYKOLAK-AS" FROM THE DROP ZONE TO THE DAMAGE ZONE...
AND TRANSFER "PRISONER BEAST" FROM THE DAMAGE ZONE TO MY HAND ...
WHAT'S MORE, THE CARD HE SWAPPED IN IS A NORMAL G-1 CARD, "PRISONER BEAST"...
NOT ENOUGH UNITS FOR A BOOST ?
DAMN. TETSU'S ON!!
I CALL PRISONER BEAST AS A REAR-GUARD TO MY VAN-GUARD!
BOOSTED WITH PRISONER BEAST,
WERWOLF SIEGER ATTACKS !!

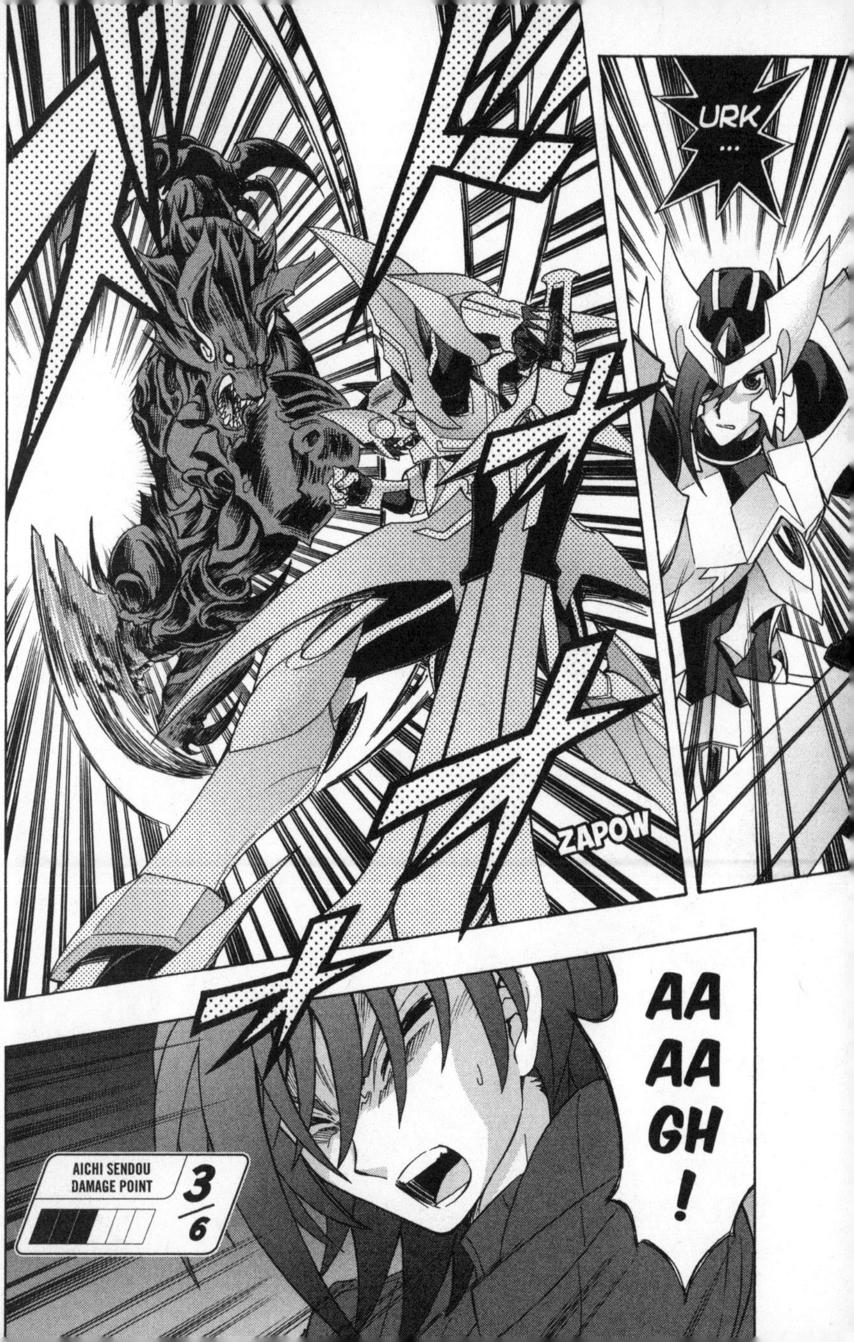
URK ...
ZAPOW
AAAAGH!
AICHI SENDOU DAMAGE POINT
3/6

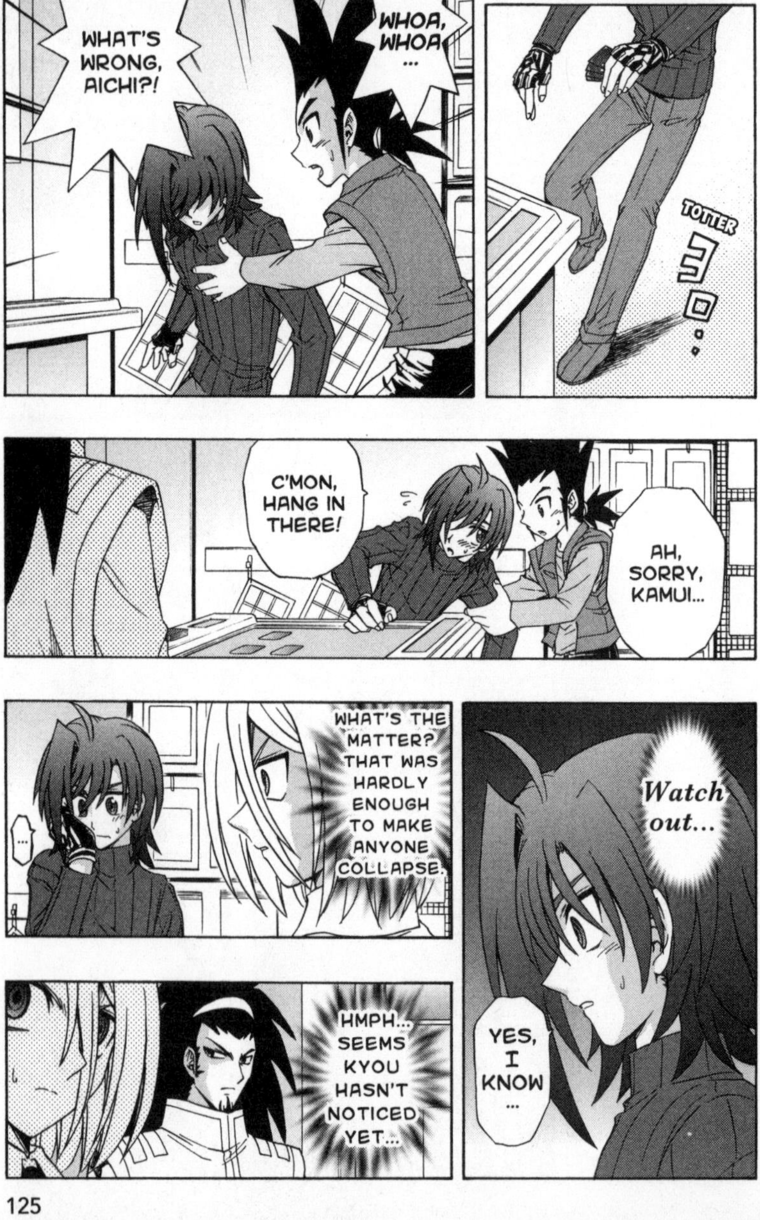
TOTTER
ヨロ
WHOA, WHOA...
WHAT'S WRONG, AICHI?!
AH, SORRY, KAMUI...
C'MON, HANG IN THERE!
Watch out...
YES, I KNOW...
WHAT'S THE MATTER? THAT WAS HARDLY ENOUGH TO MAKE ANYONE COLLAPSE.
...
HMPH... SEEMS KYOU HASN'T NOTICED YET...

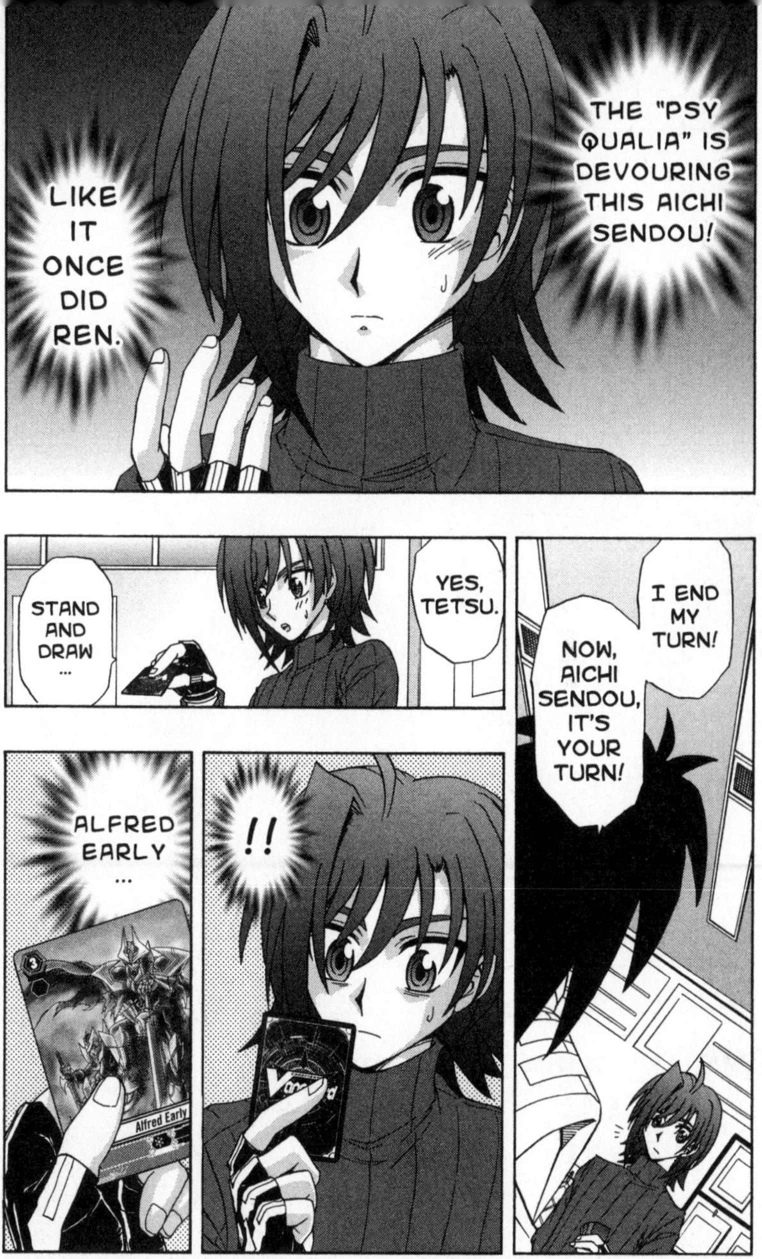
THE "PSY QUALIA" IS DEVOURING THIS AICHI SENDOU!
LIKE IT ONCE DID REN.
I END MY TURN!
NOW, AICHI SENDOU, IT'S YOUR TURN!
YES, TETSU.
STAND AND DRAW ...
!!
ALFRED EARLY ...
Alfred Early

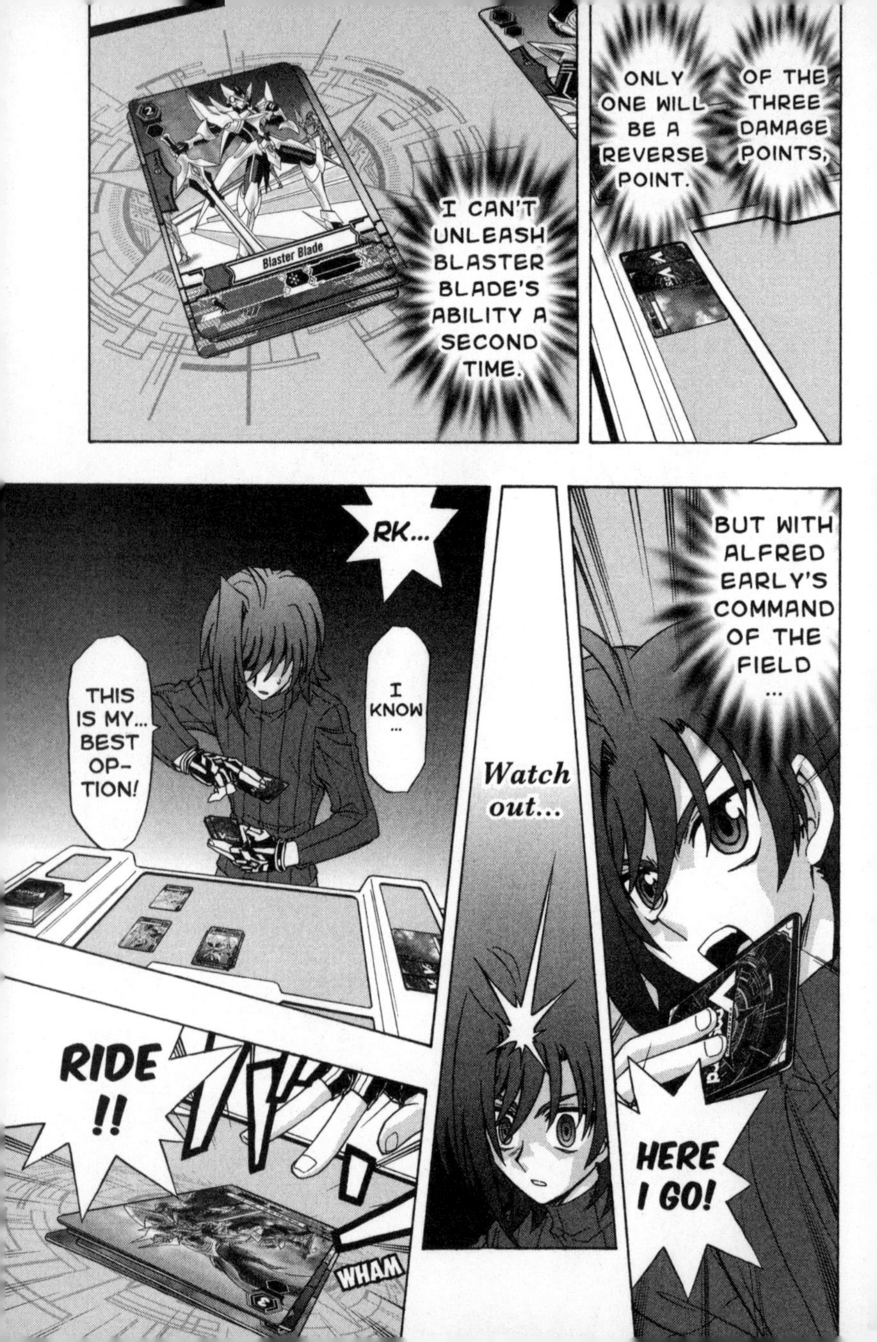
OF THE THREE DAMAGE POINTS,
ONLY ONE WILL BE A REVERSE POINT.
Blaster Blade
I CAN'T UNLEASH BLASTER BLADE'S ABILITY A SECOND TIME.
BUT WITH ALFRED EARLY'S COMMAND OF THE FIELD ...
HERE I GO!
Watch out...
RK...
I KNOW ...
THIS IS MY... BEST OP-TION!
RIDE !!
WHAM

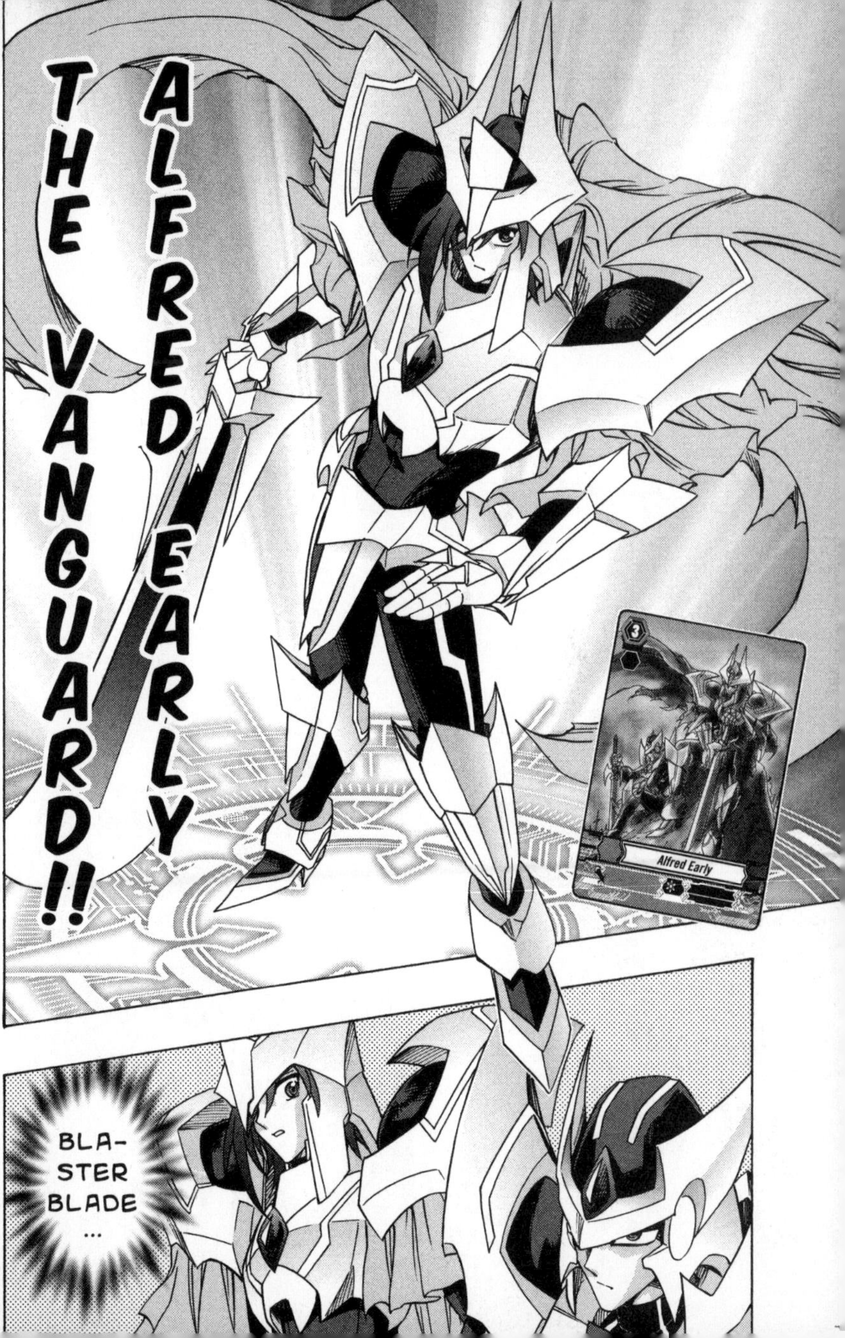
ALFRED EARLY
THE VANGUARD!!
Alfred Early
BLA-
STER
BLADE
...

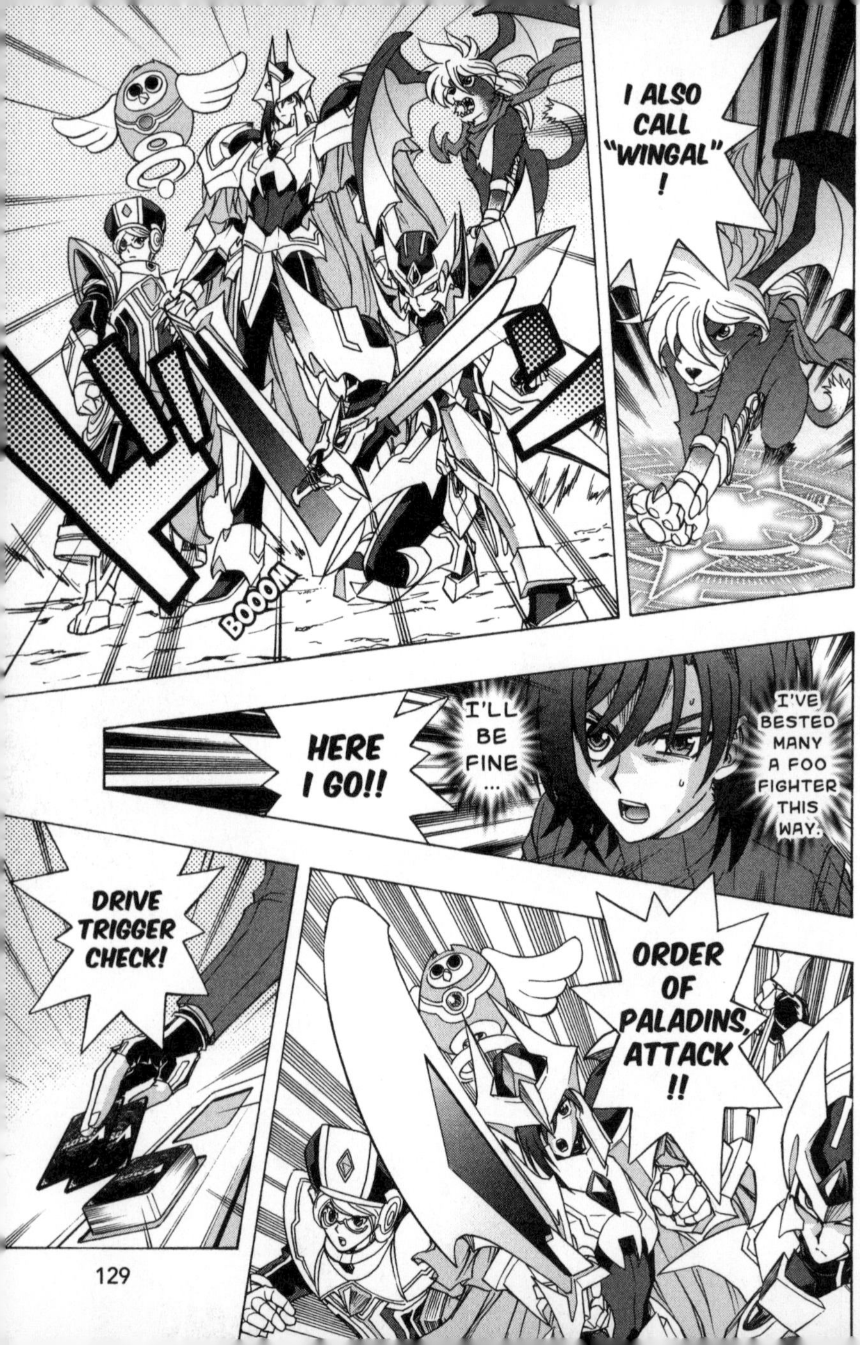
I ALSO CALL "WINGAL" !
BOOOM
I'VE BESTED MANY A FOO FIGHTER THIS WAY.
I'LL BE FINE ...
HERE I GO!!
ORDER OF PALADINS, ATTACK !!
DRIVE TRIGGER CHECK!

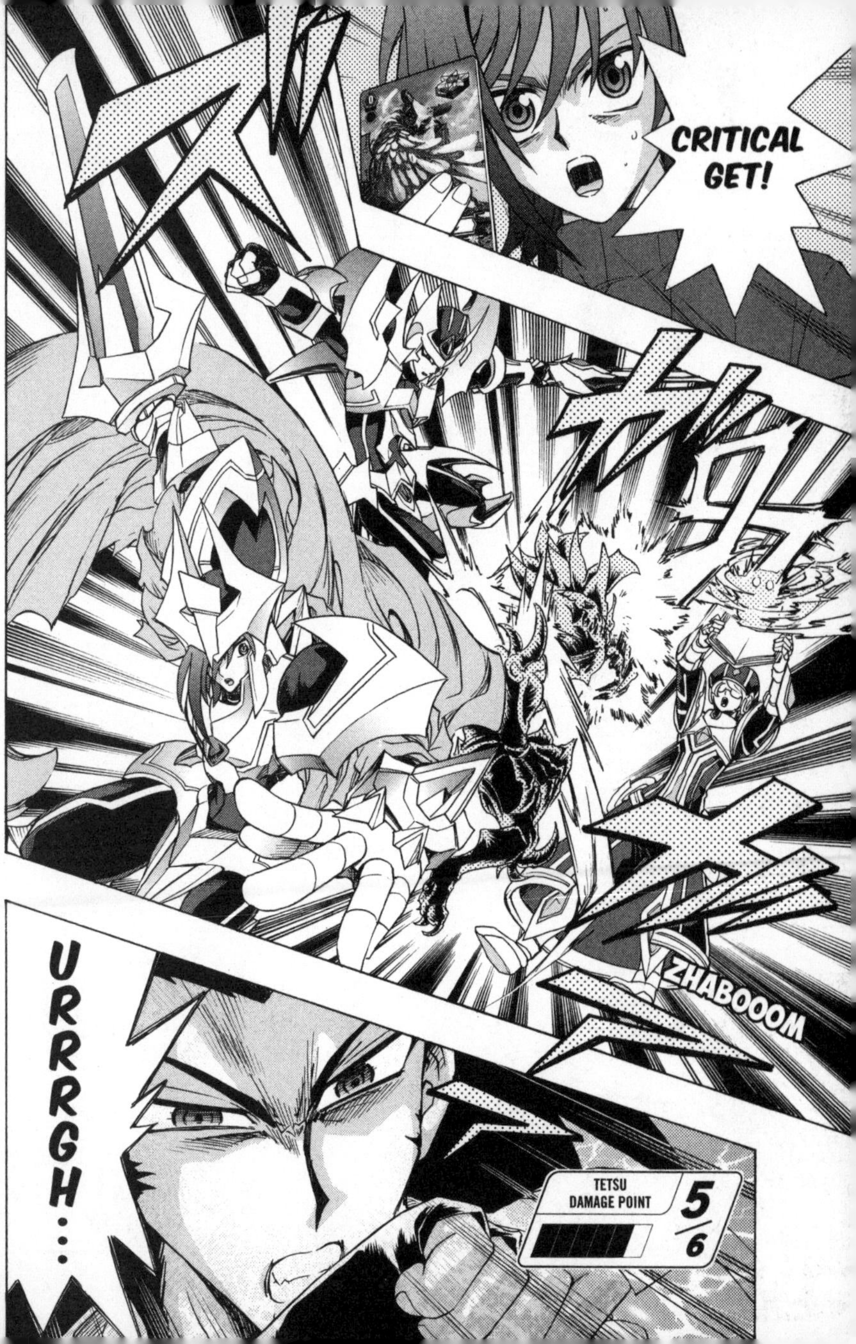
CRITICAL GET!
ZHABOOOM
URRRGH...
TETSU
DAMAGE POINT
5/6

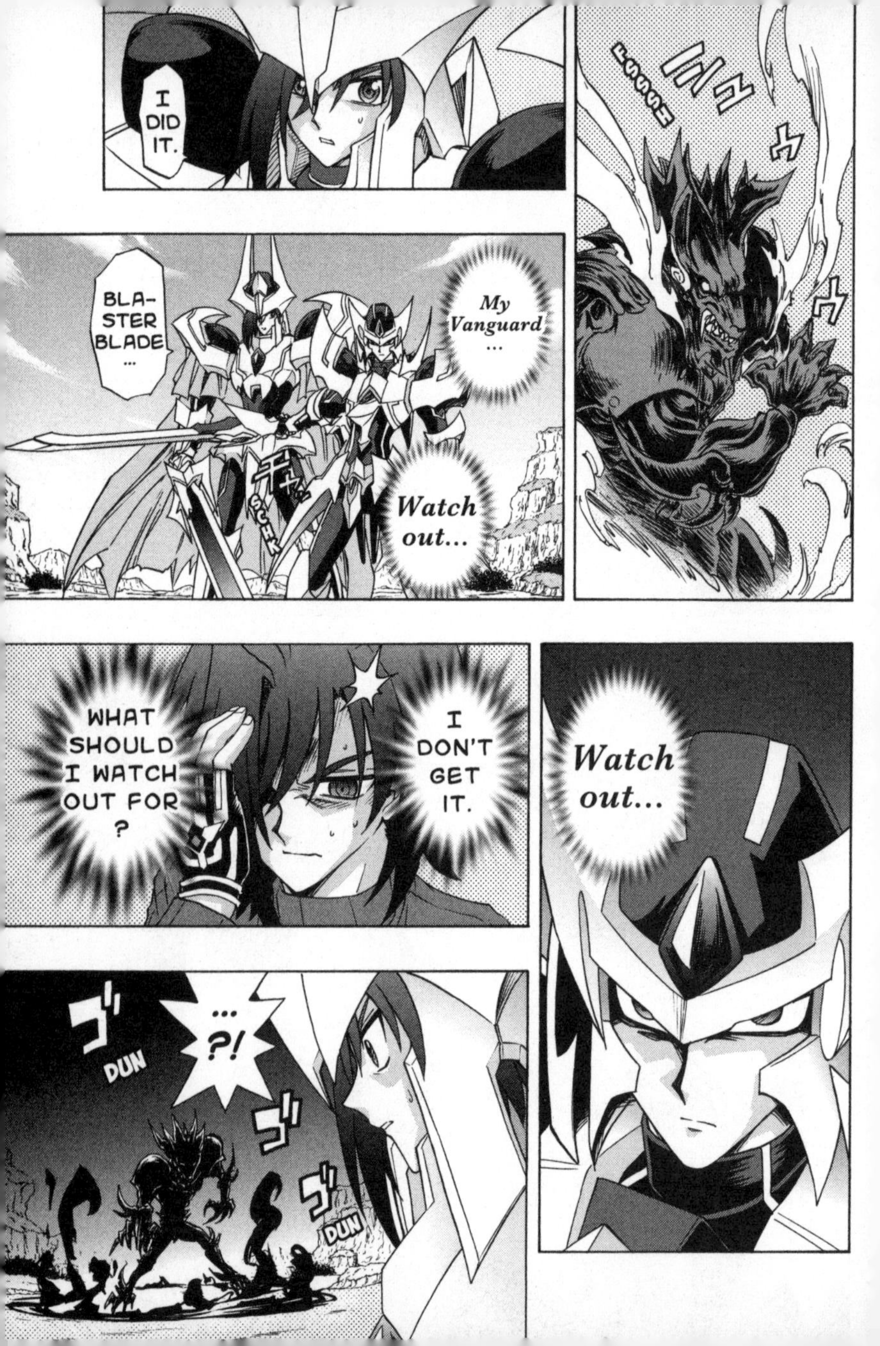
FSSSH
I DID IT.
My Vanguard ...
BLA-STER BLADE ...
SCHK
Watch out...
Watch out...
I DON'T GET IT.
WHAT SHOULD I WATCH OUT FOR ?
...?!
DUN
DUN

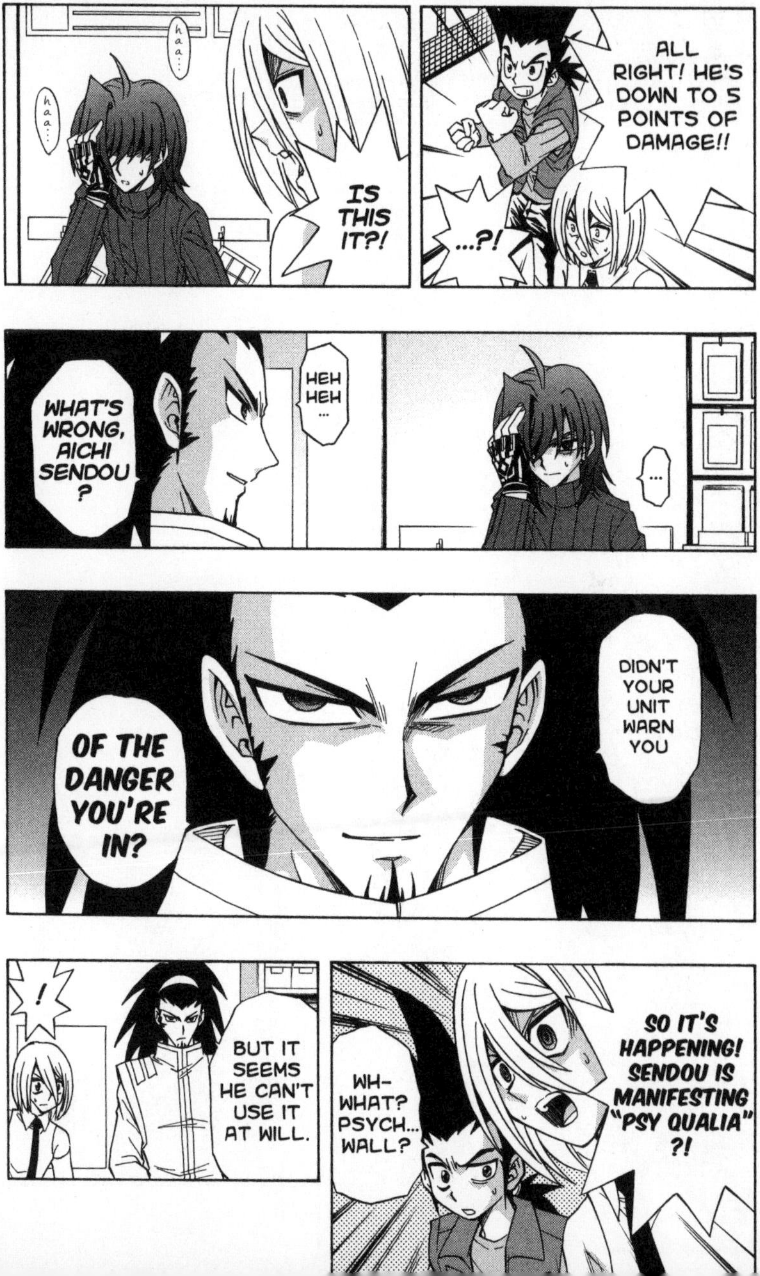
ALL RIGHT! HE'S DOWN TO 5 POINTS OF DAMAGE!!
...?!
haa...
haa...
IS THIS IT?!
...
HEH HEH ...
WHAT'S WRONG, AICHI SENDOU?
DIDN'T YOUR UNIT WARN YOU
OF THE DANGER YOU'RE IN?
SO IT'S HAPPENING! SENDOU IS MANIFESTING "PSY QUALIA"?!
WH-WHAT? PSYCH... WALL?
BUT IT SEEMS HE CAN'T USE IT AT WILL.
!

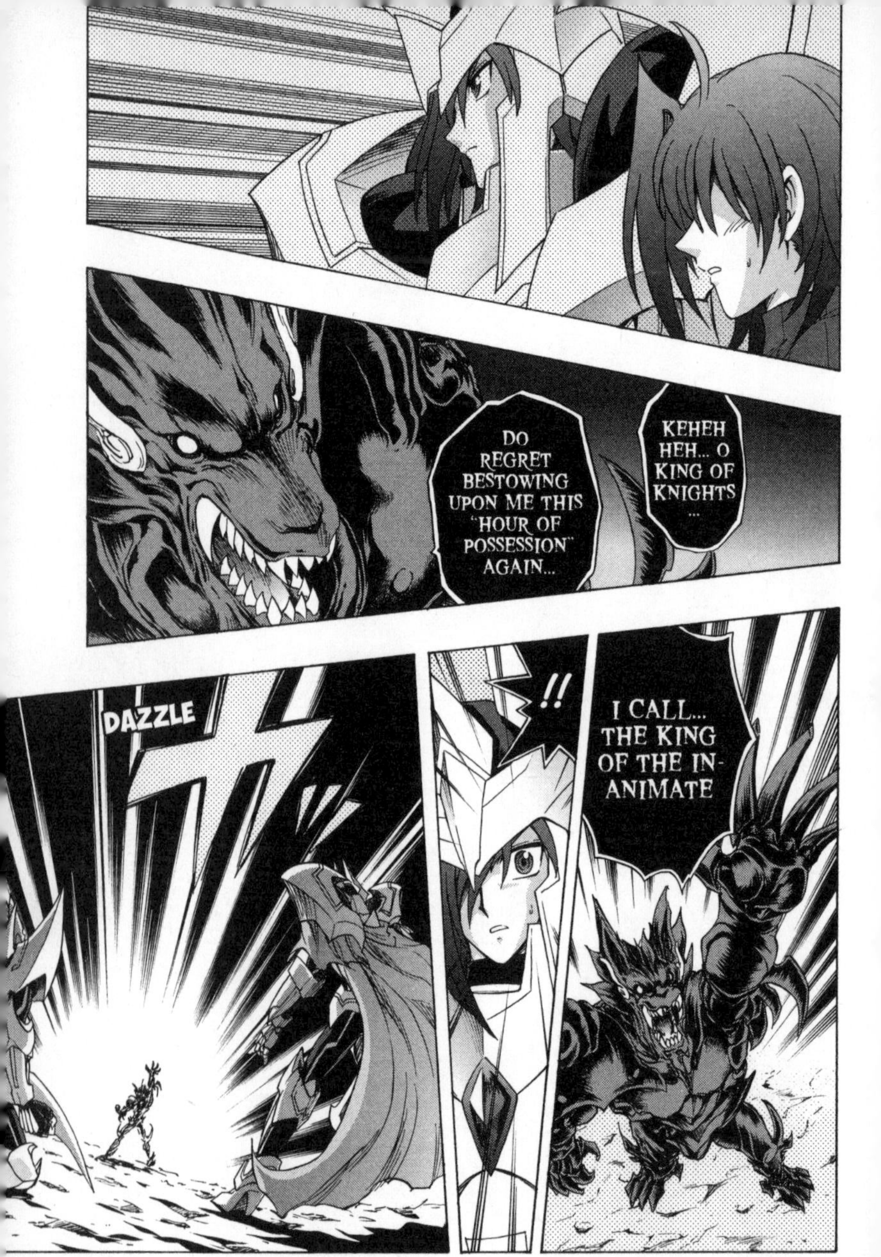
KEHEH HEH... O KING OF KNIGHTS ...
DO REGRET BESTOWING UPON ME THIS "HOUR OF POSSESSION" AGAIN...
I CALL... THE KING OF THE IN-ANIMATE
!!
DAZZLE

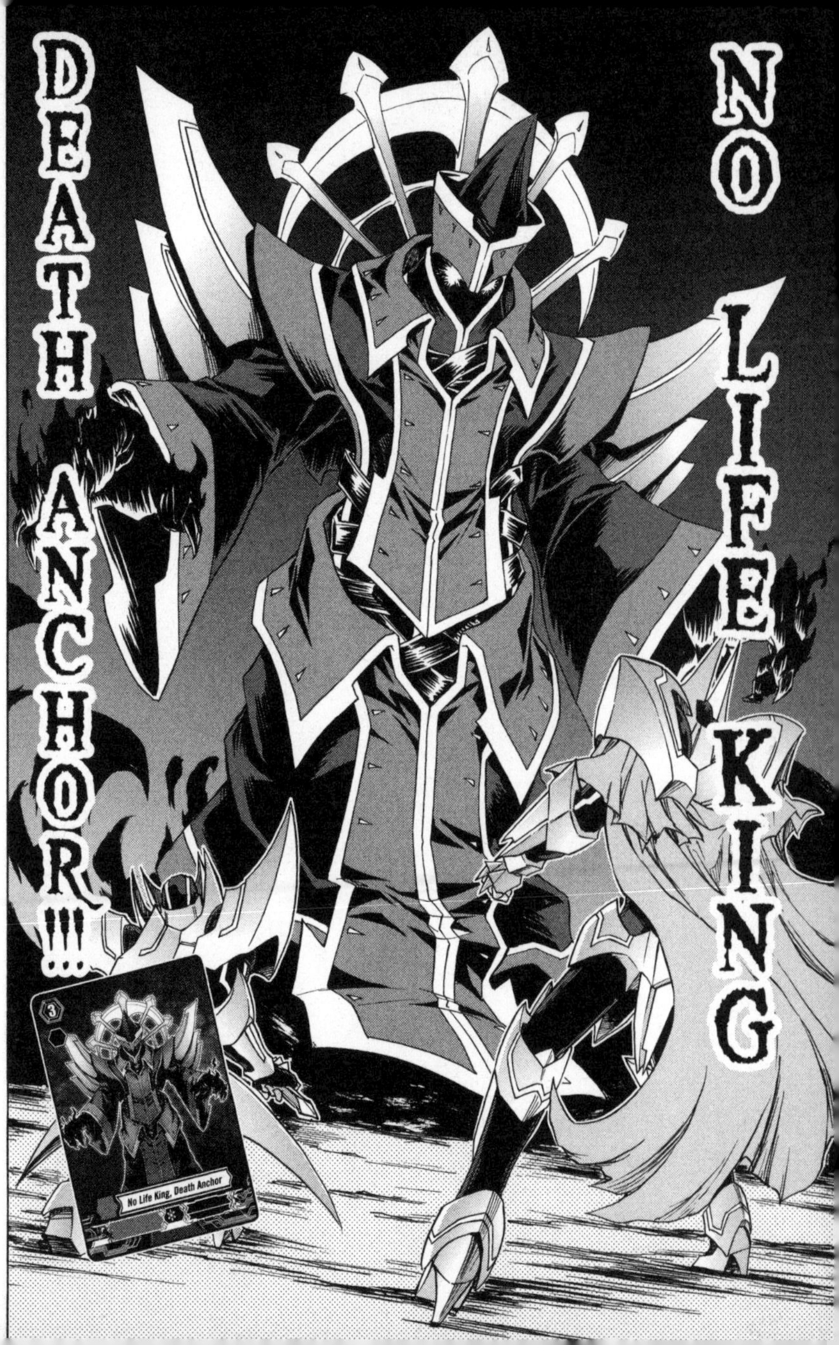
NO LIFE KING
DEATH ANCHOR!!!
3
No Life King, Death Anchor

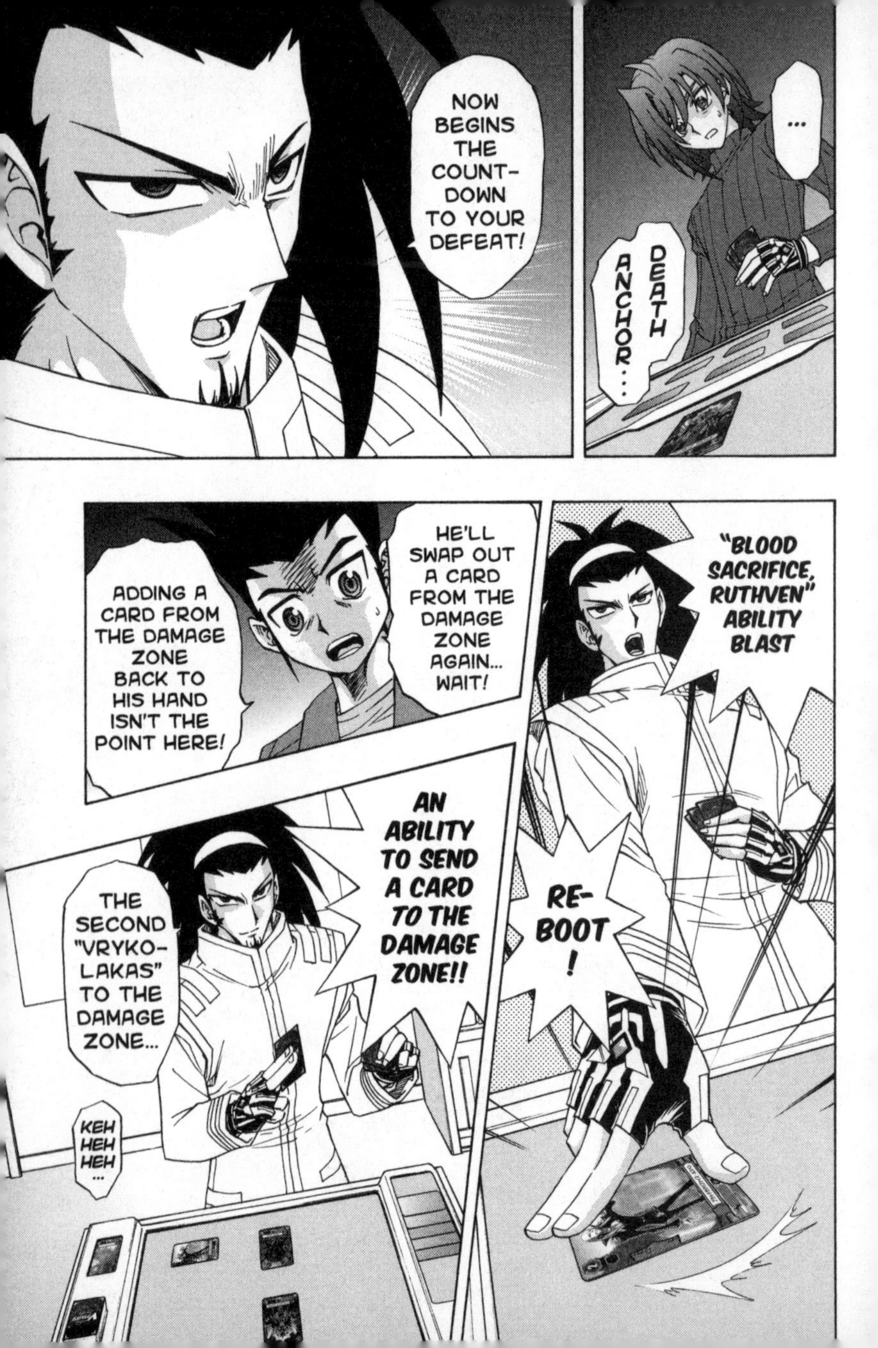
...
DEATH ANCHOR...
NOW BEGINS THE COUNT-DOWN TO YOUR DEFEAT!
"BLOOD SACRIFICE, RUTHVEN" ABILITY BLAST
RE-BOOT!
HE'LL SWAP OUT A CARD FROM THE DAMAGE ZONE AGAIN... WAIT!
ADDING A CARD FROM THE DAMAGE ZONE BACK TO HIS HAND ISN'T THE POINT HERE!
AN ABILITY TO SEND A CARD TO THE DAMAGE ZONE!!
THE SECOND "VRYKO-LAKAS" TO THE DAMAGE ZONE...
KEH HEH HEH...

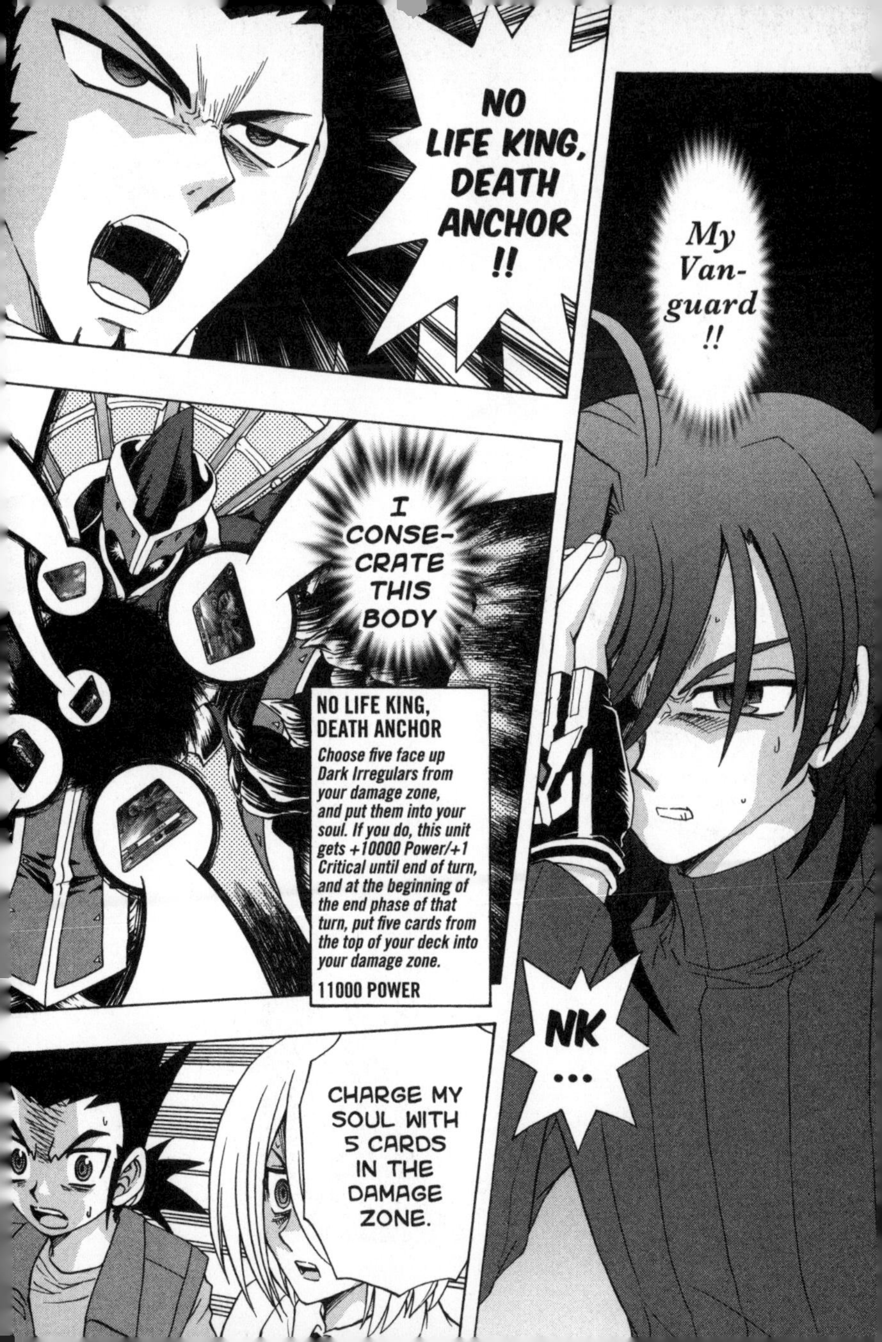

My Vanguard!!
NO LIFE KING, DEATH ANCHOR!!
I CONSECRATE THIS BODY
NO LIFE KING, DEATH ANCHOR
Choose five face up Dark Irregulars from your damage zone, and put them into your soul. If you do, this unit gets +10000 Power/+1 Critical until end of turn, and at the beginning of the end phase of that turn, put five cards from the top of your deck into your damage zone.
11000 POWER
NK...
CHARGE MY SOUL WITH 5 CARDS IN THE DAMAGE ZONE.

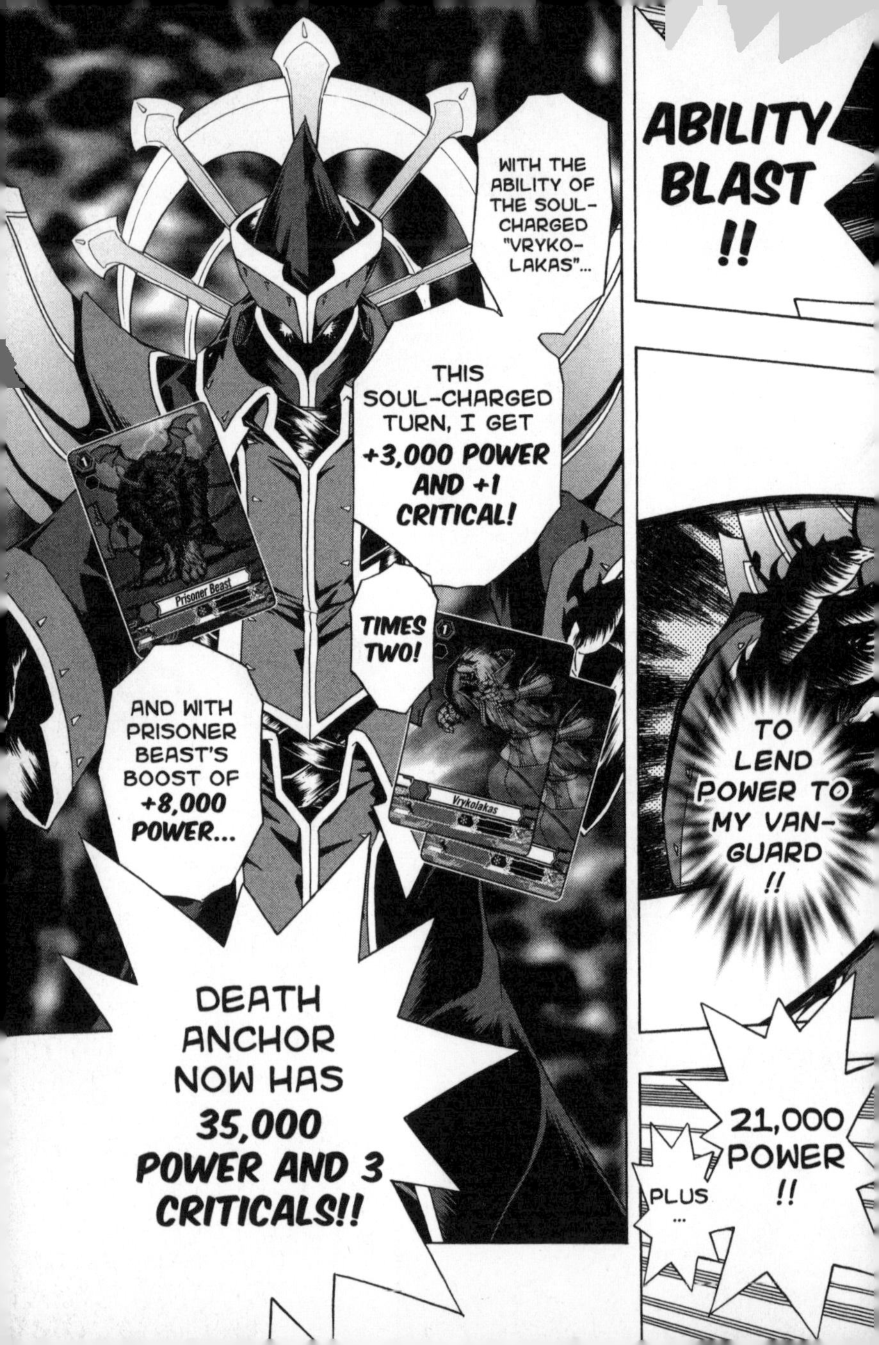
ABILITY BLAST!!
TO LEND POWER TO MY VAN-GUARD!!
21,000 POWER!!
PLUS...
WITH THE ABILITY OF THE SOUL-CHARGED "VRYKO-LAKAS"...
THIS SOUL-CHARGED TURN, I GET +3,000 POWER AND +1 CRITICAL!
TIMES TWO!
Vrykolakas
Prisoner Beast
AND WITH PRISONER BEAST'S BOOST OF +8,000 POWER...
DEATH ANCHOR NOW HAS 35,000 POWER AND 3 CRITICALS!!

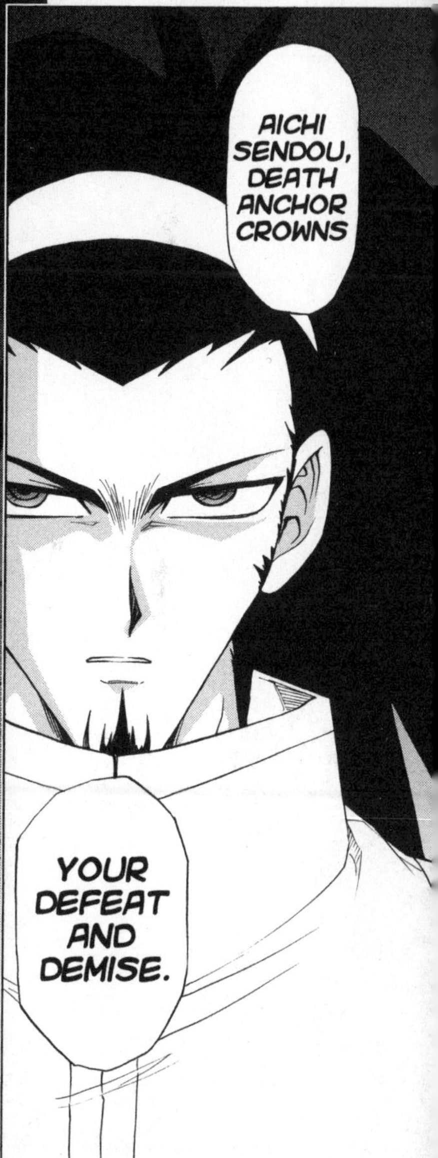
AICHI SENDOU, DEATH ANCHOR CROWNS
YOUR DEFEAT AND DEMISE.

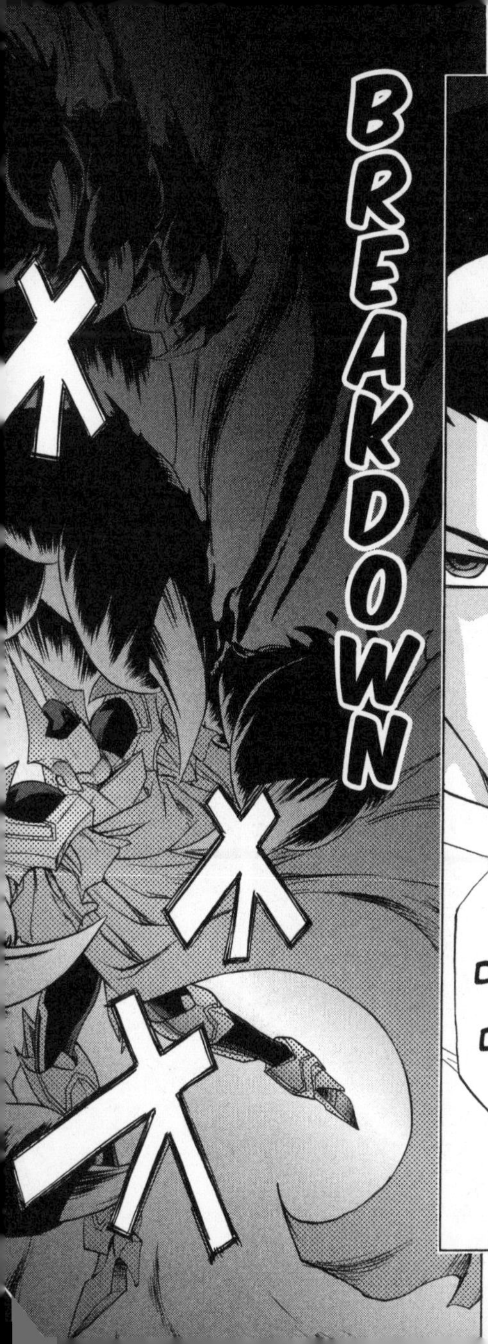
BREAKDOWN

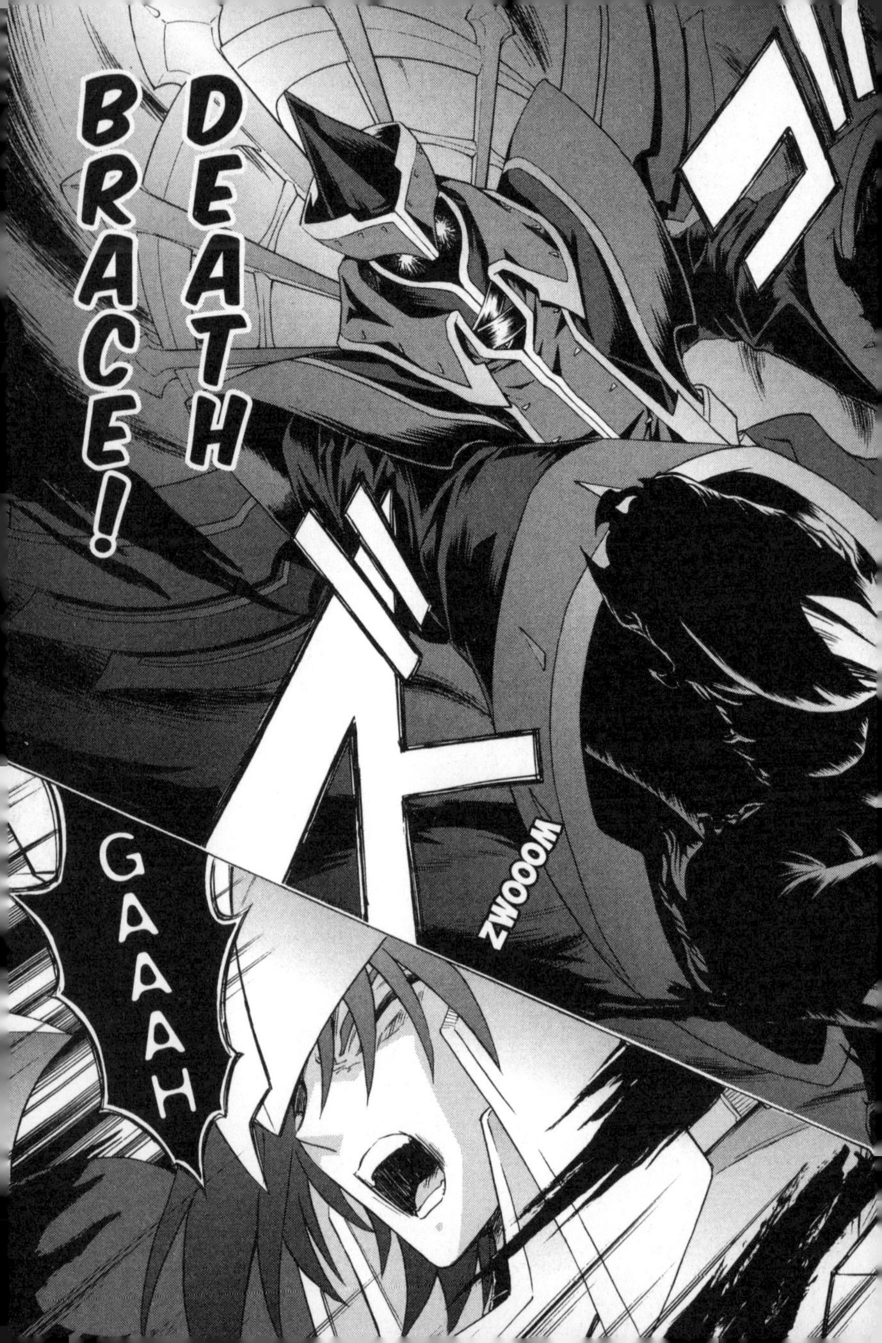
DEATH BRACE!
ZWOOOM
GAAAH

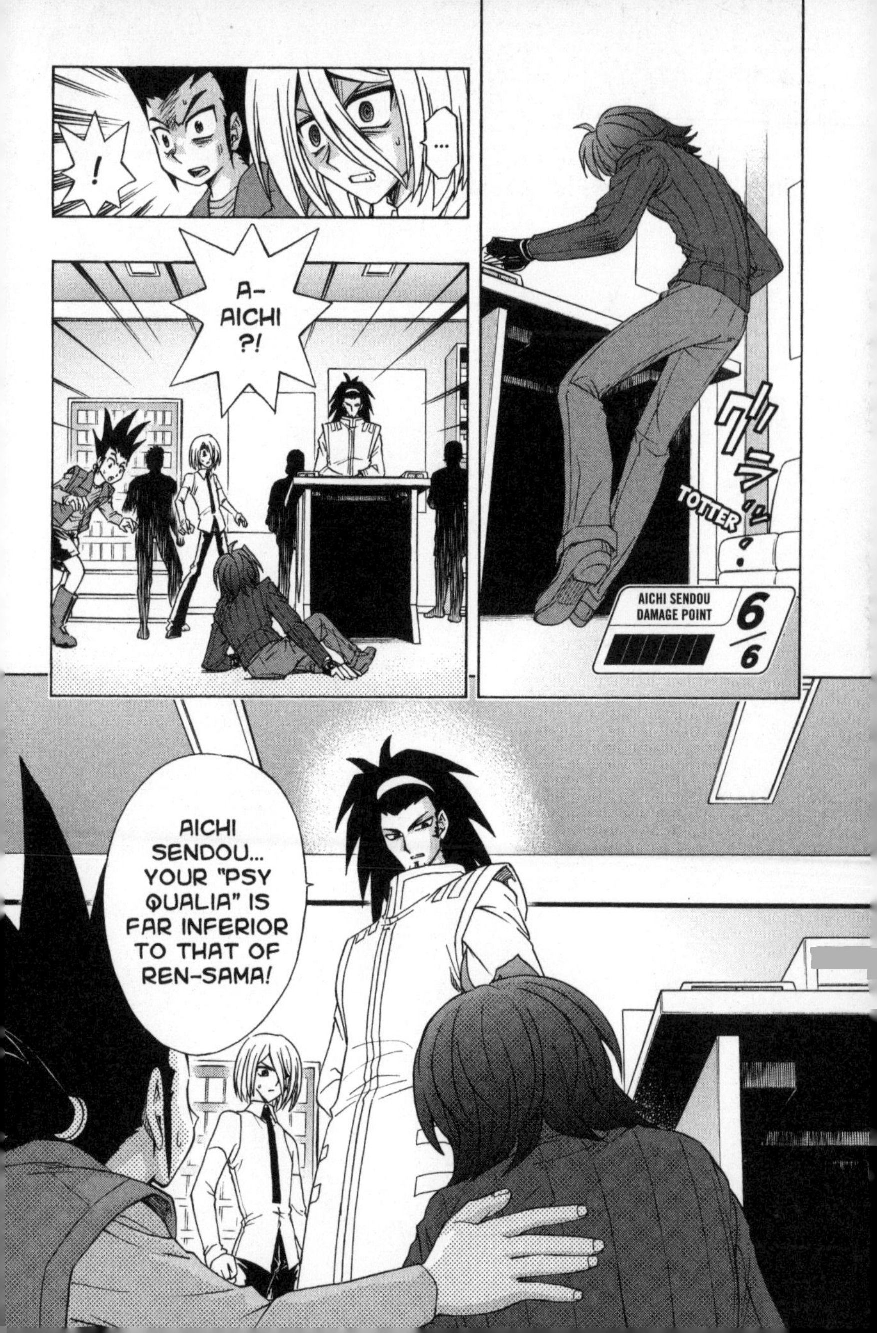

TOTTER
AICHI SENDOU DAMAGE POINT 6/6
...
!
A-AICHI ?!
AICHI SENDOU... YOUR "PSY QUALIA" IS FAR INFERIOR TO THAT OF REN-SAMA!

BONUS! CARDFIGHT!! Vanguard NEVER-BEFORE-SEEN IMAGE BOARDS

CHARACTERS

Three-Side Diagrams for Giant Figures

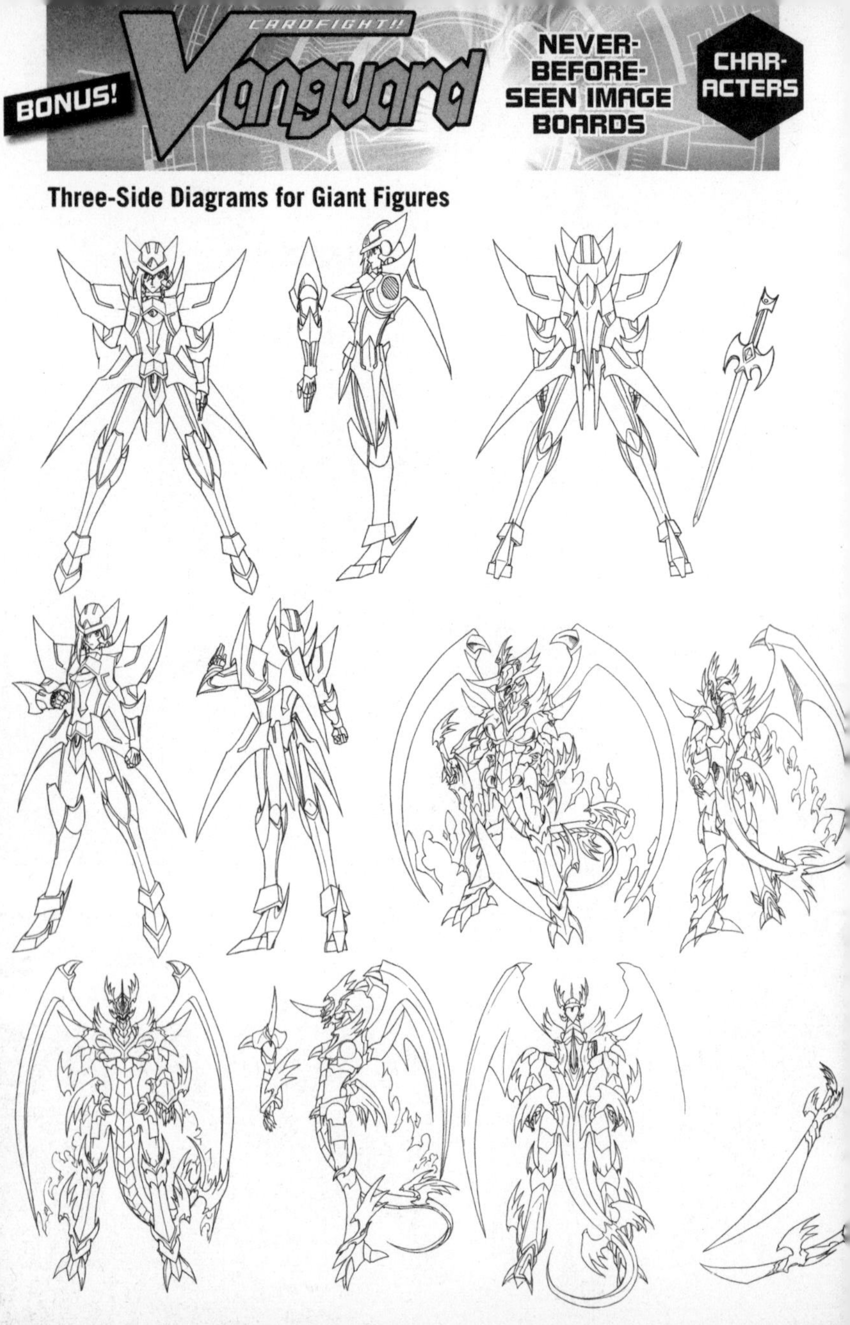

BONUS! CARDFIGHT!! Vanguard

NEVER-BEFORE-SEEN IMAGE BOARDS

CHARACTERS

New sketch

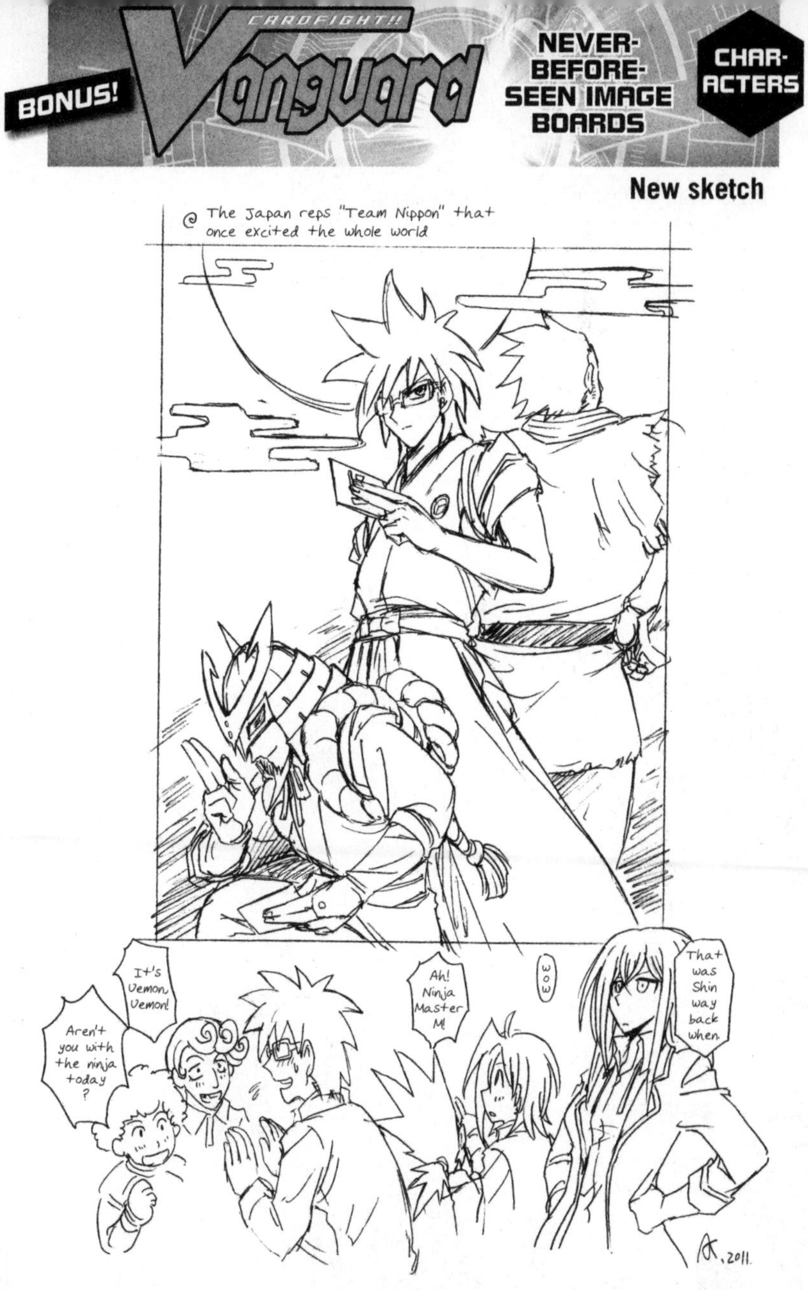

@ The Japan reps "Team Nippon" that once excited the whole world
That was Shin way back when.
wow
Ah! Ninja Master M!
It's Uemon, Uemon!
Aren't you with the ninja today?

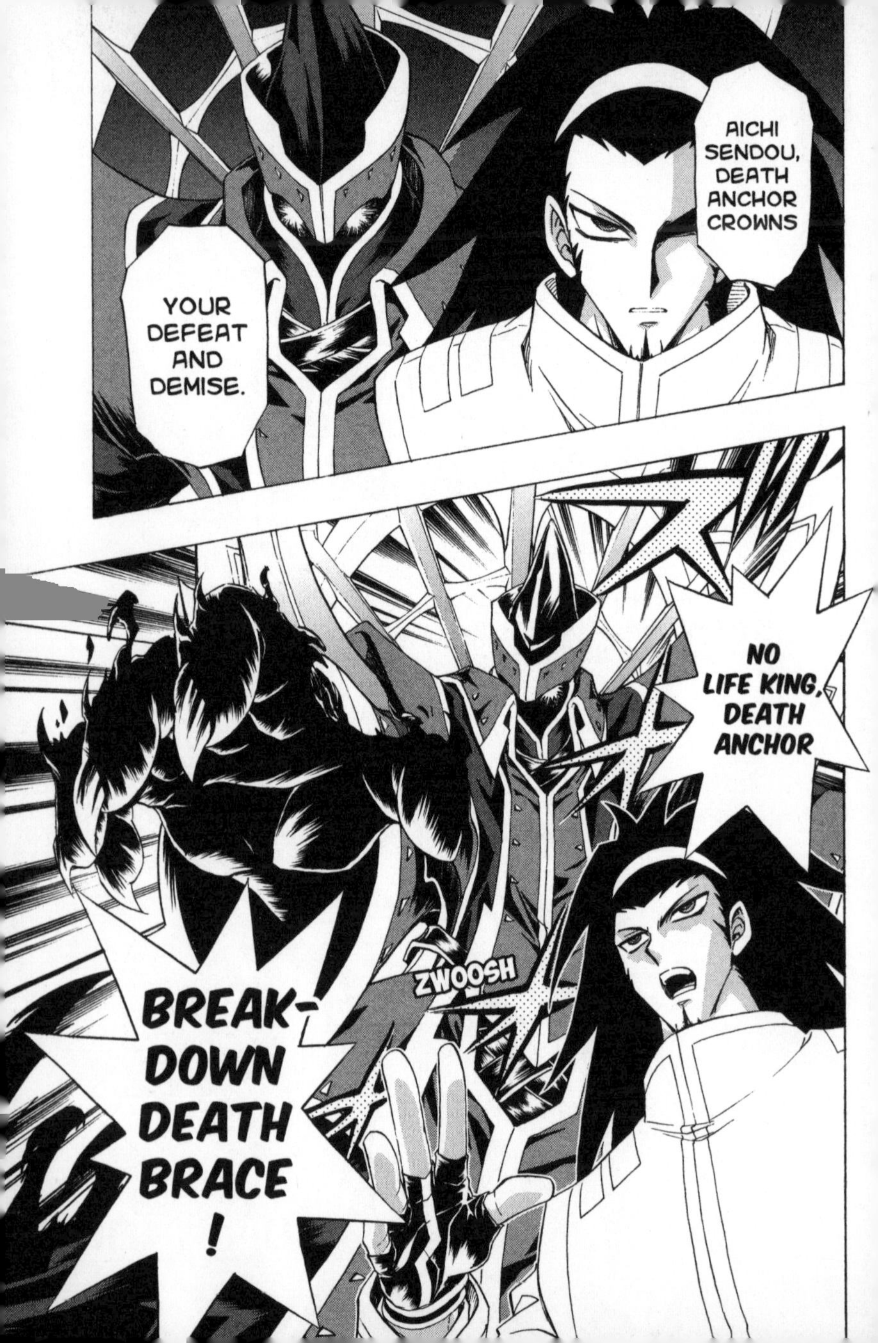
AICHI SENDOU, DEATH ANCHOR CROWNS
YOUR DEFEAT AND DEMISE.
NO LIFE KING, DEATH ANCHOR
ZWOOSH
BREAK-DOWN DEATH BRACE!

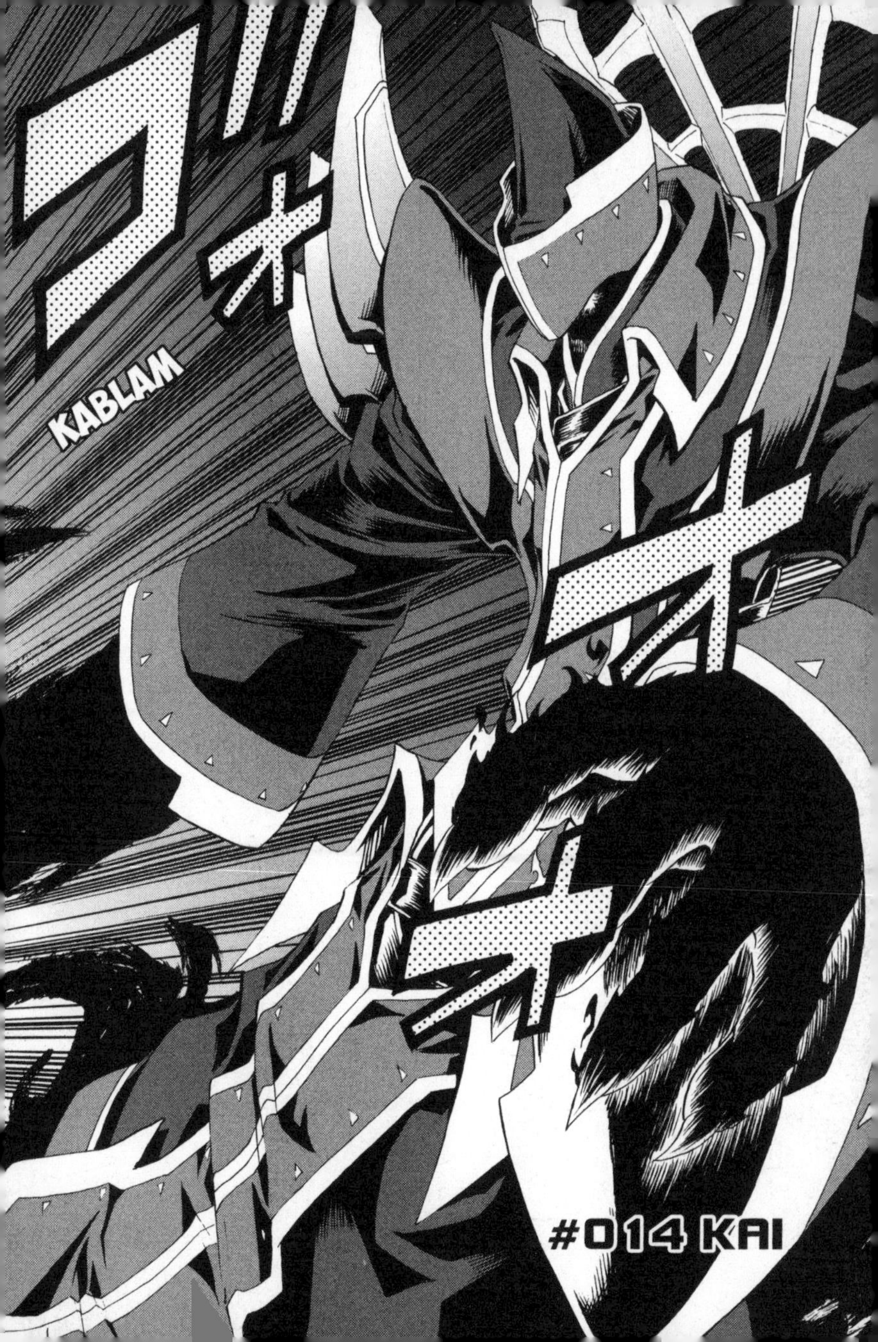
ゴオオオ
KABLAM
#014 KAI

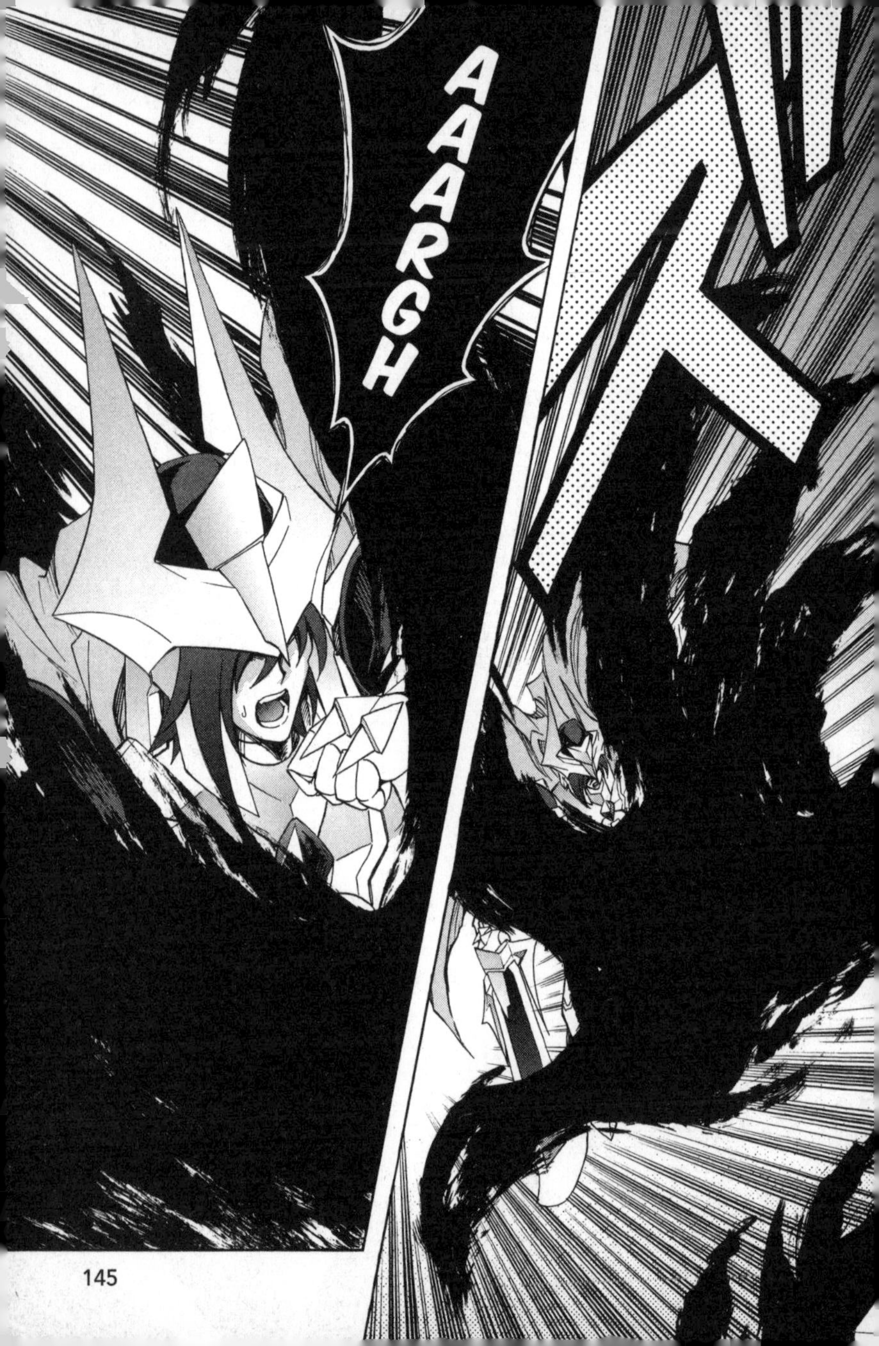
AAAARGH

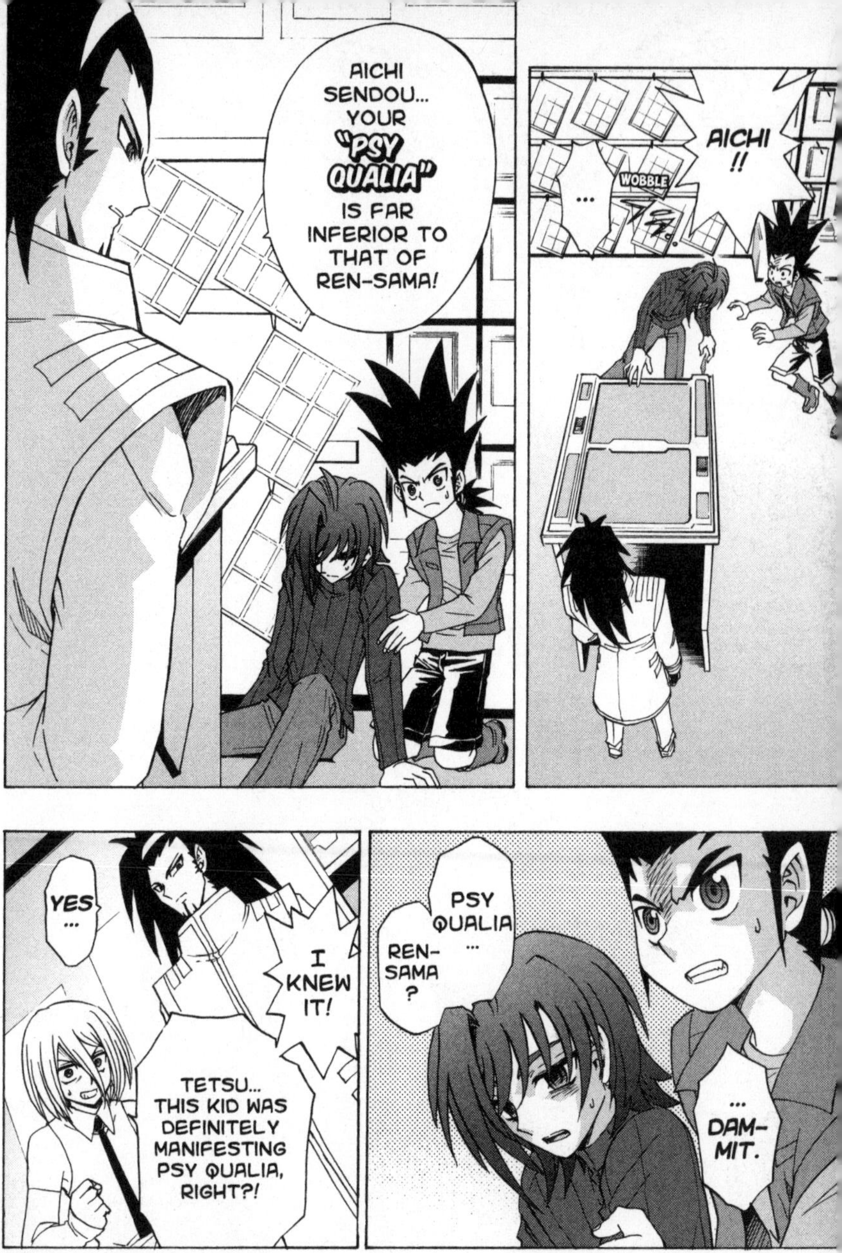
AICHI !!
WOBBLE
...
AICHI SENDOU... YOUR "PSY QUALIA" IS FAR INFERIOR TO THAT OF REN-SAMA!
PSY QUALIA ...
REN-SAMA ?
... DAM-MIT.
YES ...
I KNEW IT!
TETSU... THIS KID WAS DEFINITELY MANIFESTING PSY QUALIA, RIGHT?!

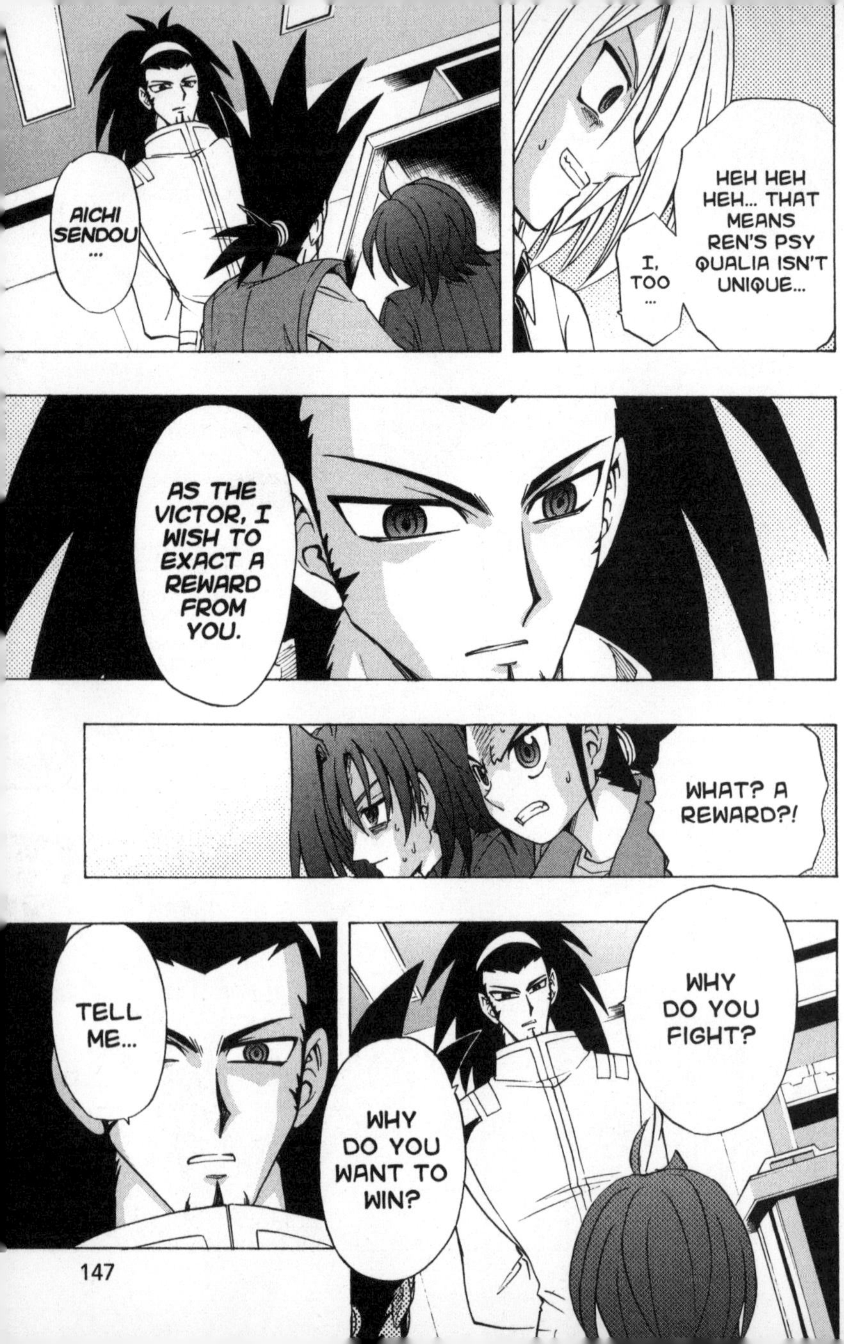
HEH HEH HEH... THAT MEANS REN'S PSY QUALIA ISN'T UNIQUE...
I, TOO ...
AICHI SENDOU ...
AS THE VICTOR, I WISH TO EXACT A REWARD FROM YOU.
WHAT? A REWARD?!
WHY DO YOU FIGHT?
WHY DO YOU WANT TO WIN?
TELL ME...

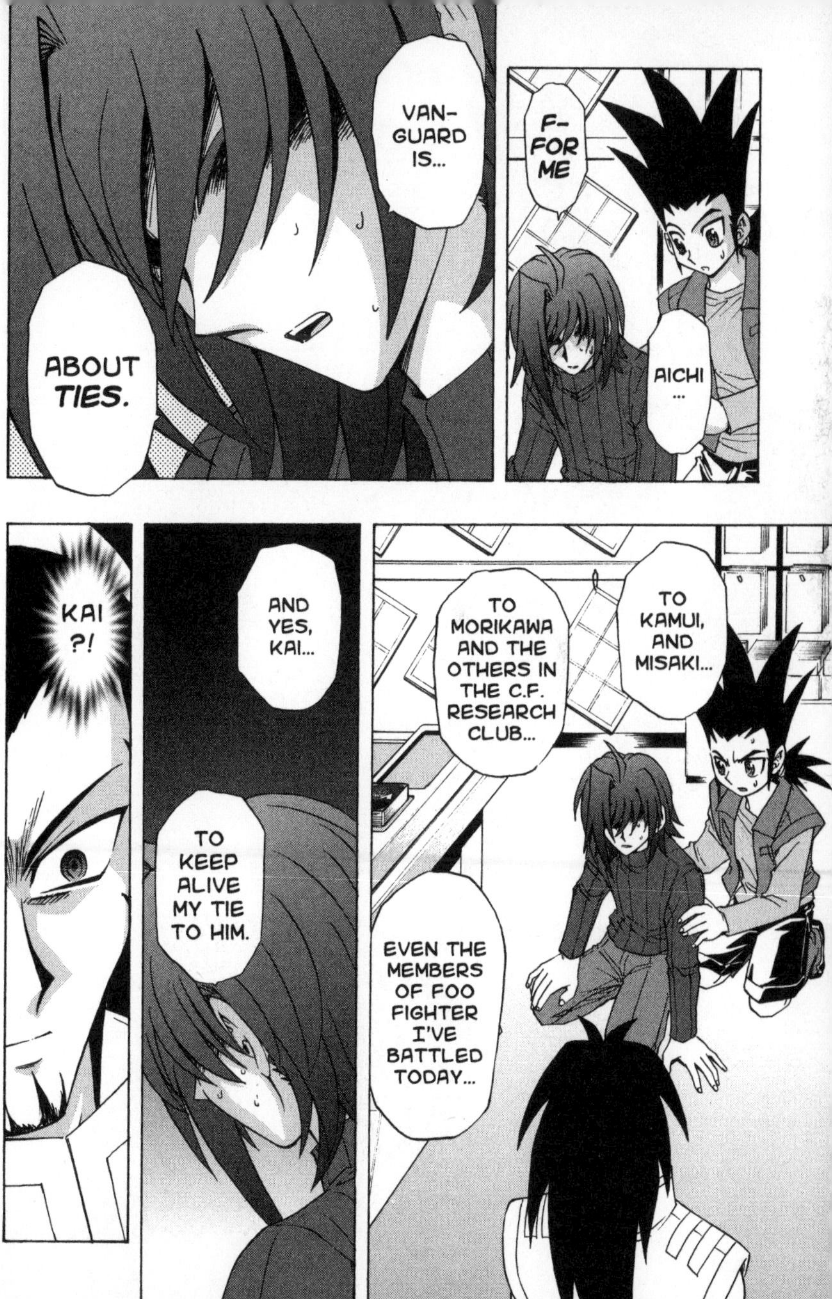

F-FOR ME
AICHI...
VAN-GUARD IS...
ABOUT TIES.
TO KAMUI, AND MISAKI...
TO MORIKAWA AND THE OTHERS IN THE C.F. RESEARCH CLUB...
EVEN THE MEMBERS OF FOO FIGHTER I'VE BATTLED TODAY...
AND YES, KAI...
TO KEEP ALIVE MY TIE TO HIM.
KAI?!

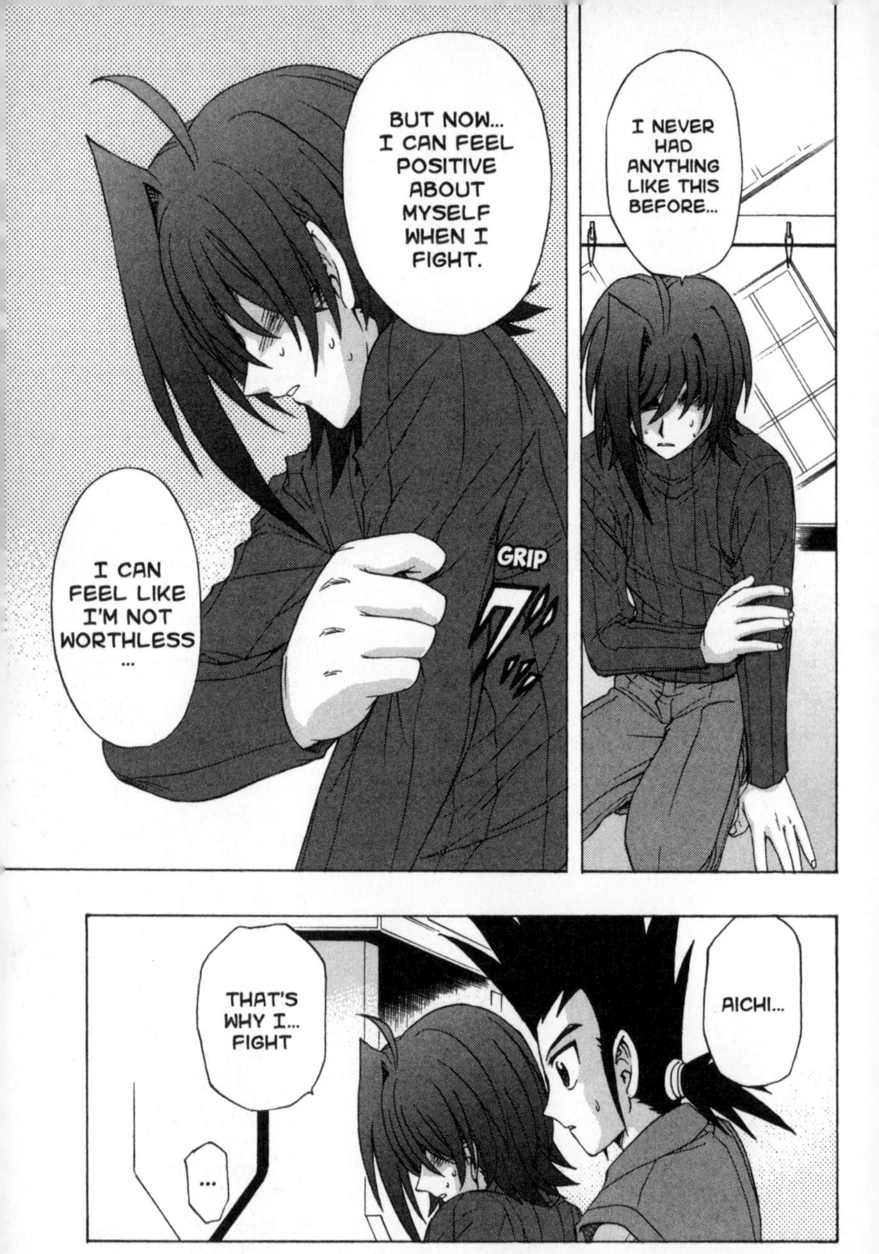
I NEVER HAD ANYTHING LIKE THIS BEFORE...
BUT NOW... I CAN FEEL POSITIVE ABOUT MYSELF WHEN I FIGHT.
GRIP
I CAN FEEL LIKE I'M NOT WORTHLESS...
AICHI...
THAT'S WHY I... FIGHT
...

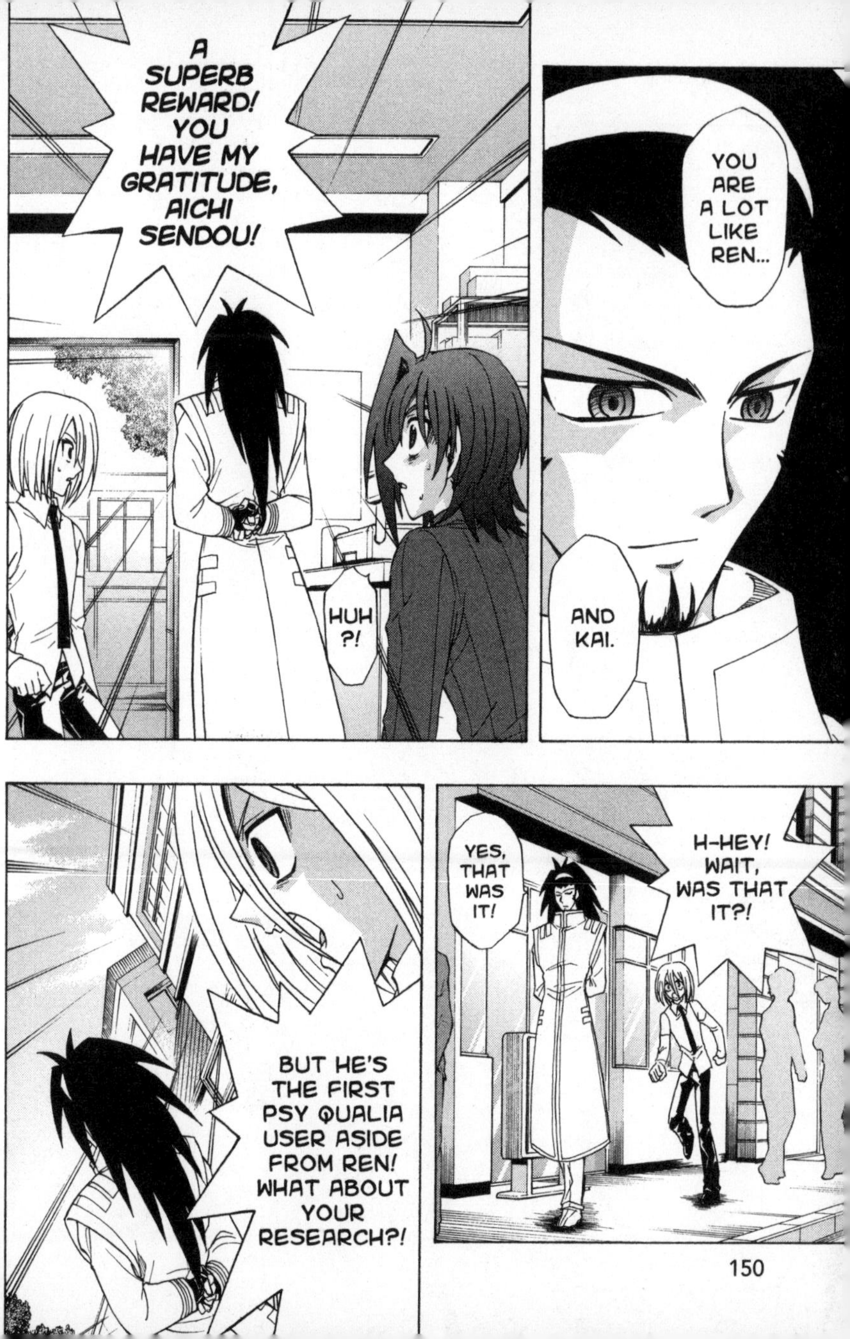
YOU ARE A LOT LIKE REN...
AND KAI.
A SUPERB REWARD! YOU HAVE MY GRATITUDE, AICHI SENDOU!
HUH?!
H-HEY! WAIT, WAS THAT IT?!
YES, THAT WAS IT!
BUT HE'S THE FIRST PSY QUALIA USER ASIDE FROM REN! WHAT ABOUT YOUR RESEARCH?!

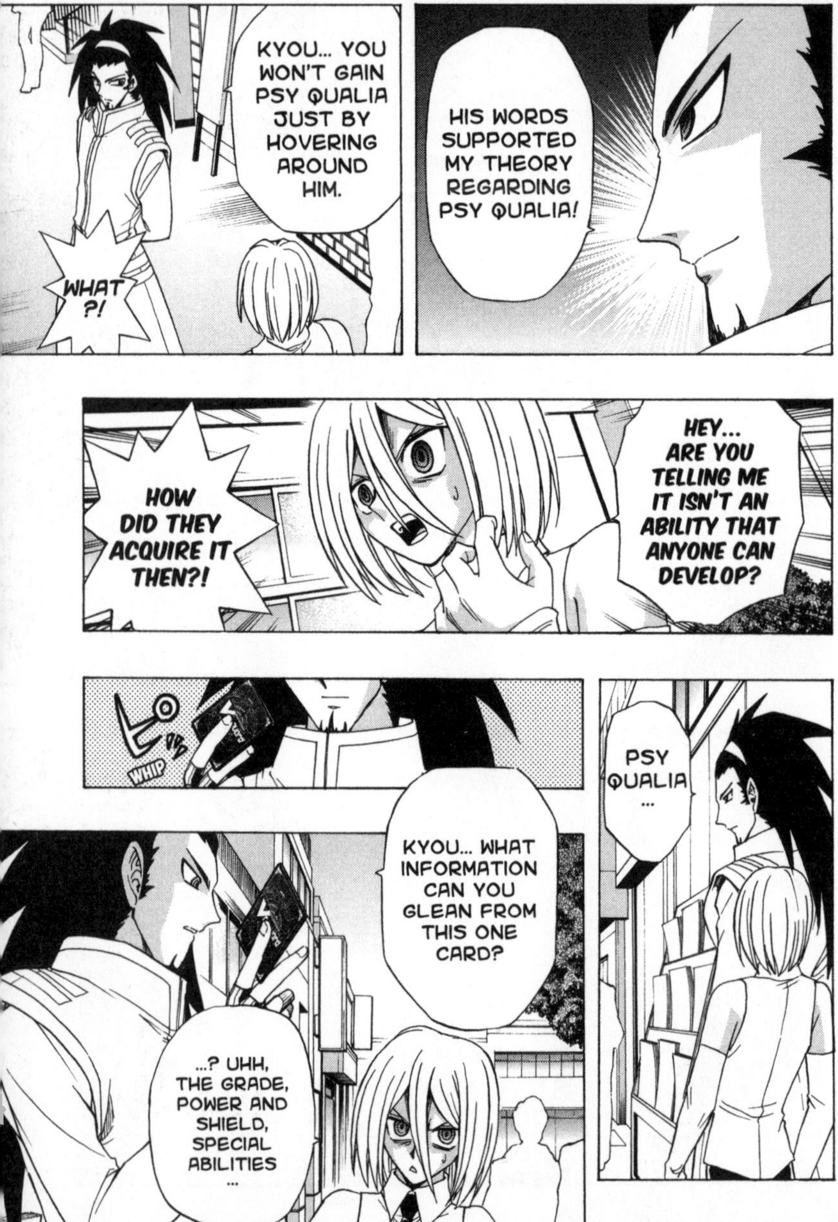
HIS WORDS SUPPORTED MY THEORY REGARDING PSY QUALIA!
KYOU... YOU WON'T GAIN PSY QUALIA JUST BY HOVERING AROUND HIM.
WHAT?!
HEY... ARE YOU TELLING ME IT ISN'T AN ABILITY THAT ANYONE CAN DEVELOP?
HOW DID THEY ACQUIRE IT THEN?!
PSY QUALIA...
WHIP
KYOU... WHAT INFORMATION CAN YOU GLEAN FROM THIS ONE CARD?
...? UHH, THE GRADE, POWER AND SHIELD, SPECIAL ABILITIES...

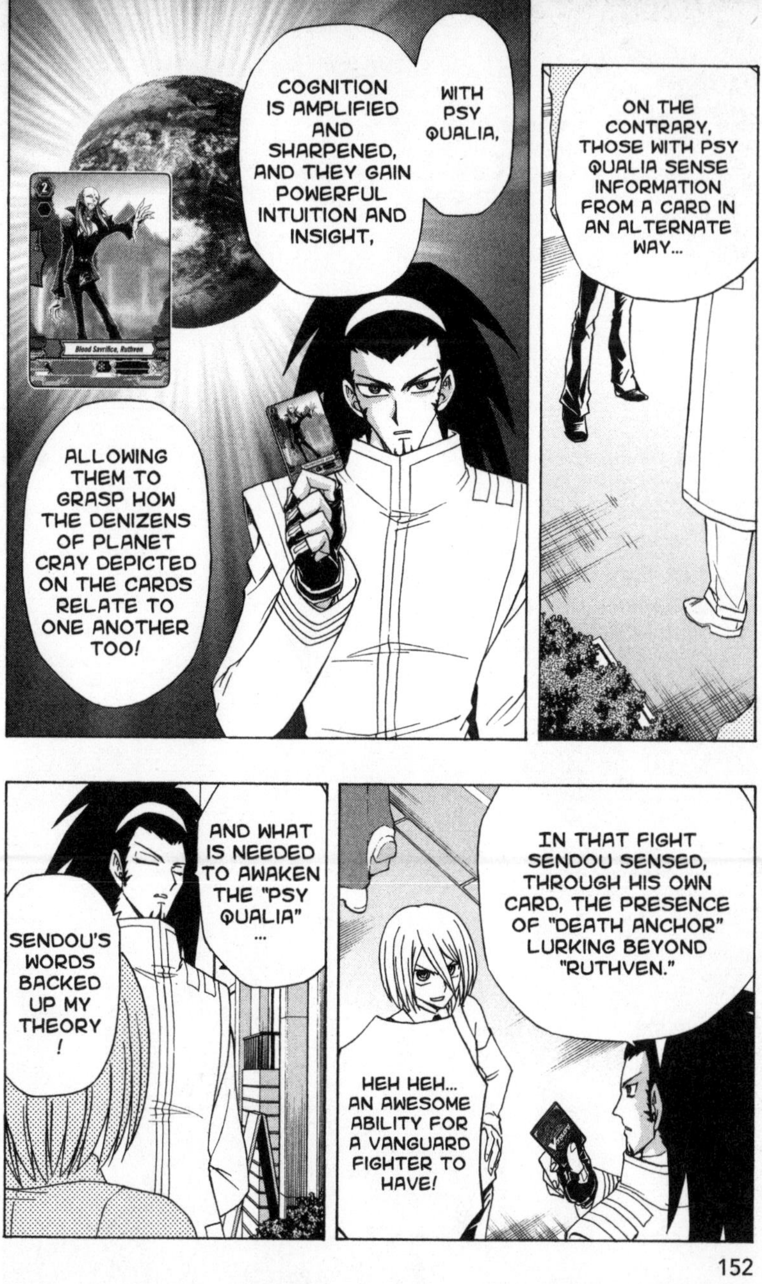
ON THE CONTRARY, THOSE WITH PSY QUALIA SENSE INFORMATION FROM A CARD IN AN ALTERNATE WAY...
WITH PSY QUALIA,
COGNITION IS AMPLIFIED AND SHARPENED, AND THEY GAIN POWERFUL INTUITION AND INSIGHT,
Blood Savrifice, Ruthven
ALLOWING THEM TO GRASP HOW THE DENIZENS OF PLANET CRAY DEPICTED ON THE CARDS RELATE TO ONE ANOTHER TOO!
IN THAT FIGHT SENDOU SENSED, THROUGH HIS OWN CARD, THE PRESENCE OF "DEATH ANCHOR" LURKING BEYOND "RUTHVEN."
HEH HEH... AN AWESOME ABILITY FOR A VANGUARD FIGHTER TO HAVE!
AND WHAT IS NEEDED TO AWAKEN THE "PSY QUALIA" ...
SENDOU'S WORDS BACKED UP MY THEORY !

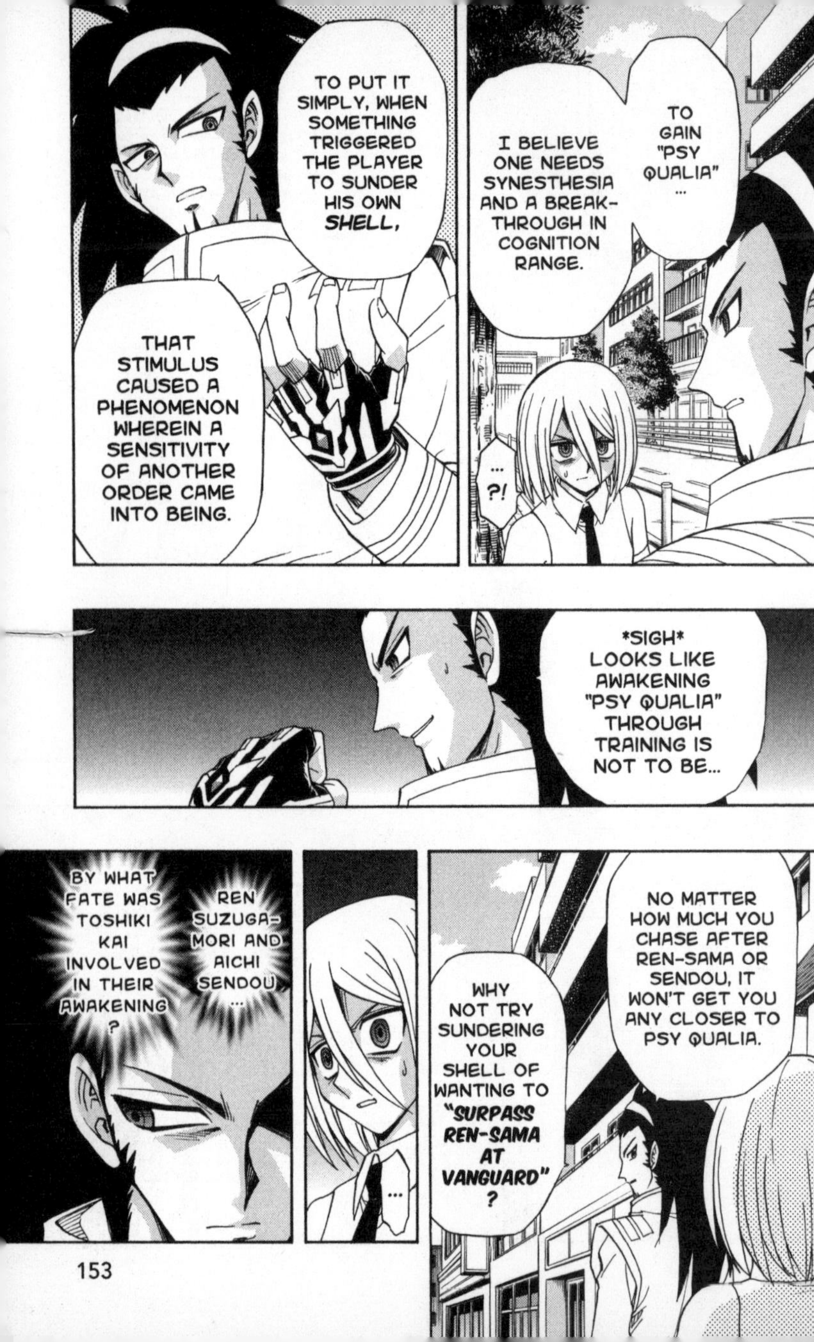

TO GAIN "PSY QUALIA" ...
I BELIEVE ONE NEEDS SYNESTHESIA AND A BREAK-THROUGH IN COGNITION RANGE.
... ?!
TO PUT IT SIMPLY, WHEN SOMETHING TRIGGERED THE PLAYER TO SUNDER HIS OWN SHELL,
THAT STIMULUS CAUSED A PHENOMENON WHEREIN A SENSITIVITY OF ANOTHER ORDER CAME INTO BEING.
SIGH LOOKS LIKE AWAKENING "PSY QUALIA" THROUGH TRAINING IS NOT TO BE...
NO MATTER HOW MUCH YOU CHASE AFTER REN-SAMA OR SENDOU, IT WON'T GET YOU ANY CLOSER TO PSY QUALIA.
WHY NOT TRY SUNDERING YOUR SHELL OF WANTING TO "SURPASS REN-SAMA AT VANGUARD" ?
...
REN SUZUGA-MORI AND AICHI SENDOU ...
BY WHAT FATE WAS TOSHIKI KAI INVOLVED IN THEIR AWAKENING ?

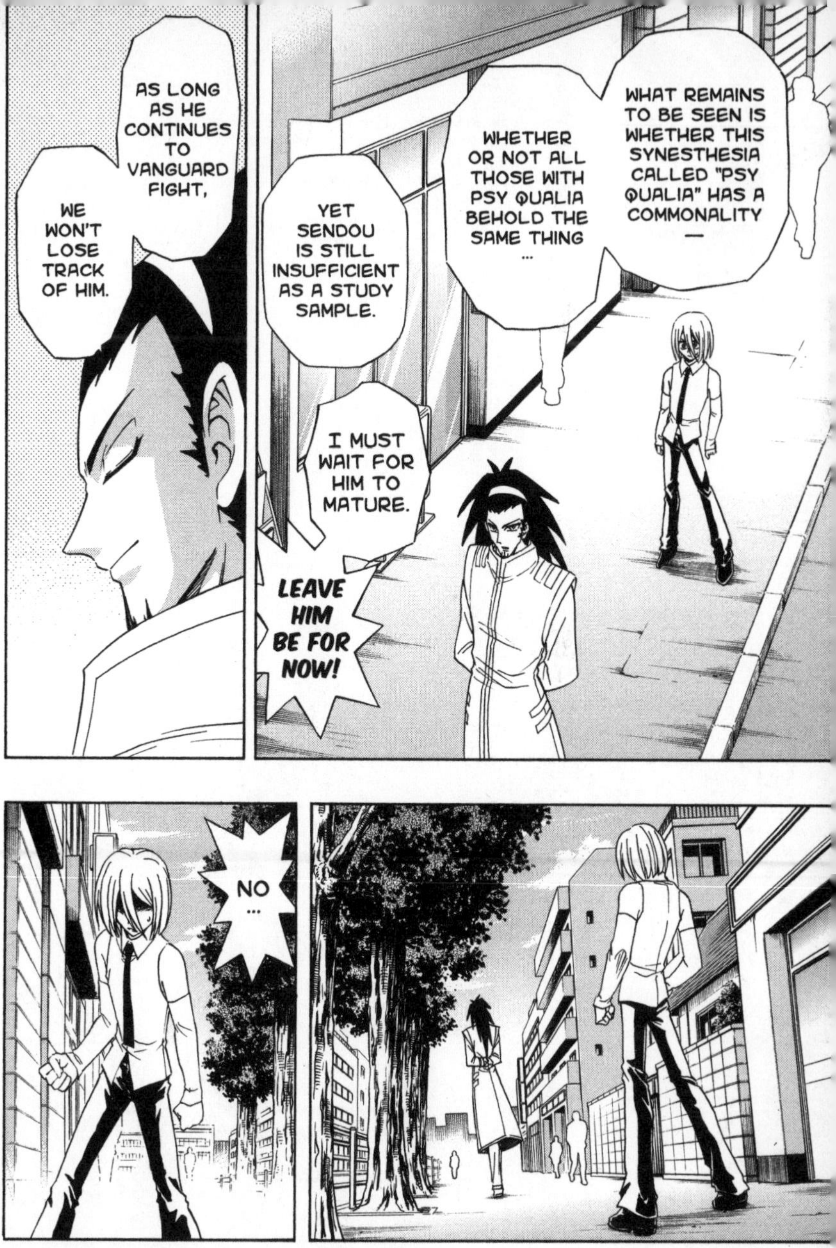
WHAT REMAINS TO BE SEEN IS WHETHER THIS SYNESTHESIA CALLED "PSY QUALIA" HAS A COMMONALITY —
WHETHER OR NOT ALL THOSE WITH PSY QUALIA BEHOLD THE SAME THING ...
YET SENDOU IS STILL INSUFFICIENT AS A STUDY SAMPLE.
I MUST WAIT FOR HIM TO MATURE.
LEAVE HIM BE FOR NOW!
AS LONG AS HE CONTINUES TO VANGUARD FIGHT,
WE WON'T LOSE TRACK OF HIM.
NO ...

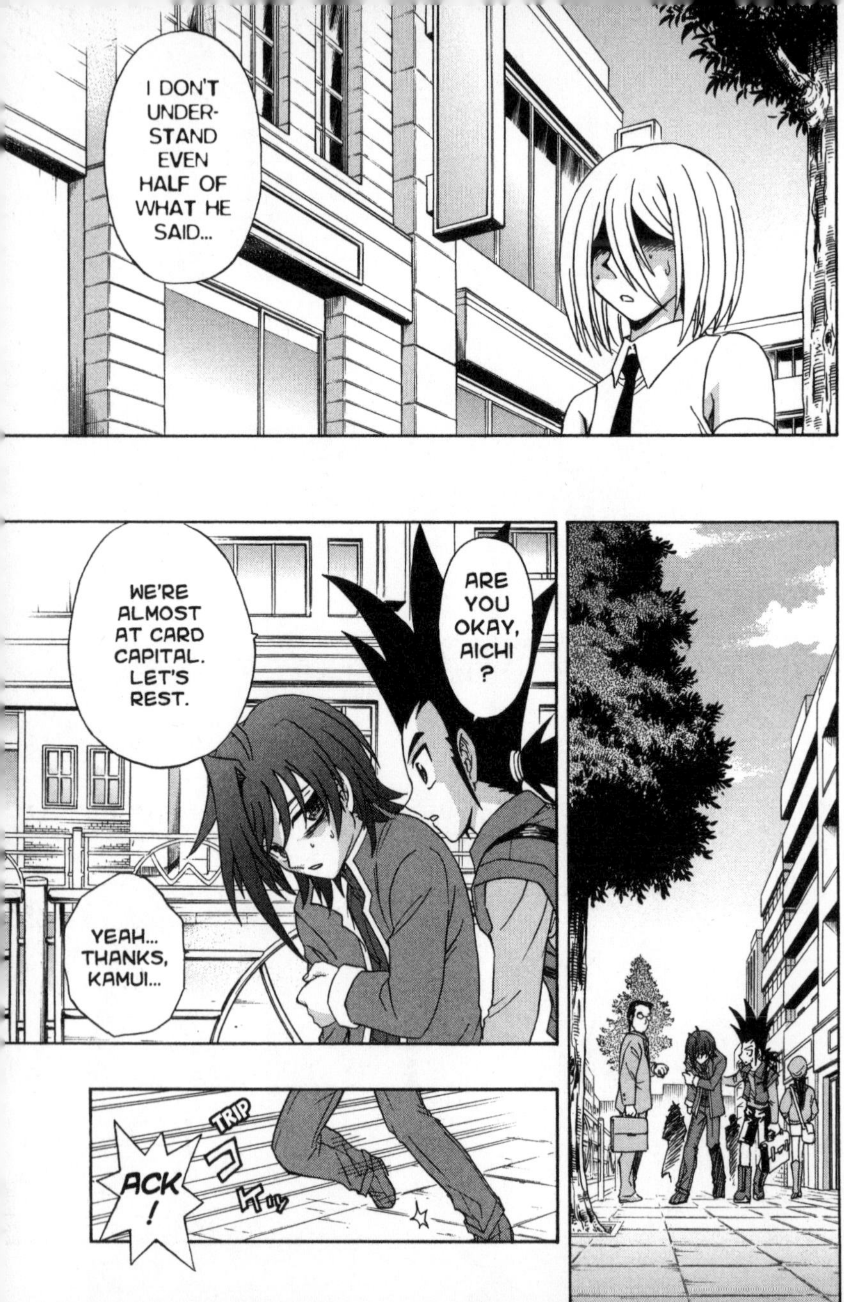
I DON'T UNDER-STAND EVEN HALF OF WHAT HE SAID...
ARE YOU OKAY, AICHI?
WE'RE ALMOST AT CARD CAPITAL. LET'S REST.
YEAH... THANKS, KAMUI...
TRIP
ACK!

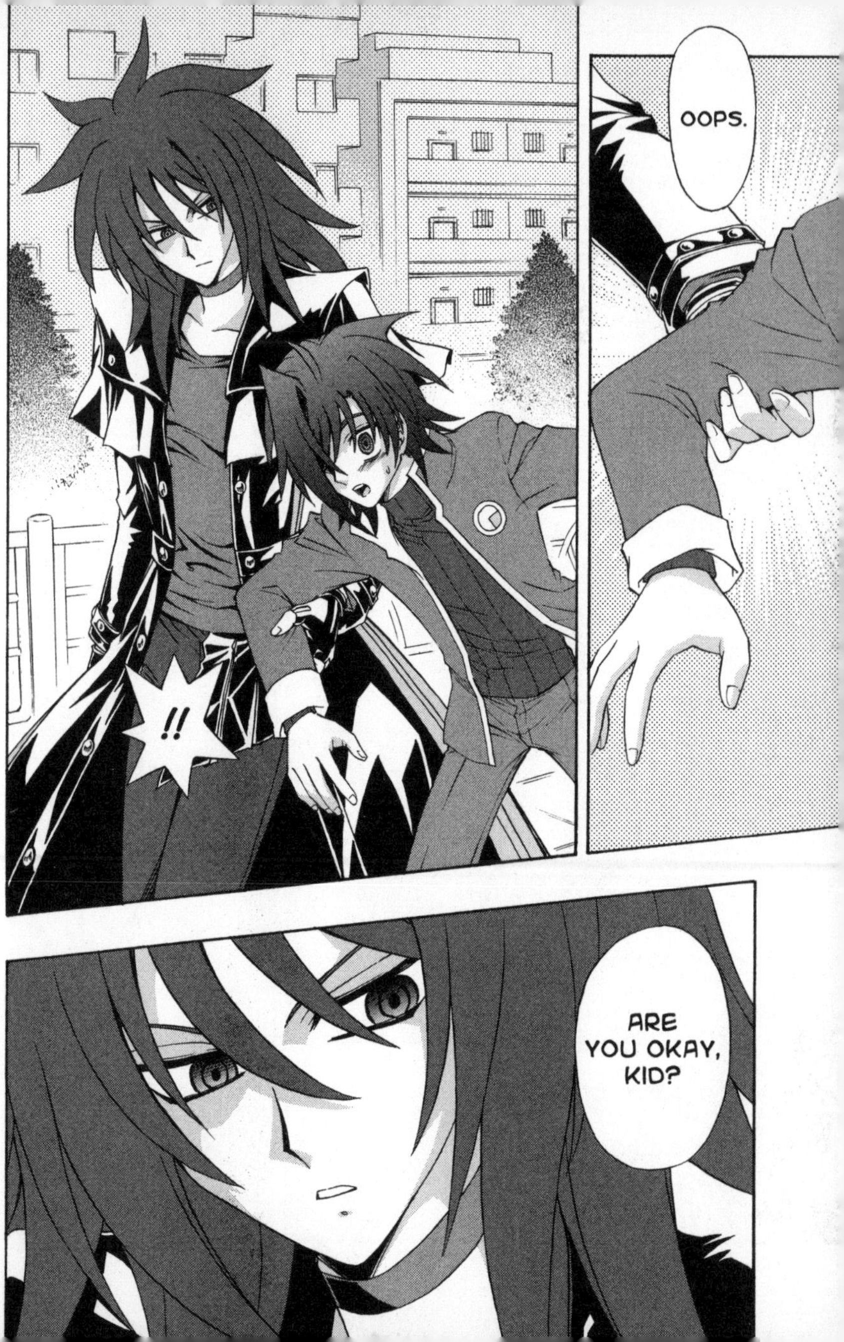
OOPS.
!!
ARE YOU OKAY, KID?

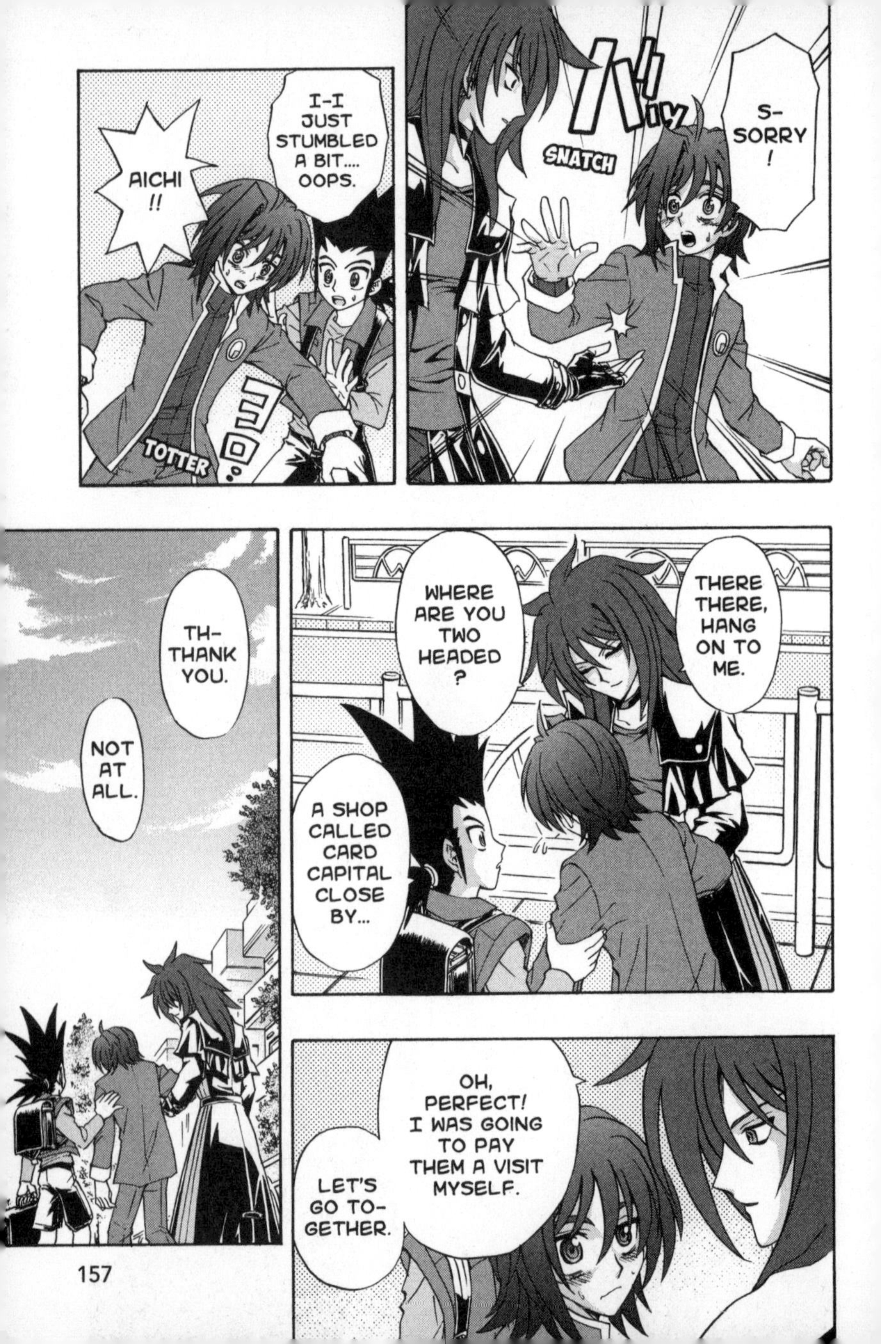
S-SORRY!
SNATCH
I-I JUST STUMBLED A BIT.... OOPS.
AICHI!!
TOTTER
THERE THERE, HANG ON TO ME.
WHERE ARE YOU TWO HEADED?
A SHOP CALLED CARD CAPITAL CLOSE BY...
OH, PERFECT! I WAS GOING TO PAY THEM A VISIT MYSELF.
LET'S GO TO-GETHER.
TH-THANK YOU.
NOT AT ALL.

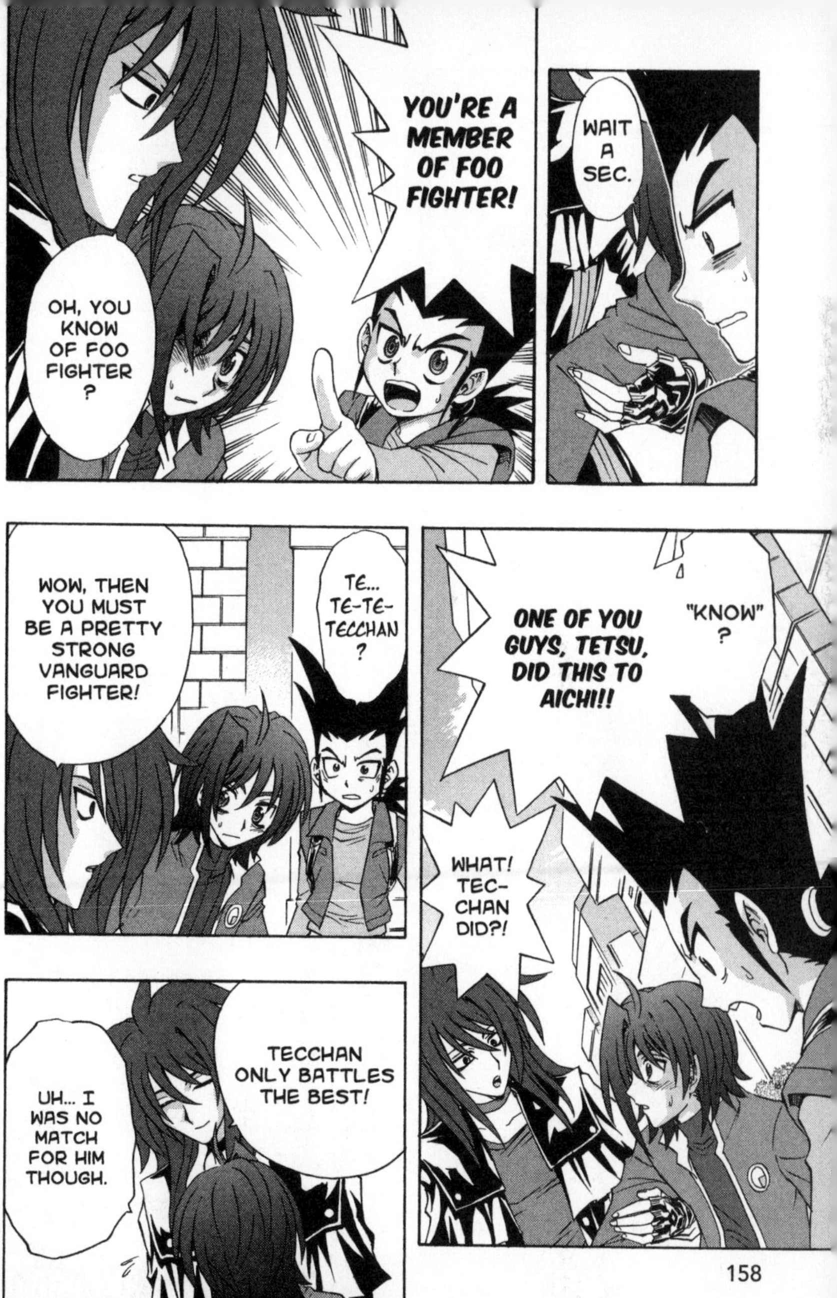
WAIT A SEC.
YOU'RE A MEMBER OF FOO FIGHTER!
OH, YOU KNOW OF FOO FIGHTER?
"KNOW"?
ONE OF YOU GUYS, TETSU, DID THIS TO AICHI!!
WHAT! TEC-CHAN DID?!
TE... TE-TE-TECCHAN?
WOW, THEN YOU MUST BE A PRETTY STRONG VANGUARD FIGHTER!
TECCHAN ONLY BATTLES THE BEST!
UH... I WAS NO MATCH FOR HIM THOUGH.

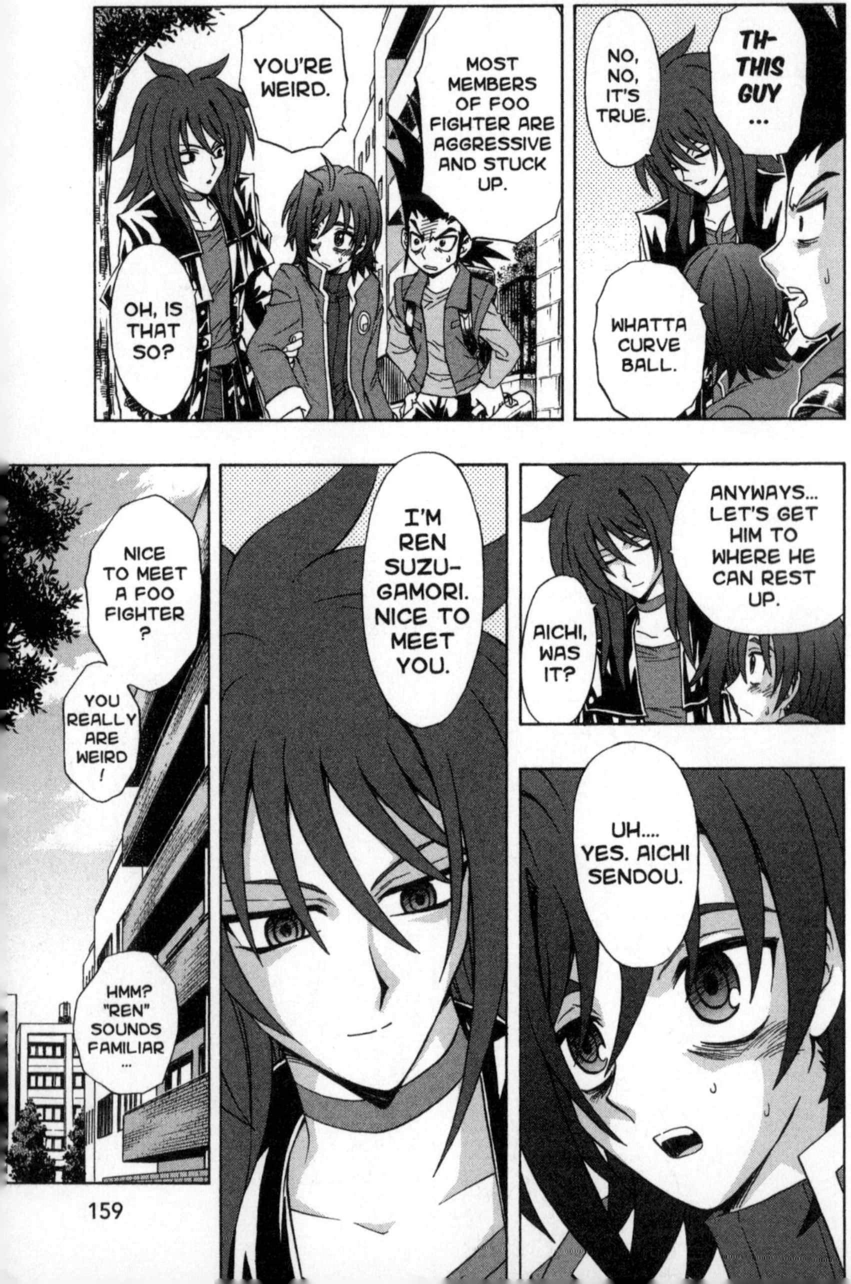
TH-THIS GUY ...
NO, NO, IT'S TRUE.
WHATTA CURVE BALL.
MOST MEMBERS OF FOO FIGHTER ARE AGGRESSIVE AND STUCK UP.
YOU'RE WEIRD.
OH, IS THAT SO?
ANYWAYS... LET'S GET HIM TO WHERE HE CAN REST UP.
AICHI, WAS IT?
UH.... YES. AICHI SENDOU.
I'M REN SUZU-GAMORI. NICE TO MEET YOU.
NICE TO MEET A FOO FIGHTER ?
YOU REALLY ARE WEIRD !
HMM? "REN" SOUNDS FAMILIAR ...

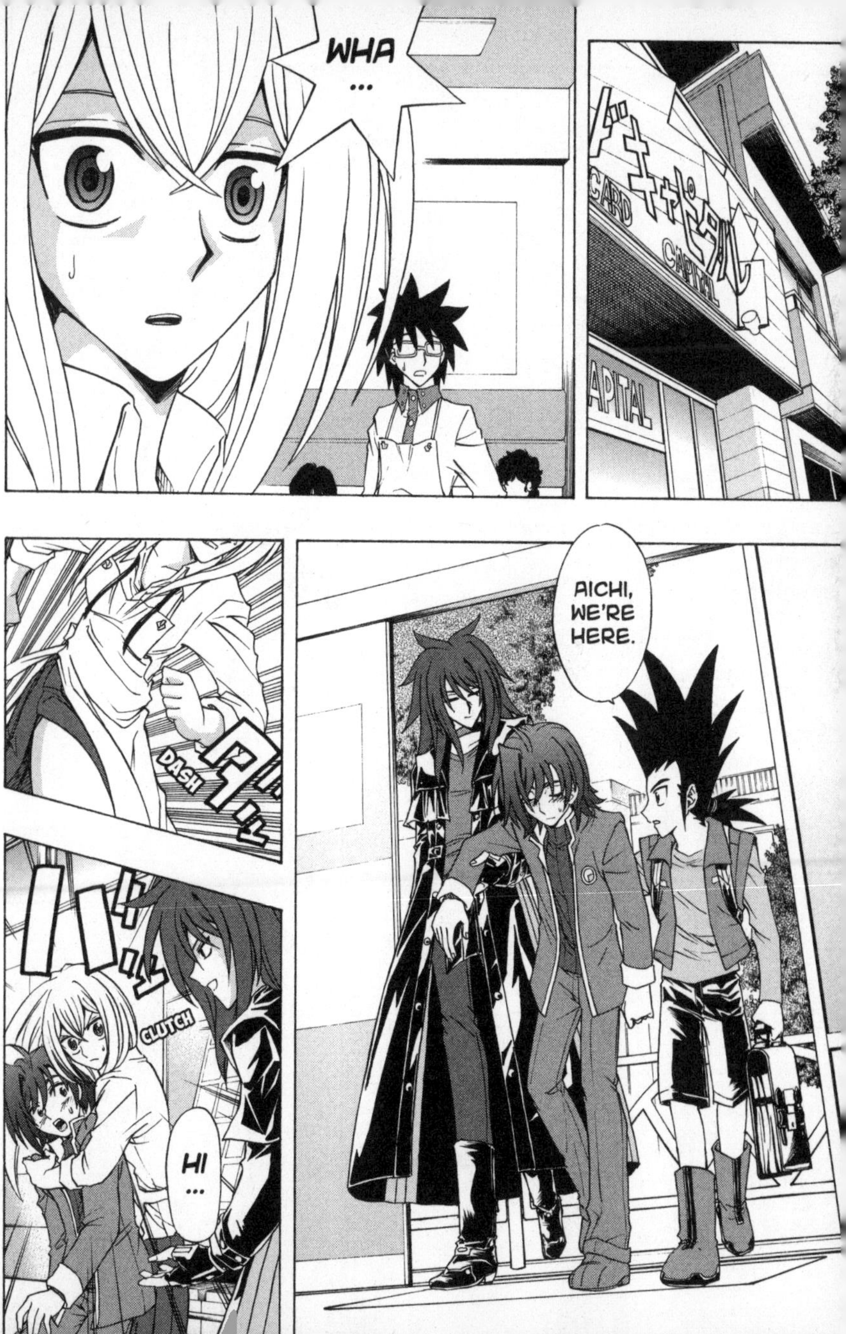
CARD CAPITAL
WHA ...
AICHI, WE'RE HERE.
DASH
CLUTCH
HI ...

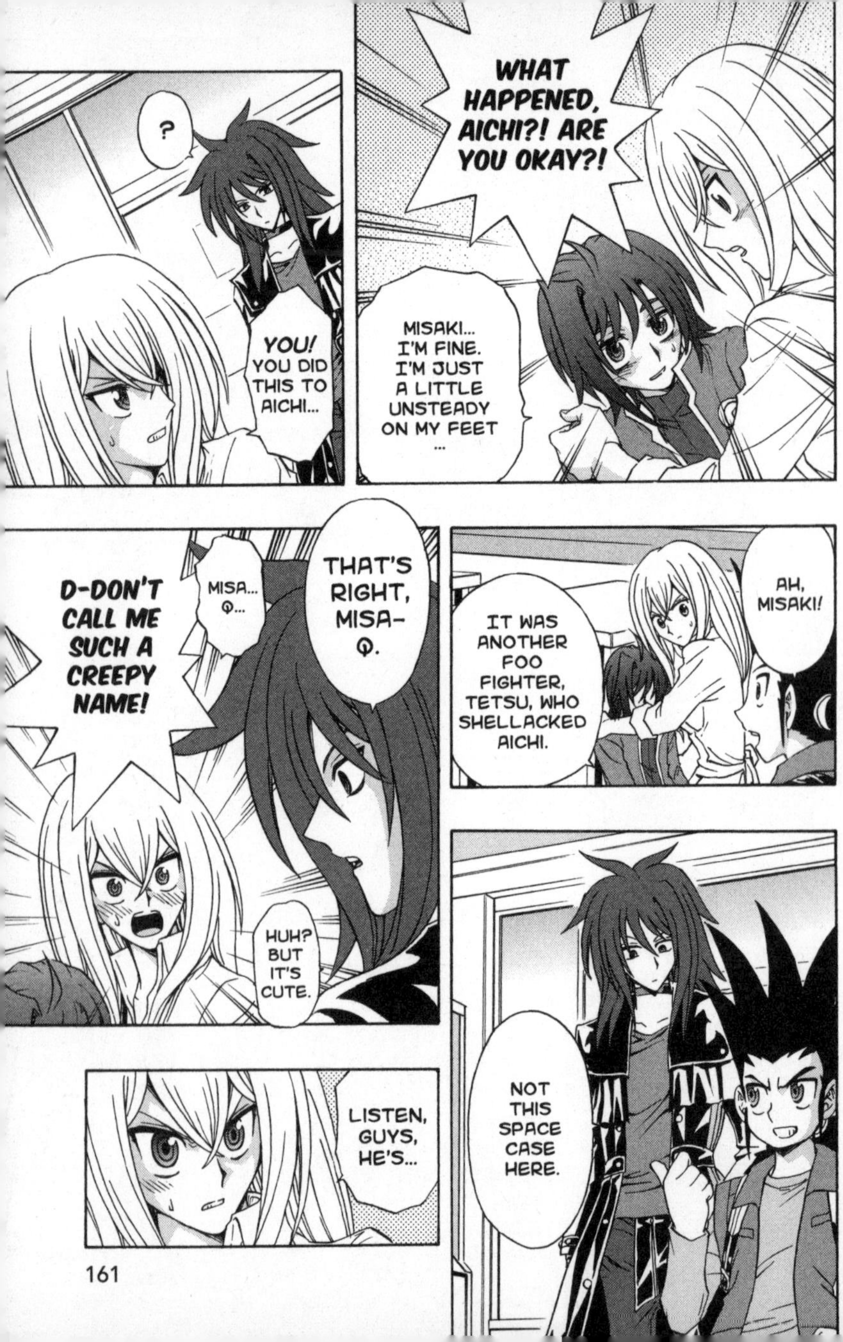
WHAT HAPPENED, AICHI?! ARE YOU OKAY?!
MISAKI... I'M FINE. I'M JUST A LITTLE UNSTEADY ON MY FEET ...
?
YOU! YOU DID THIS TO AICHI...
AH, MISAKI!
IT WAS ANOTHER FOO FIGHTER, TETSU, WHO SHELLACKED AICHI.
NOT THIS SPACE CASE HERE.
THAT'S RIGHT, MISA-Q.
MISA... Q...
D-DON'T CALL ME SUCH A CREEPY NAME!
HUH? BUT IT'S CUTE.
LISTEN, GUYS, HE'S...

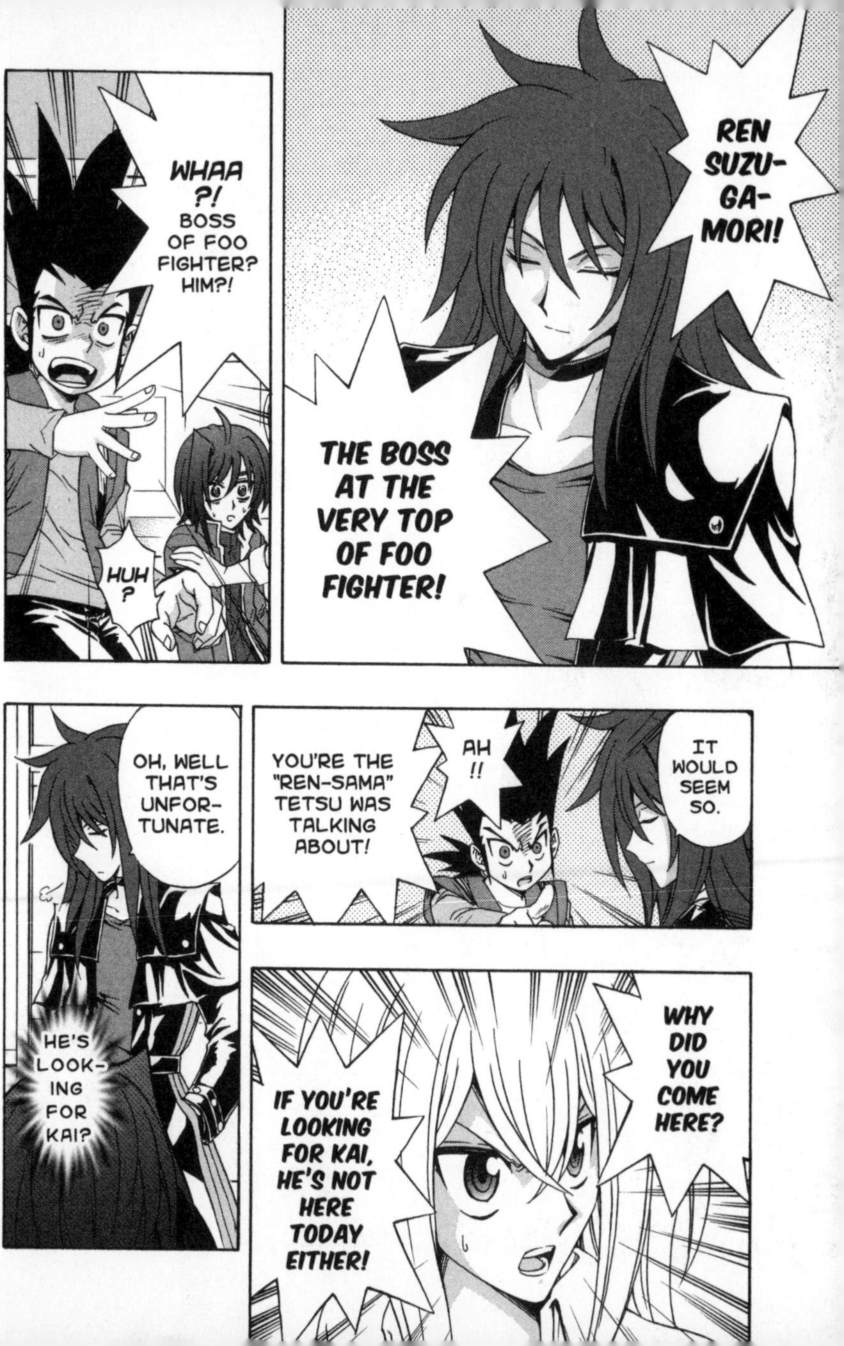
REN SUZU-GA-MORI!
THE BOSS AT THE VERY TOP OF FOO FIGHTER!
WHAA?! BOSS OF FOO FIGHTER? HIM?!
HUH?
IT WOULD SEEM SO.
AH!!
YOU'RE THE "REN-SAMA" TETSU WAS TALKING ABOUT!
WHY DID YOU COME HERE?
IF YOU'RE LOOKING FOR KAI, HE'S NOT HERE TODAY EITHER!
OH, WELL THAT'S UNFORTUNATE.
HE'S LOOKING FOR KAI?

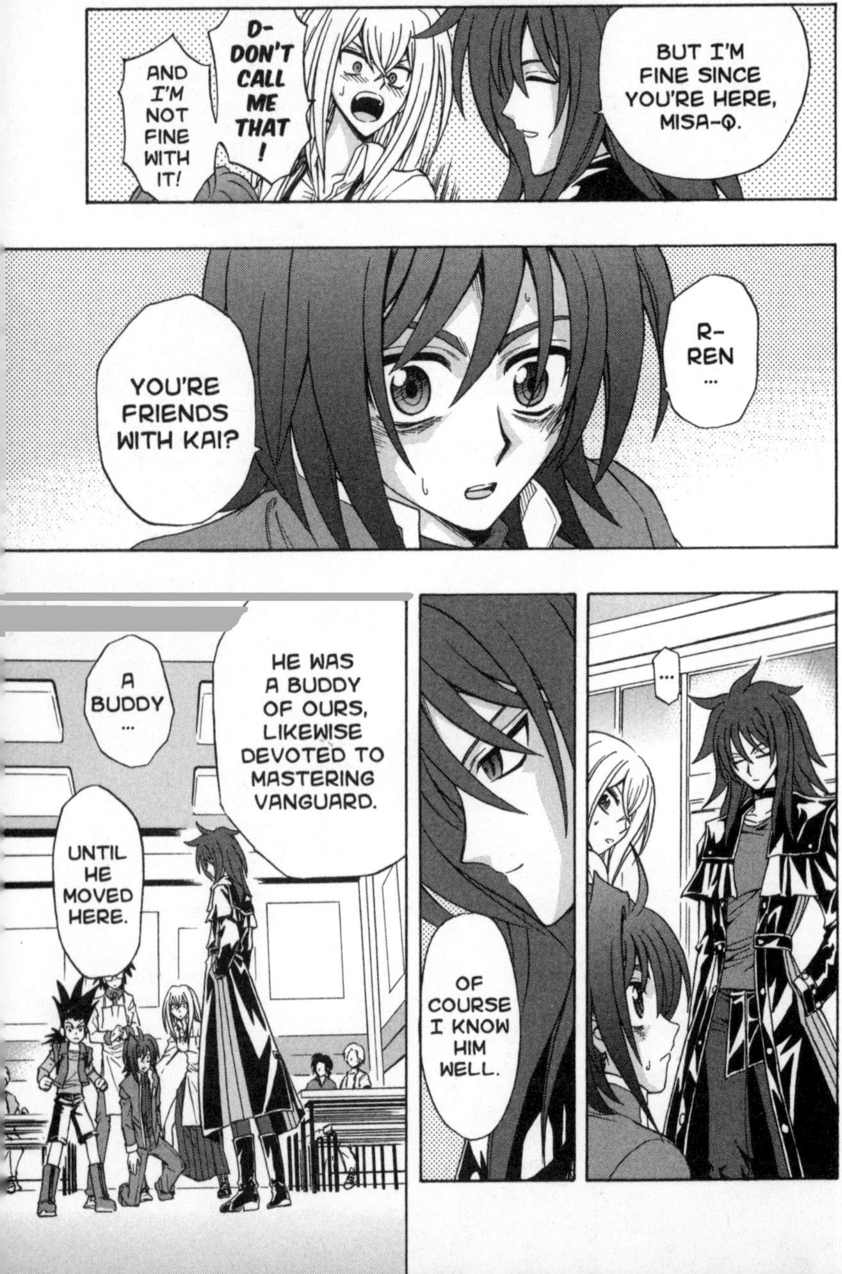
BUT I'M FINE SINCE YOU'RE HERE, MISA-Q.
D-DON'T CALL ME THAT!
AND I'M NOT FINE WITH IT!
R-REN...
YOU'RE FRIENDS WITH KAI?
...
OF COURSE I KNOW HIM WELL.
HE WAS A BUDDY OF OURS, LIKEWISE DEVOTED TO MASTERING VANGUARD.
A BUDDY...
UNTIL HE MOVED HERE.

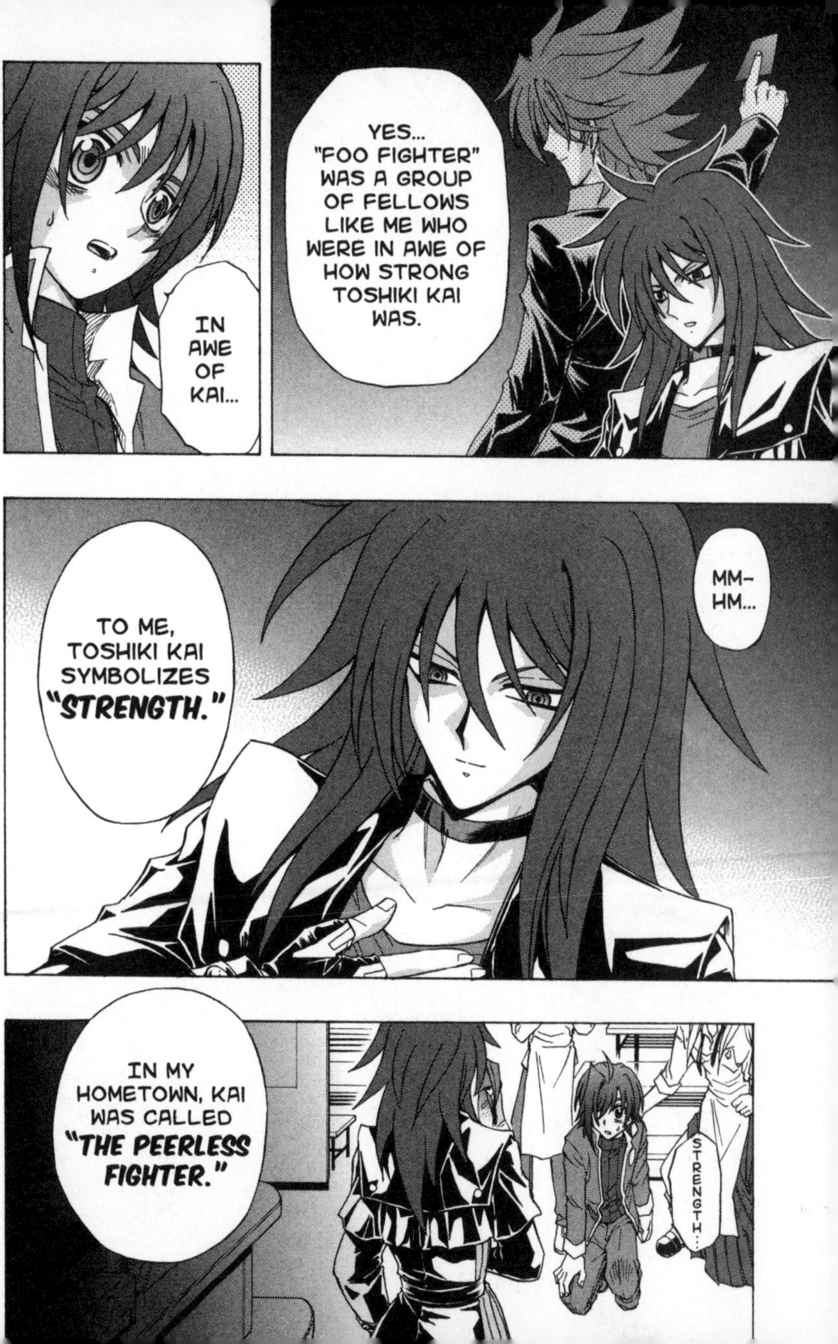
YES... "FOO FIGHTER" WAS A GROUP OF FELLOWS LIKE ME WHO WERE IN AWE OF HOW STRONG TOSHIKI KAI WAS.
IN AWE OF KAI...
MM-HM...
TO ME, TOSHIKI KAI SYMBOLIZES **"STRENGTH."**
IN MY HOMETOWN, KAI WAS CALLED **"THE PEERLESS FIGHTER."**
STRENGTH...

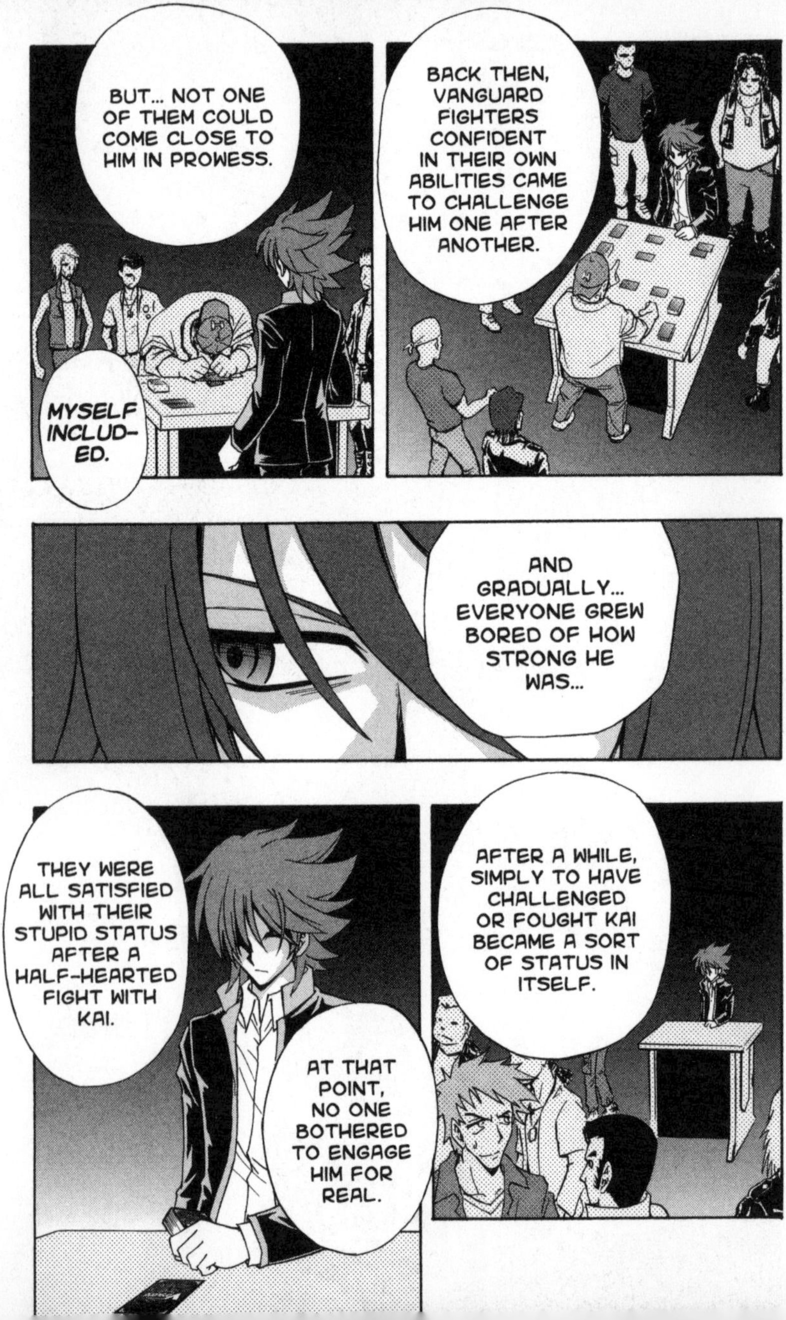
BACK THEN, VANGUARD FIGHTERS CONFIDENT IN THEIR OWN ABILITIES CAME TO CHALLENGE HIM ONE AFTER ANOTHER.
BUT... NOT ONE OF THEM COULD COME CLOSE TO HIM IN PROWESS.
MYSELF INCLUDED.
AND GRADUALLY... EVERYONE GREW BORED OF HOW STRONG HE WAS...
AFTER A WHILE, SIMPLY TO HAVE CHALLENGED OR FOUGHT KAI BECAME A SORT OF STATUS IN ITSELF.
THEY WERE ALL SATISFIED WITH THEIR STUPID STATUS AFTER A HALF-HEARTED FIGHT WITH KAI.
AT THAT POINT, NO ONE BOTHERED TO ENGAGE HIM FOR REAL.

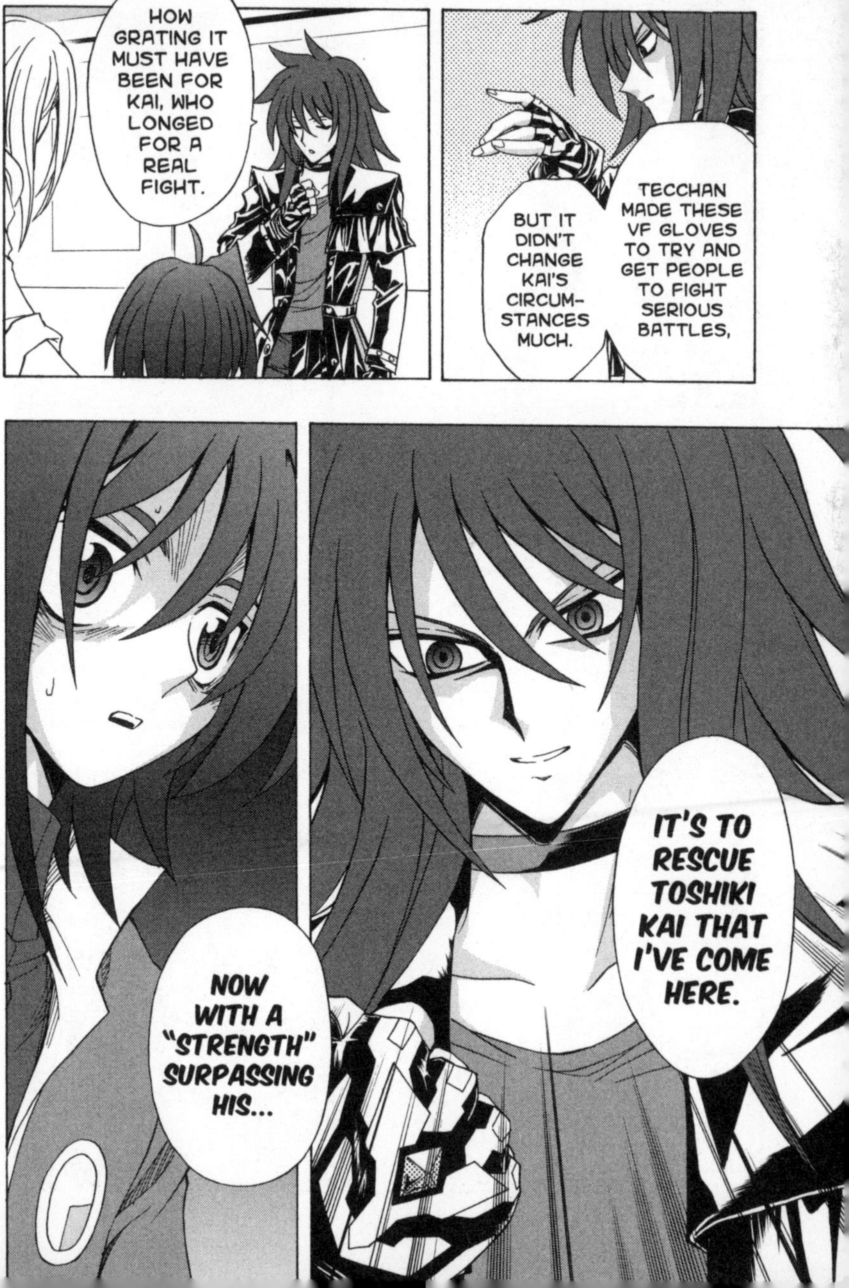
TECCHAN MADE THESE VF GLOVES TO TRY AND GET PEOPLE TO FIGHT SERIOUS BATTLES,
BUT IT DIDN'T CHANGE KAI'S CIRCUM-STANCES MUCH.
HOW GRATING IT MUST HAVE BEEN FOR KAI, WHO LONGED FOR A REAL FIGHT.
IT'S TO RESCUE TOSHIKI KAI THAT I'VE COME HERE.
NOW WITH A "STRENGTH" SURPASSING HIS...

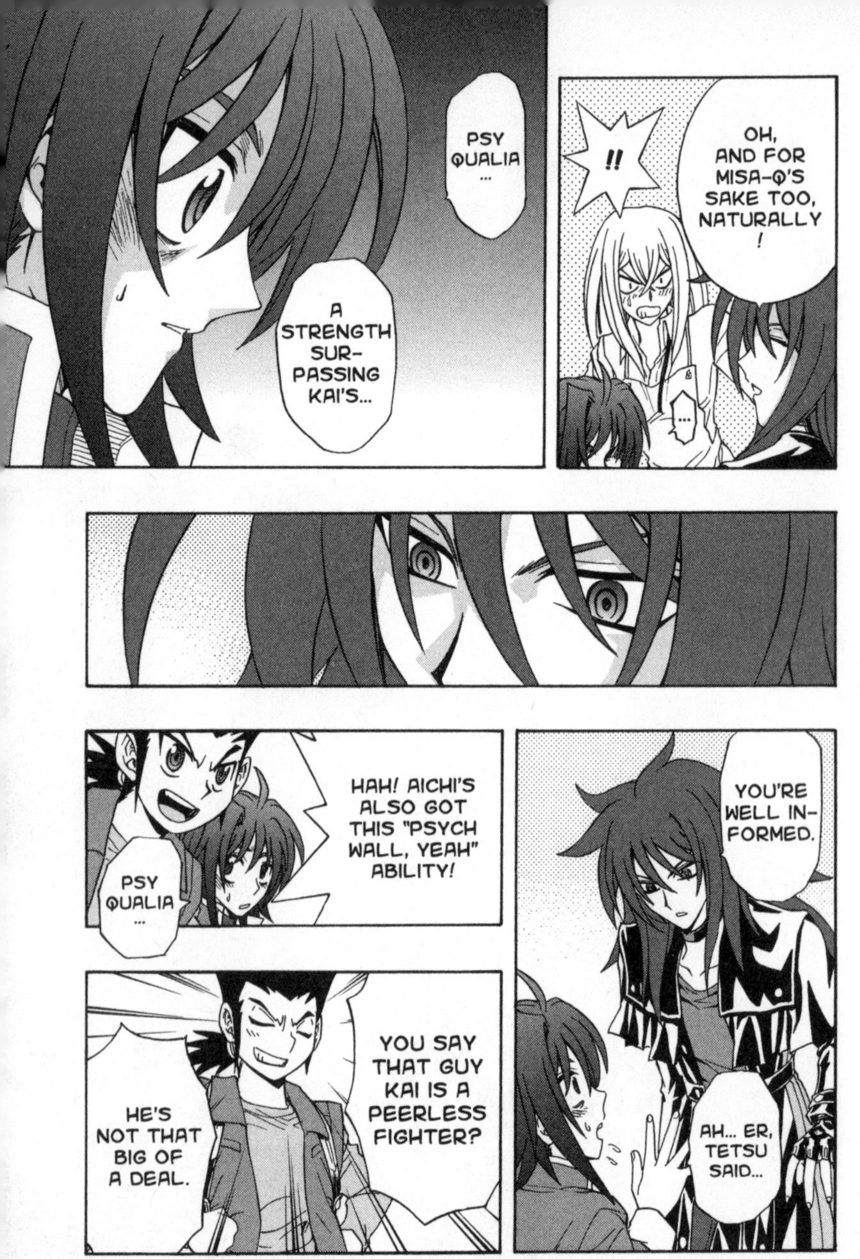
OH, AND FOR MISA-Q'S SAKE TOO, NATURALLY!
!!
...
PSY QUALIA...
A STRENGTH SUR-PASSING KAI'S...
YOU'RE WELL IN-FORMED.
AH... ER, TETSU SAID...
HAH! AICHI'S ALSO GOT THIS "PSYCH WALL, YEAH" ABILITY!
PSY QUALIA...
YOU SAY THAT GUY KAI IS A PEERLESS FIGHTER?
HE'S NOT THAT BIG OF A DEAL.

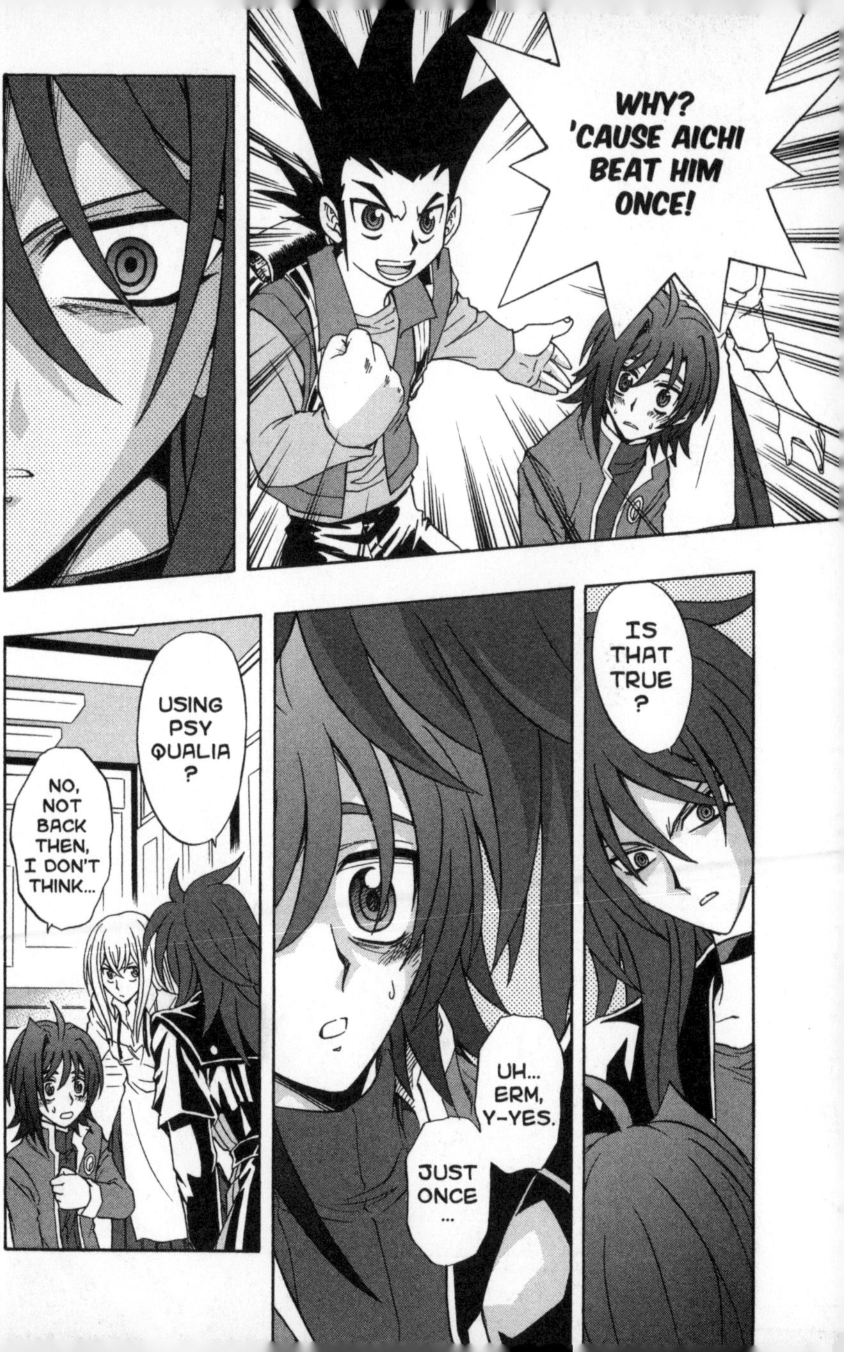
WHY? 'CAUSE AICHI BEAT HIM ONCE!
IS THAT TRUE?
UH... ERM, Y-YES.
JUST ONCE...
USING PSY QUALIA?
NO, NOT BACK THEN, I DON'T THINK...

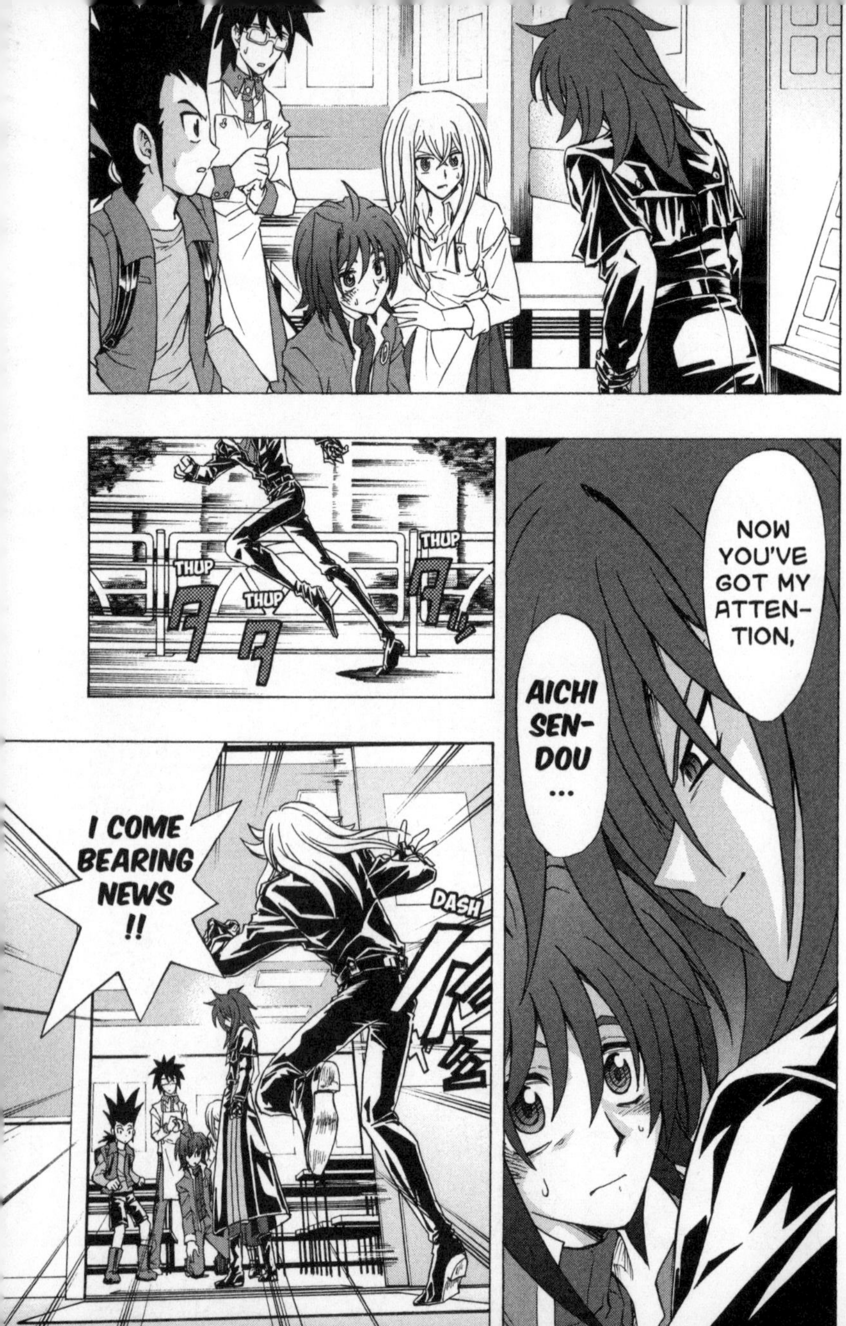
NOW YOU'VE GOT MY ATTEN-TION,
AICHI SEN-DOU ...
THUP
THUP
THUP
I COME BEARING NEWS !!
DASH

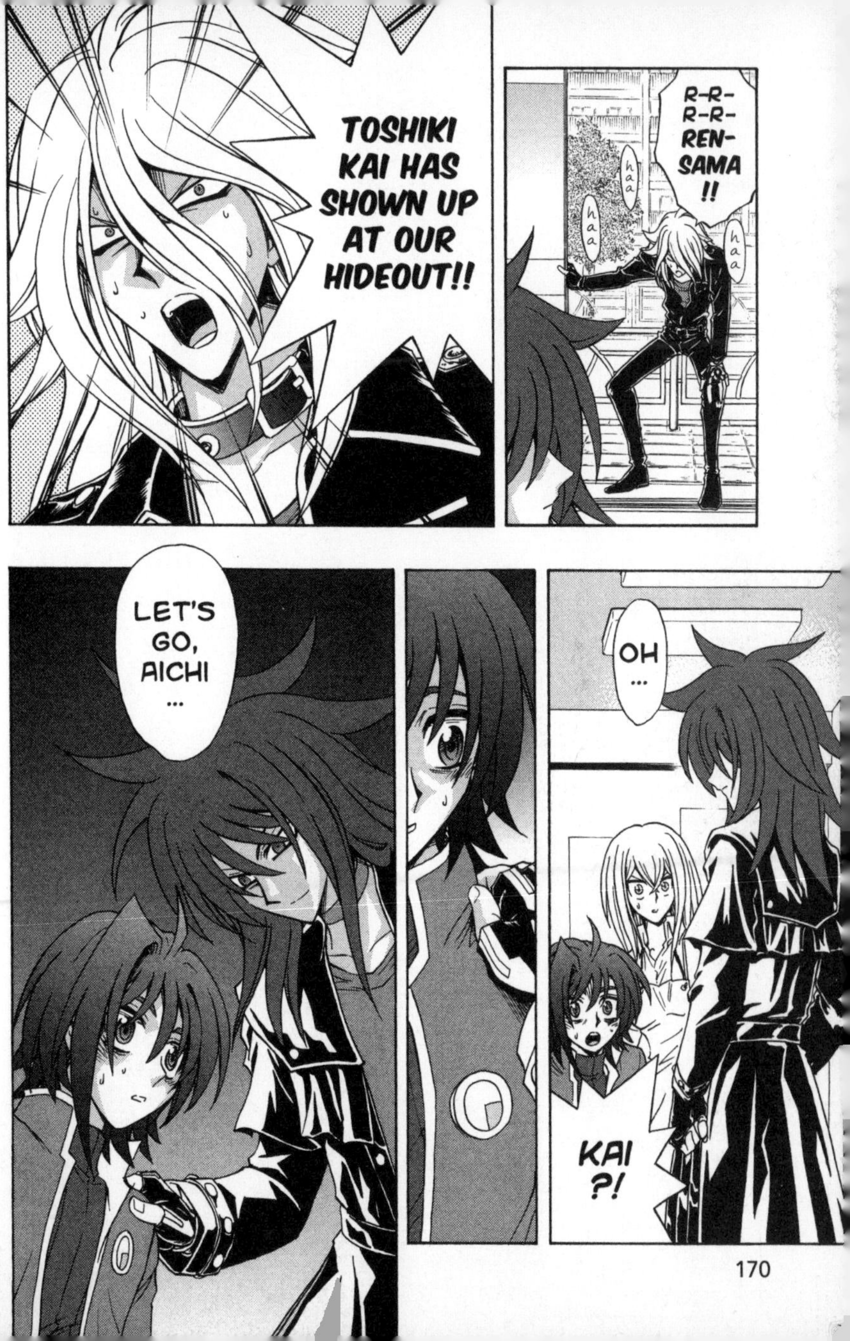
R-R-R-R-REN-SAMA!!
haa
haa
haa
TOSHIKI KAI HAS SHOWN UP AT OUR HIDEOUT!!
OH ...
KAI?!
LET'S GO, AICHI ...

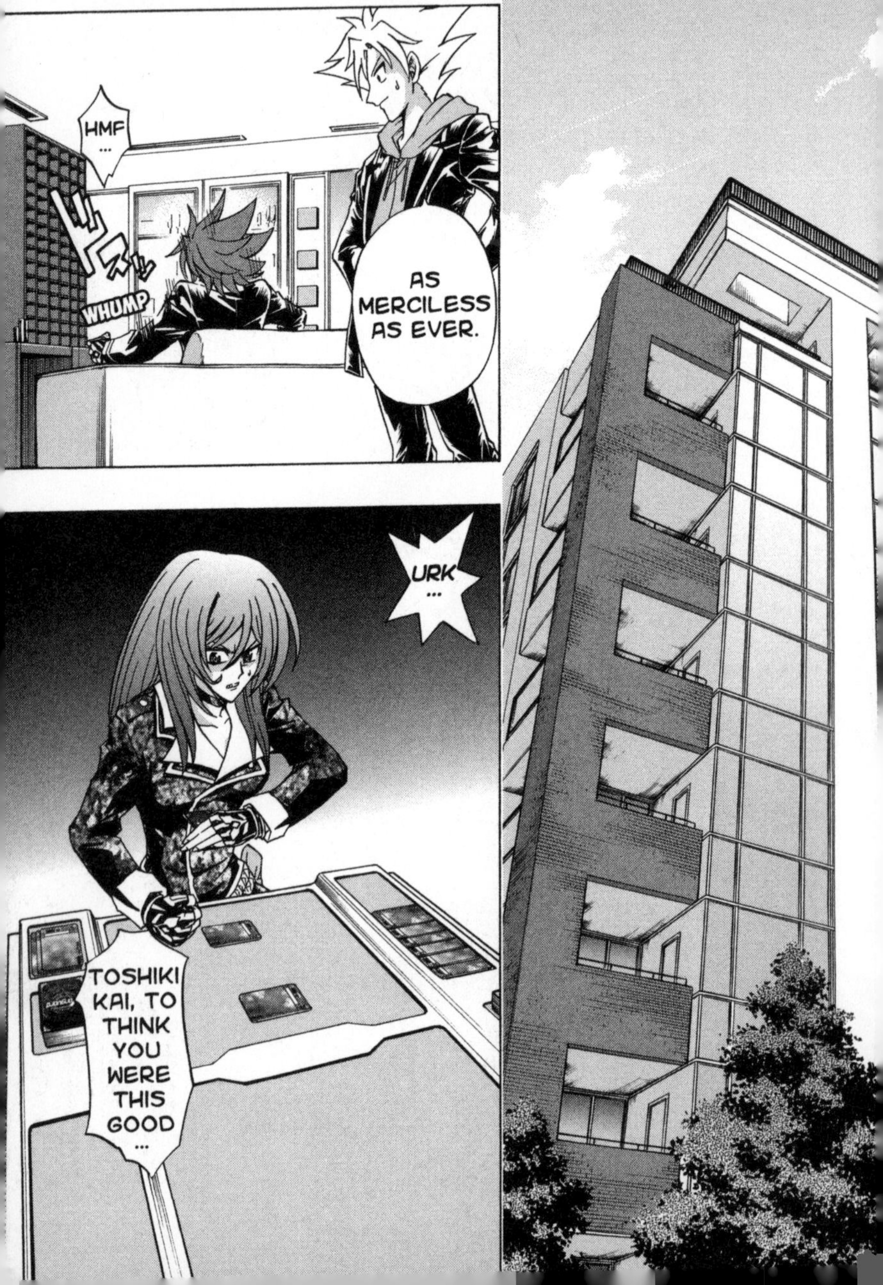
AS MERCILESS AS EVER.
HMF ...
WHUMP
URK ...
TOSHIKI KAI, TO THINK YOU WERE THIS GOOD ...

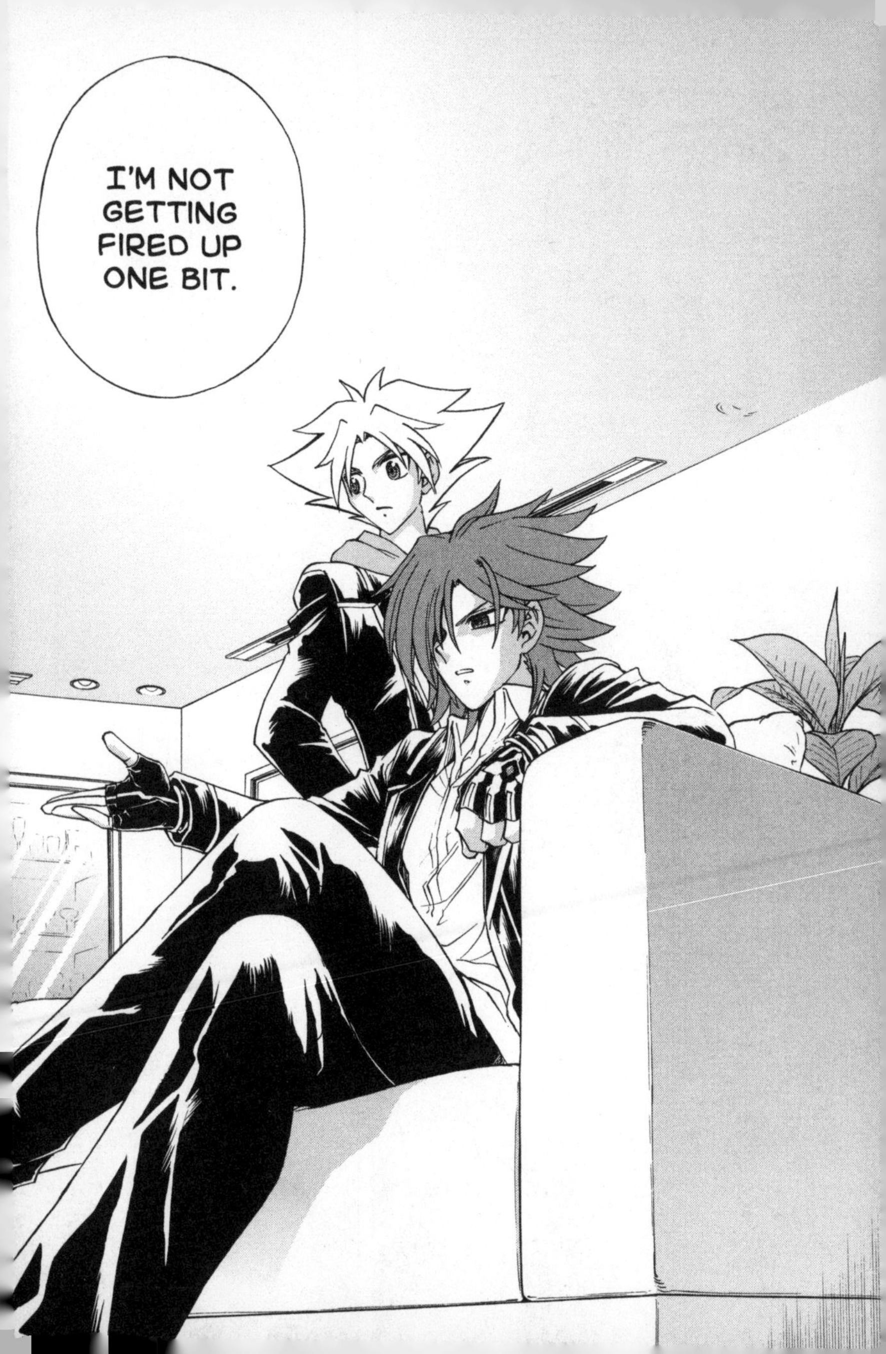
I'M NOT GETTING FIRED UP ONE BIT.

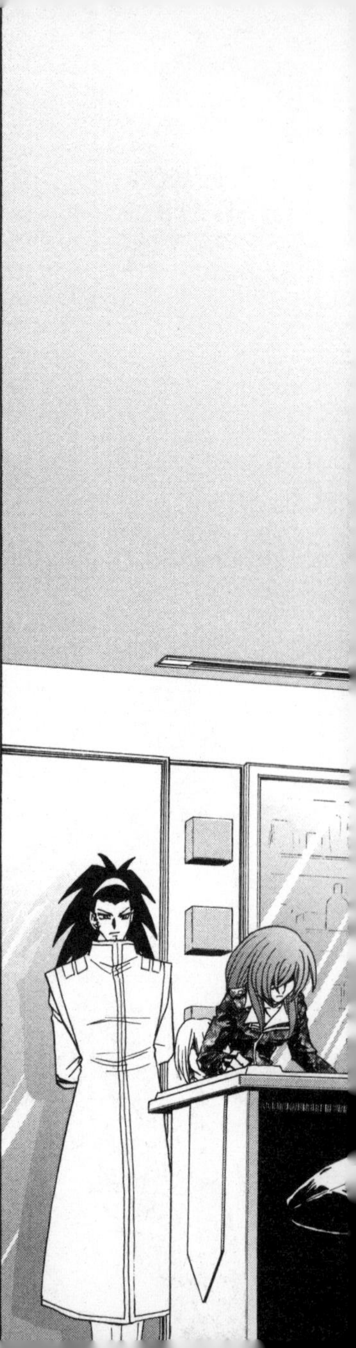

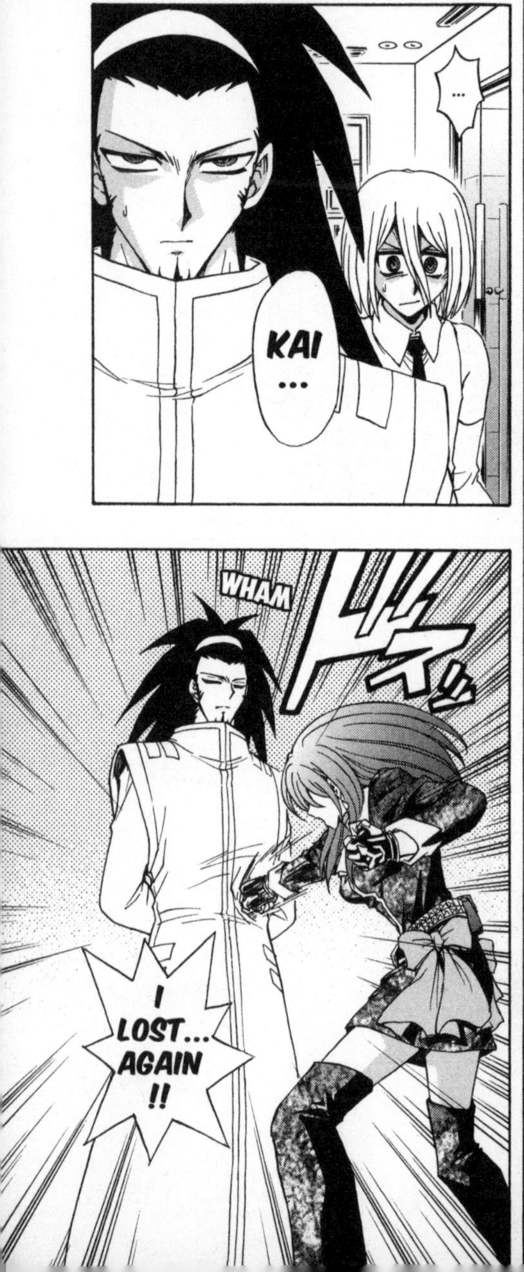
...
KAI ...
WHAM
I LOST... AGAIN !!

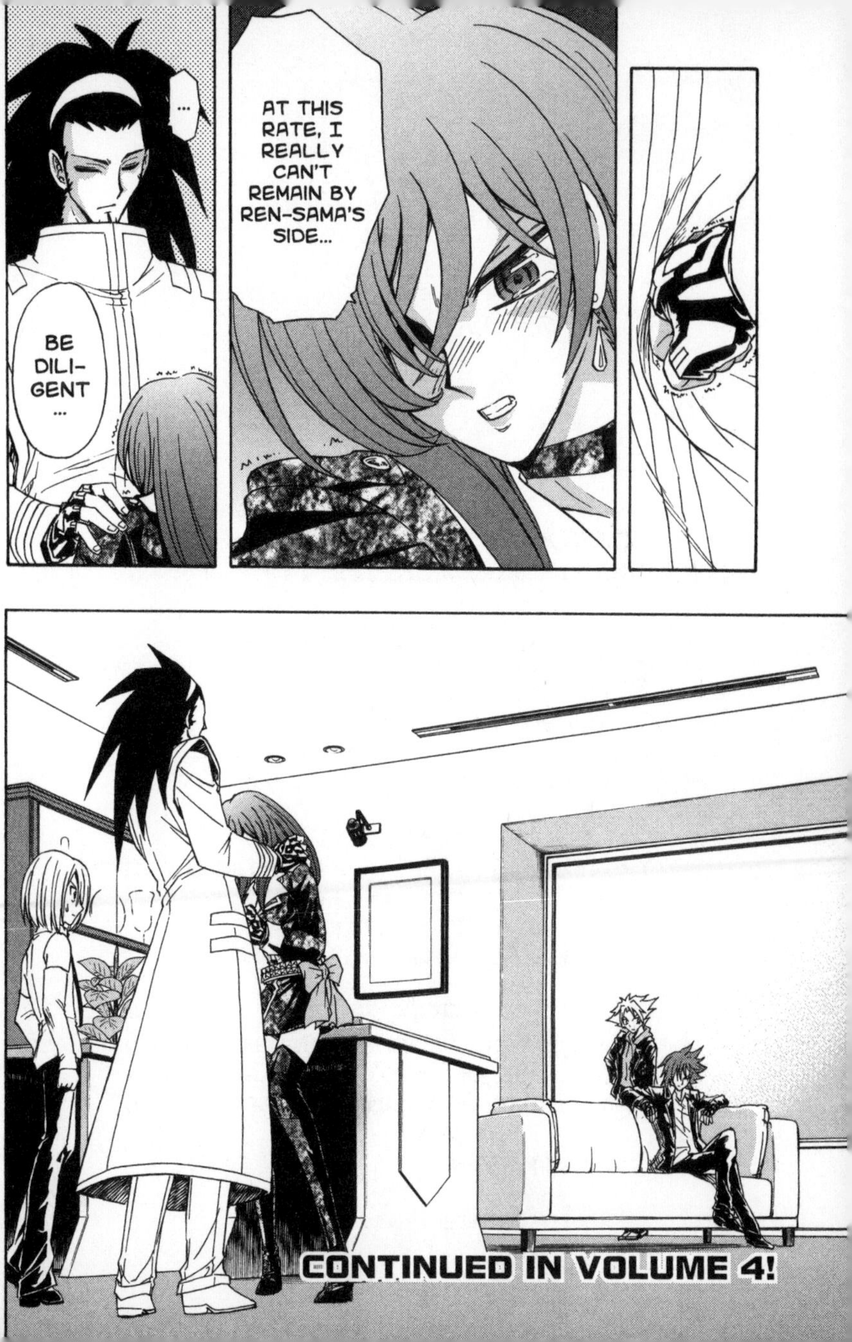
AT THIS RATE, I REALLY CAN'T REMAIN BY REN-SAMA'S SIDE...
...
BE DILI-GENT ...
CONTINUED IN VOLUME 4!

CARDFIGHT!! VANGUARD VOL. 3
ORIGINAL DESIGNS OF THE FEATURED UNITS

CHAPTER 10
Oracle Guardian, Nike / ToMo
Dark Metal Bicorn / コガラツ (kogaratsu)
Emergency Alarmer / 石田バル (Val Ishida)
Oracle Guardian, Gemini / TMS
Psychic Bird / 松島一夫 (Kazuo Matsushima)

CHAPTER 11
Luck Bird / ヨシザワ / モレシャン (Yoshizawa/Morechand)
Silent Tom / TMS
Battle Sister, Maple / NINNIN
Hades Ringmaster / ヨウイチ (Yoichi)

CHAPTER 13
Little Sage, Marron / 山崎奈苗 (Nanae Yamazaki)
Werwolf Sieger / 雨宮慶太 (Keita Amemiya)
Prisoner Beast / トニーたけざき (Tony Takezaki)
Wingal / TMS
Alabaster Owl / パトリシア (Patricia)

All Other Units / Akira Itou

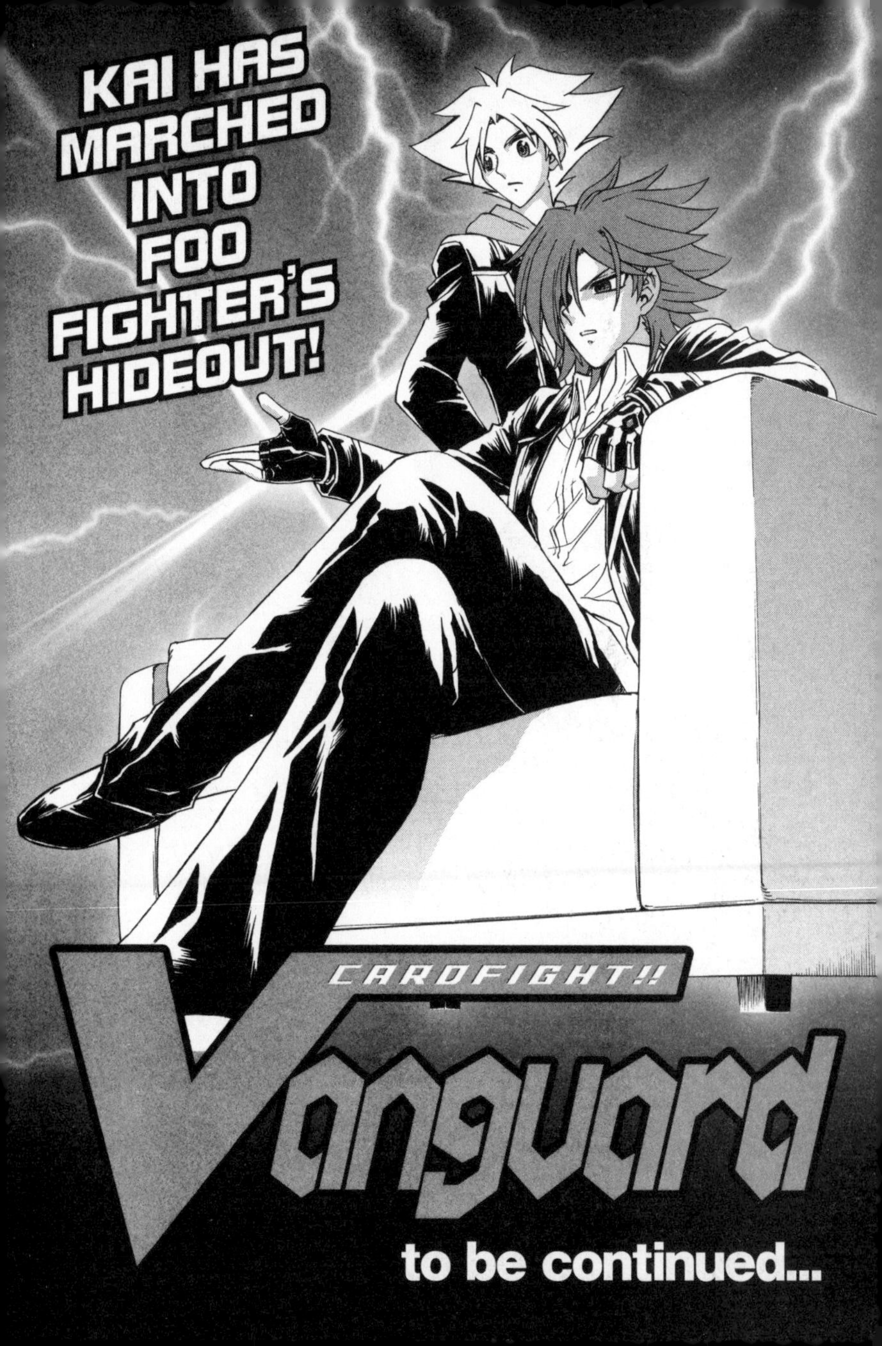
KAI HAS MARCHED INTO FOO FIGHTER'S HIDEOUT!
CARDFIGHT!!
Vanguard
to be continued...

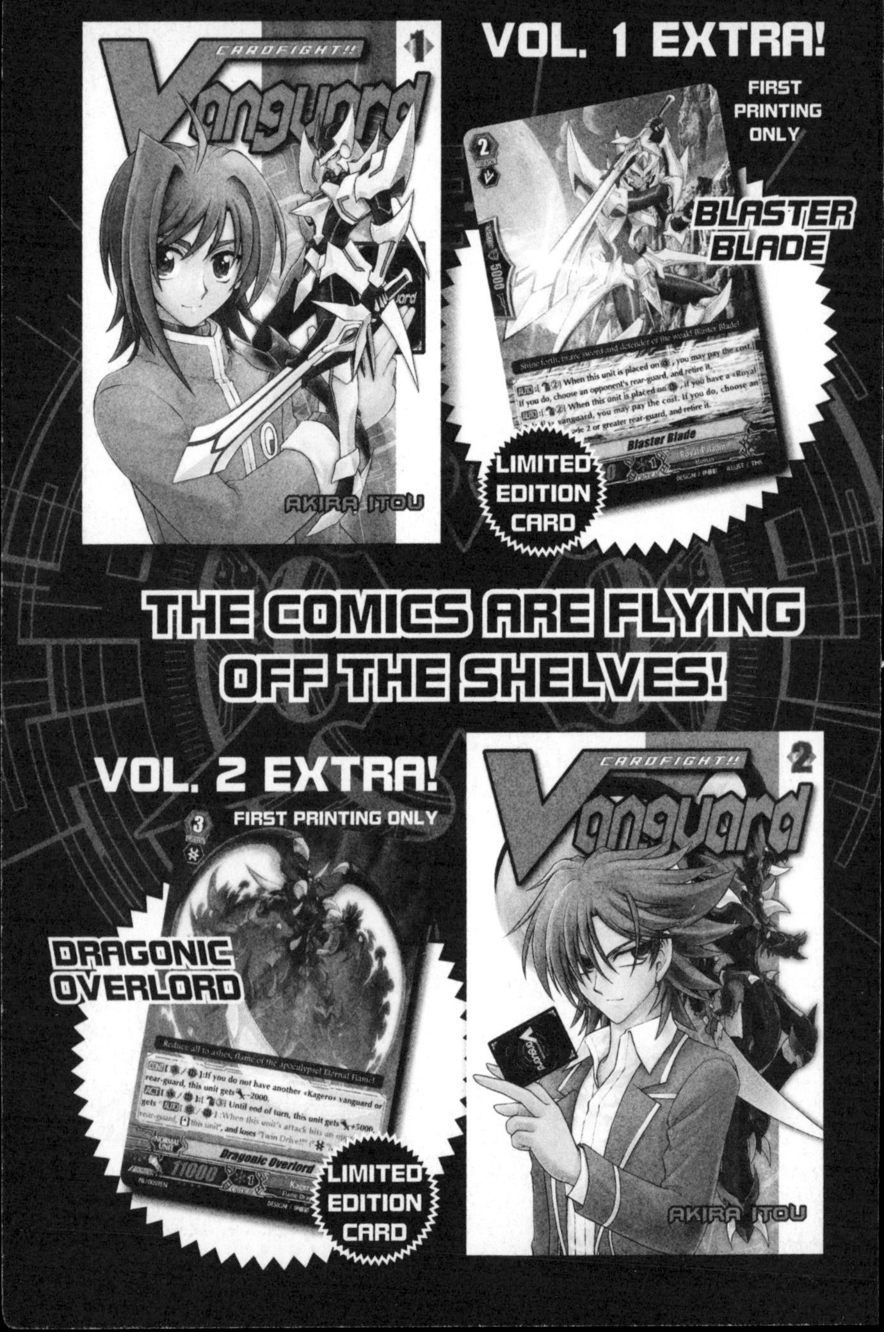

CARDFIGHT!!
Vanguard
1
AKIRA ITOU
VOL. 1 EXTRA!
FIRST PRINTING ONLY
BLASTER BLADE
Blaster Blade
LIMITED EDITION CARD
THE COMICS ARE FLYING OFF THE SHELVES!
VOL. 2 EXTRA!
FIRST PRINTING ONLY
DRAGONIC OVERLORD
Dragonic Overlord
LIMITED EDITION CARD
CARDFIGHT!!
Vanguard
2
AKIRA ITOU

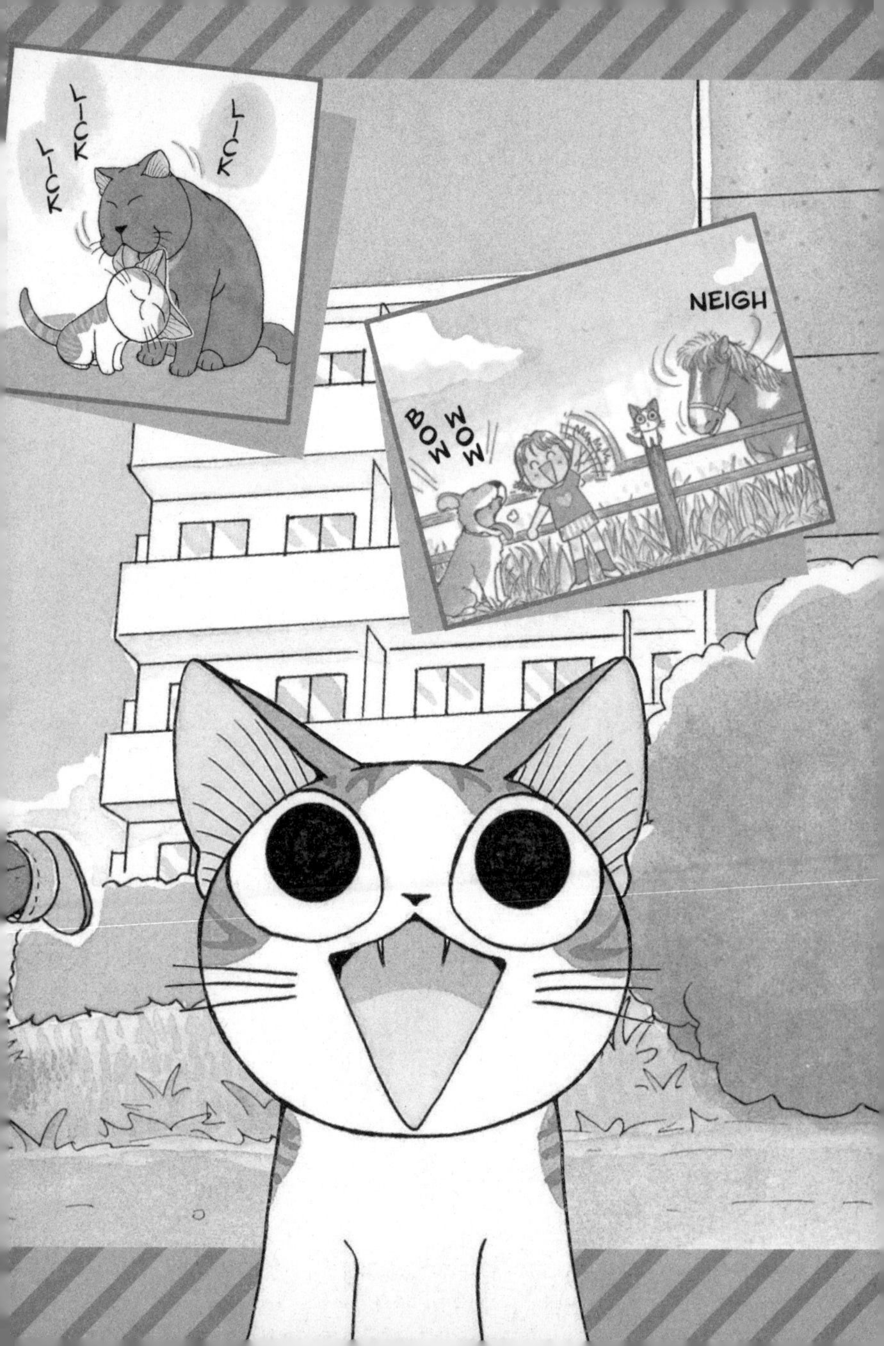
LICK
LICK
LICK
NEIGH
BOW WOW

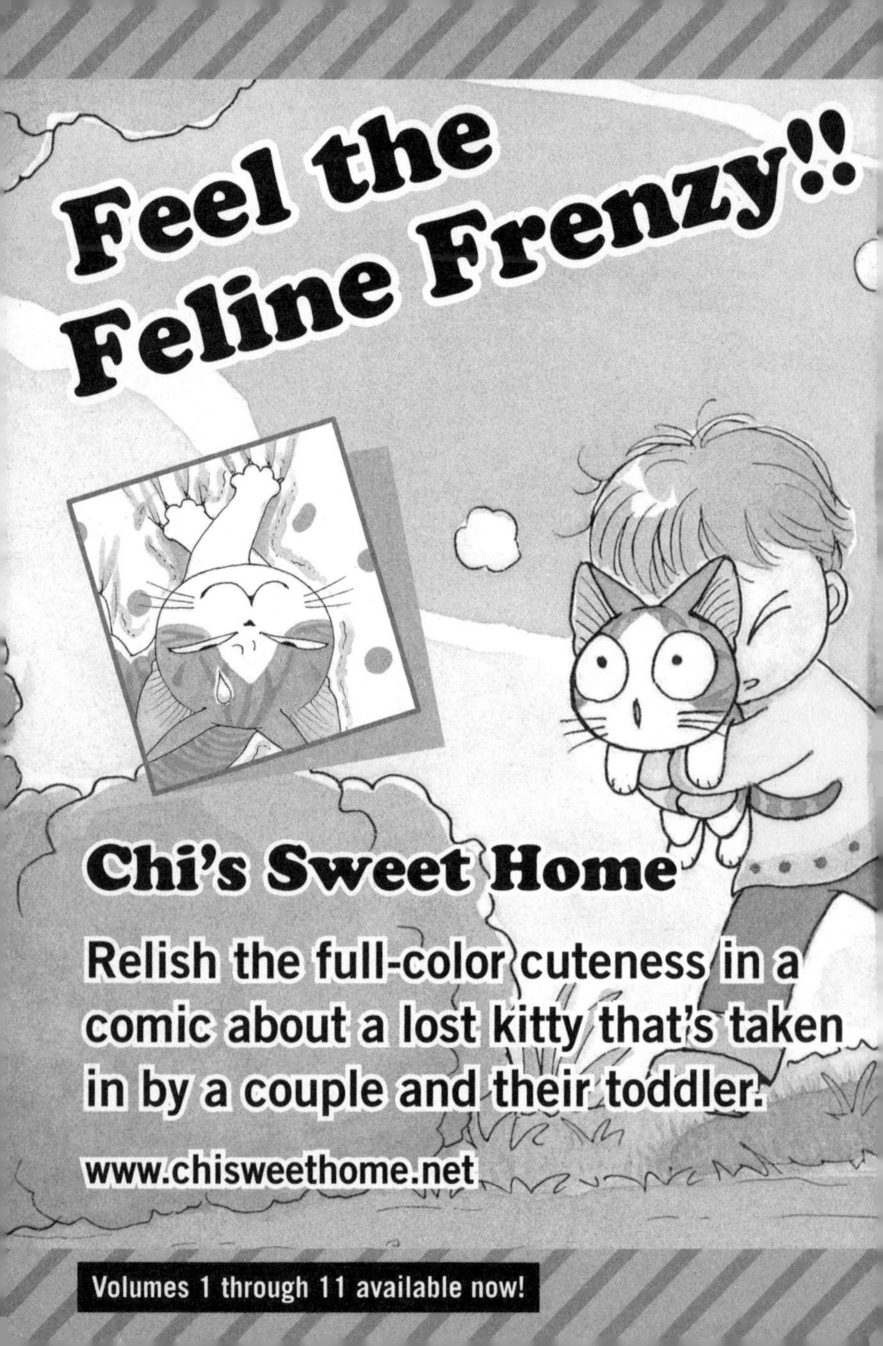

Feel the Feline Frenzy!!
Chi's Sweet Home
Relish the full-color cuteness in a comic about a lost kitty that's taken in by a couple and their toddler.
www.chisweethome.net
Volumes 1 through 11 available now!

CARDFIGHT! VANGUARD
VOLUME 3

Production: Grace Lu
            Anthony Quintessenza

Copyright © Akira ITOU 2012
            © bushiroad All Rights Reserved.
Edited by KADOKAWA SHOTEN
First published in Japan in 2012 by KADOKAWA CORPORATION, Tokyo.
English translation rights arranged with KADOKAWA CORPORATION, Tokyo
through TUTTLE-MORI AGENCY, INC., Tokyo.
English language version produced by Vertical, Inc.

Translation provided by Vertical, Inc., 2014
Published by Vertical, Inc., New York

Originally published in Japanese as *Kaadofaito!! Vangaado 3* by KADOKAWA
CORPORATION
Kaadofaito!! Vangaado first serialized in *Young Ace*, 2011-

This is a work of fiction.

ISBN: 978-1-939130-64-8

Manufactured in Canada

First Edition

Vertical, Inc.
451 Park Avenue South
7th Floor
New York, NY 10016
www.vertical-inc.com